RURAL RESOURCE MANAGEMENT

Rural Resource Management

Paul J. Cloke & Chris C. Park

CROOM HELM
London & Sydney

©1985 P.J. Cloke and C.C. Park
Croom Helm Ltd, Provident House,
Burrell Row, Beckenham, Kent BR3 1AT
Croom Helm Australia Pty Ltd, First Floor,
139 King Street, Sydney, NSW 2001, Australia

British Library Cataloguing in Publication Data

Cloke, Paul J.
    Rural resources management.
    1. Land use, Rural—Planning
    I. Title II. Park, Chris C.
    333.76'17   HD111
✓ISBN 0-7099-2037-7

Printed and bound in Great Britain
by Billing & Sons Limited, Worcester.

CONTENTS

TABLES

FIGURES

FIGURES (continued)

ACKNOWLEDGEMENTS

Our task in writing this book has been made much
lighter and more rewarding by the encouragement we
have received from family and friends while our
thoughts and energies were being directed towards its
completion. No book appears without dedicated help
from a range of people, and this is compounded when
the book appears (as this) in camera-ready format. We
are endebted to the staff of the Department of
Geography at the University of Lancaster, and to
Professor J H Johnson for allowing us to call upon the
skills of this fine team. Foremost, and deserving of
special thanks, have been Anne Jackson and Peter
Mingens who drew clear and attractive figures, and
Jean Burford and Christine Skinner who cheerfully typed
earlier drafts of the text. The high quality and fine
appearance of the printed text owes much to the skills
and efficiency of our typist Dorothy Callis, who wins
our lasting gratitude. Jean Burford typed the lengthy
index at short notice, and we thank her sincerely.
Peter Sowden, our editor at Croom Helm, has survived
the long evolution of the book with tolerance, and
we thank him for help and support in numerous ways.

Writing is a lonely and insular activity, and we have
been blessed with supportive and suitably critical
partners to whom we owe our fondest and most lasting
debt of gratitude. Chris would like to thank, with
love, his wife Angela for help and understanding through
all the good and not-so-good times : she has rare
qualities indeed. Paul would like, once again, to pay
special tribute to his wife Viv and daughter Elizabeth
for their love and understanding, and for providing
such a wonderfully supportive family setting in which
to work. William James Cloke arrived too late to see
the action ... but his time will doubtless come.

This book is dedicated to

OUR PARENTS

with grateful thanks for
their love, support and
encouragement over the
years

Chapter One

IMAGES OF AN INTEGRATED COUNTRYSIDE

The first two chapters in this book aim to establish a framework for adopting a resource management approach to planning the countryside. It is clearly necessary at the outset to define our terms of reference, and so this chapter focusses specifically on different approaches to defining the term 'rural', and to isolating the main components of 'the rural system'. Whilst many of the examples quoted refer to the United Kingdom, the framework is intended to be international in orientation, so that examples - particularly from the United States and Europe - are included in subsequent chapters.

1.1   RURAL IMAGES

> ...no comprehensive view of rural land
> use has been arrived at. In many ways,
> planning still waits for planners and the
> public to decide what kind of rural environ-
> ment they want. [1]

The future of the countryside in many developed 'areas' such as the United States and Western Europe has seemingly been in the balance for a number of years. Early concern over the rural ramifications of what Andrew Gilg has called 'the confident years of expansion in the 1950's and 1960's[2] has led to the establishment in many developed countries of forms of countryside planning machinery geared mainly towards a rather negative counteraction of growth coupled with policies of selective development. However, there has been a long - if sometimes inevitable - time-lag, between the recognition and understanding of countryside problems, and the development of suitable planning processes with which to implement suitable policy responses. Consequently,

1

the 1980's have arrived without any concomitant
evolution of countryside management away from restriction of growth and towards a positive policy of
support for the rural environment in times of economic hardship.

Perception of the Rural Environment

Many problems of countryside planning stem from the
ways in which people view the countryside - whether
these people are planners, residents, visitors or
whatever. Perception of the opportunities offered
by rural areas inevitably varies between individuals
and groups; but perhaps also perception is coloured
by national variations in population size, pressure
on land-use resources, standard of living, and the
like. In Britain, therefore, with intense pressure
on countryside resources, images of the countryside
are commonly multi-dimensional and perhaps inevitably contradictory at times.

Perceptions of agriculture in the countryside in
Britain can be used to illustrate this point. On
the one hand, the farmer is often viewed (usually by
urban-based protagonists) as 'the archetypal moaner,
feather-bedded by the taxpayer's money, but forever
pleading poverty while riding around in a new car'.[3]
The extreme environmentalist viewpoint, on the other
hand, tends to brand him as 'the destroyer of the
nation's heritage, promoting the rape of the natural
landscape and poisoning its flora and fauna in the
pursuit of Mammon'.[4] Yet, to the farmer, agriculture
is both a business and a way of life, both of which
are to be protected from the meddling of uninformed
and potentially dangerous urbanites (see Chapter 9.2).
In the United States, by contrast, images of agriculture are not so polarized, in part because land
zoning tends to separate conflicting forms of land
use, but also because overall pressures on available
land in the countryside are not so acute as in
Britain. Nonetheless, Hagood's[5] analysis of variations in the Farm Operator Level of Living Index
demonstrated substantial variations in standards of
living within and between rural farm communities
(FIGURE 1.1), suggesting that there are marked variations in social structure, and thus in likely perceptions, even within the agricultural sector.

Rural images are also strongly flavoured by differences in attitude between urban and rural dwellers.
There is a feeling, for example, that 'the countryside stands for all that is important in Britain; it

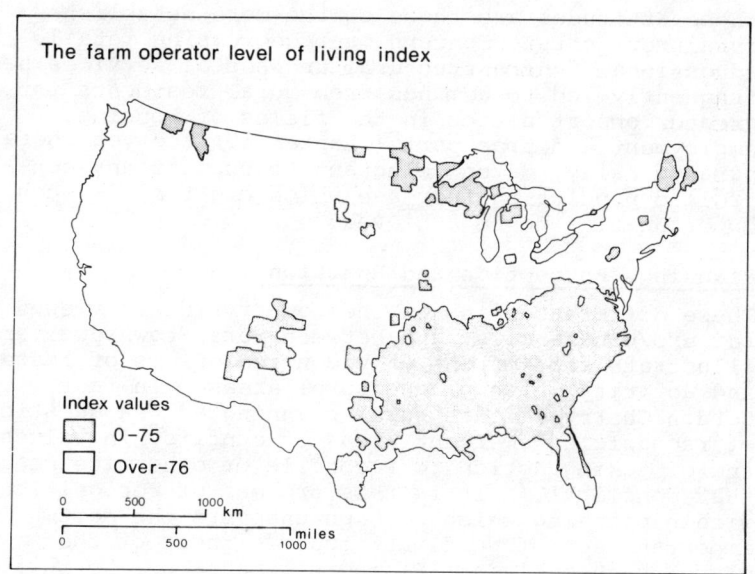

FIGURE 1.1   The Farm Operator Level of Living Index

Source: after B.E. Coates, R.J. Johnston and
           P.L. Knox, Geography and Inequality (Oxford
           University Press, Oxford, 1977):   65.

is the expression of the good life away from the
stresses and strains of the city and the symbol of
everything which is considered truly British'[6], and
this sometimes leads to conflicts of perception and
action.   Urban-dwellers are often accused of converting these deep-seated emotions into an over-use
of the countryside.   This can take many forms, such
as frequent visits to the countryside for leisure
(see Chapter 7) or taking up residence in rural settlements either as commuters or as second home owners
whose rural attachment is only seasonal (see Chapter
8).

These images are perhaps caricatures, but it is true
that urbanite ideals can become transposed as the
voice of rural people - especially when vociferous
newcomers dominate local rural politics in an attempt
to ensure that the house which they have just built
in a village is the last one to be built there, ost-
ensibly to preserve the natural rural environment
from the influx of 'outsiders'.   Counter balancing

these attitudes are those of the more established
rural residents. Concern over decreasing retail,
educational, infrastructural and social services has
frequently led to demands from rural residents for
greater opportunities in the fields of housing,
employment and transport (Chapter 10) and yet there are,
paradoxically, often reluctant to support any controlled population increase which might allow such
opportunities to be achieved.

Planning, Perception and Reaction

These differences in how the countryside is viewed by
farmers/non-farmers, and between rural/town dwellers,
illustrate some of the many contradictions of imagery
and activity which plague rural areas. In fact,
Gordon Cherry defines rural planning as ' a question
of recognizing emergent areas of conflict in values
and of taking action to reconcile or otherwise meet
that conflict'.[7] It is this process of recognition
within planning which perhaps uncovers the most
important set of rural attitudes - those of the
planners themselves. Planners' images of the rural
environment often differ markedly from those of the
politicians who they seek to influence, and from the
images of those sections of the population who are
affected by the allocation of resources within the
rural planning system.[8]

Planners' images are of fundamental importance in
two contexts. First, the adoption by planners of
'rural' and 'urban' categories clearly conditions
their assumptions and approaches to different areas.
The example of the Structure Plans prepared for the
Teeside sub-region in England demonstrates that the
area defined as urban Teeside provoked a potentially
radical growth zone response from planners while the
rural county draft plan conformed to a more traditional conservative philosophy.[9]

Secondly, even the most enlightened planner's image
of the countryside is inevitably restricted by the
inflexibility and poor resource base of current planning machinery. In Britain, for example, shire
counties and districts do not, in general, support
sufficient manpower to diversify beyond their strict
planning duties, which are on the whole mechanical
and lacking in scope for originality or lateralism,
and it seems likely that these types of problem will
be exacerbated by the onset of further public spending cuts. Thus, the likelihood of support for

experiments in positive planning at the local rural level is small and it is clear that the bureaucratic planning legislation which divides the rural environment into neat subsections - such as housing, conservation, highways, and employment - will often discourage the small-scale experiment which cuts across these artificial administrative boundaries (see Chapter 12.2). Therefore, the planner's image of the countryside rather than providing a platform for the resolution of conflicting values, tends to encourage a neglect of the connections both within the rural environment, and with surrounding urban environments.

Implications of the Rural Image

There are two possible interpretations of these conflicting images of countryside. One sees them as conscious attempts by different sectors of the community to obstruct progress in planning rural areas. The other, and perhaps more likely interpretation, is that attitudes and images from different sources are failing to keep pace with rapid changes in the society and physical environment of the countryside. One of the principal tasks for rural planners and managers in all developed countries is to reconcile and modernize conflicting attitude and action, since the more pressing problems of land use conflict may be viewed as a direct result of different groups' perceptions of the opportunities offered by the countryside.

The thesis underlying this book is that one suitable framework within which to promote a broader and more thorough understanding of the countryside by all parties is to adopt a resource-based approach. Such a framework has three main advantages:

(i)   it allows a more comprehensive view of the countryside, with possibilities for integrating the treatment of 'physical' and 'social' resources within one analytical scheme;

(ii) it aids the isolation of potential and actual conflicts between various forms of resource use, and therefore highlights underlying disharmonies of image and attitude;

(iii) it opens up various possibilities for countryside management, beginning with the provision of a concise background against which decisions about what kind of rural environment is

wanted in the future can be made, and pro-
gressing towards a full evaluation of the
suitability of various techniques of resource
management in solving particular problems of
resource conflict.

However, although rural-urban interactions should not
be discounted or ignored, our main concern is with
resources in <u>rural areas</u>. Scott Lefaver [10] argues
that rural issues need to be defined in their own
context and that the policy tools used to solve those
issues must come from the rural perspective . Task
one is to establish a working definition of rurality,
or of the concept of countryside, for use in the rest
of the book.

1.2 THE RURAL CONCEPT - IDENTITY

There are two main lines of thinking, in defining
the concepts of 'rurality' or 'countryside'. On the
one hand, many commentators conclude that 'there is
no unambiguous way of defining <u>rural areas</u>' [11] and
so any debate over such definition will, <u>ipso facto</u>,
be rather sterile. Alternatively, it is noted that
'the distinction between "urban" and "rural" areas
is deeply rooted in the psychology of most attempts
at any regional or local subdivision' [12] and so the
explanation of the rural-urban difference is of the
utmost importance. It is clear that the designations
'rural' and 'countryside' have been used by academics
and planners alike without an adequate appreciation
of how these concepts can be defined, or of the
criteria which differentiate between these concepts
and others such as 'urban, 'suburban' and the like.
These concepts and criteria form a backcloth to the
study of rural planning and management.

Definitions of Rurality

Authors have adopted three distinct perspectives in
defining 'rurality'. First, there are those who
regard countryside as synonymous with anything which
is non-urban in character (TABLE 1.1a). This negative stance conveniently transfers the onus of
definition to urban researchers, while students of
the rural environment are left to ponder over the
residuals. Such an approach assumes that the rural
environment has few specific characters or qualities
of its own. A second form of definition covers a
wide range of positive attempts to specify important
elements of rural identity (TABLE 1.1b).

TABLE 1.1 Some definitions of rurality[13]

(a) NEGATIVE DEFINITIONS

'It is the area covered by the nine-tenths or so of Britain's non-urban land surface with which this book is concerned.' (Gordon Cherry)

'The focus of rural planning activity includes all jurisdictions outside the incorporated limits of urban responsibility.' (William Lassey)

(b) POSITIVE DEFINITIONS

'Rural geography may be defined as the study of recent social, economic, land-use and spatial changes that have taken place in less-densely populated areas which are commonly recognized by virtue of their visual components as "countryside".' (Hugh Clout)

'The prime concern of the rural social geographer would be those forms of settlement ranging from isolated farmsteads to the market towns serving a tributary area.' (Gareth Lewis)

'Rural – the word describes those parts of a country which show unmistakable signs of being dominated by extensive uses of land, either at the present time, or in the immediate past.' (Gerald Wibberley)

(c) PERCEPTION-BASED DEFINITIONS

'The village can be described as a place where the countryside meets the town and where distinction between rural and urban lies very much in the eye of the beholder.' (Graham Moss)

'A village is any place which most residents think of as a village.' (Andrew Thorburn)

These attempts represent the most important input to any discussion of rural definition. However, a third type of definition has also been used, and this is based on user-perception (TABLE 1.1c).

The idea that countryside can be defined as what most people think of as countryside (or rural or village) is attractive in some respects, but in practice has proven rather an elusive notion. Measurement of the perceived countryside image, even within homogeneous groups, presents considerable methodological problems but the field is an inviting one for further study. The work of Palmer et al[14], for example, has shown that the structure of peoples' image of the countryside is not easy to explain using simple criteria. Their factor analysis (TABLE 1.2) suggested that such images are structured in

TABLE 1.2 Significant Factors in the Structuring of Countryside Images[15]

Second Order Components	First Order Factors (Loading Scores)
Recreational Enjoyment	crowding (0.7679) emotion/reflection (0.7124) accessibility (0.6344)
Recreational Environment	interest & activity (0.7126) scenery (-0.5576) contrast (-0.7496)
Evaluation	evaluation (0.9374)

composite dimensions (that is, second order factors in the analysis) rather than the more simplistic primary dimensions (which tend to be the ones most commonly used to explain the rural-urban difference). Recognition that the attitudes and behaviour of people form an important aspect of the definition of countryside and rurality has in itself broadened the horizons of interest in most aspects of countryside planning.

All-embracing definitions of the countryside have proven elusive on three grounds. First, the need to delimit the rural environment has in general stemmed from a series of specific functional purposes, and as a consequence, different narrow viewpoints on the countryside have produced different narrow definitions.

For example, an agriculturally defined countryside will differ from that perceived by planners, administrators, tourists and so on. Rural definition, therefore, depends on the <u>functions</u> designated to the countryside.

Second, attempts at definition have encountered changes over time in society's attitudes towards the countryside. A feeling of hostility towards the countryside during the nineteenth century has now evolved to sentiments connected with 'rural playgrounds' or the 'rural idyll'. Also relevant are the changing demands on the rural landscape over time which themselves are a function of social, economic and technological developments. It is clear that whatever the countryside is, it is undergoing considerable <u>temporal change</u>.

Third, the concept of countryside is subject to considerable spatial variation. At a regional scale in Great Britain, for example, there is a pronounced visual contrast between the countryside of North-West Scotland, and those of East Anglia or the Weald. At a broader international scale, the internal variations to be found within the United Kingdom appear insignificant when measured against the range of variations in countryside environments found elsewhere. Contrast, for example, the rural landscape of central Canada, wilderness regions in the United States, alpine regions of Switzerland, the polderlands of the Netherlands, and the grandeur of the Colorado Valley. Therefore, the search for rural definition has also to take account of <u>spatial differentiation</u> at every scale.

Functional Elements of Rurality

These three forbidding factors have led researchers to subdivide the rural environment into functional elements, in the hope that a series of functional definitions of countryside would, in summation, provide an approximation of the overall concept. Thus, for example, Clout [16] recognizes 'social, economic, land-use and spatial changes' as being the basic components of rural study, while Cherry [17] prefers to concentrate on economy, settlement and society as the three constituent parts of countryside.

Some of these functional elements can be considered further:

(a) <u>Land Use and Economy</u>. Wibberley[18] has described rural areas as 'those parts of a country which show unmistakable signs of being dominated by extensive use of land, either at the present time, or in the immediate past'. This definition, also used by Gilg[19], is useful in that it offers a tangible indicator of rurality (extensive uses of the land), but it highlights the existence of a 'zone in transition' in which extensive land uses have recently disappeared. This basis of definition also allows quantitative statements about the countryside to be made (eg, that 'eighty per cent of the land area of Britain is rural by use of appearance'[20].)

However, land use and agricultural economy as factors in isolation are insufficient to define the rural concept because although a clear distinction may be made between urban and rural land uses, other sectors of the rural environment are being rapidly urbanised in manners which are by no means distinct. This super-imposition of an urbanised society and economy onto an essentially rural landscape lies at the heart of problems of defining 'the countryside' in an unambiguous fashion.

(b) <u>Settlement</u>. Whereas there appears to be some concensus about rural land-use definitions, there is little evidence of agreement as to what constitutes a rural settlement. Traditionally, population size has served as an indicator to settlement type, although this criterion has unswervingly managed to confuse, rather than illuminate the issue. Moss[21] for example, advises that 'settlements falling between 200 and 5000 people are considered most likely to be villages, <u>although there are many exceptions</u>' (our italics).

The maximum size for a rural settlement, as quoted by various authors, ranges from 1000 to 15000 population (TABLE 1.3). The issue of a rural demographic threshold is further complicated by various administrative thresholds imposed by governments. Piatier and Madec[23] point out that in France all communes with more than 2000 inhabitants round the main towns are considered urban, yet if this definition were applied to Germany or the Netherlands, any "countryside" classification would disappear altogether. Similarly, in Iceland the threshold population for an administrative urban centre is 300, while in Japan it is 30,000.

TABLE 1.3   Suggested Maximum Sizes for Rural Settlements[22]

POPULATION	SUGGESTED BY	SETTLEMENT
1000	Everson and Fitzgerald (1969)	village
1500	Stirling (in Green, 1971)	
2500	Everson and Fitzgerald (1969)	country town
5000	Green	village
5000-7000	Best and Rogers (1973)	
8000	Thorburn (in Green, 1971)	
10000		Town Map Threshold
15000	Green (1971)	country town

Two further criteria need to be considered in addition to demographic size of settlement. First, function is seen to influence the nature of a settlement in that above a certain size, service and administrative levels become of an urban scale and type (however defined). Second, the character of a settlement is important as rural settlements are principally visual entities which characteristically rely on the style, shape and form of buildings as well as the relationship between these buildings and their landscapes for any distinctive identity (see Chapter 8). Recent rural settlement definitions in the United Kingdom have tended to impose upper demographic limits of 5000 and 10000[24], but in many ways Thorburn's[25] view of a village as 'any place which most residents think of as a village' remains the most telling single definition to have been proposed.

(c)   Society and Community. Definitions of rural communities are readily available. For example, Frankenberg has outlined the main differences between rural and urban communities (TABLE 1.4). Characteristics such as close-knit social networks, local power-base, and direct contact with end product of labour are an integral part of our traditional view of rural community. However, this view appears rather anachronistic when viewed against many contemporary rural societies.

Community differences of the type summarised in TABLE 1.4 were undoubtedly important when rural settlements were comparatively isolated and self-sufficient, and

TABLE 1.4 Rural-urban Community Differentials[26]

RURAL	URBAN
1. Community	1. Association
2. Social fields involving few	2. Social fields involving many
3. Multiple role relationships	3. Overlapping role relationships
4. Simple economy	4. Diverse economy
5. Little division of labour	5. Extreme differentiation and specialisation
6. Ascribed status	6. Achieved status
7. Education from status	7. Status from education
8. Close-knit social networks	8. Loose-knit social networks
9. Local power-base	9. Larger-scale power-base
10. Economic class - one division	10. Economic class - dominating division
11. Conflicting groups living together	11. Conflicting groups segregated
12. Regional focus of life	12. Occupational focus of life
13. Direct contact with end product of work	13. Detached from end product of work

when rural people were politically and socially
conservative, inward looking and economically
dependent on the land. However, with developments
in farm mechanisation, education, accessibility and
the mass media of communication, the old rural ways
of life have been radically changed:- village isolation has been reduced, the economic and social status of rural people has altered markedly, and there
has been, overall, a narrowing of the gap between
rural and urban attitudes.

Although the impact of urbanisation on rural society
should not be ignored, the notion of a "rural way of
life" continues to be viable. Evidence from the
United States for example, suggests that variations
in rates of mental distress, marriage problems and
concern for environmental quality indicate significant differences in behaviour and life-style between
rural and urban areas.[27] On the negative side, rural
communities are also united by various forms of
deprivation which are induced or exacerbated by inaccessibility and remoteness.

A Combination of Definitions. Consideration of these
various bases for characterising the countryside highlights the need to consider all of these elements
simultaneously. For the purpose of this book, 'the
countryside' should therefore be viewed as an area
which fulfils three principal criteria:

(i)   it is dominated (either currently or recently)
       by extensive land uses, such as agriculture
       and forestry, or large open spaces of undev-
       eloped land.
(ii) it contains small, low-order settlements which
       demonstrate a strong relationship between
       buildings and surrounding extensive landscape,
       and which are thought of as rural by most of
       their residents.
(iii) it engenders a way of life characterised by a
       cohesive identity based on respect for the
       environmental and behavioural qualities of
       living as part of an extensive landscape.

Doubtless, this definition is open to criticism, but
it does embrace the essential elements of resources
and their management in the countryside.

Using these terms of reference for the concept of
'countryside', three fundamental aspects of rural
areas should be stressed. First, the countryside is

composed of a complex mosaic of landscape elements, and rural areas function through processes of inter- action, change and conflict between these elements. Furthermore, the countryside is a palimpsest of com- ponents from different periods in time. It is part of a long evolution which is still occurring, and should therefore be viewed very much as a dynamic system. Finally, the countryside is a working environment rather than simply an area of escape for town dwellers. These issues reinforce the point that countryside (and the rurality it represents) is a dynamic phenomenon whose definition should be adapt- able and open to frequent re-evaluation.

The Dynamics of 'Rurality'

The dynamic nature of the countryside is clearly evident in the results of recent studies of the con- cept of rurality. For example, Cloke[28], derived an index of 'rurality' based on principal components analysis of sixteen readily available indicators settlement size, location and population character- istics (TABLE 1.5). The analysis yielded a scheme for classifying areas into various classes of rural- ity ranging from 'extreme rural' to 'extreme non- rural', on the basis of factor loadings; and this allowed the mapping of rurality levels in England and Wales (FIGURE 1.2). Rurality by this term of reference, can be viewed as representing a spectrum of states between two main types of rural area with the following characteristics:

(i) 'Those remote from the main urban areas tend to display a declining, static or only modestly increasing population; a declining number of working males; an ageing population structure often with low rates of natural increase; dec- lining employment; low female activity rates; and a high per capita cost of service provision'.

(ii) 'the dormitory or exurban areas, within com- muting distance of the major conurbations or other large towns, tend to show a rapid in- crease in population; a high proportion of workers travelling out of the area to work each day; a youthful population structure; and particularly high levels of car owner- ship.'[30]

It is clear from Cloke's analysis that rurality is a

14

TABLE 1.5 Variables used in index of rurality[29]

Variable name	Census data
1. Population density	Population/acre
2. Population change	% Change 1951-61, 1961-71
3. Population over 65	% Total population
4. Population men age 15—45	% Total population
5. Population women age 15—45	% Total population
6. Occupancy rate	% Population at 1½ per room
7. Occupancy rate	Households/dwelling
8. Household amenities	% Households with exclusive use of
	(a) Hot water
	(b) Fixed bath
	(c) Inside WC (1971)
9. Occupational structure	% in socio-economic groups
	13. Farmers—employers and managers
	14. Farmers—own account
	15. Agricultural workers

TABLE 1.5 (continued)

Variable name	Census data
10. Commuting out pattern	% Residents in employment working outside the rural district
11. In-migration	% Population resident for less than 5 years
12. Out-migration	% Population moved out in last year
13. In/out migration balance	% In/out migrants
14. Distance from nearest urban centre of 5000 population	—
15. Distance from nearest urban centre of 100000 population	—
16. Distance from nearest urban centre of 200000 population	—

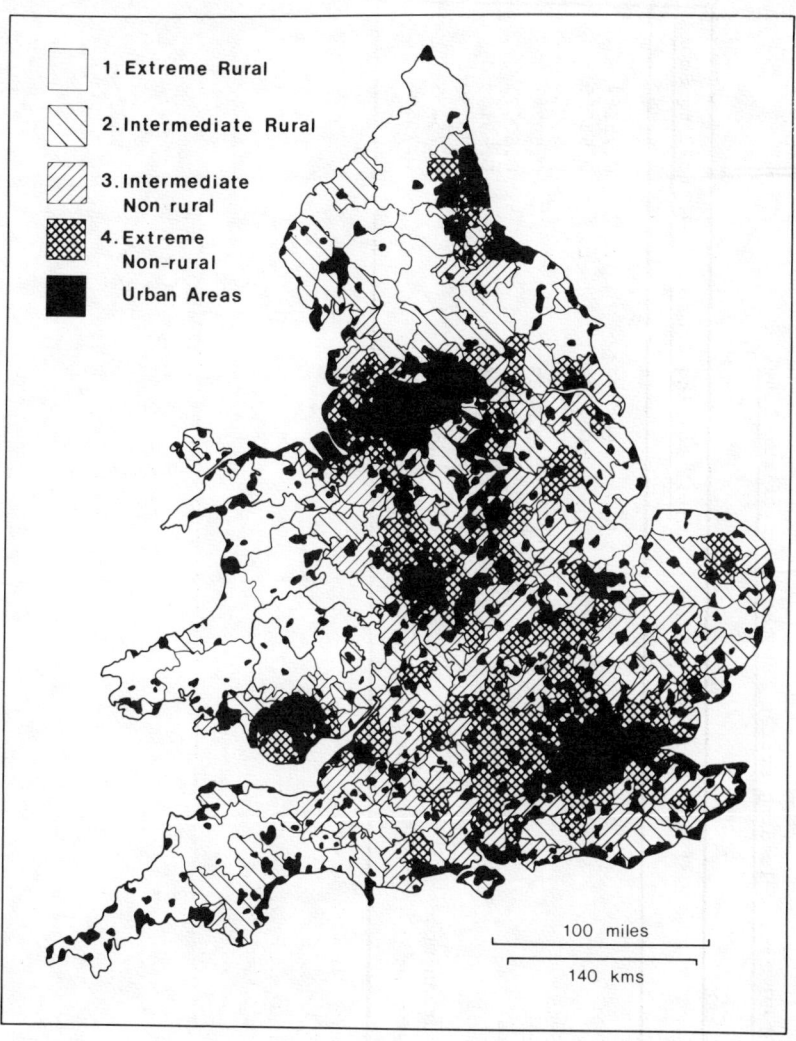

FIGURE 1.2   Spatial Variations in Rurality in
             England and Wales

Source: after P.J. Cloke, 'An index of rurality for
          England and Wales', Regional Studies 11
          (1977): 31-46.

TABLE 1.6   1961 and 1971 factor loading scores for the index of rurality[31]

Variable	1961 Loading Score	1971 Loading Score
Population change	0.73984	0.75264
Household amenities	0.73780	0.63919
Population, women 15-45	0.72098	0.81910
Commuting out pattern	0.68591	0.69741
In-migration (5 years)	0.64610	0.60671
Population density	0.59345	0.59169
Population over 65	-0.61408	-0.70138
Distance from 50000 urban mode	-0.71716	-0.76455
Occupational structure	-0.78833	-0.79594

changing concept. For example, TABLE 1.6 compares
the loading scores for significant variables in the
1961 and 1971 indices of rurality. These scores
clearly show that individual variables have become
more or less important in the explanation of the
concept of rurality over a ten year time period. For
example, the positive indicators reveal that standards of household amenities were less important as
evidence of rural character in 1971 than they had
been a decade previously. This is a predictable
result of the gradual improvement in rural housing
standards which has narrowed the rural-urban gap in
this respect (see Chapter 5). On the negative side,
the influence of retirement on rural character is
seen to have increased substantially between the
two index dates. It would appear that rural populations are progressively harbouring people of pen-
sionable age, and that this trend itself is altering
the rural character (as well as sounding a warning
for future levels of care and social services in
rural areas) (see Chapter 10.1).

1.3   THE RURAL CONCEPT - THEORIES

The theoretical treatment of the rural concept is a
vital factor in our understanding of the resources
offered by rural areas, and of the needs and requirements of rural management. An important element in
such a treatment is the extent to which rural resource management should be separate from equivalent
urban processes.

For example, Kyllingstad[32] argues that policies
developed for urban milieux create more problems in
the countryside than they solve, while Lefaver[33] concludes that 'Planning for rural areas demands a new
framework and tools quite different from those used
in urban planning. Present planning policies assume
that rural areas are no more than a part of the
urban fringe. With this bias, public officials
often attempt to solve rural problems with tools designed for urban areas. Planners must understand
that rural issues need to be defined in their own
context and that the policy tools used to solve
those issues must come from the rural perspective'.

Views on the relationships between rural and urban
areas are inextricably linked with regional and
political ideology. For example, Sigurdson[34] reports
that both India and China are challenging the traditionally exclusive linkages between urbanisation and

modernisation (thus securing a future for a separate rural identity). In eastern Europe, however, the process of urbanisation is seen as de-ruralisation (the demolition of rural identity) and one of the main stated objectives of socialism in countries such as Poland is to reduce and if possible eliminate social and economic differences between town and country.[35]

Two topics are central to an understanding of theoretical views of the rural concept:-

   (a) the relationship between 'rural' and
        'urban' areas, and changing from a rural
        to urban state.

   (b) the spatial dynamics involved in changing
        from a rural to urban state.

Rural-Urban Interdependence

Ebenezer Howard was one of the first to highlight the interdependence of town and country. He emphasised the advantages and disadvantages of town and country life. Hall[37] summarises Howard's line of argument: 'The advantages of the city were the opportunities it offered in the form of accessibility to jobs and to urban services of all kinds; the disadvantages could all be summed up in the poor resulting natural environment. Conversely the countryside offered an excellent environment but virtually no opportunities of any sort'.

Howard's solution was to combine the best elements of both types of area into the garden city idea which would maximise accessibility and environmental quality simultaneously. The inference to be gained from his thinking, however, is that existing rural areas depend on their urban counterparts for lifestyle opportunity while a reverse dependence operates for environmental opportunities.

This rather simplistic view of rural-urban interdependence has since been expanded in a variety of ways. Lassey's[38] view of the American rural environment for example, led him to conclude that: 'The urban conglomerates are much more dependent on rural based resources than are rural regions dependent on urban centres; rural areas are the principal source of food, air, water, and other raw materials on which life depends'. He might also have added that rural environments also contributed towards mental health and aesthetic values, whilst representing a locality for recreation and refreshments away from the noise, pollution and constructed environment of cities.

Doxiadis[39] in contrast, sees town and country as linked without any real discontinuity. Indeed, he has shaped the subject of ekistics out of the notion of the interrelationship of the entire settlement system, and he concluded that 'The future of rural settlements is the future for all human settlements. There is no special future for the rural versus the urban, or the small versus the large, or the rich versus the poor. It is an interdependent world and being an inhabitant of one settlement should tie each individual into the whole'.

Rural-Urban Dynamics

The theoretical nature of the rural-urban relationship may be viewed in the form of a fluid cyclical model (FIGURE 1.3) with several distinct stages. The cycle does not necessarily represent the course of changing perception through time, but it does allow various viewpoints to be synthesised.

(i) Dichotomy. The idea of 'rural' and 'urban' as two poles of a dichotomy stems from Tonnies'[41] theorisation of Gemeinschaft (community) and Gesellschaft (society). This emphasises the differences between an ideal community type where human relationships are intimate, enduring and based on a clear-cut role within society, and the large scale impersonal and contractual ties of metropolitan society. Hillery[42] illustrates this dichotomous model by comparing the village (a small agricultural settlement) with the city, which is seen as a relatively large, dense and permanent settlement of socially heterogeneous individuals.

(ii) Continuum. The next state in the cycle is the transition from dichotomy to continuum brought about by the recognition[43] that a sliding-scale between the rural and urban poles appears to reflect more accurately the real world distribution of society (and subsequently environment).

(iii) Intermeshed Continua. The continuum idea was further embellished by a realisation that one line drawn between the two poles was again an oversimplification of the rural-urban relationship, and could be replaced by a series of intermeshed continua.

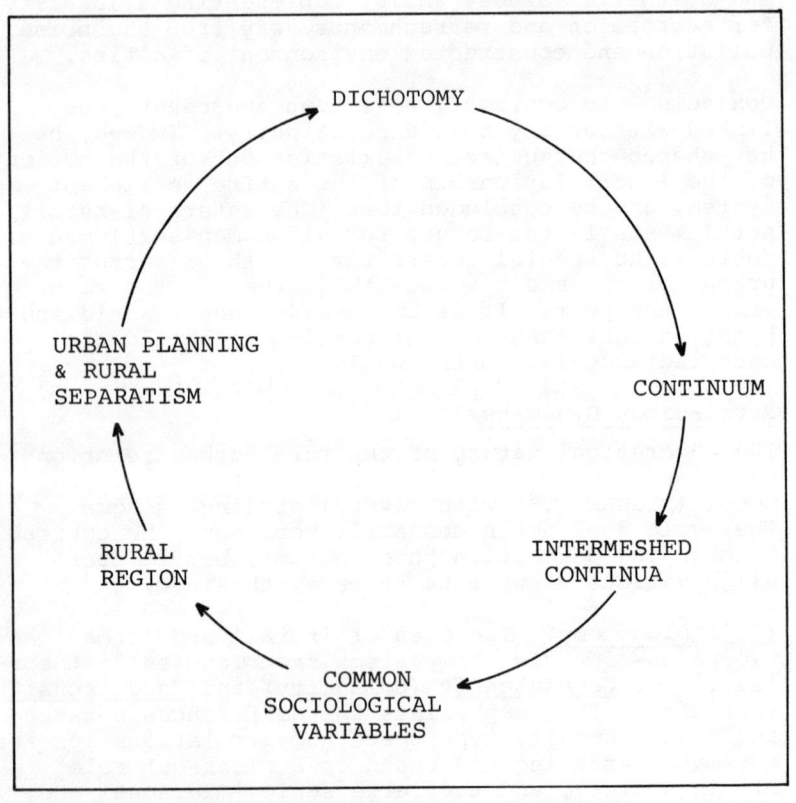

FIGURE 1.3   Cyclical Model of the Rural-Urban
             Relationship

Source: after P.J. Cloke and M.J. Griffiths,
          'Planning responses to urban and rural prob-
          lems; the case of South Wales', Tijdschrift
          vor Economische en Sociale Geografie 7 (1980):
          255-63.

This 'is composed of a series of continua, for
example social demographic, cultural, political and
economic, which need not all be present in every
situation and which do not necessarily change along
its continuum in a similar fashion'.[44]

(iv) Common Sociological Variables. A further
progression from the idea of intermeshed continua
was outlined by Bailey[45] who stressed that the
defining parameters of social problems manifest in

urban areas are the same as those occurring in the
countryside. The factors of poverty, immobility,
powerlessness and arbitrary bureaucratic control are
prevalent in all environments, and planners should
account for, and recognise the existence of, these
common sociological variables.

This stage of the conceptual cycle has proved very
attractive to resource managers and planners in that
it allows the contemplation of common solutions to
common social problems. Using this perspective, for
example, small towns might be viewed as scaled down
models or large towns.

(v) <u>Rural regions and planning separatism</u>. At
this stage on the conceptual cycle a reverse trend
came into operation, stemming from the argument that
rural management problems demand individual attention.
The sceptical commentator might reflect that this up-
turn resulted from a specific effort on the part of
academics to retain rural areas as a legitimate and
definable subject area, rather than see them merged
into a more systematic form of study.

However this trend may also be justified on two important and less pragmatic grounds. First, the agricultural base of the countryside poses distinctive
problems in terms of structural unemployment, job
retraining requirements and depopulation. Second,
the particular scale of these problems demands specific measures directed towards the basic provision of
opportunities over an extensive but sparsely populated land area. As a consequence, rural planners
have sought conceptual solace in Green's[46] regional
approach which differentiates between 'conurban' and
'rural' regions (each to be managed using very different strategies), and also in ever increasing
separatism from urban matters, with rural-urban conflicts arising over allocation of resources, prestige
and political power.

There are signs that the fairly well entrenched sep-
aratist attitude between rural and urban management
is, in itself, being broken down at the present time,
with a return to more interdependent standpoints in
the analysis of rural and urban phenomena. Perhaps
the most acceptable compromise position in this never-
ending conceptual search has been proposed by
Moseley.[47] He argues that there is a <u>rural dimension</u>,
made up of three basic characteristics:-

(i) <u>a pleasant environment</u> - which will attract the willing or unwilling unemployed.

(ii) <u>a 'spaced-out' geographical structure</u> - leading to accessibility problems and costly public services.

(iii) <u>a distinctive local political ideology</u> - favouring the market, the volunteer and the self-helper rather than public provision.

Moseley stresses, however that rurality is not the cause of social deprivation which is fundamentally similar to that occurring in urban environments (FIGURE 1.4).

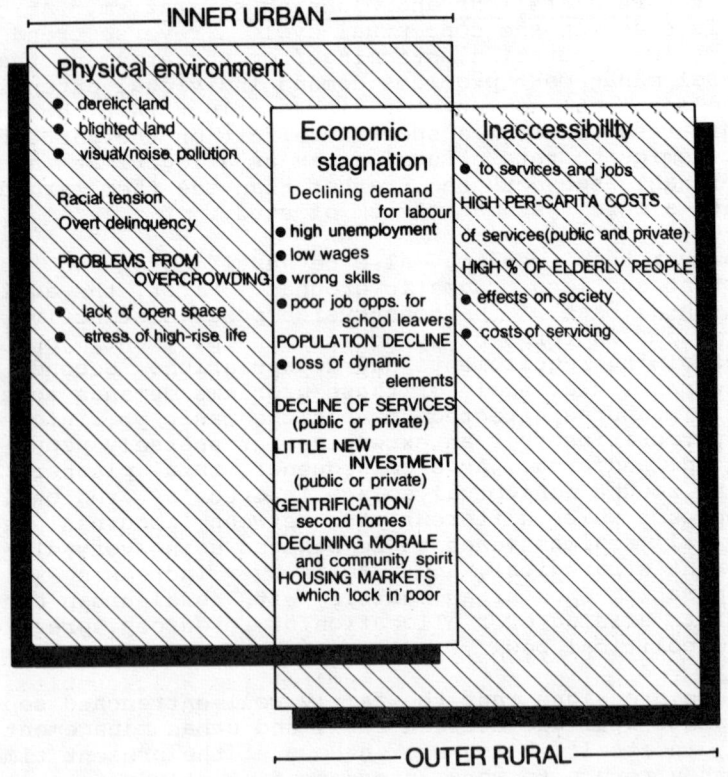

FIGURE 1.4   <u>Urban and Rural Britain - Overlapping Sets of Problems</u>

Source: after M.J. Moseley, 'Is rural deprivation really rural?', <u>The Planner</u> 66 (1980): 97.

Thus despite the acknowledgement of a set of
characteristics which may be termed rural, it does
appear that social, environmental and economic problems in the countryside may be viewed as localised
manifestations of aspatial processes. Our view of
resource management in rural areas should take note
of this point and perhaps allow it to overrule more
conventional (but less useful) conceptualisations of
the rural-urban relationship.

1.4 RURAL DYNAMICS AND CHANGE

'Each of us is familiar with areas that have
been paved over, built over, roofed over, and
completely transformed from rural to urban during our own lifetimes' [48]

It is useful to consider rural land use changes initially in this chapter, because these represent a
basic component of the dynamics of the rural resource
system. Berry and Plant[49] interpret the changing
land use situation in the United States as being one
of differing scales. Nationally, the loss of farm
land to urban use is causing some concern over the
future ability to produce sufficient food.

Transformation to Urban land uses

However, the conflict between urban growth and the
rural economy is more acute at the regional, and in
particular the local levels, where dispersed patterns
of development are seen to produce a significant
alteration in the appearance of the rural landscape,
changing it from traditionally rural to an inter-
mediate stage between rural and urban. Besides the
direct conversion of agricultural land to urban use,
the speculation in land and other spillover effects
from the urbanisation process interfere with agriculture in advance of the main wave of land use
change. Thus the formal transformation of land from
rural to urban use is preceded by the localised idl-
ing of farmland and a slow switch from high capital
investment activities (such as dairying) to other
types of farming.

Hart[50] has formalised these processes into spatial
form using the example of the Minneapolis - St. Paul
SMSA (FIGURE 1.5). When the area was first defined
in 1950, the urban fringe was relatively small, but
over the next two decades considerable lateral
expansion can be measured in various direction,

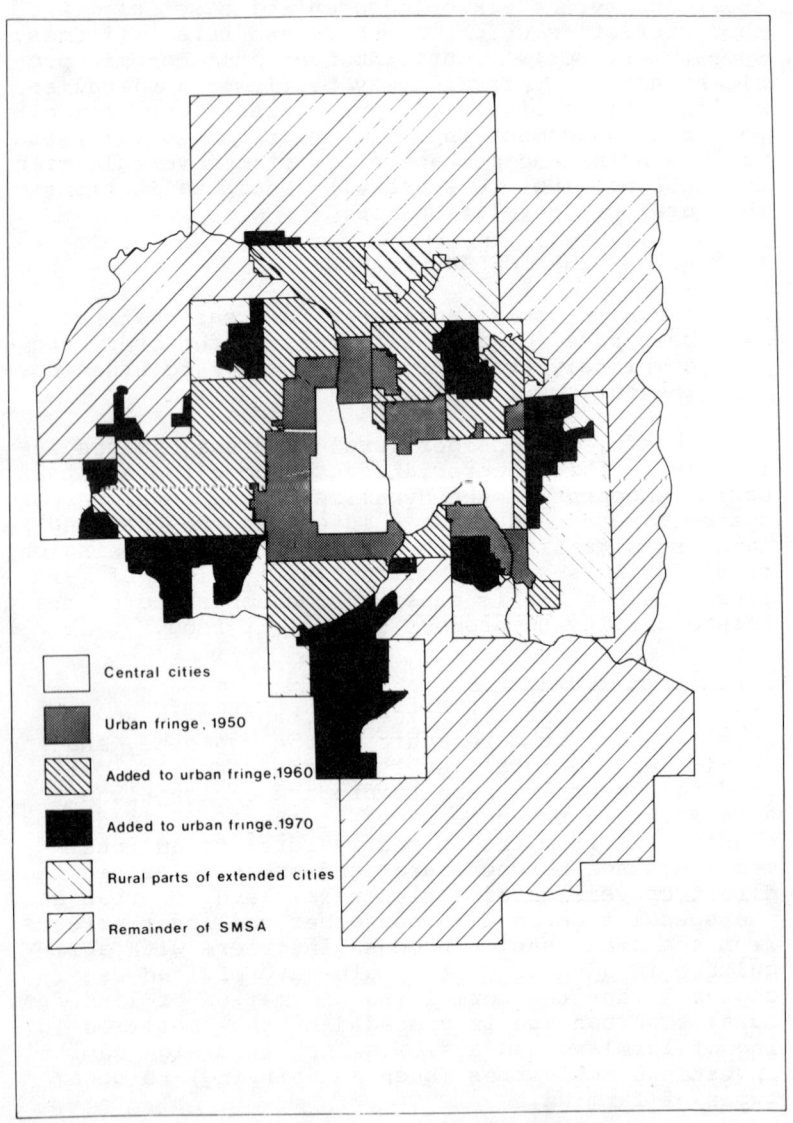

FIGURE 1.5 Rural to Urban Land Use Changes in
            Minneapolis - St. Paul

Source: after J.F. Hart, 'Urban encroachment on
         rural areas', Geographical Review 66 (1976):
         1-17.

resulting in the enlargement of the SMSA from five counties to ten in 1973. It is this type of land use change measurement which has formed the basis for modelling and theorisation of changes to the rural area.

American research in this context reflected earlier work carried out in Britain. Following the simple calculation of regional conversions of agricultural land to urban use, Best and Champion[51] developed the theme by investigating the relationship between population growth and the extension of urban land. They concluded that no such relationship necessarily exists, at least in a direct and simple form. Rather, they found that at least three factors combined to influence the urban demand for rural land:

(i) <u>National economic growth</u>, leading to land needs for industry transport and so on;

(ii) <u>Natural population growth and in-migration</u>, producing demand for new housing and associated land uses;

(iii) <u>Increasing urban space standards</u> due to rising levels of affluence exerting pressure for higher per capita land increments.

Coleman[52] sums up the effects of these factors most vividly: 'The new settlement is scattered in a loose sprawl, taking up to three times as much farmland as it actually converts to urban uses but fragmenting the remainder and subjecting it to intolerable urban pressures to the point of abandonment by the farmer'.

The Urban Influence

It is clear from this research carried out on both sides of the Atlantic that the principal occurrence of rural change is located at the urban fringe, and that the motive force behind this change is that of urbanisation. Theoretical interpretations of rural change have therefore largely adopted this perspective, although most theories have consisted of spin-off from concepts of urbanisation which have treated rural areas as mere appendages of the spreading urban mass. Consequently changes in rural areas have usually been viewed with an urban perception rather than in their own light.

Coleman[53] describes 'a chain-reaction of land use pressures spreading outward like ripples on a pond, but with a far less rapid and transitory effect'.

She dramatises this image by adding 'for ripples read shock waves which have a profoundly dislocating effect upon one zone of land use after another'. These descriptions tie in closely with the 'tidal wave' concepts of land use changes. Yet in modelling these processes, Coleman makes important secondary statements about smaller-scale changes in non-urban areas. Following the central theme of take-up of agricultural land, she emphasises two previously undervalued influences in rural change which serve to stress that the urban fringe is by no means the only rural location where important metamorphosis is taking place. First, the effects of recreation are seen to promote an accelerated urbanisation and commercialisation of the countryside. Second, the concentration of rural population into key settlements has led to the sterilisation of farmland.

The identification, use and management of various resources is further stressed by Moss[54] in the explanation of rural population change. In particular, he supports the main theme of ex-urban population movement with careful secondary observation of changes at various levels of the rural settlement hierarch. Key settlements, expanding villages, commuter villages and tourist villages are seen to come under pressure both from 'the prosperous city inhabitant who is retiring, changing employment or unwilling to remain in a decaying urban environment' and 'the poorer rural resident whose deprived lifestyle is worsening due to poor wages and diminishing government investment'.[55] Other settlements fail to attract in-migration and are therefore in danger of losing their livelihood. Although these groups are overtly stereotyped, Moss's model does begin to fill in some of the detail which was lacking in earlier broad-brush conceptualisations of rural change.

1.5 CONCLUSIONS

This brief review of examples representing diverse channels through which the conceptualisation of rural change can be approached suggests two main conclusions which are pertinent to an understanding of the overall rural concept. First, progress in providing suitable rural concepts with which to explain changes within rural areas has been tangible but slow. Only recently have researchers begun to uncover secondary aspects of change within the overall movement of urbanisation. Second, although conceptual statements in this context are of little value unless they recognize the fundamental interdependence between urban and rural matters, it is nevertheless also true that careful balancing of the urban and rural sides of the equation is required before any further progress is achieved.

On the one hand, urban-based concepts should not be used loosely in the rural context unless there is evidence to show that they are applicable in this context. On the other hand, rural conceptualisation should account for urban influences on the country-side, even if an essentially rural perspective is to be used.

What is clear is that the conceptual frameworks currently adopted do not offer a means of measuring the impact of relationships between conflicting elements in the countryside, nor do they suggest how to solve a conflict situation. It is in the attainment of these objectives that a resource-based view of rural areas offers a useful platform for advancement, both theoretical and practical.

NOTES AND REFERENCES

1. C. Doyle and R. Tranter, 'In search of vision: rural land-use problems and policies', Built Environment 4 (1978): 289.

2. A.W. Gilg, 'Needed: a new 'Scott' inquiry', Town Planning Review 49 (1978): 353.

3. For a comprehensive discussion of rural planning in general see A.W. Gilg, Countryside Planning: The First Three Decades 1945-76 (David Charles, Newton Abbot, 1978). For a specific view of the unbuilt rural environment see J. Davidson and G.P. Wibberley, Planning and the Rural Environment (Pergamon, Oxford, 1977).

4. H. Newby, C. Bell, D. Rose and P. Saunders, Property, Paternalism and Power (Hutchinson, London, 1978).

5. M.J. Hagood, 'Development of a 1940 rural farm level of living index for countries. Rural Sociology, 8 (1945): 171-80.

6. R.H. Best and A.W. Rogers, The Urban Countryside

(Faber, London, 1973): 20.

7. G.E. Cherry (ed), _Rural Planning Problems_ (Hill, London, 1976): 4.

8. D. Pocock and R. Hudson, _Images of the Urban Environment_ (Macmillan, London, 1978).

9. M.S. Cornish and S.R. Cornish, 'Planners' conceptions of rural-urban characteristics: the North Yorkshire and Tees-side Structure Plans', _Regional Studies_ 9 (1975); 169-180.

10. S. Lefaver, 'A new framework for rural planning', _Urban Land_ 37 (1978): 7.

11. M.J. Moseley, R.G. Harman, O.B. Coles and M.B. Spencer, _Rural Transport and Accessibility_ (Final Report to the Department of the Environment, University of East Anglia: CEAS, 1977: 2.

12. J.M. Shaw, 'Rural Deprivation and Social Planning: An Overview'in J.M. Shaw (ed), _Rural Deprivation and Planning_ (Geobooks, Norwich, 1979): 177.

13. Cherry, _Rural Planning Problems_ (Note 7) 2; W.R. Lassey, _Planning in Rural Environments_ (McGraw-Hill, New York, 1977): 5-6; H.D. Clout, _Rural Geography: An Introductory Survey_ (Pergamon, Oxford, 1972): 1; G.J. Lewis, _Rural Communities: A Social Geography_ (David and Charles, Newton Abbot, 1979): 22; G.P. Wibberley, 'Conflicts in the countryside', _Town and Country Planning_, 40 (1972): 259; G. Moss, 'Rural Settlements', _Architects Journal_ (18 January, 1978): 101; A Thorburn, _Planning Villages_ (Estates Gazette, London, 1971): 2.

14. C.J. Palmer, M.E. Robinson and R.W. Thomas, 'The countryside image: an investigation of structure and meaning', _Environment and Planning A_, 9 (1977): 739-749.

15. Ibid., 747.

16. Clout, _Rural Geography_ (see TABLE 1.1 and Note 13): 1.

17. Cherry, _Rural Planning Problems_ (Note 7): 2.

18. Wibberley, Conflicts (Note 13).

19. Gilg, Countryside Planning (Note 3).

20. B.J. Woodruffe, Rural Settlement Policies and Plans (Oxford University Press, Oxford, 1976): 2

21. Moss, 'Rural settlements' (Note 13): 101.

22. P.J. Cloke, Key Settlements in Rural Areas (Methuen, London, 1979): 30.

23. A. Piatier and J. Madec, 'Comment et pourquoi definir un espace rural?' Economie Rurale, 118 (1977): 3-13.

24. 5,000 by Moss, 'Rural settlements' and others (Note 13).
10,000 by Lewis, Rural Communities and others (Note 13).

25. Thorburn, Planning Villages (Note 13): 2.

26. R. Frankenberg, Communities in Britain (Penguin, Harmondsworth, 1966).

27. See in particular K.R. Tremblay and R.E. Dunlop, 'Rural-urban residence and concern with environmental quality: a replication and extension' Rural Sociology, 43 (1978): 479-491; S.D. Webb, 'Mental health in rural and urban environments', Ekistics, 45 (1978): 37-43; and K. Woodrow, D.W. Hastings and E.J. Tu, 'Rural-urban patterns of marriage, divorce and mortality: Tennessee, 1970' Rural Sociology, 43 (1978): 70-86.

28. P.J. Cloke, 'An index of rurality for England and Wales', Regional Studies, 11 (1977): 31-46.

29. Idem.

30. M.J. Moseley, Accessibility: The Rural Challenge (Methuen, London, 1979): 5-6.

31. Cloke, 'Index of rurality' (Note 28): 35, 40.

32. R. Kyllingstad, 'Tanker om landsbygdsplanlegging', Plan og Arbeid, 6 (1975): 222-26.

33. S. Lefaver, 'A new framework for rural planning' Urban Land, 37 (1978): 7-13.

34. J. Sigurdson, 'Development of rural areas in

India and China', <u>Ambio</u>, 5 (1976): 98-108.

35. K. Bajan, 'Egalisation des conditions de vie entre la ville et la campagne en Pologne', <u>Economie Rurale</u> 111 (1976): 77-9.

36. E. Howard, <u>Garden Cities of Tomorrow</u> (1898).

37. P. Hall, <u>Urban and Regional Planning</u> (Penguin, Harmondsworth, 1974): 48.

38. W.R. Lassey, <u>Planning in Rural Environments</u> (McGraw-Hill, New York, 1977).

39. See the special 'Rural Settlement' version of <u>Ekistics</u>, 43 (1977): 183-239.

40. P.J. Cloke and M.J. Griffiths, 'Planning responses to urban and rural problems: the case of S.W. Wales', <u>T.E.S.G.</u>, 7 (1980): 255-63.

41. F. Tonnies, <u>Community and Society</u> (Harper, New York, 1957).

42. G.A. Hillery, <u>Communal Organisations</u> (Chicago University Press, Chicago, 1969).

43. By Hillery himself and also, for example, by R. Redfield, <u>The Folk Culture of Yucatan</u> (Chicago University Press, Chicago, 1941).

44. Lewis, <u>Rural Communities</u> (Note 13): 34.

45. J. Bailey, <u>Social Theory for Planning</u> (Routledge and Kegan Paul, London, 1975).

46. R.J. Green, <u>Country Planning: The Future of the Rural Regions</u> (Manchester University Press, Manchester, 1971).

47. M.J. Moseley, 'Is rural deprivation really rural?' <u>The Planner</u>, 66 (1980): 97.

48. J.F. Hart, 'Urban encroachment on rural areas' <u>Geographical Review</u>, 66 (1976): 1-17.

49. D. Berry & T. Plant, 'Retaining agricultural activities under urban pressures: a review of land use conflicts and policies', <u>Policy Sciences</u>, 9 (1978): 53-178.

50. Hart, 'Urban encroachment' (Note 48): 7.

51. R.H. Best & A.G. Champion, 'Regional conversions of agricultural land to urban use in England and Wales, 1945-67', Transactions Institute of British Geographers, 49 (1970): 15-32.

52. A. Coleman, 'Last bid for land-use sanity', Geographical Magazine, 50 (1978): 820-824.

53. Idem., 820.

54. G. Moss, Rural Settlements (Note 13).

55. Idem.

Chapter Two

RURAL RESOURCES

This chapter aims to introduce the concept of
resources and resource management, and to focus
attention on the overall structure and dynamics of
the rural resource system.

2.1 THE CONCEPT OF A RESOURCE

Definitive statements on terminology within resource
management are extremely elusive because, as
O'Riordan[1] notes, there is no satisfactory definition of a _resource_, and no one definition has
remained generally acceptable through time. This
elusiveness arises partly because the very subject
of 'resources' is inherently inter-disciplinary if
not multi-disciplinary, and operational definitions
vary between interested disciplines.

Also important is the fact that a resource (in
general terms) is not necessarily a tangible object,
but it is a culturally-defined and abstract concept.
In essence, anything can be regarded as a resource
if it offers a means of attaining certain socially-
valued goals. These goals can be extremely wide-
ranging and they will vary through both space and
time. Attainment of such goals is generally influenced by the prevailing social, political,
economic and institution framework of the individual,
group or unit responsible for the decision-making
and so these elements all become important in any
resource management system.

Formulation of the Concept

The foundations for much present-day thinking within
resource management were laid down by Zimmermann[2].
He viewed a resource in terms of a functional

relationship between three things - human wants, human abilities, and human appraisal of the environment around him (using environment in its most general sense). The environment comprises both social/economic and physical/environmental elements and it offers a basic reservoir of what Zimmermann termed 'neutral stuff'.

This neutral stuff can be evaluated in terms of human wants - which are both biological (such as the provision of food and shelter and social (our sense of value and our aspirations) and human needs, at that point in time. On the basis of this evaluation, decisions might be taken to transform this aspect of neutral stuff into some form of useable resource. Whether or not this can occur, and the ease and speed of it happening, will depend largely on prevailing knowledge (that is, understanding of how to do it) and technology (having the capability to do it) (FIGURE 2.1). In short, therefore, cultural appraisal of the neutral stuff is designed to isolate opportunities offered by that environment, from the restrictions which cannot (under existing technology and/or the prevailing cultural and social system) be converted into useable resources.

Perception of Opportunities

Appraisal of opportunities depends on perception of their presence, recognition of their capacity to satisfy human wants, and development of means of utilising them to achieve socially-derived goals. Thus both technological and organisational abilities are of central concern, the latter particularly in the context in which resources are considered in this book.

The resource management system depends heavily upon the type and degree of organisation within the system - these determine efficiency of resource use and flexibility of resource management, as well as the basic functioning of the overall resource system. Once perception of the opportunities has isolated certain resources as suitable for use then alternative strategies for resource use can be evaluated (FIGURE 2.1) and final decisions made about resource management and opportunity costs.

Resources are thus created to satisfy human wants. This act of 'creation' depends on many factors, such as the identification of opportunities, the

35

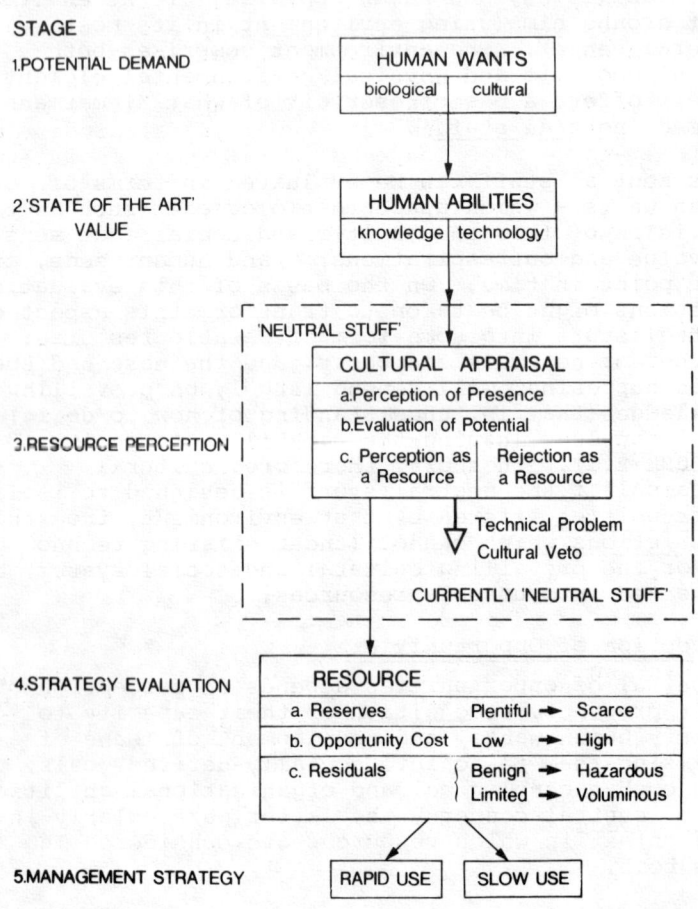

FIGURE 2.1   The Resource System - A General Model

Source: after R.M. Auty (personal communication, 1980)

characteristics of the reservoir of neutral stuff,
and on the deployment of organisational and technological abilities. To take the example of rural
land-use as a 'resource' problem, the act of
'creation' will depend on factors such as existing
land uses and evaluations of land capability for
different forms of land use; the physical properties
of the land in question, and social and economic
views on the suitability of that land for different
uses; the level and type of land management, and
development control; and levels of experience and
technical capabilities in successfully changing land
use to that required.

Zimmermann concluded that 'availability for human
use, not mere physical presence, is the chief criterion of resources. Availability in turn depends on
human wants and abilities'.[3] Thus 'resources are
not, they become; they are not static but expand
and contract in response to human wants and human
actions'.[4]

2.2   PERSPECTIVES IN RESOURCE MANAGEMENT

Within any planning situation, three basic aspects
of resources are of central value[5] - the analysis of
resource availability and status (the role of the
resource surveyor); approaches to the management of
both given and potential resources (resource manager);
and strategies for developing the resource base
(resource developer).

Inevitably, however, the emphasis given to these
three aspects of resource use varies under different
planning situations - depending, for example, on
whether one is evaluating likely resource-use through
the eyes of a developer or a planner; or whether the
planner is considering future possibilities for
development control (in which case his interest might
focus more explicitly on resource survey) or on
existing problems of land-use conflict (where he will
be concerned with the more pressing problems of
resource management).

It is likely also that the emphasis between the three
aspects of resource-use has altered over time.
O'Riordan[6], for example, has contrasted the nineteenth century preoccupation in the United States
and Great Britain with resource development (where
production and consumption of given resources were
related basically to willingness to pay and

maximisation of net private gain), with more recent
concern with resource management (where resource use
is geared more closely to optimisation of net social
benefits). This change was consequent upon the
development of welfare economics, which sees public
intervention and social control as necessary to
regulate the excesses of private action in the public
interest and it represents a basic shift of interest
within the field of resources in general. The thesis
around which this book is woven is based on resource
management rather than simply resource development,
although the two are intimately related together.

Resources are an inter-disciplinary area of study,
and they have been regarded from many points of view
(FIGURE 2.2). This inter-disciplinary foundation
does allow resource management to benefit from contact with many areas of enquiry and from a corres-
pondingly broad range of interests and concepts, but
it also creates problems in agreeing on key issues
and viable solutions. These problems arise because
of a variety of factors such as methodological
differences between individual disciplines, variations in the viewpoints and aspirations of the
individuals involved, the politics, prejudices, conservatism and flexibility of the different types of
institutions involved, and the inevitable existence
of communication gaps between even closely allied
fields of study. Such problems are highlighted in
O'Riordan's[7] study of the resource management process
in the Norfolk Broads in England which illustrates
how the different parties involved in using and
managing the area disagree on what precisely are the
main causes of environmental deterioration in the
Broads. This lack of agreement on initial causes
inevitably fosters differences of opinion on suitable courses of remedial action, and makes efficient
decision-making very difficult.

Issues and Contraints

It is clear that each of these perspectives in resource management is not of equal significance in its
potential or actual impact in decision-making. Constraints can perhaps be rationalised into a threefold
hierarchy (TABLE 2.1):

(a)   the fundamental factors (of primary importance)
      which make technical feasibility and strategic
      implications of basic importance at the outset
      in any resource management decision-making
      situation;

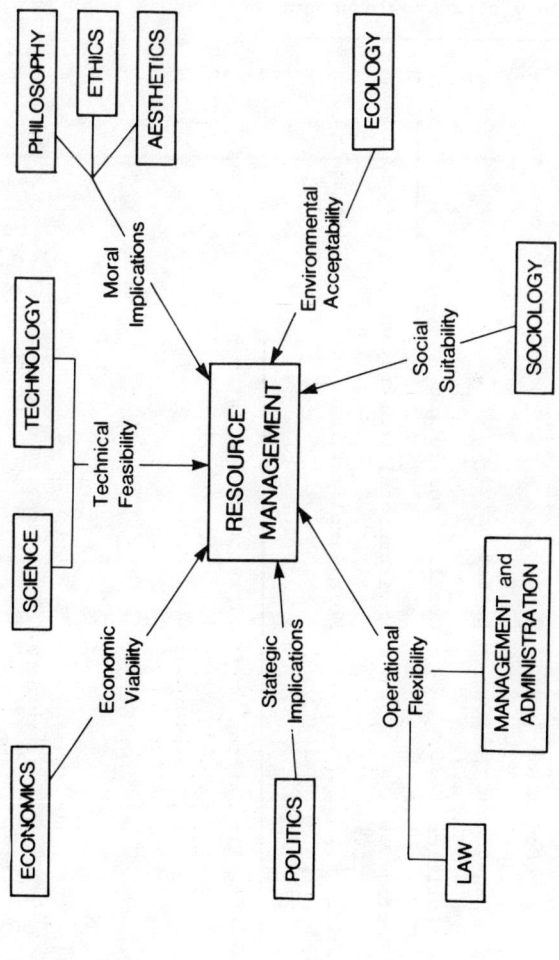

FIGURE 2.2   Some Dominant Perspectives in Resource Management

Source: after T. O'Riordan, Perspectives on Resource Management
(Pion, London, 1971): p11.

39

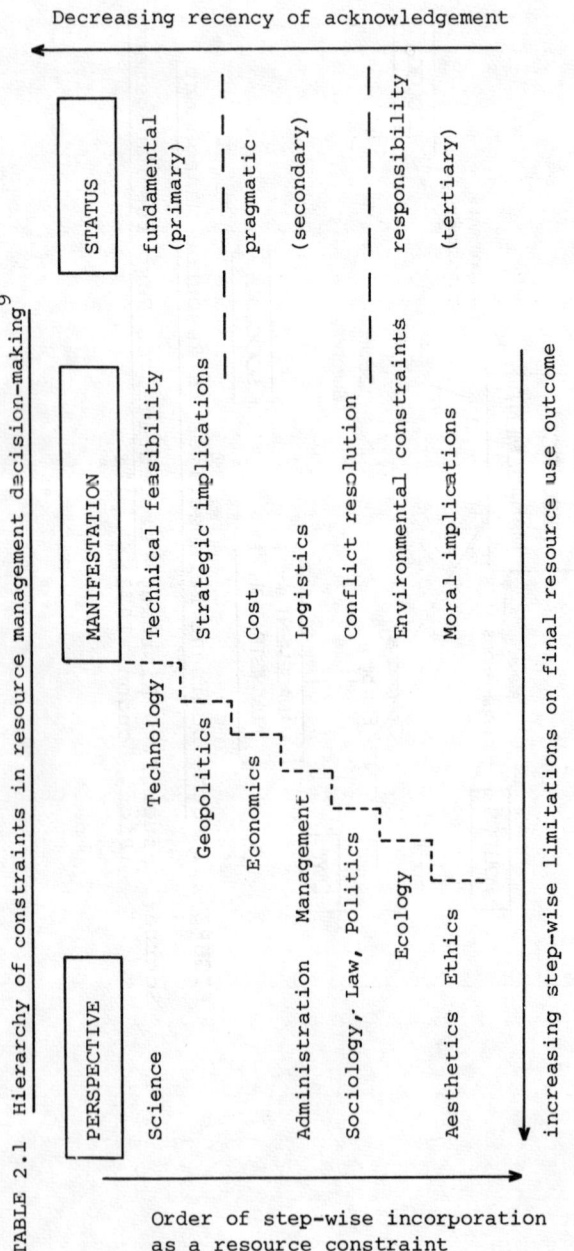

TABLE 2.1 Hierarchy of constraints in resource management decision-making[9]

(b)   the pragmatic factors (of secondary importance)
      which relate to the economic, administrative
      and social dimensions of decision-making, and

(c)   the responsibility elements (of tertiary
      importance) such as environmental and ethical
      issues.

Auty[8] has suggested that the 'fundamental' issues are
generally regarded as the most important in decision-
making. The 'responsibility' factors have been
widely acknowledged as constraints in resource-use
only recently, and then they are generally considered
after other factors have been evaluated. Within the
'responsibility' elements there appears to have been
a differential shift in emphasis over the last two
decades. Environmental constraints have clearly
shifted towards a more fundamental position since
the 1960's, with the advent and impact of environmentalism.

In addition, moral and aesthetic elements in decision-
making appeared to become more important through the
1960's and early 1970's, only to be displaced back
to their original 'tertiary' status as a constraint
after the beginnings of the energy crisis in the mid-
1970's. It seems also that such moral and aesthetic
constraints might well be suppressed by more technical, strategic and economic considerations as the
period dominated by energy shortages, economic
depression and concern for national self-sufficiency
and strategic security extends at least into the
mid 1980's.

2.3   KEY THEMES IN RESOURCE MANAGEMENT

Three themes in resource management are of particular
importance in the context of this book.

Recent Interest

The first is the relatively recent rise of interest
in resources and resource management in the developed
world. Interest has crystallised since the early
1960's, partly as a response to a growing awareness
of the possibility of large-scale and long-term
environmental disruption, and recognition of the
significance of national strategic security.[10]
Thus recent interest in resource management has
several important characteristics such as the search
for co-operative policies, increasing public

involvement, and the allied growth in number and
diversity of pressure groups. In particular the use
of formal methods of resource allocation and an
increasing role of government (with welfare consideration replacing direct profit incentives) suggest
that resource management might become more generally
accepted in all aspects of planning.[11]

Quality of Environment

A second theme is that in many developed countries,
where levels of economic development were already
relatively high (in both absolute and per capita
terms) by the early 1960's some attention within
resource management has been allowed to switch from
the basic provision of material resources for
economic growth, towards less tangible resource
issues which concern the quality of the environment
and quality of life. Chapman[12] has commented on the
implication that 'as a society reaches some threshold
of economic development, with its attendant scientific and technological capabilities, it can afford to
concern itself less with materials and quantity, and
more with the quality of life. Whether this is true
or not, and however we define our terms, attaching
utility to the quality of environment has the effect
of perceiving as resources some aspects of the
environment not previously considered to be
resources - the appearance of the landscape, wilderness, animal life, plant associations, and the like'.

This change in orientation appears to have two main
implications for rural resource management. One is
that the overall fabric and landscape of the countryside -see Chapter 4) is now seen as a resource in its
own right, even though it is less tangible as a
'resource' than other areas more traditionally
regarded as resources (such as water and mineral
resources (see Chapter 3). The other implication is
that it is now both appropriate and necessary to
take due consideration of all aspects of rural life,
work and leisure which can contribute to the 'quality
of life' of countryside resource users (regardless
of whether these users are residents, farmers,
visitors, or whatever). In many ways, therefore, it
becomes essential to take proper account of all viewpoints on what the countryside offers to various
groups of individuals or resource-users in planning
rural areas and to base resource decision-making on
broadly based images of the countryside at large
(as explored in Chapter 1).

Broadened Approaches

Theme three is a broadening in approaches to decision-making in rural resource management. Traditional approaches to resource allocation and development were based largely on the notion of cost/benefit evaluation, where the expected 'costs' incurred in developing or allocating a given resource for stated goals is balanced against the anticipated 'benefits' which would be derived from that use of the given resources.

The evaluation in traditional terms is generally based simply on economic or monetary costs and benefits - and so planners have recently started to devote some attention to deriving methods of placing monetary values on abstract resources such as wilderness (see Chapter 4.4), wildlife (see Chapter 3.4) and environmental quality.[13] This type of approach has proven only partially successful in producing socially acceptable and environmentally suitable decisions regarding resource use. The advent of welfare economics, accompanied by planners' growing recognition of the significance of social and environmental factors, has broadened the basis of decision-making, so that social and environmental elements are often considered alongside economic issues in debates about resource allocation and management. The three basic ingredients (social, economic and environmental factors) are then considered together, and although the weighting given to each factor in final analysis will inevitably depend on political administrative pressure more than on clear, objective appraisal, the very fact that all elements are considered at the outset is in many ways a critical step forward.

To some extent this broadening of the basis of resource allocation decision-making reflects also a movement away from economic theory towards a broader planning rationale, triggered off by growing awareness of the imperfections of market forces. Hines[14] has commented that 'the market mechanism cannot at the same time encourage both economic growth and the conservation of natural resources, stimulate all kinds of private economic activity and maximise social welfare, promote unrestrained economic growth and protect the environment. To assume that the market mechanism can accomplish such a wide variety of tasks, some of which are conflicting, is to endow it with an omnipotence it cannot hope to achieve'.

Sewell[15] has concluded that it is becoming increasingly necessary to consider proposals for
resource development in terms of their broad social,
environmental and institutional consequences as well
as their economic and financial effects. In addition
he identified two fundamental problems which stem
firstly from a basic incapacity to identify and
measure certain elements such as aesthetics, future
values and the like, and secondly from institutional
biasses towards some strategies rather than others.

A Resource Management Approach

There is clearly a need, therefore, for a more
broadly based approach to planning in the countryside.
This approach might be based on concepts of resource
management, and it offers a valuable opportunity to
rationalise conflicts in resource-use both between
different areas and also over time. To some extent
this represents an extension of the development of
resource management along similar lines to those
along which it appears to have developed since the
turn of the century.

Herfindal[16] has identified three important 'threads'
within the recent development of conservation and
resource management which are of relevance in this
respect:

(a)   a concern to define 'limits' to resources (in
      the form of inventories and surveys)

(b)   a concern to avoid approaching the limits of
      resource availability

(c)   recognition that use is unavoidable (emphasis-
      ing a need for constant efforts to reduce wants,
      and to encourage multi-purpose use of resources
      wherever feasible).

Principles of Resource Allocation

In essence, there are two basic principles of
resource allocation which apply to any resource
management situation, whether in the countryside or
elsewhere. The first is based on simple economic
theory, and it allows market forces to dictate
resource-use by competition between demand and supply,
based often on an economically determined cost/
benefit analysis carried out by each of the major
decision-makers involved in the allocation procedure.
The second approach demands that planning constraints

and balanced judgements which take into account
other factors such as social, cultural, strategic
and environmental impacts, dictate resource use and
allocation.

The thesis underlying this book centres on the need
for an integrated and broadly based planning system
which responds to these many types of forces in
addition to simple free-market economics for rural
resource management. But rather than simply demand
more widespread or more prescriptive planning control
in the countryside, it seems logical to demand a
countryside planning system which:

(a)   takes into account the 'image of the integrated
       countryside' and the diverse ways in which
       countryside users perceive and value the rural
       environment (see Chapter 1),

(b)   recognises the need to take stock of the assem-
       blage of 'resource' components within the
       countryside which need careful management and
       development (see Chapters 3 to 5),

(c)   focusses attention in particular on cases of
       conflict within this resource-using system (see
       Chapters 6 to 10) and considers alternative
       strategies to allocate and manage the available
       resources equitably and sensibly between com-
       peting demands (see Chapters 11 and 12), and

(d)   adopts a holistic viewpoint in dealing with
       problems of rural planning.

2.4   RESOURCE CLASSIFICATION

The simplest basis on which to classify resources is
according to their practical value, and so the
conventional distinction is between natural
resources (which have some tangible practical values)
and non-utilitarian resources (which don't). Natural
resources can be further sub-divided according to
the extent to which they can be replaced by natural
or man-made processes (TABLE 2.2) - into inexhaustible, renewable, recyclable and non-renewable
resources.

Within the context of rural planning, the non-
utilitarian types of resource must rank alongside
natural resources in significance, particularly if
intangibles such as 'quality of life' 'equity of

45

TABLE 2.2 Classification of natural resources [17]

NON-RENEWABLE RESOURCES

'are not generated or reformed in nature at rates equivalent to the rate at which we use them', eg. petroleum.

RECYCLABLE RESOURCES

'resources...which are not lost or worn out by the way we use them, and can be reprocessed and used again and again', eg. many metals.

RENEWABLE RESOURCES

'include all living things that have the capacity for reproduction and growth. As long as the rate of use is less than their rate of regeneration, and as long as their environments are kept suitable, they will go on replacing themselves. However, living communities are not necessarily renewable, if the way in which we use them is destructive. No living species can survive if we crop it at a rate more rapid than it can reproduce, or if we destroy the habitat in which it depends'.

INEXHAUSTIBLE RESOURCES

'those such as sunlight, which will continue to pour onto the earth as long as humanity will be around, whether we use it in certain ways or not'. Other examples include water resources on the world scale.

opportunity' and 'state of the environment' are high
on the list of planning priorities. The significance
of non-utilitarian resources depends largely on the
extent to which a given society regards these either
as luxuries or necessities. For example, a population with a relatively high standard of living can
readily devote greater consideration to the need for
clean supplies of air and water, and access to unspoiled recreation areas and open countryside, than
a population with food shortages, widespread unemployment and generally lower material standards of
living.[18]

Thus developed countries can afford more readily to
devote attention, resources and finances to planning
the wise use of non-utilitarian resources than their
less privileged developing counterparts; and it is
also more convenient for the developed countries to
adopt such a humanitarian approach to physical
planning at the present time than it was in past
times during their development process because of
their better material standards of living at the
present time. Whether the present period of economic
recession forces a change in attitude towards non-
utilitarian resources in countries such as Great
Britain and the United States will only become
apparent in the distant future.

This book adopts a broader basis of designating
'resources' than is more commonly used, in examining
both natural and human resources. People are a basic
ingredient of the rural resource system and they
must be considered in context. Natural resources are
introduced in Chapter 3, and human resources in
Chapter 5. Landscape resources, which represent the
interface between Natural and Human Resources, are
introduced in Chapter 4.

2.5   THE RURAL RESOURCE SYSTEM

Ashford[19] has argued that the politics of resource
allocation is now the most crucial component in the
complex relationship between cities and central
government, and he has shown how resource constraints
affect both urban policy and urban development. This
same political basis of resource allocation binds
together the countryside and central government,
although until recently 'rural' areas have tended to
be regarded as somewhat the poor cousins of urban
areas and this has been reflected in the lack of
positive planning initiatives within the countryside.

Birch[20] has observed that effective resource management '...depends on the definition of the system of relationships relative to a given resource-using situation, and thus the identification ad hoc of the structure of the relevant regional unity' and so it is important to specify the basic components in the rural resource system.

Structure of the System

It is extremely difficult to isolate each important component within the rural resource system in part because of the inter-linking and mutual inter-dependence of rural and urban systems; but also because of the complexity and multi-functional nature of the countryside as a working environment. The countryside is in many ways 'all things to all men' (see Chapter 1), and so perhaps the most basic distinction is between human and social elements in the rural system on the one hand and the physical and environmental elements on the other.

Physical elements have long been regarded as 'resources' which can be managed using conventional approaches to resource management[21] - so that, for example, management of water resources (see Chapter 3.3), mineral resources (see Chapter 3.2) and land resources can be based on the accumulated experiences of many years of resource management in both Great Britain and the United States.

The human/social elements, however, are generally not regarded as 'resources' in this same sense (see Chapter 5), and so physical planning often gets divorced from social and economic planning when alternative strategies of rural planning and development are being considered. Ashworth[22] has stressed the need for a policy for the 'human resource'; and some ways in which human resources might be integrated within an overall resource allocation framework for rural planning will be considered in Chapter 5.

This polarisation into human and environmental resources suggests, however, discrete elements within the rural resource system which are much less distinct in practice. Thus, for example, perception of the opportunities offered by the environmental resources depends heavily on 'human' elements such as population size, the aspirations and perceptions of a given population, willingness to pay for environmental resources of varying levels of utility, and so

on; whereas the opportunities which a given population offers (in the sense of actually realising the
resource potential of given environmental elements)
depends on characteristics of both the population
itself, and the actual and perceived characteristics
of the environment.

There is thus a broad common ground in between the
two 'extremes' of human and environmental resources.
This meeting ground of the human and environmental
elements lies within the actual fabric of the countryside at a given point in time - in other words, in
the prevailing mixture of environmental opportunities
offered by the 'physical' resources and realised
potential secured by the 'human' resources. This
is reflected, for example, in land use which represents a balance between the demand for land of
certain qualities and with given characteristics,
and the supply of land of suitable quality and with
prevailing characteristics. Perhaps more basically,
this meeting ground is represented by the overall
fabric of landscape in general - a theme which will
be considered more fully in Chapter 4.

Actors in the System

An alternative way of considering the rural resource
system, is to focus attention on the main groups of
resource-users in the countryside (see, for example,
TABLE 12.1). It is clear, for example, that different groups of resource-users or managers are
generally quite different. FIGURE 2.3 attempts to
rationalise the various goals which motivate the
actions of each of the major classes of resource-
users in the countryside.

Clearly rural resource use reflects a quest to attain
certain identified goals, and it reflects also the
influence of both local and national government, and
the inter-play between urban and rural populations.
The significance of a particular resource use thus
depends in part on whether the resource user is
urban-based or rural-based (see Chapter 1.2). Also,
any one type of resource-user in the countryside will
not necessarily have one single goal in resource-use
- they might well have a series of interrelated
goals, perhaps ranked in priority. This ranking of
priorities in goals itself is of significance to
rural planning - because the rankings might vary in
response to many factors such as economic, social or
political pressures (from within or outside of the

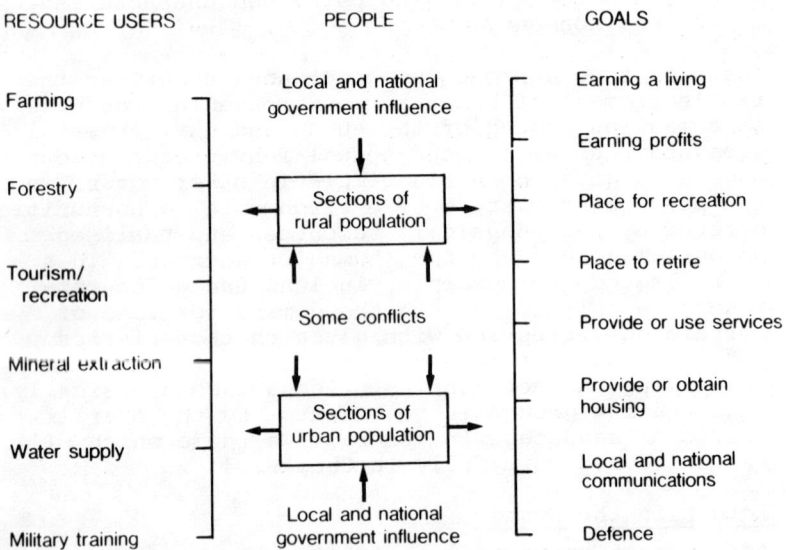

COMPONENTS OF RURAL RESOURCE USE

FIGURE 2.3   Components of Rural Resource Use

Source: after G. Clark (personal communication,1980)

local rural resource system), the age and aspirations
of the resource-user, and the resource-user's knowledge about issues of conflict within the resource-
using system.

In addition, the ranking of priorities may vary
between individuals within the same resource users
group. For example, the progressive farmer who is
keen to implement a high-technology, mechanised form
of farming, will have radically different goals to
the conservation-conscious small-holding farmer (see
Chapter 9.2) and these will be reflected in the
planning priorities he perceives and in his reactions
to given rural resource management conflicts.

Peculiarities of the System

Although it is suggested that rural planning might
profitably adopt a resource-based perspective, and

give greater consideration to the techniques of
resource allocation and management in rationalising
and resolving resource-conflict situations in the
countryside, it should be stressed that there are a
number of basic differences in the problems, policies and prospects of resource management as applied
to 'the countryside' in general, as opposed to other
resources such as water or minerals.

One difference is that the rural resource system
includes both human (see Chapter 5) environmental
elements (see Chapter 3), and both should ideally
be taken into account at all stages of the resource
allocation procedures. In addition, the rural system
has many non-utilitarian resources (such as wildlife - Chapter 3.4) and resource management has to
take these into account as explicitly as it does the
natural resources. Perhaps more fundamentally, the
countryside planning system in an area is influenced
by regional, national and even international planning
issues and goals (see, for example, agriculture in
Chapter 9.2) and the constraints of decision-makers
at each of the levels in the hierarchy can be important in local rural resource management decision-
making.

Furthermore, the rural system comprises a dynamic
mosaic of interacting resource-using situations,
some of which are compatible and others inherently
incompatible (see Chapter 12) and so conflict-reso-
lution becomes of fundamental importance. Finally,
the nature of the resource allocation process in
the rural system is not simply based on market forces
and intervention, and on normal economic processes
of supply and demand - planning (for a variety of
goals) is a basic element in decision-making. In
particular, consideration of the social incidence
of environmental costs and benefits is of undoubted
significance.

2.6 CONCLUSIONS

Manners[23] has concluded that 'natural resources can
be studied realistically only as a part of an intricate and dynamic system of interrelated phenomena
which mould their demand, their supply and their
allocation'. With many resources demand depends on
a variety of factors such as transport, economics,
technology, politics, and supply is conditioned by
environmental factors (such as geology), technology,
economics, transport and political factors. The

market allocation process in such situations is determined by the interplay of market-determined prices and administered prices (see, for example, FIGURE 3.1).

Within the rural resource system, however, demand (i.e. resource requirements) is governed by other factors in addition, such as location, development potential, and speculative or strategic interest; whereas supply (i.e. resource availability) is affected by additional factors which include existing land uses (and their compatibility with proposed changes), land quality and capability, and land ownership patterns.

In the rural system, market allocation processes are largely replaced by planning allocation processes. These take into account factors such as national and strategic policies, structure plan policies, political opinion and pressures, economic constraints and incentives, the prospects of social impacts and externalities, and the likelihood of environmental impacts and externalities.

Inevitably conflict situations commonly arise where there are competing demands on rural resources, and the planning allocation process is designed to focus in particular on rural resource conflicts - such as those which commonly occur between recreational use of the countryside and nature conservation (see Chapter 7) or between farming and forestry (see Chapter 9). These areas of conflict are of fundamental importance in rural planning; they will be considered in more detail in Section II.

NOTES AND REFERENCES

1. T. O'Riordan, Perspectives on Resource Management (Pion, London, 1974).

2. E.S. Zimmermann, World Resources and Industries (Harper, New York, 1951).

3. Idem, 15.

4. Idem, 15.

5. S. Gregory, 'The geographer and natural

resources research', <u>South African Geographer</u> 4, (1974): 374. B. Mitchell, <u>Geography and Resource Analysis</u> (Longman, London, 1979).

6. O'Riordan, <u>Resource Management</u> (Note 1): 7.

7. T. O'Riordan, 'Ecological studies and political decisions', <u>Environment and Planning</u> 11A, (1979): 805-13.

8. R.M. Auty (personal communication, 1980).

9. Idem.

10. O'Riordan, <u>Resource Management</u> (Note 1): 8.

11. Idem, 121-45.

12. J.D. Chapman, 'Interactions between man and his resources', in Committee on Resources and Man (ed) <u>Resources and Man - a Study and Recommend-ations</u> (Freeman, San Francisco, 1969): 32.

13. For example D.R. Helliwell, 'Valuation of wild-life resources', <u>Regional Studies</u> 3, (1969): 41-7.

14. L.G. Hines, <u>Environmental Issues, Population, Pollution, Economics</u> (Norton, New York, 1973).

15. W.R.D.Sewell, 'Broadening the approach to evaluation in resources management decision-making', <u>Journal of Environmental Management</u> 1, (1973): 33-60.

16. O.C. Herfindahl, What is Conservation? <u>Resources for the Future Reprint</u> No.30 (1961). Washington, D.C.

17. R.F. Dasmann, <u>Environmental Conservation</u>, 4th Edition (Wiley, New York, 1976): 6-11.

18. Chapman, Interactions (Note 12).

19. D.E. Ashford, 'National Resources and Urban Policy', in D.E. Ashford (ed) <u>National Resources and Urban Policy</u> (Croom Helm, London, 1980).

20. J.W. Birch, 'Geography and Resource Management' <u>Journal of Environmental Management</u>, (1973): 5.

21. O'Riordan, Resource Management; and Mitchell, Resource Analysis (Notes 1 & 5). See also I.G. Simmons, The Ecology of Natural Resources (Edward Arnold, London, 1974).

22. G. Ashworth, 'Natural resources and the future shape of Britain', The Planner 60, (1974) 773-8.

23. G. Manners, "New Resource Evaluations', in R.C. Cooke and J.M. Johnson (eds), Trends in Geography (Pergamon, Oxford, 1969): 159.

SECTION I

THE RURAL RESOURCE BASE: AN OVERVIEW

This section will provide the foundation stone on
which Sections II and III will build. It will be
implicit from Chapter 1 that the countryside tends
to be seen as 'all things to all men', in the sense
that the countryside represents all that is non-
urban. The countryside is looked upon by both
country folk and urban dwellers to provide space and
resources for a wide variety of functions, some
related directly to livelihood (such as farming and
forestry), others related to pleasure and relaxation (such as nature conservation, rural informal
recreation and landscape), and yet others related
to residence (such as villages and isolated farmsteads) and travel (such as access to rural areas).

The aim in this Section is to provide an overview of
the rural resource system, encompassing both physical
and social resources (i.e. the environmental and the
human viewpoints), and to integrate these by considering landscape in the countryside.

Chapter 3 deals with the natural resource base of the
countryside, and it seeks to establish which parts of
the physical environment are the most important to
life and livelihood in the countryside. The discussion centres on three types of natural resource -
mineral resources, water resources and ecological
resources - because these figure most prominently in
many resource-use conflicts.

The physical environment offers a series of non-
utilitarian resources of use to man in various ways,
and Chapter 4 focusses on landscape as a resource in
order to illustrate how human use of the environment,
and the physical character of the environment, are
inherently linked together.

This leads in turn to an exploration of the human resource base in Chapter 5. The social/human resource elements are of basic importance within the countryside, because rural areas offer employment and homes to a great many people and their needs and aspirations are paramount in the allocation of rural resources. The discussion in Chapter 5 centres on three levels of resource use, spanning primary resources (the individuals and their community), secondary resources (settlements and labour pools), and tertiary resources (including housing, education and employment).

It is stressed that the human element must be considered alongside the environmental elements, and that planning of resource allocation within the countryside must recognise both the environmental resource base and its suitability for exploration and exploitation in given ways, and the socio-economic position and life-style requirements of those who live in and are committed to the countryside. The concepts of environmental quality, human deprivation and opportunities, and perception of the rural environment figure largely throughout this section.

The basic argument is established that each element in the rural resource system, be it an environmental or a human factor, has values which must be recognised and incorporated within rural planning systems. It is implicit throughout the three chapters that the countryside is often called upon to meet several needs simultaneously, yet it is equally clear that most parts of the countryside can cater for some needs better than others. This might be because of environmental differences (eg. in soil type or bedrock), differences in past land use and land management, or because of the inherent incompatibility of some of the demands being made on limited land resources. The human dimension lies at the very heart of the debate, for a countryside starved of human interest and sterilised of human concern will in the long term satisfy few of the genuine social and economic demands being placed on it.

Conflict is an inevitable result of unequally powerful users seeking equal opportunities to use limited countryside resources in their own self-interest. Such conflicts arise in a wide variety of ways, some of which are explored in Section II. Conflict, in turn, requires resolution and some accommodation of vested interests between the different parties and

56

groups involved. Some of the more viable policy and management options are introduced in Section III.

Chapter Three

NATURAL RESOURCES

The countryside offers a broad spectrum of opportunities to a wide range of users. It is seen as a
place to live or work; a place to escape from the
bustle of city life and to paint and write about; a
place to grow food and trees and a haven for wildlife; a collecting ground for water supplies and a
reservoir of raw materials. There is a feeling that
'the countryside stands for all that is important in
Britain; it is the expression of the good life away
from the stresses and strains of the city, and the
symbol of everything that is considered truly
British'[1].

Whilst the links between town and country are deep
rooted, long lived and all embracing, Lassey has
stressed that 'the urban conglomerates are much more
dependent on rural based resources than are rural
regions dependent on urban centres; rural areas are
the principal source of food, air, water and other
raw materials on which life depends'[2].

This chapter will focus on some important aspects of
this rural resource base, concentrating in particular
on the natural resources which are so important to
life and livelihood. Landscape, an important non-
utilitarian resource in the countryside, will be
considered in Chapter 4, and Chapter 5 will explore
the importance of social resources within rural
resource management.

3.1 NATURAL RESOURCES – UTILITY AND CHARACTER

Natural resources were defined in Chapter 2 as those
'which have some tangible practical value', and three
types of natural resource (mineral resources, water
resources and ecological resources) will be

considered here. Whilst these three are not the
only natural resources which could be considered,
they are included because they illustrate the most
important dimensions of the natural resource base,
and they figure large in resource-use conflicts (see
Chapters 6 to 10).

Common properties of the resources

All natural resources, including the three isolated
here, share certain characteristics which in turn
influence how those resources are used. First, all
natural resources derive ultimately from the natural
environment, and so there is a limit to the total
quantity of those resources which will be available.
Whilst many natural resources can be recycled, the
overall resource base is finite (unless technological
developments make recycling or substitution more
viable). Secondly (as noted in Chapter 2) all
resources are culturally defined. Therefore different aspects of the natural environment might be
regarded as 'resources' in the future if the framework of this cultural definition changes. Resources
are thus those parts of the natural environment which
are useable under present-day technical, economic
and cultural conditions; if one or more of these
conditions changes then some things which are presently regarded as 'resources' will cease to warrant
this utility connotation, and others will become
'resources'.

The third important property of natural resources is
their uneven distribution. Few natural resources
have ubiquitous distributions between and within
countries - the quantities, qualities and characteristics of the natural resource base varies in space
as well as time. Certain economic minerals (such as
iron and copper) have markedly uneven distributions,
and the quantity and quality of other natural resources such as fertile soil, commercial forests and
fresh water show distinct spatial variations over
even small distances.

Finally, natural resources need to be allocated carefully to ensure equitable distributions, sustainable
levels of use, and patterns of use compatible with
long term social and environmental objectives (such
as reduction of environmental pollution). The allocation of natural resources is complex. In an ideal
situation simple economic theory allows market
forces to dictate resource use by competition between

supply and demand - this inter-play is often judged via economic cost-benefit analyses carried out by each of the major decision-makers involved in the allocation procedure[3]. However the market mechanism is not a suitable basis on which to allocate countryside resources because of imperfections in market forces, and the need to include welfare and equity considerations alongside purely economic factors[4]. Planning intervention thus demands constraint and rational judgements in balancing factors such as social, cultural, strategic and environmental impacts of proposed changes in deciding on the allocation and use of natural resources.

Intervention in resource allocation is required to foster attainment of certain culturally-defined goals (such as preservation of cherished landscapes (Chapter 4.2) or scientifically important ecological habitats (Section 3.4 in this Chapter)), accommodation of both local and national government policies (such as the national need for mineral resources versus the local concern about landscape despoilation and pollution which often stem from quarrying activities (see Chapter 6.1)), and harmonisation of conflicting interests of urban and rural populations (such as the conflict between urban demand for water, and rural resistance to flooding of upland valleys for reservoir construction)[5].

The chosen natural resources

Mineral resources are included in this chapter because they offer a suitable illustration of the problems of dealing with non-renewable natural resources. Once used, non-renewable resources cannot be harvested again, so that enlightened resource management is required to ensure optimum benefit from resource development and use. Moreover, use of non-renewable resources often triggers off environmental impacts such as pollution and reduction of scenic quality, so that the wider repercussions of mineral extraction (see Chapter 6.3) must be taken into account at all stages of resource-use decision-making.

Water resources and ecological resources are included as illustrations of renewable natural resources which will last indefinitely if properly managed (see Chapter 2.4). Both water and ecological resources highlight a recurrent problem in managing renewable resources which is that the quality of the resource base is often impaired (sometimes very seriously) by inadequate or inappropriate management. This arises, for example, via pollution of water resources, and depletion of plant and animal stocks through over-intensive use, such as recreation use (see Chapter 7.5) or through intentional removal or persecution, such as via changing farming practices (see Chapter 9) or via mineral extraction activities (see Chapter 6). Each of these natural resources influences landscape as a resource (Chapter 4) as well as providing the ultimate resource base for social and cultural use of the countryside (Chapter 5).

3.2   MINERAL RESOURCES

The Resource Base

Mineral resources have played an extremely important role in the evolution of human society, and to a large extent the present high standard of living in industrial countries such as Western Europe and the United States has been possible and is presently sustained by the exploitation of mineral resources. Evidence of mineral exploitation is impressed in both the course of evolution of human societies (hence the important Bronze and Iron Ages of the prehistoric past) and in the present day landscape of many rural areas. Thomas argues that most peoples' mental image of Wales is dominated by 'hundreds of derelict mines, formerly extracting iron, lead, zinc, copper, manganese or gold ores, (which) dot the countryside'[6].

Like most types of natural resource, minerals are only seen as resources when a use for them is perceived, and after the development of techniques for extracting them, removing impurities, and manufacturing useful materials or products from them. Stanford and Moran point out that all presently-prized economic minerals (such as petroleum, nickel and uranium) have been around for millions of years, yet they have only been regarded as useable (thus worth exploiting) in recent decades as a response to human needs and developing technologies[7]. Unlike many natural resources, however, minerals tend to be non-renewable so that the overall resource base is fixed by geological events of the remote past. Since the total resource base cannot be extended, increased use of mineral resources has been accommodated largely by switching to progressively lower grade mineral ores (although increased exploration for previously unknown reserves has temporarily halted this trend in

the case of some minerals such as petroleum and oil
and gas). Copper illustrates the trend quite
clearly[8]. The very first copper mines, some 3000
years ago, took relatively pure copper by digging it
out of surface rocks. This was very high grade ore
(which could be processed by the primitive technologies then available), and mining stopped when surface deposits ran out. By the late eighteenth and
early nineteenth centuries growing demand for copper coupled with improved mining and refining technologies, made it possible and viable to extract
lower grade ores from deeper mines. By 1900 copper
smelters could handle ores with concentrations as
low as 10%; by the late 1970's ores with concentrations down to 0.5% have become viable. This natural
progression from high to low grade ores has also
occurred with minerals like iron and aluminium, although certain mineral ores (such as lead, zinc and
mercury) do not conform to this trend.

Mineral resources include both metallic minerals
(such as iron, copper and lead) and non-metallic
materials (such as cement, coal and water). TABLE
3.1 lists a classification of mineral resources
based on how the different materials are used.

TABLE 3.1 Classification of mineral resources[9]

(a) METALLIC MINERAL RESOURCES

1. Abundant metals; such as iron, aluminium, manganese,
   titanium, and magnesium.

2. Scarce metals; such as copper, lead, zinc, tin, tungsten,
   gold, silver, uranium and mercury.

(b) NON-METALLIC MINERAL RESOURCES

1. Minerals for chemical, fertilizer and special uses; such
   as sodium chloride, phosphates, nitrates.

2. Building materials; such as cement, sand, gravel, gypsum,
   asbestos.

3. Fossil fuels; such as coal, petroleum, natural gas and
   oil shale.

4. Water; lakes rivers and ground waters.

This sort of classification highlights the wide
variety of types of mineral resources; water resources will be dealt with separately in Section 3.3.

The distribution of mineral resources

From the point of view of resource management in the
countryside, minerals are important because inevitably they can only be extracted from locations with
suitable deposits. Thus mineral extraction is generally concentrated spatially, with little latitude
for selection between possible extraction sites.
Geological factors account for the distribution of
mineral resources. These factors include the com-
pression of plant and animal remains to yield fuel
minerals (oil, gas and coal), igneous intrusions
which emplaced many important metallic minerals
(such as copper, gold, lead and zinc), chemical
weathering under tropical climates (to produce
bauxite through chemical breakdown of clay minerals),
and mechanical weathering and erosion which create
placer deposits of rare metals such as gold or
platinum[10].

Few mineral resources are ubiquitous (unlike many
ecological resources, for example). Some, such as
chalk and brickclays, occur quite widely in Britain
so that there can be an element of choice concerning
which areas are to be quarried, and which deposits
can be most efficiently extracted at a given time.
Other minerals such as fuller's earth are very limited in distribution, so there is rarely scope for
choice in where to locate extractive operations.

Warren points out that although the resources are
fixed in location, quite often a choice has to be
made between them[11]. Problems arise particularly
where rare minerals occur in areas of high amenity
value (especially the upland areas); yet ironically
the same geological factors (regional metamorphism
and igneous intrusions) account for the existence of
the mineral emplacements and the resistance (hence
presence today) of the upland masses. This is highlighted in areas like the Western Isles off north
west Scotland, where regional metamorphism in the
geological past has created both resistant landscapes
(of high amenity and scenic value (see FIGURE 4.2))
and mineral emplacements which are worthy of exploitation if only on a limited scale[12].

For many mineral resources, therefore, there is a

marked spatial concentration of impact and extraction. This arises from various factors, such as the local- ised distribution of many resources, lack of complete knowledge of overall distributions (through inade- quate or incomplete exploration), and from the hist- orical legacy of past investments in existing mines and quarries (FIGURE 3.1). A further important factor for many minerals is the high cost of trans- port of the product. Some minerals such as diamonds and platinum, have high market values and can sus- tain transport over long distances. Others, such as gravel and bricks, are bulky and have low market values, so that it is not economic to transport them over long distances. Extraction in such cases is closely orientated around local demand. Thus, for example, most brickworks in areas like the Oxford clay vale in England, have traditionally been located very close to the working faces of local clay pits[13], and most gravel pits have been worked close to urban centres which generate demand for cement and aggre- gates[14] (see Chapter 6.4).

Because of the real possibility of working out exist- ing quarries, switches in locations of extraction are common. Such switches are also promoted by changes in the viability and economic efficiency of alternative sites for a given mineral resource through time (triggered off by changes in factors such as market forces and production costs, and in working efficiency through investment in new plant). Lomas and Gleave[15] have charted a post-war change in the location of gold mining in South Africa, with decline in the older fields around Johannesburg and a rise in importance of newer fields to the south west. The older fields suffer from exhaustion or near-exhaustion of payable ores in the fact of fixed revenue (the price of gold) and rising working costs (deeper mining and the working of lower grade ores), and the industry recognised the need to exploit rich- er grades of ore to maintain profitability.

The importance of mineral resources

The importance of mineral resources within the rural resource system centres upon the wide variety of uses for minerals in most spheres of economic and industrial activity. Skinner has stressed that 'maintenance of the earth's huge population is now totally dependent on continuing supplies of natural resources; fertilizers to increase crop yields, water to drink and irrigate crops, metals to build

65

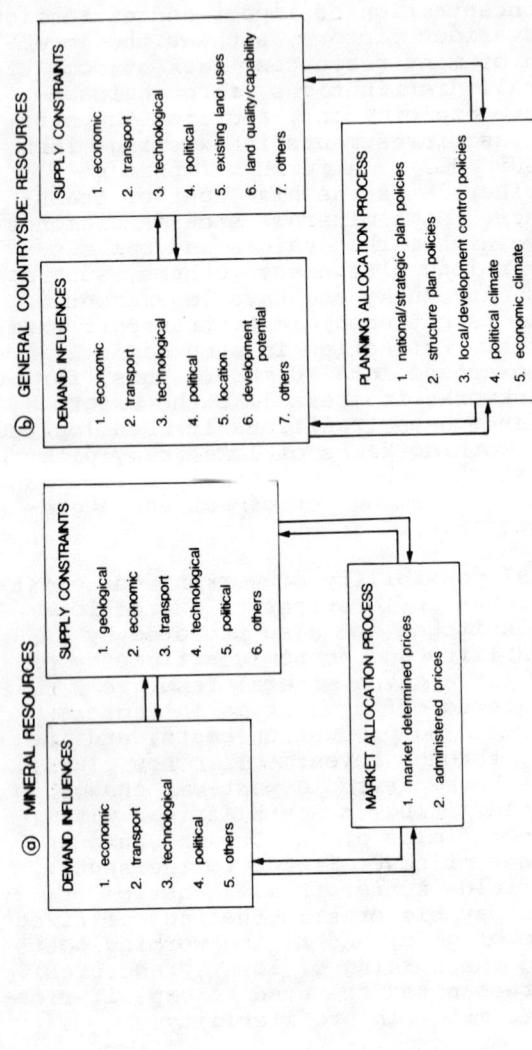

FIGURE 3.1 Some Differences Between Countryside Resource Systems and Mineral Resource Systems

Source: after G. Manners, 'New resource evaluations', in R.U. Cooke and J.H. Johnson (eds) *Trends in Geography*, (Pergamon, London, 1969).

machines, fuels to energise them, and a myriad of
other materials. Without continuing supplies civil-
ised society must collapse and the population
wither'[16]. Uses for mineral resources fall into
three broad groups, reflecting the three classes of
mineral resources - metallic minerals, non-metallic
minerals, and energy resources (TABLE 3.1).

Metallic Minerals. The metallic minerals are widely
used in industrial processes and in the manufacture
of goods and machinery[17]. For example, iron accounts
for over 90% of all metals consumed, and it is combined with various forms of alloy to produce steel
with specific properties. Aluminium is more abundant
as a resource than iron, and its high resistance to
corrosion and good electrical conduction make it a
versatile and much demanded resource. Other uses
are made of the scarce metallic minerals, such as
tin. silver and mercury which are found in low
concentrations and thus have high prices.

Non-Metallic Minerals. The non-metallic minerals
are used in two main ways - as a basis for the production of fertilizers and chemicals and as material
for use in building and construction[18]. Fertilizers
are clearly of world-wide significance for food production, and most of the mineral components (nitro-
gen, potassium and phosphorus) are quite abundant
and widely distributed. Building materials represent the largest volume of all mined minerals, and
include those materials which can be used directly
from source (such as building stone, gravel and sand)
and those which need processing before use (such as
clay for bricks and raw materials for cement).

Energy Resources. Without doubt the most important
mineral resources are those which yield energy
supplies, such as coal, crude petroleum, natural gas,
uranium, peat and wood. The fossil fuels play an
important role in twentieth century society, and
emphasis has switched progressively since the
Industrial Revolution from coal to petroleum and
natural gas[19]. Coal benefits from being the best
energy source for use in smelting iron ore, being
cheaper per tonne than petroleum, and being perhaps
the most flexible energy source (in providing both
heat and motive power); but it suffers the drawbacks
of low energy content per unit mass, difficulties
and costs of transportation, and the impurities
released on combustion (such as sulphur) which leads
to air pollution.

The hydrocarbons (petroleum and natural gas) are
easier to transport (by pipeline), have higher
energy contents per unit mass, and are relatively
clean burning as fuel sources. Crude oil has few
direct uses as a fuel or raw material, and most is
broken down by refining to yield both fuels (such as
petroleum for motor vehicles) and non-fuel products
(such as lubricants and various petrochemicals).
Natural gas has become more important as a fuel
source in Western Europe after the discovery and
development of North Sea reserves during the 1970's[20].

In Canada the construction of the Trans-Alaska Oil
Pipeline, designed to carry oil overland across
permafrost country some 1270km from Prudhoe Bay on
the North Slopes of Alaska, to Valdez in the Gulf of
Alaska, during the 1970's, was surrounded by considerable controversy. This controversy centred on
the possible environmental impacts of the pipeline,
and the possible impacts on the lifestyles and livelihoods of native peoples along the routeway of the
pipeline and in the oilfield area[21] (see Chapter 10.4).

Resource dynamics

Mineral resources figure largely in many debates
within rural resource management because of the continued growth in demand for such resources. Demand
for most mineral resources had continued to grow
during the present century - urban development
demands cement and aggregates, domestic and industrial energy policies demand coal, oil and natural
gas, rising standards of living fuel the demand for
more precious metallic minerals such as gold, and
so on.

Recent demand projections for Great Britain[22] show
increasing production of sands and gravels, limestone, chalk, salt, clays, fluorspar, igneous rock
and sandstone, and they underline the need to increase working of domestic supplies of metalliferous
ores. The quest for self-sufficiency in mineral
resources, for both economic advantage and strategic
security, threatens the depletion of some intensive-
ly-worked mineral reserves. Ratcliffe, for example,
notes that 'pressure on the economy demands that
home supplies of minerals be used, and perhaps the
biggest danger to the countryside is from the trend
towards the total extraction of some of the more
localised materials'[23].

Continued expansion of demand for mineral resources, coupled with continued reduction in the availability of high grade mineral deposits, has encouraged larger scale operations and changing mining practices. One clear manifestation of this is the switch from underground workings towards opencast pits. In the past underground working was common. It involved high development costs, and high operating costs through the need to pump water and mud from operating areas. Such activities are labour intensive. Open cast, or strip mining, is based on removal of all over-burden material followed by rapid wholesale removal of ore-bearing country rock. Such operations can be mechanised to a greater degree, but open cast mining often provokes intense public opposition because of its large size and its destructive nature.

Opposition to open cast mining in remote areas generally focusses on loss of good quality farmland, loss of amenity in and access to the mined areas. Opposition in populated areas often concentrates on landscape and visual intrusion of contemporary and past workings[24].

To enhance efficiency and maximise returns on investment, open cast works tend to be extremely large - massive open pit mining of lignite (brown coal) in West Germany is carefully landscaped and screened in order to reduce offensive and visible environmental impacts[25]. Despite the economic advantages of larger open cast mining, there are cases where this trend has been reversed. The post-war increase in production of ironstone around Corby and Scunthorpe in England was made possible by replacing open cast workings by mining eastward dipping strata. This was necessitated in part because of the escalating costs of moving large amounts of overburden from the downward-dipping strata as extraction continued[26].

Extraction of mineral resources creates conflict within the rural resource system, because of the intrusive nature of the quarries, and because of the destructive nature of the activities and environmental impacts associated with extraction. This theme will be explored more fully in Chapter 6.

3.3 WATER RESOURCES

Water in the environment

Water provides a useful example of environmental

69

resources which require careful management because
it occurs in limited quantities yet demand for water
of specified qualities has been rising throughout the
present century[27]. As a natural resource water has
many uses and values, including water supply, maintenance of hydrological balance, use in food production, an important element of scenic diversity and
andscape attractiveness, and important habitats for
wetland and freshwater species of plants and animals.

Water occurs in the environment in many different
habitats, and freshwater wetlands include rivers,
lakes, reservoirs, canals, flooded gravel pits, ponds,
bogs and other marshy areas. Pressures on the water
resource base of most countries have mounted and
diversified considerably in recent decades, and they
include freshwater pollution, urban and industrial
development, agricultural improvement, flood protection schemes, water supply and recreational use
of wetland areas.

Water resource management is a major area of public
responsibility in the United Kingdom for three principal reasons[28]. The first is that water is available in limited quantities, yet demand for water continues to rise. Secondly water is most readily
available in locations distant from the main centres
of demand; in Britain it rains more in the north and
west, yet most of the population is concentrated in
the south and east, so that water resource distribution systems are required to balance supply and
demand in both space and time. The third reason is
that water is required for a variety of purposes,
only some of which are compatible with one another,
so that allocation of available resources between
competing claimants becomes essential.

Water resources share the property of uneven spatial
distribution with most other types of natural
resource, but they have two unique characteristics
which influence the way in which the resource is used:

(a)   because water is a 'flow resource' in the sense
      that it moves across the landscape there are
      many opportunities for repeated use of the same
      water as it moves downstream; water can thus be
      a multi-phase resource as well as a multi-funct-
      ional one.

(b)   the different elements of the water resource
      system are intimately linked together by these

flows, so that groundwater and surface water are closely associated in both space and time; the use of one component of water resources thus markedly influences the other components.

Water resource management and allocation

There are three broad aims to water resource management in countries like the United Kingdom and the United States - the development of new reserves of water, allocation of existing resources, and recycling of water (FIGURE 3.2). The overall aim is to ensure that sufficient quantities of water of suitable quality are available at appropriate times in

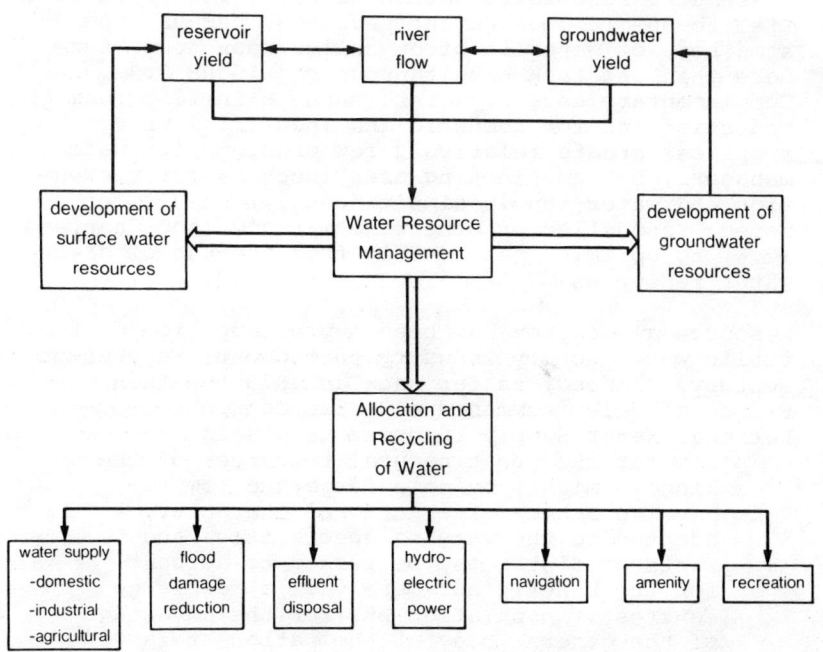

FIGURE 3.2   The Water Resource Management System

Source: after E. Porter, Water Management in England and Wales (Cambridge University Press, London, 1978):   p4.

correct places, in order to meet the demands of water

users. Water supply to agriculture, industry and
domestic users is a central service of the water
industry; the other main services are flood damage
reduction, effluent disposal, navigation, generation
of hydro-electric power, amenity and recreational
use of waterways and wetlands. In the United Kingdom
inland water navigation is very limited, and hydro-
electric power generation is restricted to a small
number of upland streams, principally in Scotland.
Flood damage reduction[29] and effluent disposal[30] are
major areas of public investment and general concern,
and increasing attention is being devoted to the potential uses of waterways, lakes and reservoirs for
recreation and amenity uses[31].

This multi-functional nature of water resources gives
rise to special management problems, because the
same body of water is often called upon to perform
more than one task simultaneously (FIGURE 3.3).
Complementary uses of water (such as in flood damage
reduction and for domestic and industrial water
supplies) create relatively few problems for water
managers, but conflicting uses (such as for recreation and water supply simultaneously) need to be
zoned, reconciled or otherwise managed (see Chapter
12.6) to optimise net benefit from the use of given
water resources.

Resource allocation has been a preoccupation of the
public water supply industry throughout the present
century. Indeed, as far back as 1878 the then
Prince of Wales summoned a Public Congress on
National Water Supply in order to discuss
> how far the great natural resources of the
> kingdom might, by some large and compre-
> hensive scheme of a national character,
> adapted to the varying specialities and
> wants of districts, be turned to account
> for the benefit not merely of a few large
> centres of population but for the advantage
> of the general body of the nation at large[32].

The evolution of water management in the United
Kingdom is discussed in greater detail elsewhere[33],
but it is important to highlight some recent changes
in attitudes towards water resources which have been
encompassed within the most recent structural and
legislative changes.

Two developments in the 1960's were to have a
particularly marked impact on water management. One

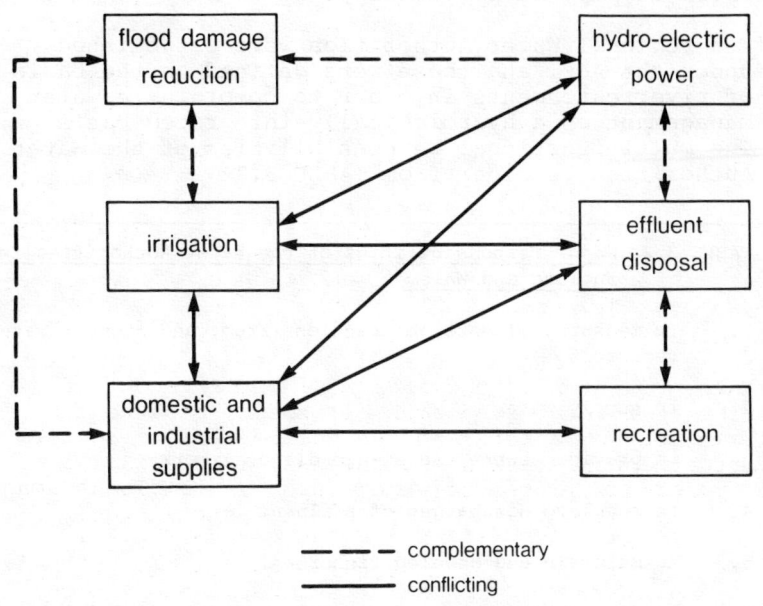

FIGURE 3.3   Complementary and Conflicting Uses of
             Water Resources

Source: after E. Porter, Water Management in
          England and Wales (Cambridge University
          Press, London, 1978): p11.

was a growing awareness, and feeling of unrest, over
the inadequacies of existing legislation (in particular the 1963 Water Resources Act) to deal effectively with water pollution, which had increased measurably during the 1960's on many British rivers. More
important, from the point of view of the countryside
in general, was the mounting public concern over the
preservation of land and landscape (see Chapter 2.5
and Chapter 4.2) and public opposition to planning
proposals for new water-resource projects (especially
new reservoirs in upland areas) was well orchestrated
and formed a strong and effective amenity/conserva-
tion lobby. Both of these issues were in part addressed in the 1973 Water Act which served overall
to diversify the responsibilities of the water industry to include water supply, water quality management and amenity use of water (rather than simply

water supply, as previously).

Ten regional Water Authorities were established under the Act, and these were defined on the basis of river catchments in order to co-ordinate water management on a hydrologically-integrated basis. The multi-functional responsibilities of the Water Authorities is clear from TABLE 3.2

TABLE 3.2 Major responsibilities of the Water Authorities in England and Wales[34]

1. To measure, licence abstractions from, and augment water resources

2. to supply water

3. to provide sewers and sewage disposal works

4. to regulate discharges of effluent

5. to maintain and develop fisheries

6. to direct land drainage functions (through regional land drainage committees)

7. to exercise these functions so as to allow recreational use of water

8. to have due regard to the desirability of preserving amenities of and public rights of access to areas of natural beauty, historic and other interest

9. to survey water quality, use and estimated future demands in, and make plans for new developments for water.

Resource Dynamics

Like most natural resources, water has been demanded in ever-increasing quantities in recent decades. Evidence on levels of water use in England and Wales since 1960[35] show a continued steady growth in public water supplies in response to rising total population, increasing per capita consumption of water, increasing industrial activity and changing farming practices (such as spray irrigation).

In the light of such rising demand for available water resources, the water industry has given serious

consideration to the need for a national strategic
plan for water resources to ensure reliable supplies
up to the year 2000 A.D.[36]. The National Water Plan
assumed that most of the predicted increases in industrial demand for water could be met from private
sources, through improved recycling within industry
and through re-purification of water polluted with
effluent. Expected increases in domestic demand
were to be met by a combination of additional surface
storage, improved use of existing storage capacity
and more coordinated use of underground storage.
The plan aimed to inter-link major river systems in
England and Wales by aqueduct and pipeline, to form
a water grid[37] and to generate an optimum pattern of
reservoir storage.

From the point of view of impact on the countryside,
the most visible component of the Water Plan was the
need to improve inland reservoir storage potential.
This phase of the plan envisaged the construction
of five new large reservoirs and the substantial enlargement of five existing reservoirs. Each proposal was fiercely opposed by local residents and
various environmental and amenity-based lobbies who
argued that such large scale developments in scenic
upland valleys would be destructive, intrusive and
unwelcomed.

Water and Resource Management

Water resource management can have wide-ranging significance to rural resource management in general
for two main reasons. The first centres on the
direct impact of water resource activities - such as
reservoir construction and related developments - on
other issues such as landscape, recreation and amenity opportunities, and land availability for other
uses (such as agriculture or forestry). The second
relates to the unity of drainage basins in general,
and of the water cycle in particular. Changes in
one part of a drainage basin (triggered off perhaps
via land use changes or mineral extraction (see
Chapter 6)) can be transmitted via altered streamflow
and sediment yields to other parts of the same drainage basin. The water cycle links together the other
major environmental systems (the energy system,
nutrient cycle, and the sediment system), and all
parts of the land surface in temperate areas belong
to one drainage basin or another[38].

The corollary is that land within the catchment area
of water supply schemes in the countryside can often

75

not be used in ways which might be incompatible with
the principal objective of water collection. Many
forms of land use markedly influence water chemistry
and quality, perhaps not so badly that the water
resources are classed as 'polluted', but at least
badly enough to require costly purification before
they can be used for domestic supply. Agricultural
land use (Chapter 9) can seriously reduce water
quality via washout of chemical fertilisers added to
fields to enhance crop or grassland productivity[39].
For example, much debate in recent years has centred
upon the significance of intensive farming methods
in East Anglia in producing water quality problems
in waterways and streams around the Norfolk Broads[40].
Recreation (Chapter 7) can also seriously affect
water quality and hence suitability for supply use -
water based recreational pursuits affect water quality via direct impacts of pollution from boats (from
sewage, oil leaks etc.) and via litter, bank collapse
and shore-based activities[41], whilst land-based pursuits around wetland and waterways have impacts via
accelerated erosion, litter and general intrusion[42].

The association between water resource management and
resource management in the countryside also arises
through the inadvertent impact of various forms of
land use on water quantity and quality. Purposeful
management of water resources influences the countryside in many ways - such as via dam construction -
but the impacts on water and wetlands of environmental management geared towards other objectives
(such as agriculture and urban development) are often
of greater magnitude and longer-term importance.
Water resource management is planned, whilst indirect
impacts are not; the former involves conscious
decisions according to defined objectives whereas
the latter are more incidental.

American studies during the 1930's yielded evidence
of accelerated erosion and effects on runoff of destruction of protective vegetation cover by fire, tree
felling, heavy grazing, smelter fumes, forest clearance, road and railway construction and various cultivation practices[43], and many other more recent
studies have illustrated the magnitude and diversity
of such man-induced changes.

Vegetation removal often triggers off accelerated
erosion, and this in turn promotes environmental
impacts near and downstream from the area of removal.
Impacts in the sediment source areas produce problems

for soil management and soil conservation, so that land treatment practices and structural controls are often required[44]. There are many areas in Britain where gully development has been induced in historic times through partial or complete destruction of former heathland vegetation by overgrazing or over use. One such area is the southern Pennines, where gully development in blanket peat over the last 200 years has been attributed to a variety of possible factors such as overgrazing by sheep, moorland burning for heather management, peat cutting, peat trenching to mark land boundaries, trampling of peat by pack-horse traffic, and impacts of military traffic on manoeuvres during World War One[45].

The various ways in which land management through forestry practices, land use changes, land drainage, water resource management schemes and urban development, can influence water quantity and quality are reviewed more fully elsewhere[46], but it is worthwhile to underline several conclusions about these indirect influences on water resources. Whilst resource-using activities such as agriculture and forestry (see Chapter 9) have significant effects on water quality and quantity, and on sediment yields from catchments, national and local policies tend to ignore the wider environmental impacts of large scale drainage, planting and land management. If the water resource base is to be conserved for optimum use in the future, rural planning and environmental management must recognize the significance and widespread nature of these forms of indirect impact on river systems, along with side-effects of water resource management policies such as reservoir development and inter-basin water transfers and urban development.

3.4 ECOLOGICAL RESOURCES

Ecology, resources and survey

Ecological resources refer to 'all plant and animal resources in terms of individuals, species, communities, habitats and ecosystems, other than those managed specifically for financial gain (such as commercial forestry operations and agriculture in general)'[47]. Whilst ecological resources which are managed for commercial gain are, strictly speaking, forms of ecological resource, attention here will be devoted to 'wildlife' ecological resources.

77

Managed ecosystems, such as agricultural ecosystems[48], have considerable value to wildlife and conservation, and in a crowded country like Britain it would indeed be hard to find ecosystems which have not been affected to some degree in the past by human intervention or interference. It is implicit, however, that natural species, habitats and ecosystems have greater value for nature conservation than managed or artificial ones. The importance of ecological resources has grown considerably during the present century in all developed countries because of changing attitudes to the environment, but also because of mounting threats to the survival of many species and habitats.

The stability and survival of natural ecosystems in many areas are being threatened by the deliberate exploitation of ecological resources (such as via hunting, fishing and shooting sports, and via commercial cropping of species such as whales), the reduction if not wholesale removal of ecological habitats (such as the Tropical Rain Forest), and environmental pollution (such as water pollution through nutrient enrichment, which often leads to outbreaks of algal blooms and eutrophication of the aquatic habitat). Stability in vegetation is closely related to successional stage (FIGURE 3.4), so that the pressures on ecological resources vary considerably from place to place.

The ecological resource base is extremely important, yet in many countries little consideration is given to establishing what constitutes the resource base, yet alone how it is being threatened. Terborgh has stressed that 'preserving diversity in a world of rapidly shrinking land resources will require a prompt and universal response based on an appropriate application of ecological knowledge. Every nation should possess an inventory of its biological endowment'[49]. There is clearly a pressing need to evaluate ecological resources in order to provide direct inputs into the planning decision-making machinery, and to identify the need for and appropriate approaches to the conservation of ecological resources. Taylor[50] has underlined the need to measure the ecological resource base before it can properly be managed, and he argues that whilst land use and vegetation maps are now available for many local areas and for sites currently threatened with or in the process of development in Britain, there is still a need for a comprehensive, disinterested survey of land resources in Britain. Such a

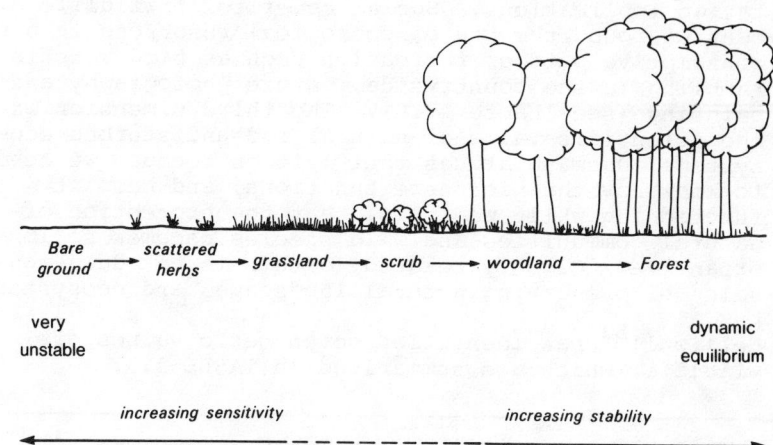

| Bare ground | scattered herbs | grassland | scrub | woodland | Forest |

FIGURE 3.4   The Relationship Between Successional
             Stage and Stability in Vegetation

Source: after F.B. Goldsmith, 'Ecological effects
          of visitors in the countryside', in
          A. Warren and F.B. Goldsmith (eds)
          Conservation in Practice (Wiley, London,
          1974).

resource survey is essential as an input into the
formulation of realistic and effective resource
management policies, and as a baseline against which
to measure changes in the size and composition of
the ecological resource base through time.

The importance of ecological resources

Interest in ecological resources rests upon recognition of the values of wildlife and the need to
conserve it as an environmental heritage for the
benefit of future generations. This interest is an
amalgamation of various dimensions of concern for
wildlife and ecological resources. Moore[51] identifies two value judgements which underlie much interest in conservation - one is that wildlife must
be conserved because it has intrinsic value, and the
other is that we conserve wildlife because it is of
value to man who is himself valuable.

The ethical basis of concern thus rests on the

premise that wildlife must be cherished and conserved without necessarily any specifically utilitarian implications. Social benefits of wildlife
centre around the use of ecological resources in non-
consumptive outdoor recreation such as bird watching,
rambling in the countryside, nature photography and
painting (see Chapter 7.6). The third dimension is
the scientific value of natural and undisturbed ecosystems; Dasmann argues that ' it is because we need
to know how the biosphere functions, and keep it
functioning while we learn, that the protection of
natural communities and wild species becomes so important'[52]. Closely related to this is an educational
value of preserving natural landscapes and ecosystems.

Helliwell[53] has identified seven basic values of
wildlife, which are summarised in TABLE 3.3.

TABLE 3.3   Values of wildlife and ecological resources
proposed by Helliwell

(a)   Direct returns; the direct material and financial returns
derived from hunting, shooting, fishing, berry
picking, etc.

(b)   Genetic reserve; the values of maintaining a reserve of
genetic material from which new varieties of crop-
plants and animals might be bred in the future

(c)   Ecological balance; the values of maintaining natural
populations of animals and plants as a buffer
against unnaturally large increases in pest species

(d)   Educational value; the values of educating children and
adults in a direct way about the manner in which the
biological world functions

(e)   Research; the value of facilities for research into
biological problems, and for the training of
research workers

(f)   Natural history interest; the value of catering for interesting hobbies for the amateur naturalist,
photographer, artist, poet etc.

(g)   Local character; the value of maintaining the visual
character of an area.

Ecological resources represent an important element

within the rural resource system for a number of
reasons. One is the inherent value of preserving
natural habitats and ecosystems. There is also the
need to ensure that landscape changes triggered off
by resource-using activities recognize and accommodate the need to disturb wildlife as little as possible. A third need is to create new habitats for
species of plants and animals and birds which are
displaced through land use changes. Most forms of
resource use trigger off impacts on wildlife, and
many of these are harmful or destructive.

However, some types of activity actually benefit
wildlife. This is the case, for example, with
enlightened management of broad-leaved woodland
and carefully planned agricultural developments
(other than intensification and mechanisation of farming)(see Chapter 9). Most forms of water resource
management schemes (see Chapter 3.3) can also benefit
wildlife through regulating public access to water
collecting grounds, or through preventing ecologica1-
ly destructive developments within catchment areas.

Whilst many types of resource extraction inevitably
have destructive effects on wildlife (see Chapter
6.3) through removal of habitat or disturbance of
species, these adverse impacts can be localised and
short-lived (depending on the time-scale and life-
cycle of the extractive operation) and with careful
site restoration some sites can become more attractive as wildlife habitats after use than they were
originally. Many flooded gravel pits around urban
centres offer valuable habitats for wading birds,
freshwater fish and plant species, and the nature
conservation potential of such sites is often greater than in the adjacent farmland (see Chapter 6.5).
There are a variety of situations in which 'man-made'
environments can be beneficial to wildlife in general,
and to specific species in particular. Davis[54] has
outlined some ways in which wildlife can adapt to and
exploit man-made environments because except in the
most highly disturbed areas recolonisation and
secondary succession is generally possible, and this
can occur quite quickly.

Kelcey[55] has identified various types of industrial
development sites which offer considerable potential
for wildlife, including linear habitats (such as
road verges and canal banks and pathways) which
serve as corridors along which plants and animals can
migrate; discrete sites (such as chalk quarries,

industrial waste sites and sewage works) which are
often better protected against public access than
even nature reserves, and which can provide safe
areas in which both common and rare species can survive and reproduce in both rural and urban areas.

Ecology and Resource Management

Problems arise in dealing with ecological resources
in the countryside for two main reasons. The first
is that whilst ecological resources are classified
as renewable natural resources (see Chapter 2.4 and
TABLE 2.2) (because of the ability of plants and
animals to reproduce and thus replace members of the
population who have been destroyed for whatever
reason), in many senses they become non-renewable
resources because the rate of loss of individuals
from a given area is often so high that it prevents
natural regeneration of that population locally by
natural processes of reproduction and growth. Sup-
plementation of local populations by migrant newcomers (a process which can be rapid for birds and
animals but extremely slow for recolonisation by
plant species through secondary succession[56]) might
go some way towards offsetting local losses, but
rarely is this strategy of recovery fully successful
in ecological communities.

The second problem centres around the fact that most
forms of resource-using activities in the countryside
destroy or adversely affect ecological resources.
For example, intensive recreational use of many habitats such as grassland, woodland and open moorland
can have marked effects on soils, plants and animals
within the area (see Chapter 7.5); mineral extraction
is destructive of habitat in the working-phase of
the development (see Chapter 6.3); and many farming
practices involve the removal or marked modification
of previously natural habitats (Chapter 9.4).

The human impact

In Britain, as elsewhere, there appear to be relatively few parts of the countryside (even in remote
areas), where the ecological resource base has not
been affected to some extent by human activities.
The human impact arises in a wide variety of ways.

One is by purely destructive actions designed to
remove ecological resources in the pursuit of other
resource-using objectives. Thus, for example, many
aspects of land management such as forest clearance,

hedgebank removal and modern farming practices, lead
to direct destruction of vegetation and the concomitant removal of ecological habitats for birds,
animals, invertebrates and so on (see Chapter 9.4).

Introduction of species into an area, either by
accident or by design represents a different dimension to the human impact. For example Jarvis[57] has
evaluated the intentional introduction of exotic
plants into England during the period 1550 to 1700,
especially from North America, as a result of increased variety of plants available to horticultural-
ists, a climate of fashion and taste which encouraged
the cultivation of plant rarities and curiosities,
and a contemporary tendency to enlarge the ornamental components in gardens, parks and forest groves.

Other human impacts include over-collecting of plants
by visitors to the countryside. An extreme example
is the edelweiss plant which was previously common
on dry rocky alpine slopes above the timber-line,
and has been markedly reduced in distribution in
recent years simply through the direct impact of
over-collecting[58].

Considerable attention has been devoted to the impact of human activities - particularly via habitat
changes - on the distribution of particular species
of plant, animals or birds. For example, Wells[59]
relates the contracting distribution of formerly
common meadow plants such as the Pasque flower to
progressive ploughing of chalk and limestone areas
of lowland England, and Duffey[60] associates the extinction of the Large Copper Butterfly from Woodwalton Fen National Nature Reserve in Huntingdonshire,
to drainage of the Huntingdon Fens over the last two
centuries.

The main pressures on ecological resources stem from
land use changes and from environmental pollution.
Whilst the latter topic is beyond the terms of reference of this book, it is worth pointing out that
pollution from either nutrient enrichment (stemming
perhaps from intensive farming practices) or from
release into the environment of toxic or harmful
materials (stemming perhaps from industry) can
markedly affect ecosystems and individual species.
The ecological impacts of pollution include excessive production in some species (such as via eutrophication in aquatic ecosystems), impaired repro-
ductive success in others, as well as behavioural

and/or metabolic changes in individuals exposed to
pollution, and direct mortality once lethal concentrations of the damaging pollutants have been
reached[61].

NOTES AND REFERENCES

1. R.H. Best and A.W. Rogers, The Urban Country-
    side (Faber & Faber, London, 1973).

2. W.R. Lassey, Planning in Rural Environments
    (McGraw Hill, London, 1977).

3. See, for example, A.J. Harrison, Economics and
    Land Use Planning (Croom Helm, London, 1977),
    and J. McInery, 'The simple analytics of
    natural resource economics', Journal of
    Agricultural Economics 27 (1976): 31-52.

4. L.G. Hines, Environmental Issues - Population,
    Pollution, Economics (Norton, New York, 1973).

5. C.C. Park, 'The concept of resources in rural
    geography', in G. Clark (editor) The Changing
    Countryside (GeoBooks, Norwich, 1984).

6. T.M. Thomas, 'Wales - land of mines and quar-
    ries', Geographical Review 46 (1956): 59-81

7. Q.H. Stanford and W. Moran, Geography - a study
    of its physical elements (Oxford University
    Press, Toronto, 1978).

8. Idem.

9. B.J. Skinner, Earth Resources (Prentice-Hall,
    New Jersey, 1976): 10.

10. Stanford and Moran, Geography (see Note 7).

11. K. Warren, Mineral Resources (Penguin,
    Harmondsworth, 1973): 30.

12. C.C. Park, 'Timeless Hebrides face the future',
    The Geographical Magazine April (1981): 437-442.

13. P.R. Healey and E.R. Rawstrom, 'The brickworks
    of the Oxford Clay Vale', East Midland
    Geographer 4 (1955).

14. A. Coleman, 'Landscape and planning in relation to the cement industry', Town Planning Review 25 (1954): 216-30.

15. P.K. Lomas and M.B. Gleave, 'Recent changes in the distributions of production in the South African gold mining industry', Geography 53 (1968): 322-6.

16. B.J. Skinner, Earth Resources (Note 9): 1.

17. Stanford and Moran, Geography (Note 7).

18. Idem.

19. Idem.

20. See, for example, N.R. Ball, 'The east coast of Scotland and North Sea Oil', Geography 58 (1973): 51-3; and J. Fernie, 'The development of North Sea Oil and gas resources', Scottish Geographical Magazine 93 (1977): 21-31.

21. See, for example, R.B. Norgaard, 'Petroleum development in Alaska - prospects and conflicts', Natural Resources Journal 12 (1972): 83-107; and R.B. Weeden and D.R. Klein, 'Wildlife and oil - a survey of critical issues in Canada', Polar Record 15 (1971): 479-94.

22. R.A. Healing and M.C. Harrison, United Kingdom Mineral Statistics 1973 (HMSO, London, 1973).

23. D.A. Ratcliffe, 'Ecological effects of mineral exploitation in the United Kingdom, and their significance to nature conservation', Proceedings of the Royal Society of London A339 (1974): 368.

24. K. Warren, Mineral Resources (Note 11).

25. H. Goedecke, 'Design of large open pit lignite mines to lessen their environmental impacts', Bulletin of the International Association of Engineering Geology 18 (1978): 131-8.

26. D.C. Pocock, 'Britain's post-war iron industry', Geography 51 (1966): 52-55.

27. See, for example, T. Dunne and L.B. Leopold, Water in Environmental Planning (Freeman, San

Francisco, 1978); and H.C. Pereira, Land use and water resources in temperate and tropical climates (Cambridge University Press, London, 1973).

28. See, for example, E. Porter, Water Management in England and Wales (Cambridge University Press, London, 1978); and D.J. Parker and E.C. Penning-Rowsell, Water Planning in Britain (George Allen and Unwin, London, 1980).

29. See, for example, G.E. Hollis, 'River management and urban flooding', 201-216 in A. Warren and F.B. Goldsmith (editors) Conservation in Practice (Wiley, London, 1974).

30. See, for example, D.E. Walling and B.W. Webb, Water quality' 126-172 in J. Lewin (editor) British Rivers (George Allen & Unwin, London, 1981); and D.J. Parker and E.C. Penning-Rowsell, Water Planning (Note 28): 104-151.

31. M.F. Tanner, 'The recreational use of inland waters', Geographical Journal 139 (1973): 456-461.

32. Cited by C.C. Park, 'The supply of and demand for water', 129-145 in R.J. Johnston and J.C. Doornkamp (editors) The Changing Geography of the United Kingdom (Methuen, London, 1983).

33. Idem.

34. Idem.

35. See, for example, Central Water Planning Unit, Analysis of trends in public water supply (CWPU, Reading, 1976) and Water Data Unit, Water Data 1976 (Water Data Unit, Reading, 1978).

36. Water Resources Board, Water Resources in England and Wales (HMSO, London, 1973): some implications of the plan are discussed by J.A. Rees, 'Rethinking our approach to water supply provision', Geography 61 (1976): 232-245.

37. See, for example, V. Gardiner, 'The Yorkshire Water Grid', Geography 65 (1980): 134-36; the Lancashire Conjunctive Water Use Scheme is described by C.C. Park, The Supply of (Note 32).

38. C.C. Park, 'Drainage Basin Planning, Water
Resources and Environmental Management in Great
Britain', paper presented at Third British-
Hungarian Geographical Seminar, University of
East Anglia, September 1982.

39. See, for example, D.E. Walling and B.W. Webb,
Water Quality (Note 30).

40. B. Moss, 'Conservation problems in the Norfolk
Broads and rivers of East Anglia, England;
phytoplankton, boats and the causes of turbidity', Biological Conservation 12 (1977): 95-114.

41. M.J. Liddle and H.R.A Scorgie, 'The effects of
recreation on freshwater plants and animals -
a review', Biological Conservation 17 (1978):
183-206.

42. J. Tivy and J. Rees, 'Recreational impact on
Scottish lochshore wetlands', Journal of Bio-
geography 5 (1978): 93-108.

43. See, for example, W.C. Lowdermilk, 'Acceler-
ation of erosion above geologic norms',
Transactions of the American Geophysical Union
25 (1934): 505-509.

44. D.A. Davidson, Soils and land use planning
(Longman, London, 1980).

45. J. Radley, 'Peat erosion on the high moor of
Derbyshire and West Yorkshire', The East Midland Geographer 3 (1962): 40-44.

46. C.C. Park, 'Man, river systems and environmental impacts', Progress in Physical Geography
5 (1981): 1-31.

47. C.C. Park, Ecology and Environmental Management
(Butterworth, Borough Green, 1981): 173.

48. D.F. Smith and D.M. Hill, 'Natural and agricultural ecosystems', Journal of Environmental
Quality 4 (1975).

49. J. Terborgh, 'Preservation of natural diversity
- the problem of extinction prone species',
Bioscience 24 (1974): 715-722.

50. J.A. Taylor, 'The ecological basis of resource

management', Area 6 (1974): 101-106.

51. N.W. Moore, 'Experience with pesticides and the theory of conservation', Biological Conservation 1 (1969): 201-207.

52. R.F. Dasmann, 'A rationale for preserving natural areas', Journal of Soil and Water Conservation 28 (1973): 114-117.

53. D.R. Helliwell, 'Valuation of wildlife resources', Regional Studies 3 (1969): 41-47.

54. B.N.K. Davis, 'Wildlife, urbanisation and industry', Biological Conservation 10 (1976): 249-291.

55. J.G. Kelcey, 'Industrial development and wildlife conservation', Environmental Conservation 2 (1975): 99-108.

56. C.C. Park, Ecology (Note 47): Chapter 4.

57. P. Jarvis, 'North American plants and horticultural innovation in England, 1550-1700', Geographical Review 63 (1973): 477-499.

58. M. Moyal, 'Endangered and threatened plant species', Scottish Forestry 30 (1976): 182-185.

59. T.C.E. Wells, 'Land use changes affecting Pulsatilla vulgaris in England', Biological Conservation 1 (1968): 37-44.

60. E. Duffey, 'Ecological studies on the Large Copper Butterfly (Lycaena dispar Haw. batanus Obth) at Woodwalton Fen National Nature Reserve, Huntingdonshire', Journal of Applied Ecology 5 (1968): 69-96.

61. C.C. Park, Ecology (Note 47): 216-7.

Chapter Four

LANDSCAPE AS A RESOURCE

> On property we grow pigs or peanuts. On
> land we grow suburbs or sunflowers. On
> landscape we grow feelings or frustrations.[1]

Landscape offers a convenient framework for integrating the human dimension of resource use, and
natural resources in the countryside. The countryside can be viewed as a mosaic of social and environmental resources fundamentally linked together.
O'Riordan has defined resource management as 'the
process of striking a balance between improving the
well-being of people and causing undesirable environmental change'[2]. By this term of reference landscape is a basic component of the rural resource
system.

Landscape, as used in this chapter, refers to both
land-use and scenery in an area - indeed, Linton
specified the two basic elements of scenic resources
as the form of the ground, coupled with the 'mantle
of forests and moorlands, forms and factories,
natural vegetation and human artefacts by which the
hard rock body of the landscape is clothed'.[3]
Problems arise in dealing with the landscape as a
resource, however, in part because landscape is a
product of complex popular culture operating over
a long period of time, it is created in an uncon-
scious manner on the whole, and it remains largely
unperceived as a resource by the main groups and individuals who shape it.[4]

4.1 LANDSCAPE AS A RESOURCE

Type of Resource

There is little doubt that landscape, or scenery, can

be viewed correctly as a natural resource. The exact
type of resource, adopting the classification scheme
outlined in TABLE 2.1, is perhaps difficult to
specify, if - indeed - specification is either necessary or of value. Some landscapes can be viewed as
a renewable natural resource, in the same that they
can be created, managed or modified (by landscape
planners and architects, for example). Natural landscape is clearly a non-renewable natural resource,
however. On the other hand, landscape can be regarded as a non-utilitarian resource, with social and
aesthetic value of greater importance than its purely
practical values. Regardless of how the resource
base is classified, Linton has stressed that

> like other natural resources, it is a potential
> asset that becomes actual only when valued and
> exploited by a society that has reached a
> particular cultural and economic level. For
> something more than a century there have been
> people of sufficient sensibility to set store
> by scenic variety or splendour, and of suf-
> ficient wealth and leisure to travel in search
> of them.[5]

As with many non-utilitarian resources, interest in
the resource base has only awoken consequent upon a
change in attitudes towards the environment at large,
away from a strictly economic view of what the
environment offers, towards a more overtly moral or
aesthetic concern for present and future environment.[6]

The landscape resource has also evolved in importance
because of the planner's tendency to separate the
environment into three discrete policy areas - the
protection of physical and mental health; the enhancement of economic value; and the preservation of sensory and participatory pleasure[7] - to each of which
landscape can be of immediate and lasting significance.

Landscape and countryside planning

Dower[8] has isolated landscape as one of the eight
principal functions of open country, and he has
stressed the importance of landscape in all countryside planning. Dower lists four main objectives in
countryside planning:

(a) provision of access and facilities for open-air
    enjoyment;

(b)   fostering the gradual evolution of farming, forestry and other land-uses;

(c)   conscious planning of changes in characteristic landscapes;

(d)   suitable protection of wildlife, buildings and places of architectural and historic interest.

There is clearly a symbiotic association between the landscape resource base (and the ways in which this is managed and developed) and each of these objectives, in that the resource base both offers opportunities and provides constraints for achieving the various objectives. At the same time any steps towards attaining the objectives will inevitably change the character and value of the landscape resource base. This type of inherent conflict situation permeates many aspects of countryside resource planning (see Chapter 2).

An illustration of the significance of the landscape resource is afforded by the Table Mountain National Monument in South Africa.[9] Table Mountain offers a small pocket of unspoiled countryside set within the heart of an extensive residential and business area (FIGURE 4.1). The National Monument inevitably provides a focus for local informal recreation, and visitor use in recent decades has been extremely high. One impact of this visitor pressure has been widespread and in places very severe erosion (FIGURE 4.1A) - to such an extent that the very landscape resources which attract visitors are under threat of irreversible damage.

A management scheme to alleviate some of these problems has been proposed (FIGURE 4.1B), which involves some small additions to the National Monument area, but more importantly - a zoning of recreational use of the entire resource into high and low import areas. The upland central portion of Table Mountain, with the highest landscape values and the greatest threats of over use, is zoned for low intensity visitor use.

Protection of landscapes is an important issue in many cases of conflicting land-use demands, and examples like that of Table Mountain can readily be found in most countries. Jacobsen[10], for example, has evaluated the situation in Denmark, where eight

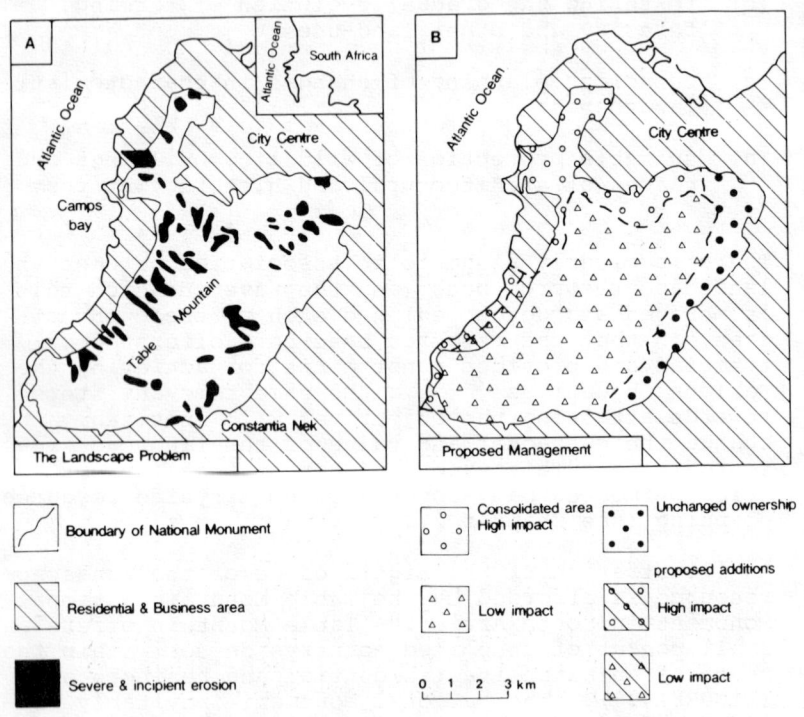

The Landscape Problem

Proposed Management

Boundary of National Monument

Residential & Business area

Severe & incipient erosion

Consolidated area
High impact

Low impact

0 1 2 3 km

Unchanged ownership

proposed additions

High impact

Low impact

FIGURE 4.1   Table Mountain National Monument, South Africa.

Source: after E.J. Moll et al., 'A mountain in a city - the need to plan the human usage of the Table Mountain National Monument, South Africa', Biological Conservation 13 (1978): 117-31.

areas representative of natural landscapes in the country as a whole were selected to assess optimal patterns of land use in terms of ecosystem tolerance, possibilities for improvement, necessary management, and scope for re-establishing destroyed environments.

Landscape Resource Problems

As a resource, landscape offers four broad problem areas which are not conventionally met in resource economics.[11]

One relates to a family of problems associated with the irreproducibility of unique phenomena - natural landscapes, for example, cannot be replaced by other natural landscapes. A second problem area is that whilst the supply of natural landscape resources cannot readily be enlarged by man, demand is rising, and the utility to individuals of direct association with wild, unspoiled landscapes is unquestionably increasing (see Chapter 7.2). In addition, in many situations the real costs of refraining from converting remaining rare natural environment may not be very high - and economic arguments about landscape resources may not be very convincing. Finally, if planning in particular, and behaviour in general, are motivated by a desire to leave some form of 'landscape estate' for future generations, some part of that estate will need to be in assets which yield collective goods of appreciating future value.

Sensitive landscape planning management and protection are thus basic necessities, particularly with a view to long-term preservation of the landscape resource base. Ashworth has stressed that 'ironically, planners have rarely been involved in discussions on the long-term allocation of resources nationally or locally, but have been rather more involved with short or mid-term allocation.'[13]

In addition to these specific resource problems, landscape as a component of countryside planning and management provides difficulties to the resource manager for four main reasons:

(a) the countryside is a palimpsest of landscape elements from different periods in time - reflecting a long sequence of change and evolution to which contemporary land use change and structural developments add the final touches. The dynamics of the countryside, with flux and change as basic ingredients (see Chapter 1.4) are of critical importance.

(b) the countryside is a complex mosaic of landscape elements (such as trees, fields, rivers, settlements) in close juxtaposition, again highlighting interaction, conflict and dynamics.

(c) the countryside in general (except in strictly protected areas) is a 'working' system, where the landscape considerations of change are generally subservient to the needs of agriculture,

93

access, employment, and the like. Few areas
are blessed with planning systems where landscape as such is the dominant focal point of
resource planning.

(d) there is often a feeling - as expressed in
William Cowper's maxim that 'God made the
country and man made the town' - that countryside landscapes should be preserved largely for
the enjoyment of urban dwellers (see Chapter
10.4), and that the most pressing planning
problems are those of the urban areas themselves.
In some ways, particularly in Great Britain until relatively recently, the countryside has
been seen as the residual part of a planning
system orientated more closely around urban
problems and priorities (see Chapter 1.4).

Landscape - Evolution, attitude and variability

The landscape resource base is characterised by inherent diversity - indeed this variability from place
to place and through time encourages the distinct-
iveness of individual landscapes, and leads to the
mosaic form of landscape variations when viewed at
the large (eg. national) scale. Variability through
time relates to both the changing face of landscape
over time in a given area, and the changing attitudes that people have of the environments and landscapes open to them.

The history of landscape changes through the ages in
Great Britain is well documented.[14] Contrast the
late seventeenth century movements towards landscaping, field enclosure and timber planting, with
landscape changes brought about as a result of the
Industrial Revolution in the mid-eighteenth century.
The latter include the opening up of coal mines to
provide fuel for new factories; forest felling for
wood to be used as fuel and in building; the spread
of factories into previously remote rural areas; the
transformation of small remote villages by terrace
housing and new factories; the spread of mineral
extraction and quarrying into hitherto countryside
areas; the construction of waste tips by factories
and spoil heaps by industrial workings; the effects
on vegetation, over wide areas, of extensive air
pollution related to the new industrial activities.[15]
Projected landscape changes in the United States over
the period 1950-2000 also reflect the dynamics of
the resource base, and highlight the ongoing nature

LAND USE	PROJECTED CHANGE 1950-2000 ($\times 10^3 km^2$)	PERCENT OF CHANGE	PROBABILITY OF CHANGE APPROXIMATELY TO EXTENT AND DIRECTION INDICATED	KINDS OF ADJUSTMENT THAT WILL BE MADE IF PROJECTIONS OF DEMAND AND SUPPLY RESPONSES ARE IN ERROR
Urban purposes	+97	+141	Very high	Area used will change proportionately
Public recreation	+198	+107	High	Some area adjustment; mostly adjustment in intensity of use
Agriculture	-81	-4	Low	Adjustments in area, intensity of use foreign trade, and consumption all readily possible
Forestry	-117	-6	High	No major changes in area, but in intensity and consumption
Grazing	-81	-3	High	No major changes in area, but in intensity of use and output
Transportation	+20	+20	High	Area will change proportionately
Reservoirs and water management	+40	+100	High	Area will change proportionately
Primarily for wildlife	+24	+43	Moderate	Area will change proportionately
Deserts, swamps, mountain tops	-101	-29	Low	Area will change proportionately

TABLE 4.1 PROJECTED LAND-USE CHANGES, UNITED STATES A.D. 2000+ [16]

of change (TABLE 4.1)

Attitudes towards landscapes have also altered
radically over time. In rural China, for example,
peasant farmers have traditionally worked in harmony
with the landscapes around them, as witnessed by a
lengthy history of successful land management (involving, for example, irrigation; terracing; intensive cultivation; and forest felling). In post-1949
China, however, attitudes towards landscape have
changed markedly.[17] With pressing needs to increase
agricultural production, along with an ideological
commitment to change the environment, has developed
an attitude in which land is now seen as subservient
to industrial development and agricultural change.

Variability of landscape in the spatial dimension
arises at a variety of spatial scales. At the local
scale the configuration and relative abundance of
individual landscape components, such as streams and
waterways; field boundaries; vegetation form and
density; roadways and access routes; and buildings,
serve to influence landscape character and encourage
landscape diversity. At a larger, and more generalised scale of analysis, the individual landscape
components cease to be of such relevance, and the
overall landscape is coloured by dominant land forms
and dominant land-use. The distribution of major
land-use landscapes within an area like Scotland
(FIGURE 4.2), for example, demonstrates this scale
of variability and highlights the fact that variability of landscape character (as measured in terms
of the range of landscape classes encountered within
a unit area) does widely vary throughout a region.

4.2   THE VALUES OF LANDSCAPE

As stressed by Linton[18] and pointed out earlier
(section 4.1), the potential of landscape resources
can only be realised in practice when the resource
is valued and exploited for some goal or goals.
Value in the sense used here refers to the benefits
of landscape resources overall, as distinct from the
scenic evaluation of individual landscapes in order
to identify the most attractive landscapes, or those
most worthy of preservation.

Unlike many types of resource, the value of landscape
can be assessed in a variety of ways other than the
purely economic evaluations commonly employed in
resource-use decision-making.[19] Although attempts

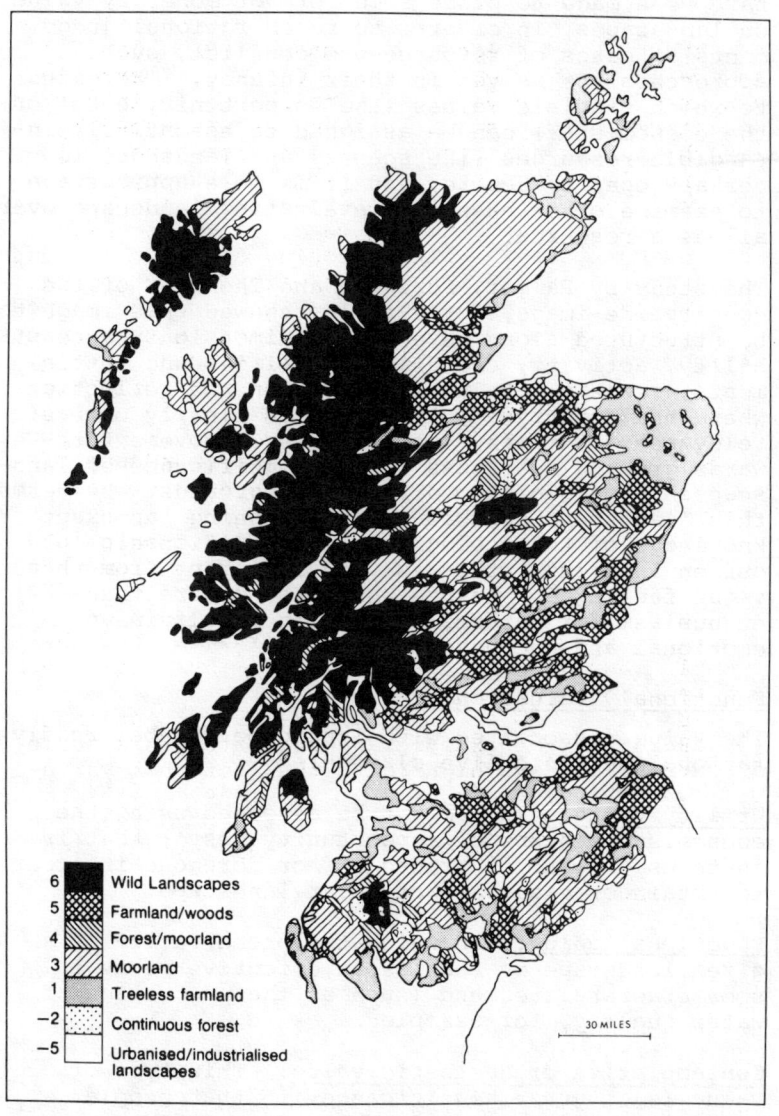

FIGURE 4.2   Land Use Landscapes in Scotland, based
             on the Linton landscape evaluation scheme.

Source: after D.L. Linton, 'The assessment of
          scenery as a natural resource', Scottish
          Geographical Magazine 84 (1968): 223.

have been made to place some form of monetary values
on landscapes, in efforts to reach rational judgements in cases of resource-use conflict, such
approaches are as yet in their infancy. The extent
to which tangible values (the 'opportunity cost' of
the economist[20]) can be assigned to essentially intangible resources like scenery and landscape is
perhaps open to debate, and it is more appropriate
to examine other bases for evaluating landscape overall as a resource.

The study by Palmer, Robinson and Thomas[21] of the
countryside image, for example, showed this image to
be structured along seven broad dimensions (accessibility, activity, crowding, facilities and settlements, scenery, evaluation, emotion and reflection),
where the countryside landscape is clearly of basic
relevance. Mattern[22] has detected a movement towards growing awareness of the significance of landscapes to people from diverse backgrounds. He terms
this 'landscape consciousness', meaning 'an exact
knowledge of the ecological interrelationships of
our environment: this is very different from that
vague feeling for nature which is no more than an
enthusiasm for nature, expressing itself in an
emotional and uncontrolled manner.'[23]

Functional Evaluation

The values associated with landscape can be broadly
rationalised into five classes:[24]

Utility value: This might be assessed using the
economists concept of 'opportunity cost'; that is,
in terms of what is traded off or foregone in order
to obtain or visit a particular landscape.

Functional value: In which the preservation of a
given landscape is seen as an effective means to
some other related end (such as the protection of
water quality, for example).

Contemplative or aesthetic value: This type of
value is of great significance, in that people
appreciate and respond to what they regard as
'attractive' scenery (however evaluated); they enjoy
recalling past visits and anticipating future visits;
and they cherish the thought that attractive landscapes exist even if it will probably never be
possible for them to visit such places.

Recreational value: Landscapes offer varying types
and qualities of recreational opportunities (eg. the
case of Table Mountain in South Africa, FIGURE 4.1);
and this form of 'value' encompasses both functional
and contemplative.

Ecological value: Landscape offers perhaps the most
visible evidence of ecosystem forms and functions,
and preservation of landscape is an important element
in habitat preservation, in maintenance of ecological
diversity, and in ecosystem conservation in general.
Again, this value encompasses the functional value.

The aesthetic values are without doubt the most abstract ones, and the intangible nature of these contemplative benefits underlies recent debates about
what types of landscape are the 'most attractive'
and hence most deserving of preservation (see Section
4.3). Yet, as Leopold and Marchand stress, 'on
landscape we grow feelings and frustrations'[25].
Thayer[26] has sought to evaluate the aesthetic foundations of interest in landscapes, and he suggests a
five-fold hierarchy of levels of aesthetic significance (TABLE 4.2) ranging from the concrete to the
behavioural.

Growing awareness of the significance of aesthetic
and behavioural responses to different landscapes in
part reflects an allied growth of public concern
over the environment in general, and over landscape
in particular (see, for example, Chapter 9.3). In
both Great Britain and the United States, for example,
there is evidence[28] of growing emphasis on amenity
groups, preservation societies and general environmental lobbies of opinion, as well as on public
participation in statutory planning.

Environmental and amenity groups represent a wide
range of interests and fears, but Means[29], for
example, regards many as representing a social
movement with distinct characteristics. His results
from the United States suggest that people from all
walks of life belong to such groups; that on the
whole they are not just sentimentalists or 'pure
preservationists'; and that their attentions are
focussed not only on the 'Great Outdoors' but also
on the wider moral/aesthetic aspects of the environment in general. Other studies from the United
States[30] on the other hand, suggest that the movement is primarily urban-based, and dominated by

TABLE 4.2   Hierarchy of levels of aesthetic significance of landscape as proposed by Thayer[27]

LEVEL	AESTHETIC RESPONSE	COMMENT
1.	Concrete, or presentational	influenced by the visual composition (colour, form and texture) of a landscape.
2.	Associative, or representational	objects and spaces within a landscape are associated with their functional origins and uses.
3.	Emotive or affective	elements of a landscape evoke emotional responses (such as pleasure, sadness, boredom and inspiration).
4.	Rational or symbolic	where all or part of a given landscape is intentionally measured in relation to our value system; the landscape might also symbolise something more abstract.
5.	Behavioural or activating	a combination cf all the preceding levels; where the landscape provckes identifiable behavioural patterns.

upper middle class (particularly professional)
people.

Landscape Preference and Taste

This growing awareness also reflects enhanced understanding of the associations between perception, reaction and behaviour. Lynch[31], for example, describes attempts to evaluate the 'sensory quality' of
an area in terms of sounds, smells, tactile sens-
ations and the like, arguing that human reactions to
the landscape and environment surrounding them should
be explored as an integral part of the planning and
administration of a given area.

The 'New Environmentalism' school of thought in planning during the 1960's in the United States (with
roots in nineteenth century positivism, the Utopian
Socialists, the Garden City movement and the philosophy of New Town development) was based on the
belief that by careful manipulation of the physical
environment it is possible to bring prescribed
changes in peoples' patterns of behaviour.[32]

Aesthetic values also relate to landscape tastes,
which can inevitably vary in both time and space.
Rees[33] has charted the evolution of what he terms
'The Scenery Cult' in terms of the changing interest
in wild or mountain landscapes over time in England
and the United States. Early attitudes towards
mountains ranged from indifference to dislike (because of possible danger, inconvenience and super-
stition), but in England between the Restoration and
the mid-eighteenth century dislike of mountains reflected fashion (which was not in favour of Gothic
architecture, or the classical ideas of order, reason
and restraint).

A marked shift of attitude, and allied change of
taste, in favour of mountainous landscapes from the
mid-eighteenth century onwards can be related to
artistic developments in the post-Romantic Movement,
growing appreciation of the wider aspects of nature
(through exploration and discovery), and an interest
in newly-available, non-Biblical time-scales for
landscape evolution.

Differences in landscape take over space, between
countries, are also apparent. Lowenthal[34] has isolated three dominant elements in the idealised image
of the American landscape - size (the scale of the

landscape, and the objects in it); wildness (the relative absence of human artefacts); and formlessness (a generally indefinite structure in many landscapes).

Contrast this with the caricature of the typically English scene offered by Sayer: 'rurally romantic scenes of picture-book prettiness, adorned with cosy cottages, bursting cornfields, and roses twining around every porch in sight'[35]; and the conclusion of Lowenthal and Prince that 'the English landscape is altogether so tamed, trimmed and humanised as to give the impression of a vast ornamental form, as if the whole had been designed for visual pleasure.'[36]

4.3 LANDSCAPE ANALYSIS

As with all other types of resources, planning and management of landscape demands detailed analysis of the resource base as a prerequisite to plan formulation, strategy evaluation or resource use. Two basic aspects of this analysis are important - inventory and evaluation.

Landscape Inventories

The most basic form of landscape analysis is the listing of what is present, in a value-free manner (i.e. without placing value-judgements on the resource). Base-line surveys are common in all resource management situations - such as those involving ecological resources for example[37] - although spatial coverage is often patchy and perhaps of variable quality.

Inevitably the availability and detail of landscape inventories varies markedly from place to place within any one country, and between countries. It is quite likely that time, effort and resources have been invested largely in the grand, the spectacular, the unique and the unusual landscapes, at the expense of the commonplace. It is also inevitable that the best surveyed and most comprehensively documented landscapes are those that offer direct utility values (popular recreation areas, for example), and those faced with the prospects of radical change through development (such as proposed reservoir sites, motorway routes, or new settlement sites).

This form of selective bias in inventory status implies that the less well-known landscapes or areas

are perhaps less worthy of preservation, and that it
is easier to justify the investment of resources in
preserving the better-known and more widely cherished landscapes. Examples of the more comprehensively
surveyed types of landscape are the National Parks
in England (FIGURE 4.3). Indeed, one of the reasons
for establishing a system of National Parks, and
equivalent areas in Great Britain, under the 1949
National Parks and Access to the Countryside Act, was
to encourage the preservation and enhancement of
areas of high landscape value (see Chapter 10.4).[38]

The landscapes in most other parts of England and
Wales have also been classified in one form or
another within the last decade, as a basic input to
structure plan formulation (see Chapter 11). Turner
concludes that 'the advent of the structure plan
would seem to have provided an opportunity to add
landscape to land-use and social and economic
factors in the drawing up of planning strategies'[39].
There is as yet, however, relatively little uniformity of approach to such classifications between
Authorities, so that nation-wide comparisons are
somewhat difficult.

The Land Use Survey of Great Britain, initially
carried out during the 1930's under the direction of
Dudley Stamp[40], and revised during the 1960's under
the direction of Alice Coleman[41], offers a base-line
survey of landscape resources which is spatially
complete and uses a standardised approach, but at
local and national scales there have been many and
varied landscape changes within the last two decades
which limit the utility of these earlier surveys.
With this recent change in mind, the Countryside
Commission[42] in the late 1960's launched a Changing
Countryside Project to collect reliable data on the
type and rate of landscape change for use in long-
term policy formulation. Field trials between 1966-
69, however, revealed the complexity, cost, and time
consuming nature of the task, and the project was
abandoned late in 1969.

Interest in the compilation of landscape inventories
at the national level was encouraged during the
1970's by the International Union for Conservation
of Nature and Natural Resources (I.U.C.N.), which
launched a major study geared towards the production
of a Green Book of Outstanding Landscapes to comple-
ment existing Red Data Books on Endangered and
Threatened Species. The purpose of the Green Book

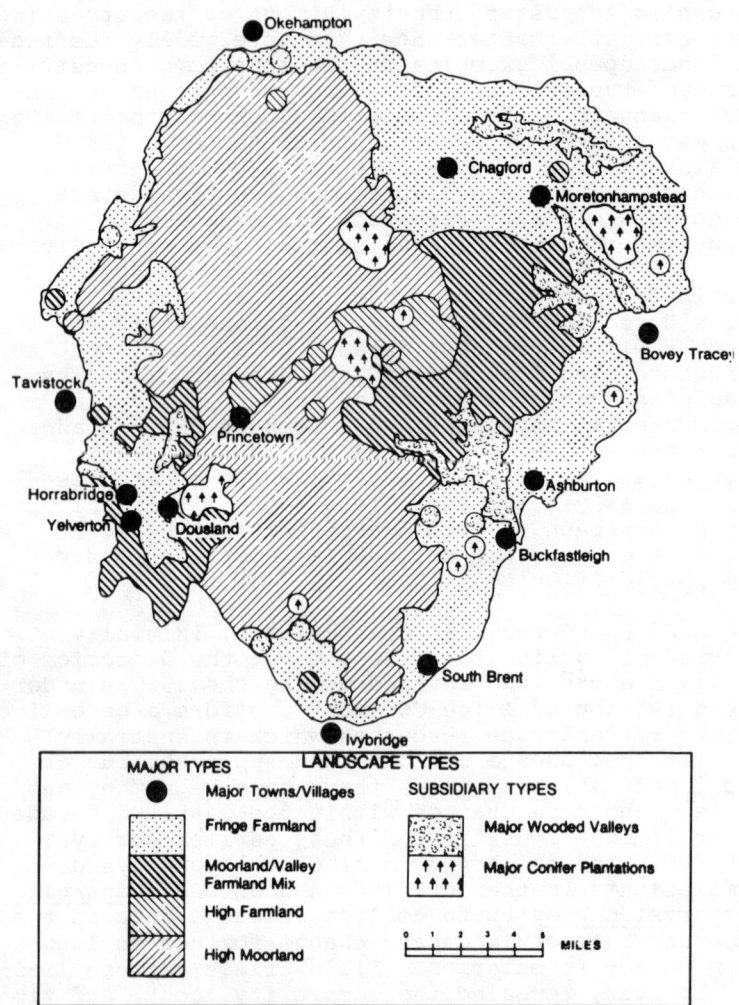

FIGURE 4.3   The Landscape Mosaic of the Dartmoor
             National Park

Source: after Dartmoor National Park Authority,
          Dartmoor National Park Plan (Exeter,
          Dartmoor National Park Authority: 1975).

was 'to provide an inventory and description of cultural landscapes as a basis for such action as may be
necessary to conserve them' [43] at the world-wide scale.
In the pilot programme for the study, a representative sample of countries were each invited to sub-
mit inventories of 10 'outstanding landscapes'. For
example Ireland[44] collected information on 138 possible landscapes as its national overview, and classified this list into seven landscape types based on
areas of low relief (terrestrial; lakes; river valleys; marine; and islands) and high relief (terrestrial; and marine). Unfortunately, as with the
Countryside Commission project, constraints of limited financial and manpower resources forced the
I.U.C.N. to abandon the study after the pilot phase.
Whilst the exercise did stimulate interest in landscape inventories in some countries, the overall
aims were far from realised.

Landscape Evaluations

The compilation of inventories has been complemented
by the development of approaches to provide comparable bases for identifying 'attractive' landscapes,
and ranking landscapes in a given area on the basis
of scenic merit. Such evaluations are of value in
five main contexts[45]: they provide:-

(i)   a statement of landscape resources in terms
        of character and/or quality and/or rarity.
        This is one of the basic inputs in determin-
        ing land-use and development strategies;

(ii)   comparisons of the character and/or quality
        and/or rarity of different sites, as a guide
        to development control decisions;

(iii)   an indication of the zone of visual influence
        of suggested developments, again useful in
        making development control decisions;

(iv)   an indication of the susceptibility to change
        of different landscapes; and

(v)   an evaluation of the suitability of the land-
        scape for different roles (such as residential
        use, or wilderness).

Much has been written about landscape evaluation in
recent years and this is reviewed elsewhere.[46] It
is useful, however, to distinguish at least two
broad approaches to the problem of evaluating
countryside landscapes. One approach is based on
ranking a series of individual sites or landscapes

on the basis of their relative scenic merits. The
evaluation might be designed to:

(a)   select which sites are most worthy of inclusion
      in a landscape preservation system;

(b)   isolate which sites are least suitable for a
      proposed development which is not necessarily
      area-specific (such as an upland water-supply
      reservoir); or

(c)   simply rank the sites along a given dimension
      of landscape quality such as uniqueness, natur-
      alness, diversity or grandeur. Leopold main-
      tains that 'landscape which is unique - that is,
      different from others or uncommon - has more
      significance to society than that which is
      common'[47].

The alternative approach seeks to rank all sites or
landscapes within a given area, on the basis of
relative scenic merits. If all parts of an area are
evaluated it is possible to construct a map of variations in landscape quality across the study area.
Such maps are of considerable value both in establishing where preservation or development control
policies might be required, although, as Linton has
stressed 'we must remember that it (the map) makes
no decisions for us. It offers nothing but information about the extent and location of our scenic
resources. Decisions must be made as to what action
should be taken regarding those resources'[48]

An example of landscape evaluation in practice is
offered by the Hampshire County Council,[49] faced with
the problem of designating an Area of Outstanding
Natural Beauty in eastern Hampshire, based on subjective criteria. Their approach is based on identifying elements in the landscape which have an apparent influence on scenic quality; whether these
elements enhance or reduce this visual attractiveness. Detractive elements were taken to include
such things as electricity distribution lines; derelict mine workings; and unsuitable farm buildings.
Attractive elements include striking topography;
'tidy' agricultural land with isolated copses of
trees; the presence (but not the dominance) of woodland; natural and semi-natural land-uses; and
special types of landscape such as country parks.

All approaches to landscape evaluation commonly adopted seek to provide an objective assessment of

scenic merit, but as Craik[50] and others have demonstrated, appraisal of intangible resources like
landscape is underlain by psychological factors which
are often deeply rooted in the personality and
character of the individual or individuals involved.
Penning-Rowsell[51] has reviewed over thirty different
approaches to landscape evaluation grouped into two
broad types, depending on the extent to which the
attitudes and preferences of landscape users are
taken into account. The approaches which are independent from the landscape users are generally based
on subjective evaluations drawn up by the resource
planners or managers. In practice this often means
that the evaluations are carried out by professional
groups like landscape architects, planners and highway engineers, who profess to bring a rationality
and objectivity into the decision-making process
which would not necessarily emerge in group-concensus
evaluations amongst samples of resource-users.[52]

A number of studies of the factors underlying peoples'
assessment of natural scenery have sought to
identify which elements of the landscape are important in colouring perception and preference. An
example is the semantic differential evaluation reported by Calvin, Dearinger and Curtin[53]. Their
principal components analysis of the responses of
psychology students to a series of colour slides of
different landscapes suggested two basic dimensions
of assessment:

(i) Natural scenic beauty: measured along a
      scale from scenic (colourful, beautiful,
      natural and primitive landscapes) to ugly
      (drab, ugly, artificial and civilised);

(ii) Natural force factor: measured along a scale
      from powerful (turbulent, loud, rugged, com-
      plex types of landscapes) to tranquil
      (tranquil, hushed, delicate, simple).

In most decision-making involving landscapes, the
pressures of seeking to optimise resource use in the
face of competing demand for land generally rule out
detailed consideration of relatively intangible issues such as perception of, and preference for given
landscapes, and the resource manager generally has to
base decisions on specially prepared landscape evaluation maps. Such maps can be used in four basic
ways:-[54]

Landscape

(i) <u>Landscape preservation</u>: The identification
of areas of countryside to be designated as
worthy of preservation in a state as close as
possible to that presently existing;

(ii) <u>Landscape protection</u>: Similar to (i), but
less restrictive to planned landscape change;
the aim is to link development control decisions to available landscape resources, and
resolve conflicts between the two;

(iii) <u>Recreation policy</u>: Seeking to preserve areas
of high landscape quality as sanctuaries
from recreation, and to develop prescribed
areas as foci for most outdoor recreation;

(iv) <u>Landscape improvement</u>: Based on identifying
those elements in the landscape which are
doomed to detract from scenic quality (such
as derelict land), and suggesting appropriate
management policies.

4.4 WILDERNESS

The term <u>wilderness</u> evokes different images and
feelings in different people. The Concise Oxford
Dictionary, for example, is singularly unilluminat-
ing in defining wilderness as 'desert, uncultivated
and uninhabited trace-part of garden left wild'. In
landscape terms, wilderness refers to residual areas
of completely undeveloped land, which probably still
carry original or nearly-original vegetation cover,
are relatively remote and often inaccessible, and
are protected from large scale intrusions of human
artefacts by legislation and/or management agreements.

Simmons maintains that 'from the status of an
economic resource which had to be developed for gain
by felling, mining or farming, wilderness has now
become to some a treasured remnant which must at all
costs, save national security, be protected from such
uses'.[55] The underlying importance of wilderness is
stressed by Lucas, who states that, 'the wilderness
resource is not just a composite of conventional
resources (soil, vegetation, water and wildlife),
although these exist in wilderness. Rather it consists of naturalness and solitude, qualities that can
only be found in unmodified, uncrowded land'[56].

Preservation of Wilderness

Reasons for preserving certain tracts of land as wilderness are many and varied, but they relate to two broad beliefs:[57]

(i)   Wilderness is culturally desirable. The perpetuation of unspoiled landscapes is regarded, at least in developed countries, as spiritually uplifting in itself; and there are growing pressures to preserve such areas for use in informal recreation as an escape from the pressures of late twentieth-century society (see Chapter 7.2 and Chapter 10.3).

(ii)   Wilderness is scientifically necessary. Large, undeveloped areas need to be protected because they assist in the maintenance of general environmental stability and in the conservation of genetic diversity in plant and animal species; they are also essential for the study of plants and animals in their natural habitats, and as an educational resource (see Chapter 3.4).

The main impetus for preserving wilderness landscapes has stemmed from the United States, and it reflects both the greater availability of extensive open areas there than in, for example, Western Europe, and a long history of concern to preserve remnants of the 'original' landscape fabric of the nation, typical of the United States in pre-European settlement times. In Great Britain, for example, there are few areas sufficiently large, remote and undeveloped, to fulfil even in general terms, the cultural and scientific criteria outlined above. Pressures on previously 'natural' landscapes from agricultural expansion, evolution of settlements, spread of extractive industries, changes in communications etc. have been long and widespread (see, for example, Chapter 12.1) so that remnant 'wild' areas in Great Britain are now largely confined to upland Scotland and remote islands.[58]

An American concern to preserve a heritage of wild landscapes both for the benefit of future generations and the pleasure of existing 'wilderness seekers' aspiring to taste the joys and fears of their forebearers faced with opening up an entire continent, is reflected in the lengthy history of formal actions to ensure this preservation.[59] The designation of

the Yellowstone National Park in 1872, as 'a public
park or pleasuring ground for the benefit and enjoyment of the people', reflects an early sense of concern and commitment. This is seen also in the setting up of the U.S. National Park Service, under the
Department of the Interior, in 1916 'to conserve the
scenery and wildlife in such a way they will be un-
impaired for enjoyment of future generations.'

By 1929 the U.S. Forest Service had recognised the
need to designate parts of the National Forest
System as <u>Primitive Areas</u> (to be maintained free from
development or disturbance) and in 1939 the U.S.
Department of Agriculture designated some of the most
spectacular areas under its control as <u>Wilderness
Areas</u> (but with relatively little formal long-term
protection offered in the designation). The post-
war boom in countryside visitors produced mounting
pressures on existing areas (see Chapter 7.2) and in
the early 1960's the Outdoor Recreation Resources
Review Committee was set up to evaluate the wilderness resources of North America. The committee's
report, in 1962, recommended that Congress introduce
legislation to ensure the permanent preservation of
a national system of wilderness areas.

Hence the 1964 Wilderness Act[60] established a
<u>National Wilderness Preservation System</u> 'to secure
for the American people of present and future generations the benefits of an enduring resource of
wilderness'. The Act also formalised the basis for
defining a Wilderness Area in terms of extent of
human impact, opportunity for solitude, convenience
of size, and particular values; and it grants Congress the authority to establish wilderness areas
on federally owned public lands. The distribution
of areas within the system is shown in FIGURE 4.4.
Four federal land-managing agencies have jurisdiction over the public lands: the U.S. Forest Service,
the National Park Service, the U.S. Fish and Wildlife Service, and the Bureau of Land Management
(TABLE 4.3). Each is responsible for preserving the
wilderness character of the land under its administration.

This preservation generally prevents the construction
of roads, dams, buildings and other permanent
structures; forest felling; and the operation of
motorised vehicles and equipment (with the general
exception of those associated with fire fighting,
emergencies, health and safety). The legislation

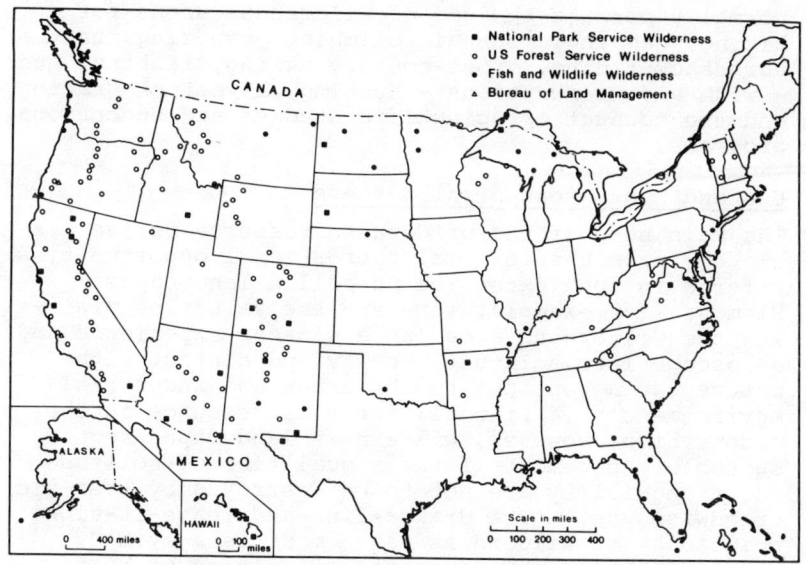

FIGURE 4.4   Distribution of Wilderness Land in the
United States National Wilderness
Preservation System (1978)

Source: based on data provided by The Wilderness
Society

TABLE 4.3 The United States National Wilderness Preservation
System.

Status of the N.W.P.S. as at 31 December 1978[61].

AGENCY	WILDERNESS SYSTEM	WILDERNESS AREA $(X10^3 km^2)$	PERCENTAGE OF TOTAL AREA OF WILDERNESS SYSTEM
U.S. Forest Service	110	63	80.56%
National Park Service	25	12	15.38%
Fish and Wildlife Service	52	3.1	4.00%
Bureau of Land Management	3	0.05	0.06%
TOTAL	190	78.3	100.00%

normally permits the use of wilderness areas for
hiking, camping, mountain climbing, canoeing, rafting,
horseback riding, cross-country skiing, fishing, and
- with a few exceptions - hunting, livestock grazing,
and the conduct of scientific studies and educational
programs.

Use and Management of Wilderness

The main uses of the wilderness resource derive
closely from the informal recreational opportunities
offered in such extensive unspoiled landscapes.
Simmons, for example, stresses the values of visiting the wilderness area 'as a pioneer experience and
an escape into solitude, beauty and contact with
nature, as a contrast to the urban and industrial
environment'[62]. Like all forms of resource in the
countryside, however, wilderness landscapes require
suitable management if their qualities of solitude
and tranquillity are not to be destroyed by over-use
or unwise use. 'The draw-a-line-and-leave-it-alone
philosophy of wilderness management is a myth'[63],
concludes Lucas, who suggests principles of both
ecological management and social management:

(i) Ecological management: (a) to maintain as
much of the integrity of the basic ecological
resource as possible (without preventing
further natural ecological changes by fossil-
ising the landscape at some prescribed stage
of development).

(b) to control vis-
itor impacts, ideally by non-structural remedial practices (such as the reseeding of worn
areas), and enlightened visitor management
(to influence the behaviour, distribution,
and impacts of the visitors).

(ii) Social Management: Aimed at protecting or
enhancing the quality of the wilderness experience for the visitor. Guidelines include:

(a) develop an oppor-
tunity spectrum - to cater, for example, for
those who would be content with visiting a
'semi-wilderness' area.

(b) manage the sur-
rounding landscapes sensitively.

(c) respect the vis-
itors' freedom - for example, apply necessary
controls or access points rather than in the

wilderness area, and avoid the use of controls
if the provision of information, education
and/or persuasion could produce similar
results.

(d) provide opportun-
ities for solitude.

The scope and need for suitable 'social management'
in the wilderness area is particularly important in
the light of the types of wilderness users, and their
aspirations (see, for example, FIGURE 7.2). The intangible, and essentially personal, nature of 'the
wilderness experience' means that it is extremely
difficult to characterise the objectives and aspirations of wilderness users unambiguously, although a
series of studies of the characteristics of this
group of landscape resource users yield interesting
findings.

Shafer and Mietz[64], for example, sought to evaluate
the importance of five types of experience associated
with the use of wilderness trails in the White Mountains and Adirondacks; and they found that in each
area hikers responses favoured aesthetic, emotional,
physical, educational and social experiences by
decreasing order of perceived importance. Studies
of the characteristics of wilderness-uses by the
United States Department of Agriculture Forest
Service[65] highlight the dominance of small family
groups, generally from urban centres, led by highly
educated seniors with abundant experience of wilderness recreation.

These sorts of user-profiles suggest that visitors
consciously plan their trips with care and anticipation; that they frequently return to wilderness
areas; and that they derive values which are much
more personal and inner-orientated than simply the
physical or social values generally associated with
informal outdoor recreation (see Chapter 7.2).

One of the most intensively studied wilderness areas
is the Boundary Waters Canoe Area, on the Canadian
border of northern Minnesota[66]. This is an area of
over 4300km^2, some 18% of which is occupied by lakes
and river systems, offering over 2000 km of canoe
routes through a roadless area. The area is managed
by the U.S. Forest Service, which allows limited
timber harvesting and limited use of motors (eg. in
motor-boats). The major resource conflicts in the
wilderness area stem from over-use by recreationists,

and relate to threats to ecosystem stability and
diversity (caused by excessive trampling and use of
preferred routes), and the visual and aesthetic intrusions of crowded conditions on the heavily-used
routes. The Forest Service has recognised the pressing need to formulate management policies which
prevent ecological deterioration and enhance user
satisfaction, and they have sought to develop a travel behaviour model for testing the suitability of
different forms of controls (based on either regulation or manipulation of visitor use).

Wilderness thus offers an important dimension of
landscape resource-use which highlights the problems
of conflict, value preservation and sensitive management which undertake many countryside planning situations. Thorsell[67] stresses two distinctive properties of the wilderness resource, however. First,
wilderness is not an absolute dimension; rather it is
a state of nature as perceived in a cultural context
(TABLE 4.4). Secondly, most users of wilderness do

TABLE 4.4 The Wilderness Continuum[68]

'Wilderness' is seen as the end-point of a spectrum of states
of landscape naturalness, which might include the following
elements in the United States:

1. the completely structured, artificial landscape
2. the small garden lawn, or penthouse garden of the inner
    city
3. the downtown park (one block or less in size)
4. larger lawns and parks of the suburbs
5. open spaces of the agricultural countryside; and heavily
    used county, state and regional parks/camp grounds
6. forest and range lands (uncultivated and sparsely populated,
    but still managed for material production)
7. National Parks and other large reserves (which have been
    withdrawn from 'economic use' and are preserved for their
    recreational and/or scenic values)
8. Wilderness Areas (those portions of parks and reserves
    from which all walks of man are deliberately excluded).

---

not use the areas to experience wild nature, or unspoiled landscapes, but to enjoy a brief break from
civilisation that is both pleasurable and safe.

4.5 SOME IMPLICATIONS

It is clear from this chapter that landscape can
rightly be regarded as an important resource in the
countryside. Landscape represents the physical manifestation of interactions between man and environment, and hence between human resources and physical
resources. Landscape per se has little tangible
value - only when valued by society according to one
of a variety of bases for evaluation, does the landscape resource have any real meaning for planning.

Landscape is generally viewed as a residual element
in countryside resource management, in that it is
generally created unconsciously as a result of resolving other resource-use conflicts (such as recent
agricultural changes, see Chapter 9). Many of the
values of the landscape resource are related to
aesthetic appreciation of 'fine scenery', and so the
preferences and perceptions of landscape resource-
uses can assume considerable importance in conflict
resolution.

However, Lowenthal and Riel[69] stress that planners
should not base decisions regarding landscapes simply
on what people say they prefer, because the way we
think we see the world is in many respects not the
way we do actually see it, and because stated preferences to hypothetical situations are often either
reversed or radically altered when the reality is
confronted.

Landscape differs from many resources in the countryside resource system in the extent to which it is
replaceable. Whilst entirely 'natural' or 'pristine'
landscapes cannot be reconstructed once they have
been destroyed or markedly altered, nonethless a wide
variety of approaches to the management of landscape
resources are available (TABLE 4.5). In particular
management schemes orientated around the conservation,
re-creation, creation, replacement, elimination or
development of particular landscapes are important
in the landscape resource system; and, again, they
reflect the interface of human and physical resource
systems in the countryside.

TABLE 4.5   Some possible approaches to the management of landscapes[70]

(A)   TRADITIONAL MANAGEMENT

Landscape Use		Management Approach
(i) Moorland, grassland:	rough pasture for cattle, sheep and deer grazing.	- felling, grazing and uncontrolled fires.
(ii) Heather Moor:	grouse shooting.	- felling, controlled fires, grazing and draining.
(iii) Improved Farmland:	crop and stock production	- felling, enclosure, soil modification, crop introductions, stocks and fertilisers.

(B)   FUTURE MANAGEMENTS

Landscape Use		Management Approach
(i) Conservation:	nature reserves, scientific study, species preservation	- prevent fires and grazing, limit access.
(ii) Re-creation:	wildlife parks	- eliminate fires and domestic animals; reintroduce locally extinct animals.
(iii) Creation:	safari parks	- replace indigenous wildlife exotic animals
(iv) Replacement:	conifer plantations, limited recreation	- eliminate fire and grazing, introduce exotic plants, limit access.
(v) Elimination:	urban, mining, industrial and reservoir development	- destroy ecosystems.
(vi) Development:	recreation centres, deer farming, cattle ranching	- use existing resources.

NOTES AND REFERENCES

1. L.B. Leopold and M.O. Marchand, 'On the quantitative inventory of the riverscape', Water Resources Research 4 (1968): 709-19.

2. T. O'Riordan, 'Ecological studies and political decisions', Environment and Planning A 11 (1979): 805-13.

3. D.L. Linton, 'The assessment of scenery as a natural resource', Scottish Geographical Magazine 84 (1968): 223.

4. J.E. Vance, 'Ordinary Landscapes', Landscape 24 (1980): 29-33.

5. Linton, 'Assessment' (note 3): 219.

6. This line of argument is explored by T.A. Heberlein, 'The Land Ethic realised - some social psychological explanations for changing environmental attitudes', Journal of Social Issues 28 (1972): 79-87, and by J. Black, The Dominion of Man - the search for ecological responsibility (Edinburgh University Press, Edinburgh, 1970).

7. Suggested by T. O'Riordan, 'Some reflections on environmental attitudes and environmental behaviour', Area 5 (1973): 17-21.

8. M. Dower, 'The function of open country', Journal of the Town Planning Institute 50 (1964): 132-40.

9. E.J. Moll, B. McKenzie, D. McLachlan and B.M. Campbell, 'A mountain in a city - the need to plan the human usage of the Table Mountain National Monument, S. Africa', Biological Conservation 13 (1978): 117-31.

10. N.K. Jacobson, 'The balance between agriculture, forestry, urbanisation and conservation - optimal pattern of land-use', in M.W. Holdgate and M.J. Woodman (eds) The Breakdown and Restoration of Ecosystems (Plenum Press, London, 1978): 391-409.

11. Suggested by J.V. Krutilla, 'Conservation

reconsidered', American Economic Review 67
(1967): 777-86.

13. G. Ashworth, 'Natural resources and the future
    shape of Britain', The Planner 60 (1974): 774.

14. For example, W.G. Hoskins, The Making of the
    English Landscape (Penguin, Harmondsworth, 1979).

15. Summarised in C.C. Park, History of the Conserv-
    ation Movement in Britain (The Conservation
    Society, London, 1976).

16. M. Clawson et al, Land for the Future (John
    Hopkins University Press, Baltimore, 1960).

17. R. Murphy, 'Man and nature in China', Modern
    Asian Studies 1 (1967): 313-33.

18. Linton, 'Assessment' (Note 3).

19. B. Mitchell, Geography and Resource Analysis
    (Longman, London, 1979).

20. A.V. Kneese, Economics and the Environment
    (Penguin, Harmondsworth, 1977).

21. C.J. Palmer, M.E. Robinson and R.W. Thomas,
    "The countryside image - an investigation of
    structure and meaning', Environment and Plan-
    ning A 9 (1977): 739-50.

22. H. Mattern, 'The growth of landscape conscious-
    ness', Landscape 16 (1966): 14-20.

23. Idem. 14.

24. This is based on the scheme proposed by
    D. Berry, 'Preservation of open space and the
    concept of value', American Journal of Economics
    and Sociology 35 (1976): 113-24.

25. Leopold and Marchand, Quantitative inventory
    Note 1).

26. R.L. Thayer, 'Visual Ecology - revitalising the
    aesthetics of landscape architecture',
    Landscape 20 (1975): 37-43.

27. Idem.

28. P.D. Lowe, 'Amenity and equity: a review of local environmental pressure groups in Britain', Environment and Planning A 9 (1977): 35-58.

29. R.L. Means, 'The New Conservation', Natural History 78 (1969): 17-25.

30. J. Harry, R. Gale and J. Hendee, 'Conservation - an upper-middle class movement', Journal of Leisure Research 3 (1969): 246-54.

31. K. Lynch, Managing the Sense of a Region (London: MIT Press, 1977).

32. J.H. Bradbury, 'Walden Three: new environmental-ism, urban design and planning in the 1960's', Antipode 8 (1976): 17-28.

33. R. Rees, 'The scenery cult: changing landscape tastes over three centuries', Landscape 19 (1975): 39-47.

34. D. Lowenthal, 'Is Wilderness "paradise now"? Images of nature in America', Columbia University Forum (Spring 1964): 34-40, and D. Lowenthal, 'The American Scene', The Geographical Review 69 (1968): 61-8.

35. D. Sayer, Wild Country, National Asset or Waste? (CPRE, London, 1970): 5.

36. D. Lowenthal and H.C. Prince, 'The English landscape', The Geographical Review 65 (1964): 325.

37. C.C. Park, Ecology and Environmental Management (Butterworths, London, 1981).

38. I.G. Simmons, 'Protection and development in the National Parks of England and Wales: The role of the physical environment', Geographia Polonica 34 (1976): 279-90.

39. J.R. Turner, 'Applications of landscape evaluation: a planner's view', Transactions of the Institute of British Geographers 66 (1975): 156-62.

40. L.D. Stamp, The Land of Britain; its use and misuse (Longman, London, 1962).

41. A. Coleman, 'Is planning really necessary?', The Geographical Journal 142 (1976): 411-37.

42. Countryside Commission, Changing Countryside Project - A report (Countryside Commission, Cheltenham, 1971).

43. International Union for the Conservation of Nature and Natural Resources, Some Outstanding Landscapes (IUCN, Morges, 1978).

44. An Foras Forbortha, Inventory of Outstanding Landscapes in Ireland (National Institute for Physical Planning and Construction Research, Dublin, 1977).

45. Turner, 'Applications' (Note 39).

46. Mitchell, Resource Analysis (Note 19).

47. L.B. Leopold, 'Quantitative comparison of some aesthetic factors among rivers', United States Geological Survey Circular 620 (1969): 5. See also Leopold and Marchand, Quantitative inventory (Note 1).

48. Linton, 'Assessment' (Note 3): 258.

49. Hampshire County Council, East Hampshire Area of Outstanding Natural Beauty (Hampshire County Council, Winchester, 1968).

50. K.M. Craik, 'Psychological factors in landscape appraisal', Environment and Behaviour 4 (1972): 255-66.

51. E.C. Penning-Rowsell, Alternative Approaches to Landscape Appraisal and Evaluation (Middlesex Polytechnic Planning Research Group, Enfield, 1973).

52. E.H. Zube, Rating everyday rural landscapes of the north eastern United States', Landscape Architecture 63 (1973): 370-5.

53. J.S. Calvin, J.A. Dearinger and M.E. Curtin, 'An attempt at assessing preference for natural landscapes', Environment and Behaviour 4 (1972): 447-70.

54. E.C. Penning-Rowsell, 'Constraints on the

application of landscape evaluations', Transactions of the Institute of British Geographers
66 (1975): 149-55.

55. I.G. Simmons, 'Wilderness in the mid-twentieth
century U.S.A.', Town Planning Review 36 (1966):
249.

56. R.C. Lucas, 'Wilderness - a management framework', Journal of Soil and Water Conservation
28 (1973): 151.

57. F. Fraser-Darling and N.D. Eichorn, Man and
Nature in the National Parks (The Conservation
Foundation, New York, 1967).

58. T. Huxley, 'Wilderness' in A. Warren and F.B.
Goldsmith (eds) Conservation in Practice (Wiley,
London, 1974): 361-76.

59. This history is traced, for example, by R.F.
Dasmann, Environmental Conservation (Wiley, New
York, 1976).

60. The Wilderness Act, Public Law 88-577,
3 September 1964.

61. Based on data supplied by The Wilderness Society,
Washington D.C. (1980).

62. Simmons, Wilderness (Note 55): 251.

63. Lucas, Wilderness (Note 56): 154.

64. E.L. Shafer and J. Mietz, 'Aesthetic and
emotional experiences rate high with north-
east wilderness hikers', Environment and
Behaviour' (1969): 187-97.

65. J.C. Hendee, W.R. Callon, L.D. Marlow and C.F.
Brockman, 'Wilderness users in the Pacific
North West - their characteristics, values and
management preferences', United States Depart-
ment of Agriculture, Forest Service Research
Paper PNW 61 (1968).

66. Described by C.G. Gilbert, G.L. Peterson and
D.W. Lime, 'Toward a model of travel behaviour
in the Boundary Waters Canoe Area', Environment
and Behaviour 4 (1972): 131-57, and R.C. Lucas,
'Wilderness perception and use: the example of

the Boundary Waters Canoe Area', <u>Natural Resources Journal</u> 3 (1964): 394-411.

67. J.W. Thorsell, 'The new wilderness and park planning', <u>Alternatives</u> 6 (1977): 24-6.

68. N. Helburn, 'The Wilderness Continuum', <u>The Professional Geographer</u> 29 (1977): 333-7.

69. D. Lowenthal and M. Riel, 'The nature of perceived and imagined environments', <u>Environment and Behaviour</u> 4 (1972): 189-207.

70. B.J. McLean and R.A. Pullan, 'Man and the changing wildscape', <u>The Geographical Magazine</u> (October 1975): 36-7.

Chapter Five

SOCIAL RESOURCES: THE HUMAN DIMENSION

5.1 HUMAN RESOURCES IN RURAL AREAS

Within the past five years more and more
chief executive officers have accepted the
fact that the quality of their professional
and managerial resources largely determines
both short-term and long-range profitability
and growth. Consequently, the human resources
function, staffed by a fully qualified professional, is coming into its rightful place as
an integral part of the top management team.[1]

The Resource Context

Nowhere has the terminology and concept of
'resources' been so overused yet ill-defined as has
been the case in the study of society, social change,
and social management. Robert Desatwick's translation of 'dealing with people' as 'the human resources function' is symbolic of the jargon-ridden
state of resource conceptualisation in the social
sciences. Equally, in the narrower field of study
concerning social phenomena in rural areas the term
resource has been used in widely differing contexts
with various inferred meanings. A glance at any
rural planning text, for example, will yield a harvest of such usage:

While the countryside must be economically
healthy if it is to cope with all the demands
placed on it, there is evidence that the pen-
dulum has swung too far in favour of resource
development. [2]

Nationally, it may appear that there is ample
land for accommodating the excess housing and
recreational needs of the nation's urban

> population and that the demands they put on
> the countryside hold out the possibility of
> a welcome transfer of <u>resources</u> from the towns
> to the country. [3]

> All parts of the country wanted similar numbers
> of villages designated key settlements because
> of the <u>resources</u> they were supposed to attract. [4]

While this point may seem rather laboured, the very
fact that most researchers dealing with rural communities and social planning have adopted a rather
liberal and generalised approach to the resource concept means that it is far less easy to equate rural
social resources with the body of theory and concepts
suggested in Chapter 2 than has been the case with
natural resources. Yet if the notion of resources
can realistically be identified as a basis for more
integrated study of rural management, the definition
of social resources is an important task both despite
the difficulties of current semantic usage, and indeed because of these very difficulties.

Two principles expanded in Chapter 2 hold the key to
just how much of rural society and its trappings can
be seen in a resource perspective.

<u>Principle One</u>: <u>'a resource may be viewed as a
functional relationship between human wants, human
abilities and a human appraisal of the holistic
(that is 'physical' and 'human') environment.'</u> The
idea of a holistic relationship between man and environment naturally accords well with the heart of
traditional geographical thinking. Moreover, social
geographers believe that this relationship functions
around the three influences of physico-geographical
conditions, economic forces, and (significantly)
societal structures. Thus we are presented with the
idea not only that man and environment interlink
economically, but also that a similar social link
may be established. Indeed, Dennis and Clout[5] argue
that 'social relationships are.....advanced by social
geographers as forming a kind of missing link or an
area of mediation between the natural milieu and the
processes of economic production.'

There are two fundamental ways of looking at these
three elements of the man-environment relationship.
First, social values are not resources themselves
but are seen to perform acts of arbitration on the
use of other, more tangibly physical resources. In

nations where rural areas constitute vast stretches
of relatively unpressured land, this arbitration role
is paramount.

The land use program for Ontario, Canada, for example,
notes a shift in social values towards rural land:

> There is a growing consciousness of the natural
> environment and concern with natural environ-
> mental consequences of urban development. The
> public relates to the preservation of agricul-
> tural land and the treatment of rural land as
> a natural resource rather than a resource for
> urban use.[6]

In this case, prevailing social values do not recognise the importance of existing community structures
as integral parts of the resource base under discussion. Rural land is viewed as a natural resource
by an environmentally conscious urban population,
and rural society is seen to exist on top of the
rural resource base.

This concept of society as being grafted onto a
foundation of natural and environmental resources is
supported by the idea of 'urban resources' as expressed by authors such as Perloff[7] and MacNeill[8].
Here, the natural elements of the urban system (such
as space, topography, climate and surroundings) are
defined as urban resources which support a variety
of interrelated life systems, including man.

The second perspective on the interaction of environment, economy and society stems from the idea that
as economic links between man and environment can be
seen in resource terms, there is no logical reason
why social links cannot similarly be classed as
resources. In this way, society and community are
part of the rural resource base rather than separate
phenomena which parasitically sit astride the natural
facets of rural areas. This symbiotic relationship
between man and environment might thus be seen as a
useable resource with which to generate social,
cultural and economic objectives.

Even the overused maxim 'resources are not, they
become' (see Chapter 2.1) applies here in that the
utility and viability of rural communities will depend on the political will of nations to maintain
and develop an alternative to urban life-styles by
promoting equality of opportunity amongst groups of

different class, race and affluence to live in a
rural environment. In broad terms, then, rural
communities may be viewed as a primary resource without which more tangible natural resources in rural
areas could not be exploited, and through which the
human wants, abilities and environmental appraisal
can take place against the background of a choice of
living milieux. It is this second view of the en-
vironment/economy/society relationship which is
adopted in this book.

Principle Two: 'anything can be regarded as a resource if it offers a means of attaining certain
socially valued goals'. If it is accepted that society and community in rural areas can be viewed as
an integral part of the primary resource base (that
is an essential ingredient of the value and utility
of the rural environment) then it follows that any
item required to sustain the needs of rural communities can itself be labelled as a resource.

There is an interesting divergence of interpretation
here of the 'means' by which socially-valued goals
may be attained. Whitby and Willis[9] define resources
as 'the means for producing goods and services that
are used to satisfy wants'. They subdivide resources
into three categories:

Natural resources: All those gifts of nature such as
land, air, water, minerals, forests, fish, quiet
pleasant landscape and so on.

Labour: All human resources, mental and physical,
inherited or acquired.

Capital: All equipment, including everything man-
made which is not consumed for its own sake, but
which may be used up in the process of making other
goods.

This taxonomy is well suited to the economic analysis
adopted by Whitby and Willis but is less so for other
purposes, such as Spitze's[10] analysis of the progress
of rural people (both as economic and human beings)
into 'productive, participating and satisfying roles
in our society and economy.' To this end he proposes
an overall function to define the human resource:

$$Rh = f \ (A,E,H,Ie,Kf,M,Fe,Ei)$$

where (Rh) stands for a resource, a human being in a

productive participating, and satisfying role in a
free society; (A) for inherent abilities; (E) for
family and cultural environments; (H) for physical
and mental health; (Ie) for investment in education;
(Kf) for knowledge of factor markets; (M) for mobility; (Fe) for factor entry-exit; and (Ei) for employment level. Although Spitze uses this framework as
a basis for quantification, a task which may be
regarded as overambitious and of little explanatory
value it does at least provide a nucleus for the
consideration of some of the resources required to
sustain the primary resource of human beings and
their communities in rural areas.

The Human Resource Hierarchy

Whether the broad categories of capital and labour
are accepted, or whether a longer and more detailed
list of the means of attaining socially-valued goals
in rural areas is preferred, it is clear that the
human resource in rural areas requires a series of
secondary and tertiary resources for its sustenance
and survival. A simple view of these various levels
of resources is offered in FIGURE 5.1.

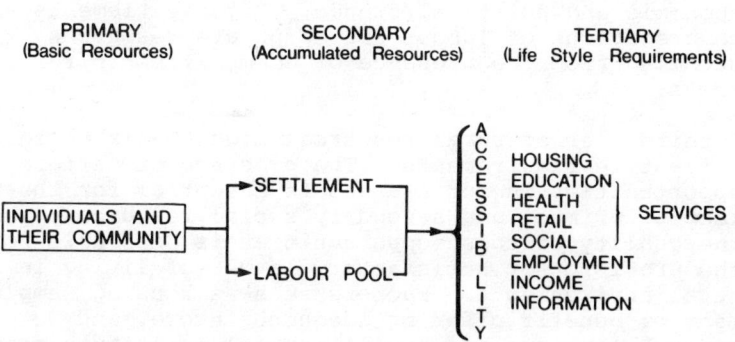

FIGURE 5.1 Levels of Resource Use for Social
Resources

The primary social resource in rural areas consists
of rural people and the communities they establish.
This represents the opportunity of an alternative

living environment (and in some cases life-style)
from that offered in urban areas and as such is
closely linked to the natural and landscape resources
discussed in Chapter 3 and 4. Primary social resources are useful strategically (providing habit-
ation of land areas), economically (providing labour
with which to make use of other non-human resources)
and socially (both as a basis for alternative living
and as a servicing network for transient recreationists and tourists wishing to make temporary use of
rural landscape resources).

The existence of primary human resources leads to an
accumulation of what might be termed secondary means
of attaining socially valued goals. The physical
vestiges of the rural built environment (see Chapter
8) have evolved to serve the needs of rural communities, but are themselves subject to changing
trends of fashion and economic raisons d'etre. Many
rural settlements in Britain are viewed as under-
used resources[11] because of the public and private
sector propensity to rationalise investment into
ever larger rural growth centres. Smaller settlements falling outside of this growth allocation
scheme may have substantial capacity for the receipt
of new development should this potential be recognised by resource managers. A similar resource
accumulation occurs with the rural labour pool, which
is equally subject to the ebb and flow of socio-
economic and political trends. Both settlements and
congregations of labour are corporate resources
stemming from the presence of communities in rural
areas.

A third tier of rural resources might be labelled as
life-style requirements. The presence of certain
opportunities in rural areas is essential for the upkeep of primary and secondary social resources, and
the quality of these opportunities is desirable for
the provision of satisfactory levels of living in
rural environments. Factors such as housing, employment or benefit offering adequate income, and
various services and facilities all constitute means
of attaining the valued goals of rural society.
Moreover, the extent to which rural dwellers are
granted access to these resources (see Chapter 10.1)
and to information which they require to continue
their life style aspirations represents a crucial
intervening filter to this set of tertiary resources.

This simple breakdown of the levels at which resource

concepts can be applied to the human geography of
rural areas is neither innovative nor mutually exclusive. Rather it attempts to provide a context for
themes which will be given further analysis in the
remainder of this chapter.

5.2 PRIMARY RESOURCES

If the primary social resource in rural areas is rural people and the communities they establish, it
should immediately be recognised that these resources
exist in a state of flux. A brief attempt to define
the distinctive characteristics of rural communities
was made in Chapter 1, but a realistic understanding
of communities as a resource can only be gained by
placing rural social groups in a wider context of
social and demographic change.

Two main strands of contextual theory are important
here dealing with macro- and micro-structures res-
pectively.

Macro-scale Social Change

Macro-scale social change is prompted by the ebb and
flow of growth, which O'Riordan[12] defines as being
characterised by increases in four aspects of consumption and production:

(i)   increases in goods and services produced and
         consumed;

(ii)   increases in human capital, through education,
         training, experience and the dissemination of
         socially useful knowledge and information;

(iii)   increases in non-human capital through invest-
         ment and the application of science and
         technology, and

(iv)   improvements in economic organisation and
         management through the application of organ-
         isational theory and techniques.

Clearly, the outcomes of an _absence_ of growth in
rural communities are as crucial as those prompted by
the _presence_ of growth in various forms. O'Riordan
stresses that

        economists have always believed that growth
        cannot continue indefinitely and that event-
        ually (though the actual timing is highly
        debatable) increases in wealth must give way

> to improvements in spiritual and other
> aspects of non-monetary well-being'[13].

This recognition of the transient nature of wealth
and growth crystallises the issues of how dependable
and how pressured social resources actually are in
rural areas. These communities and the areas in
which they are situated can be seen to represent a
valued spatial milieux for non-monetary well-being
and psychic income, but at the same time they are the
areas least well equipped to cope with the market-
oriented trends of rationalisation and concentration
which have accompanied growth processes in many
western societies. It could be argued therefore
that the life-style represented by rural communities
should be maintained, if needs be artifically, so
that a primary resource base will be readily available when the time comes to trade wealth and growth
for the spiritual improvement postulated by
O'Riordan.

Another issue is of parallel importance here. The
survival of communities per se in rural areas does
not guarantee equality of opportunity for social
groups of all age, class, wealth and health levels
to participate in rural living. Current trends of
gentification in rural areas suggest that some rural
settlements are only being maintained because of a
polarisation of the affluent and the mobile within
them. Those sections of the community who are unable to purchase housing and accessibility in un-
supported rural settlements are being forced to
migrate to those centres where such opportunities
are more readily available and attainable. It
therefore appears important to maintain rural communities in which equality of opportunity is inherent (see Chapter 10.1), so that the psychic income
they offer will not be of a distributional nature.

The distribution and dependability of primary social
resources in rural areas will be dependent on these
issues. It should not be found surprising, therefore,
that analysis of macro-scale structures of social
change tends to be political in nature and subject
to ideological dogma. In particular the Marxist
approach has found favour with many geographers[14],
who thus view societal change through the dialectical
kaleidoscope whereby continuous improvements in the
means of production inevitably lead to discontinuous
changes in the structure of society which itself
becomes increasingly incompatible with production

technology. Within this format, the <u>management</u> and <u>organisation</u> of productive growth are seen to create divisions of class, affluence and decision-making power, and thus perpetuate social problems caused by disadvantaged elements in any community.

The implications of these processes for current Western society are clearly summarised by Dennis and Clout[15], who note that

> the problems of capitalism cannot be 'cured' by applying policies consistent with the overall ideology of capitalism. The ultimate downfall of capitalist society and its re-placement by a new form of social organis-ation is thereby guaranteed.

The Marxist approach has received criticism both from those who would label themselves as 'radical' think-ers and from more conservative elements. Represent-ing the former group, Muir[16] rejects Marxist pers-pectives as being subject to economic determinism and as emphasising ends over means, activism over intellectualism and party over individual. He in turn values the academic freedom to adopt items from various ideologies as and when they can be supported by observed reality. According to this approach societal change may well be structured and class-ridden, but policy alternatives aimed at im-proving this situation are not confined to the over-throw of capitalism. It follows that the <u>management</u> and <u>organisation</u> of production and growth can be performed with equity and beneficial outcome, thereby tackling rather than perpetuating social problems. A more conservative ideology would place significant stress on management processes as essential mechan-isms of social and economic control.

Interpretation of macro-scale social change affect-ing rural primary resources will ultimately depend on which of these ideological stances is adopted by the individual analyst. In effect, we need to follow Perelman's[17] prompting to study the way in which society <u>chooses</u> to employ scarce resources.

Micro-scale social change

Within these macro-scale interpretations of social change, some attempts have been made to model micro-scale processes and movements affecting rural com-munities. For example, Lewis and Maund[18] offer a

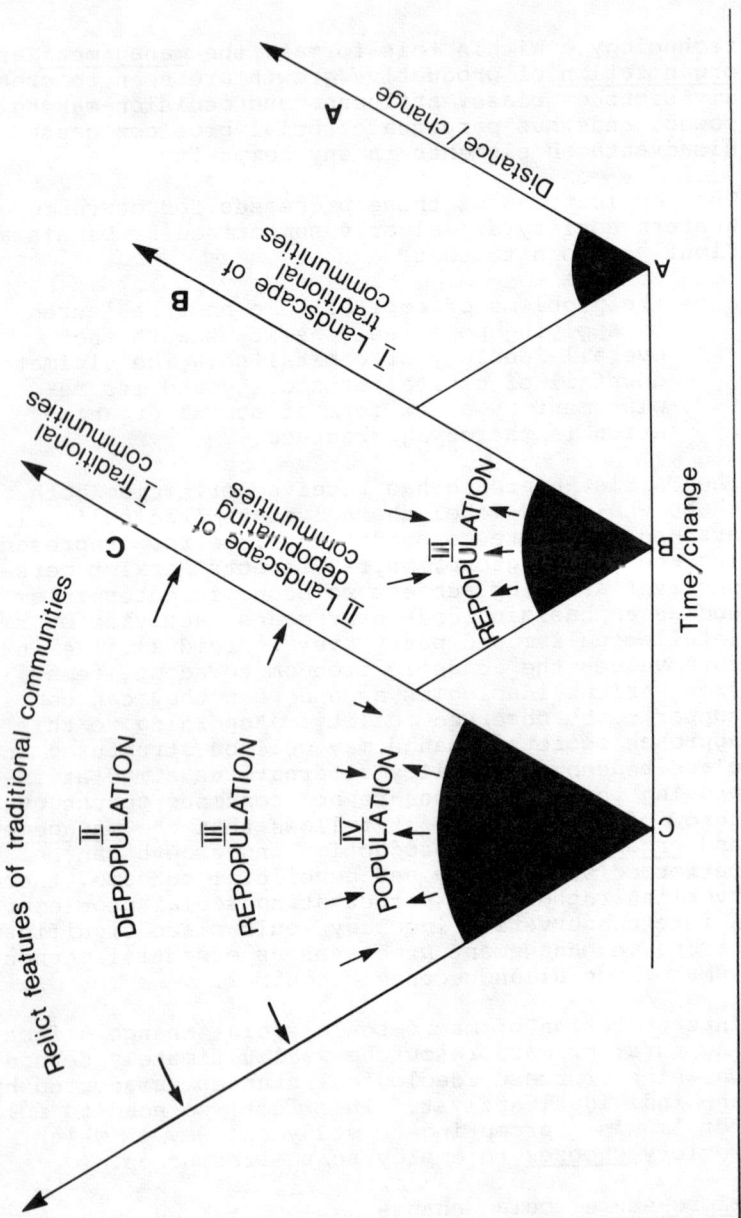

FIGURE 5.2   A Time-Space Order of Urbanisation

Source: after G.J. Lewis and D.J. Maund, 'The urban-
          isation of the countryside - a framework for
          analysis', Geografiska Annaler 588 (1976):17-27.

time-space framework of community changes in the countryside (FIGURE 5.2). The traditional landscape of A, with urban centres differentiated from small communities, is replaced by B in which depopulation occurs from rural settlements and, at a smaller scale, repopulation of peri-urban settlements is brought about by commuting trends. Stage C demonstrates continuing depopulation but an accelerated rate of repopulation sponsored by early retirement among high income executives and by improved transportation systems.

The 'observed reality' of these phenomena of depopulation and repopulation has produced evidence of a range of rural community diagnoses in different parts of the developed world. Rural areas of the USSR, for example, are still characterised by processes of depopulation and rationalisation[19], although some small scale comminuting links are beginning to appear[20]. By contrast, parts of North America show strong signs of repopulation and community growth[21], a process mirrored by the 1981 Census in Britain[22]. Perhaps most central to the resource concept is whether any distinctive rural communities are being maintained during the superimposition of urbanisation trends (see Chapter 1.4). There appears to be a strong realisation of the need for this special primary resource, with Adams[23] amongst others arguing that a modern technological civilisation is not inevitable and that a strengthened rural community structure is needed as a failsafe in case of urban breakdown.

This realisation, however, should be tempered by the overwhelming evidence which suggests that considerable changes are taking place in rural communities and that the primary human resource base in rural areas is by no means a static phenomena. The diehard reports of small town social life being appreciably different to that found in urban areas[24] are far outnumbered by evidence of changing rural values[25] and the disturbance of rural community structures.[26]

Kyllingstad[27] even argues that the concept of rural community is now a museum piece. Typical of the research evidence on this subject is that offered by Mogensen et al[28] on changes in Danish rural communities. They relate that most rural settlements in Denmark have received population growth in recent years and that communities have become increasingly prosperous and less dependent on localised employment.

As a result, living conditions in villages have become similar to those in other residential areas and parallel erosion has taken place in community differentials.

Two riders should be introduced at this point. First, the variations in scale between nations causes difficulties in the interpretation of the rural trends outlined above. Vast land areas such as those in Canada, USSR and USA will inevitably include extremely remote rural communities which are less radically altered by urban pressure than areas closer to major urban centres. By comparison, the rural areas of a small nation such as Denmark might be seen as peri-urban in scale and therefore liable to different trends of structural change in community. The rurality of communities is thus a relative concept and should be viewed as such.

Second, any expectation that rural communities should remain untouched by technological advance and increasing life-style expectation ignores the fact that very few areas of the developed world have stood still in development terms over the past few decades. In most cases rural areas have simply grown less quickly than their urban counterparts, and are now in some instances catching up some of that lost ground. The idea that rural communities should not evolve is therefore a rather false one, although the specific search for a simpler life-style may in some cases artificially induce this outcome.

The Definition of Rural Communities

An understanding of the effects of these widely varying changes in primary human resources in rural areas depends at least partially on an ability to unravel the semantic difficulties attached to the notion of rural communities. Newby[29] outlines three interpretations:

(i)   a small number of people living together in a rural location usually in a nucleated pattern

(ii)   the pattern of social relationships which exist within this locality

(iii)   a disembodied 'spirit' of community, a sense of belonging, of sharing a social identity in a spirit of friendliness and common emotional experience.

The changes taking place in rural areas have affected the second and third of these definitions. Repopulation processes have brought adventitious population groups into close physical contact with indigenous rural people (originally connected with agriculture). Social relationships between these groups are often strained and lack cohesion[30].

In terms of shared social identity and common emotional experience, the classic view of rural community stems indomitably from previous economic regimes. Newby points out that agricultural communities created close-knit and overlapping social ties:

> The village inhabitants formed a community
> because they had to: they were imprisoned
> by constraints of various kinds, including
> poverty, so that reciprocal aid became a
> necessity. The village community was,
> therefore, to use Raymond Williams's term,
> a 'mutuality of the oppressed.'[31]

Urbanisation of the countryside, however, has transformed many rural areas into predominantly middle class territory[32]. Moreover, resource allocation policies which systematically disadvantage the rural poor usually attract the democratic support of these middle class groups (see Chapter 10.1). As a consequence, the dominant classes do not share the mutuality of the oppressed, and thus find it difficult to share the social identity of indigenous rural people. Indeed, the deprivation among non-affluent rural groups is perpetuated by the influx of adventitious newcomers[33].

At a broader level, it has been argued that the urbanisation of rural communities and rural values has constituted a 'dehumanisation' of primary rural resources. Weissman[34] suggests that if future human settlements are to be habitable in terms of environmental satisfaction, a reverse process of humanisation will be necessary to counteract the current overemphasis on short term economic growth, and technical and economic efficiency. These ideas accord with the increasingly steady flow of people who have opted out of high pressure urban living and moved to rural areas in search of a more relaxed and self-sufficient life-style.

This movement towards voluntary simplicity[35] is one part of the currently accepted package of futures for primary rural resources. Uhlmann et al[36] consider it unreal to plan for a stabilisation of absolute population numbers in rural areas. Rather there is a need to maintain the living conditions of those who in the long term wish to live within the rural environment, and voluntary simplicity of life-style is certainly one option for the attainment of this need.

In addition, however, it appears equally desirable (if not essential) to ensure a rural future for population groups who wish to sell their labour while continuing to live in the rural milieux. This goal is far less easily met and is particularly prone to deficiencies in tertiary human resources such as employment and adequate income. Thus the dependability of primary resources relies in turn on the mismatch which often occurs between secondary and tertiary resources in rural areas.

5.3 SECONDARY RESOURCES

FIGURE 5.1 suggests that two rather more tangible collections of resources may be viewed as accumulating from the primary base of individuals and their community. These were nominated as secondary resources and represent the physical accretions of settlement and the human accretions of the rural labour force.

The Rural Labour Force

Hodge and Whitby attach considerable significance to labour resources in rural areas:

> rural labour markets are at the core of the
> problem of rural depopulation in developed
> countries: the success of policies seeking
> to moderate the process of population de-
> cline will be closely related to the policy-
> maker's ability to influence labour markets
> constructively. [37]

In essence, it can be argued that economic viability is usually a necessary ingredient of social survival in rural areas, and that the size and nature of the labour force offered by rural communities has to be recognised as a current and future resource in the achievement of viability.

Classic labour market theory has tended to concentrate on demand factors[38], focussing particularly on the employer's hiring behaviour. The supply elements of labour market theory are less well developed and study has been based on the rather outmoded concept of individual workers moving from job to job in a search for aggregated advantages of financial and non-pecuniary benefit.

Traditionally, rural labour forces have been placed in the context of agricultural employment, and have thus been trapped in a low income sector. Four major reasons have been advanced for this position[39]:

(i) the low income elasticity of demand for food, which implies that agricultural incomes do not grow as fast as aggregate natural income;

(ii) flexibility in expansion of output, primarily due to the availability and adoption of new techniques;

(iii) the low price elasticity of demand for food which causes wide fluctuations in price in response to moderate changes in output;

(iv) the low supply price of agricultural manpower, that is the low level of acceptable earnings below which labour will switch into altern- ative occupations.

Thus where agriculture is the dominant user of rural labour forces, rural communities are encouraged to sell their labour at a low rate of return[40], this being the principal function of the 'mutuality of the oppressed' discussed in Section 5.2.

In many western nations, however, the numbers of agricultural workers have dwindled to the extent that in Britain they now represent less than 5% of the total labour force (see Chapter 9.2). Rural labour resources are thus not only facing problems of being tied to a low-pay industry, but also that this industry's demand·for labour is declining. As a consequence, economic viability in rural areas depends on replacing agricultural employment with other opportunities.

Gilg[41] argues that the matching of labour and employ- ment opportunities requires different priorities of action in different types of rural area. For example, urban dominated areas are blessed with industrial and office growth which alongside strong community trends lead to a basically suburban labour force in a rural setting. <u>Intermediate areas</u>, which often represent lowland sub-regions[42] have also proved well capable of attracting entrepreneurs into their usually attractive rural environments. Here, rural labour pools are offered some opportunities outside the agricultural sector.

It is in the <u>extreme rural areas</u> where the decline in agricultural and other primary sector jobs has <u>not</u> been offset by new users of rural labour resources. Attempts to attract new manufacturing industries as alternative labour users have been less than successful, for by definition these areas are often too remote from external manufacturing linkages and the labour supply is often too dispersed for effective industrial concentration. Furthermore, a labour force rejected by agriculture may neither be suited to industrial employment nor willing to refrain for that purpose.

The future of rural labour forces is in the balance. Unless alternative uses of rural labour are found, rural communities will be polarised towards the self-employed, the retired, or the long-distance commuter, and these groups will increasingly dominate the residual community elements who depend on the <u>localised</u> sale of labour.

Moreover, any attempts to secure localised employment will encounter strong conflict from the conservationist lobby. Gilg advances their case as follows:

> these are often the most attractive and unspoilt areas of the country and in such a crowded island as Britain it is self-defeating to seek urban and industrial development everywhere. Holidaymakers do not travel from Birmingham to see the same landscape in Cornwall, Snowdonia or the Scottish Highlands. Physical planning should seek to retain regional differences in landscape not reduce them.[43]

The conflict between spoilation of physical and environmental resources in the countryside and the maintenance of human life-style through the utilisation of rural labour resources will be a recurrent theme in this book.

Rural Settlements

The other secondary or accumulated human resource in
rural areas is that of settlement. A cluster of
buildings in rural areas has usually served to cater
for the shelter and congregational demands of rural
communities, particularly with respect to primary
economic functions such as agriculture, forestry,
fishing and mining.

The fact that rural settlement patterns are historically derived and reflect particular economic
functions means that they too are susceptible to the
socio-economic changes currently taking place within
overall processes of depopulation, repopulation and
urbanisation. In rural societies where agriculture
still dominates or flourishes, settlement planning
and social planning are inextricably linked in
schemes of village renewal and land consolidation.[44]
Elsewhere, settlements have become more detached from
their original raison d'etre and tend to personify
a group of rural people rather than a unified socio-
economic experience (see Chapter 8).

The importance of settlement resources in rural areas
lies in their dual role both as indicators of human
life-style needs and as potential locations for the
supply of opportunities to meet those needs. Smith[45]
argues that 'the geographical perspective may be
summarised as a concern with who gets what, where
and how', and this preoccupation with spatial inequality tends to be focussed on settlements in
rural areas, as compared to areas within settlements
in the urban context.

Inevitably, the value of rural settlement resources
is also entangled with the a priori assumption that
any part of the rural environment should be deemed
worthy of conservation regardless of how restrictive this assumption might be in terms of preventing
development which is needed to sustain other human
resources (see Chapter 8.3). Thus settlement is
used as a surrogate both for communities and for
physical environment in rural areas, and conflicts
between these perspectives are commonplace.

Settlement Dynamics. It should be noted that rural
settlements are by no means permanent phenomena.
For example, Roberts reports on over 2000 deserted
Medieval villages in England (FIGURE 5.3) and
accepts that 'the numbers of deserted villages are

such that we are quite clearly dealing with something more fundamental than the mere accidents of
history'[46]. This fundamental process represents a

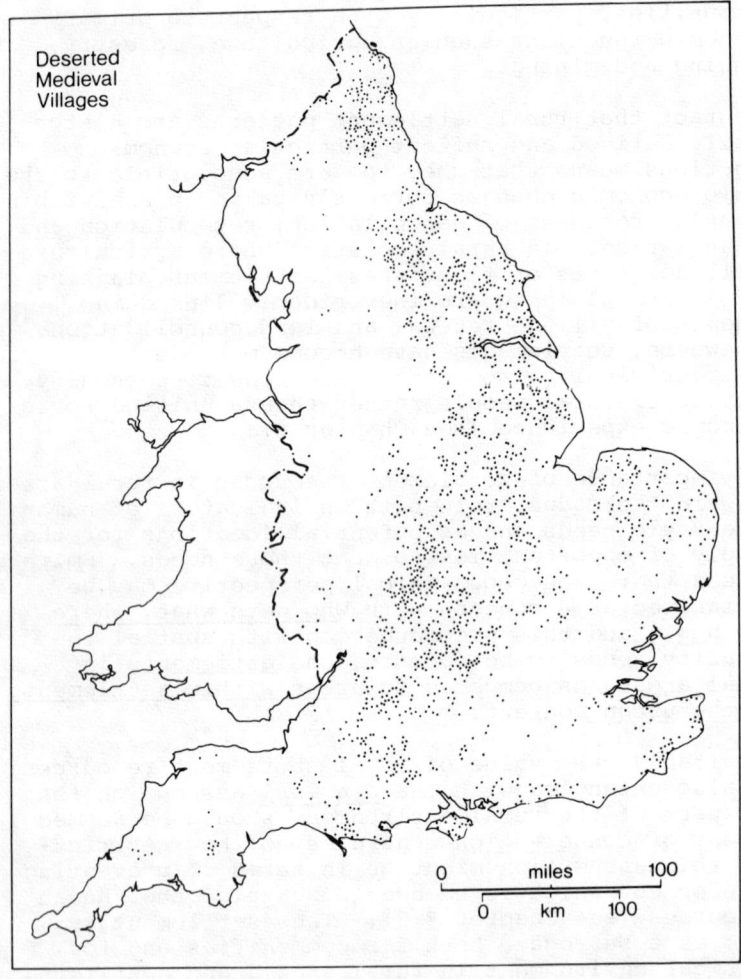

Deserted
Medieval
Villages

FIGURE 5.3 Deserted Medieval Villages in England

Source: after B.K. Roberts, Rural Settlement in
Britain (Hutchinson, London, 1979).

constant adjustment of patterns of rural settlement

to changing circumstances, and these changes have
been evident in most rural areas of the developed
world at various points of their history. Indeed,
the Durham County Council plans to demolish the so-
called 'D' villages during the 1960's provide a
recent example of this trend[47]. In this case, several settlements linked with redundant mining enterprises were perceived by planners as having reached
the end of their useful life, and were designated
for demolition. Following considerable public
reaction against this decision, which was seen to
ignore the social capital still remaining in the villages, the demolition policy was replaced by one
which merely declined to place any further public
investment in these locations.

Any understanding of the dependability and permanence
of rural settlement resources will necessarily have
to take account of this evolutionary perspective.
One view is that 'desertion is a phenomenon of settlement, a normal, possibly even healthy phenomenon,
usually occurring in response to changing needs'[48].

A logical extension of this attitude is to accept
depopulation trends from remoter rural settlements
as an inevitable and in some cases 'healthy' movement. Modern society, however, appears increasingly
disposed to reject this notion of 'natural' growth
and decline, preferring to attach value to antiquity
and to the perception of bucolic rural idyll. Moreover more political note is now taken of the social
ramifications of 'natural' desertion trends, so much
so that rehousing of residual households has generally become a public, not a private, responsibility.

Given these circumstances, it is not surpising that
the preservation of rural settlements is often supported by conservationists and social planners alike,
although their reasons for support and their visions
of what the settlement should be like are usually
poles apart (see Chapter 8.3).

Building and Design. Concern for the future of rural
settlements stems from an uneasily interactive appreciation of buildings, invested capital, and social
fabric. Rural buildings offer a curious symbiosis
with physical resources in the countryside. Most
primary building materials stem from rural land and
the collection of traditionally clad buildings in a
rural setting is irresistable to the conservation-
minded. In addition, a positive promotion of the

use of traditional materials might be seen as the method of promoting growth in primary rural indust-[49] ries connected with mining and quarrying. Weller's suggestion that a Rural Building Resources Group be established to further these interests is indicative of the strength of emotion involved in these matters in the British context. Similarly in the USA, rural buildings and settlements are cherished:

> A functional and harmonious relationship exists between a rural area's buildings and villages and their surrounding open space because traditionally the setting, types and design of rural developments were heavily influenced by topography, climate, and indigenous building materials.[50]

Stokes'[51] recognition of the rural conservationist ethic is accompanied by sponsorship for cultural resources surveys which would provide archaeological, cultural and historical data necessary for the establishment of preservation goals throughout rural America. It is clear, therefore, that settlement resources are perceived as valuable an account of their constituent buildings alone.

Capital Investment. The second theme inherent in rural settlement resources is economic in nature. Although the decline and desertion of settlements is historically undesirable, this modern age of seemingly finite physical and social resources has tended to place a premium on the utilisation of existing settlement resources rather than the construction of new settlements in the rural environment.

Despite the transient favour enjoyed by new towns, and to a much lesser extent new villages, there appears to be an increasing recognition of the worth of capital invested in existing settlements. For example, the concentration/dispersal debate in rural settlement planning in Britain[52] has been characterised by an opposition to planned rationalisation of rural opportunities into large centres because of the capacity for growth represented by existing investment in smaller villages. Gilder's[53] work in the Bury St. Edmunds area of East Anglia has produced convincing evidence both that significant spare capacity exists in small villages, and that this resource is not appreciated by planners.

This economic theme is strongly linked to social

aspects of rural settlement resources. The notion that life-style opportunities in small villages should be restricted to these elements of society who can afford the additional costs of accessibility and housing premiums (see Chapter 10.1) is anathema to any ideology which encompasses equality of opportunity, or preservation of rural life as a failsafe for urban failure.

In any nation where such opportunities are provided or controlled by the public sector, some degree of choice exists as to whether or not resource allocation is distributional in nature. That choice depends in turn on the philosophy of supply and provision of tertiary human resources in rural areas.

5.4 TERTIARY RESOURCES

The upkeep of primary and secondary human resources in rural areas rests largely on a number of life-style requirements which range between necessity and desirability depending on the definitions of these terms accepted by different governments in different societies (see FIGURE 5.1).

Contributory Factors

Access to these life-style requirements has been influenced by a number of dynamic factors in rural areas, the interaction of which has created a collective impetus for change of far greater magnitude than the combined influence of the individual components. Five factors appear to be most important:

(i) <u>Decline in traditional labour forces</u>. The wholesale decline in traditional forms of rural employment has had a number of effects on rural communities. In some areas, out-migration has been fuelled by job losses and the structural reform of agriculture[54]. Elsewhere, in cases where farmworkers remain the kingpin of rural society, the limited employment opportunities have led to low income levels and a poor quality of life. Indeed, Keating[55] argues that the major task of New Zealand's rural planners is to improve life-style quality through income levels.

(ii) <u>Mobility and energy</u>. The traditional isolation of rural communities from urban centres and their consequent attributes of self-sufficiency have been gradually broken down since the turn

143

of the century by increased personal and public
mobility. Easier access to jobs and services
in urban locations has prompted the removal
of _in situ_ opportunities in villages, and the
outcome of this dependence on urban resources
has been distributed unequally with the decline
in public transport services brought about by
the market dominance of car ownership. The
losers in this respect are those non-mobile
elements of rural communities who have no access or only partial access to personal transport (see Chapter 10.1).

(iii) Resource rationalisation. In most rural areas
of the developed world there has been a tendency for facilities, services and opportunities
to gravitate away from small and scattered rural settlements towards the more viable markets
offered by larger urban centres. The cross-
cultural implications of these trends have
been fully documented. In Britain, for
example, the Standing Conference of Rural
Community Councils[56] has uncovered an alarming
pattern of service decline in rural areas, and
particular emphasis has been placed on the
plight of everyday village functions such as
the primary school.[57]

French researchers have also been active in
the investigation of how services can be
organised in the context of a scattered rural
population[58], and evidence of the withdrawal
of rural opportunities is seemingly emerging
from most rural areas. TABLE 5.1 for example,
shows the results of a study of Etetahuna, a
small Wairarapa County in New Zealand, and
although the administrative labels are culturally confined, the underlying trend is
extremely familiar.

The rationalisation of resources is partly a
'natural' process, as private sector operators
chase economies of scale, and partly a planned
process in which public sector agencies (often
dealing with relative decreases in expenditure)
find themselves increasingly inclined to concentrate investment into larger central places.
Thus, although different balances of public
and private responsibility occur within different political frameworks, the underlying
structures of rationalisation are similar in

terms of economics and pragmatism.

TABLE 5.1   Eketahuna: Closures and Transfers, 1960-1977.[59]

Year	Event
1960	District High School closed. Resident Vet Surgeon moved out.
1969	Resident F.C.D.C. Agent moved out.
1970	Power Board Line staff moved out. Office closed 1942.
1971	Haywrights closed. Newman School closed. Post Office Depot closed.
1972	Kaiparoro and Rongokakako Schools closed. Saleyards closed. Humua and Hukanui Schools closed.
1974	Pest Destruction Board merged with Wairarapa Board. All staff moved out. One returned in 1977.
1975	Borough and County merged.
1976	Nireaha Casein Factory closed. At least four families moved. Dispensing Chemist closed.
1977	Maternity Hospital closed.
Unknown	Ministry of Works Depot closed.
1960-1977	Number of farms decreased from 331 to 265.

(iv) <u>Environmental quality</u>. As a counterbalance to the promotion of out-migration through resource rationalisation, rural environments can also be seen to have displayed a magnetism for in-migration either because of their perceived environmental quality or because of the price suitability of housing in those settlements which are less in vogue than others. This in-migratory motive is an important piece of the rural jigsaw because in some cases in-migrants themselves utilise opportunity resources which might otherwise have been available to local residents.

(v) <u>Land use and land ownership</u>. Any building development in rural areas will inevitably involve the take-up of productive agricultural land, and may therefore either be jeopardised

by the conservationist ethic or may itself
endanger the adequacy of future supply of land
resources for food production. This conflict
is complicated by localised land ownership
attitudes,[60] whereby some landowners will be
willing to release land for housing development whereas others will resist this pressure
even if new housing resources are required to
sustain local community viability.

Underprovision and Deprivation

Differing combinations of these changes have led to
the resulting rural conditions of depopulation,
social polarisation, narrow political interests and
rural deprivation. The latter is crucial in that it
highlights sections of the rural community where access to tertiary resources is underprovided.

Rural deprivation is not a modern phenomenon, in that
privilege and underprivilege have been constant companions in the history of rural areas. It is, however, a 'hidden' process whereby poverty, unemployment, poor living conditions, social stress and
physical isolation are far less easily identified
in small and scattered rural communities than in the
larger and more newsworthy urban environments.

Despite a vast literature on the subject[61], the concept of deprivation has proved difficult to define
and grasp. Wibberley poses the central question:

> Should we be mainly concerned about ab-
> solute poverty or deprivation, that is, an
> absence of some or all of the necessities
> of life? Even this absolute situation is
> hard to identify and measure because of
> the shadowy distinction between absolute
> and conventional necessities.[62]

It is clear that both poverty and deprivation stem
from an underprovision of various tertiary resources.
A convenient summary of the components of these deficiencies is to be found in Shaw's[63] outline of three
categories of deprivation:

Household deprivation. Indicates a low level of
ability to make use of available opportunities in
rural areas. The major constraint on individuals
and families in this context is a paucity of income,
from which it may well be difficult to escape without

migrating to more remunerative urban employment. A parallel problem is that of securing adequate housing in a rural settlement. In Britain, a combination of sparse rented accommodation and steeply rising costs of owner occupation created by urban demand for rural housing has meant that low-income families have found it increasingly difficult to find accommodation in their local rural area. Thus the dual outcome of income and housing factors has been to discriminate against low income families who wish to remain in rural settlements.

Opportunity deprivation. As well as these personal attributes of discrimination, the changing location of several amenities and facilities also serves to disadvantage particular groups within the rural community. The trends of resource rationalisation and declining demand for rural labour outlined above have ensured that localised opportunities for employment and for various education, health, retail and social services have disappeared over the last two or three decades (see Chapter 10.1). Even where shops and services remain in rural locations, the rural resident pays a high price for food and generally incurs additional expenses in the achievement of a similar standard of services as those available to urban people. Once again, these various forms of opportunity deprivation present the least well equipped rural households and individuals with the harsh choice either of incurring the additional costs of gaining access to centralised services or of migrating to larger settlements where opportunity resources are more plentiful.

Mobility deprivation. Suggests that those members of rural communities who have least access to personal mobility find it most difficult to adapt to the withdrawal of opportunities from rural settlements. Clearly there is a high degree of overlap between those suffering household deprivation caused by low income, and those who equally cannot afford to purchase mobility, and it is this self-reinforcing nature of deprivation which presents significant problems for planners and other agencies wishing to ensure an adequate provision of tertiary resources in rural areas.

The Association of County Councils note that

> children from low income families in poor
> rural housing, suffering from the added

disadvantage of limited educational
provision and inaccessible further education
facilities, are not likely to acquire the
skills necessary to obtain employment offering the opportunity of a higher standard of
living for their own families.[64]

This brief view of how a lack of tertiary resources
can create distributive deprivation in rural communities echoes the important issue raised in Section
5.2 concerning the type of rural society which should
be preserved as a primary resource. If we are solely
interested in ensuring that some population is retained in rural areas so that an alternative living
environment is preserved, then the adequacy of the
tertiary resource base is relatively unimportant. In
most developed nations rural areas will be saved from
abandonment by the wealthy and the powerful (or both)
whose status and purchasing ability will ensure them
a place in the countryside, whether this be on a
permanent or transient basis. If, however, the aim
is to permit a wider upkeep of communities and their
labour and settlement components, then some provision
has to be made to ensure the supply of essential tertiary resources to all rural groups whatever their
age, race, affluence or status. Whether this task
is approached via income levels, to allow deprived
households to raise their spending power, or through
the statutory provision of necessary services to
those who are disadvantaged by the locational outcomes of the market system, it represents a goal that
will only be achieved by positive intervention
through resource allocation mechanisms.

5.5   RESOURCE ANALYSIS AND ALLOCATION

This array of social resources in rural areas provides a fertile habitat for conflict both between
different social needs and between social and physical resource usage. Some of these conflicts are
dealt with in Chapters 6-10 and management mechanisms
which have evolved to cope with resource clashes are
reviewed in Chapters 11-12. There are, however,
certain generalisations which require elucidation at
this point.

Politics, Ideology and Resources

Social resources are inevitably entwined with political economy and ideology. As a consequence, the
analysis and allocation of resources in the social

sphere cannot be viewed 'objectively' but rather are subject to the differential perspectives offered by individual and collective viewpoints. For example, the lack of adequate tertiary resources to support the primary and secondary base of the countryside has been bemoaned in widely differing political and cultural regimes.

The resource deficiencies under the British mix of capitalism tempered by some degree of public sector social intervention has been well documented[65]. As a result, some authors have turned to overtly social-ist systems in the search for a more equitable res-ource distribution pattern. Barkin[66], for instance analyses the Cuban attempt to bridge the rural-urban resource gap. Viewing the history of capitalist society as a growing chasm between town and country, he reports that:

> The Cubans attacked this problem frontally from the very beginning. The earliest redistributive measures forced a re-alloc-ation of resources from the urban areas to the countryside. Since then Cuba has moved much further in the direction of directly attacking the causes for these divisions.[67]

In similar vein, Nolan and White[68] draw an unfavour-able comparison between socialism, and post-Mao economics, in China. They describe the egalitarian nature of rural differentials in the early 1970's which stemmed from the basic socialist elements of the Chinese political economy and from the left-wing policies of the leadership during this period. By contrast, they foresee a considerable increase in rural inequalities under the growth-oriented policies of the post-Mao leadership.

These two contributions apparently underwriting socialism as a basis for rural resource distribution should, however, be set against studies such as that by Fuchs and Demko[69] which suggest that social and spatial inequalities remain largely undiminished even in areas professing an ideological commitment to capitalism.

Human Resource Allocation

Clearly the macro-scale analysis of social resources in rural areas is ideologically constrained. There are, however, focal points of interest to all those

interested in the analysis and allocation of rural
resources.

Resource analysis: Depends on the identification
and measurement of poverty and inequality within
rural communities, yet such judgements are notor-
iously difficult to make. Smith's review of quantitative measures of inequality leads to a recommendation of upmost caution in this matter:

> The necessary, if regrettable, conclusion
> from this is that it is extraordinarily
> difficult to make precise comparisons of
> the degree of inequality experienced in
> different parts of the world.....It is
> important to bear in mind these tech-
> nical difficulties, that predispose the
> student of inequality to extreme caution.
> We must always beware of asking more of
> our data than its accuracy and the tech-
> niques at our disposal can legitimately
> yield.[70]

Similarly, qualitative assessments of inequality are
liable to encounter the ideological difficulties
expressed above, particularly in the examination of
minimum acceptable resource levels in rural areas
and in the degree to which rural-urban resource
differentials are a valid basis for comparative
resource analysis.

Resource allocation: Depends on the equity and
efficiency of resource analysis. Some of the pit-
falls of the analysis/allocation relationship are
evident in Lassey's[71] list of seven tasks for human
resource planning, American-style:

1. Identifying the basic problems of major
   social categories of the population.

2. Measuring the existing human service provisions for each subcategory.

3. Establishing 'ideal' conditions in the form
   of general goals to be achieved.

4. Measuring the gap between 'existing' conditions and the 'ideal' conditions, to
   develop specific operational objectives
   or targets.

5.   Designing procedures or programs, and locating sources of funding, by which objectives can be met in some order of priority.

6.   Helping to monitor and guide the programs toward reaching the objectives.

7.   Measuring results, progress, or failure.

The identification of 'problems' in Step 1 relies on an appropriate social categorisation of rural people (and indeed potential rural people) as well as the political definition of the concept of problem given that rural-urban migration, for example, will be viewed by some as a problem and by others as an inevitable and tenable result of social-economic change. The measurement of service levels in Step 2 may seem a straightforward exercise, but tends to gloss over the situation wherein services might be provided but at too high a level of cost to be used by non-affluent groups.

The difficulty ties in with the issue of 'what is a problem?' For example, one of the basic criticisms to be levelled at rural accessibility studies in Britain concerns their assumption that if access to services and facilities is available then the problems of rural people disappear. This, however, ignores the ability of those people to pay the cost of access and broaches the underlying issue of income and wealth deficiencies.

Step 3 invokes the establishment of 'ideal conditions' which will again be subject to the achievement of an acceptable collective vision for the rural future, but the measurement of the gap between 'ideal' and 'existing' (Step 4) involves both technical difficulties and the political decision of how much priority should be attributed to which particular gap between present state and future vision. Step 5 clarifies this problem further by suggesting that the availability of funding for particular projects is an important factor in the attachment of policy priorities, and the monitoring processes of Steps 6 and 7 again present problems for the resource allocator.

Should performance be measured against the problems of Step 1, the improvements made to existing conditions in Step 2, the visions expressed Steps 3 and 4, or the value for money suggested by Step 5?

Lassey's statement of intention, therefore, highlights the complexities and interactions of these
many factors.

5.6 SOME IMPLICATIONS

The allocation of rural resources is too vast a
subject to be discussed in detail here, and more
considered accounts are available elsewhere[72].
Various themes are picked up throughout this book,
but the authors in general argue that merit and
common good should be replaced by need and equity of
opportunity as the bases for resource differentiation.
We further suggest that the notion of spatial injustice, that is the unfair treatment of rural areas as
opposed to urban and of some rural settlements as
opposed to others, tends to mask the much more
crucial notion of social injustice in which the
needs of individuals and groups within communities
are paramount wherever their spatial location. By
concentrating on the rural environment we have
recognised a rather arbitrary spatial differentiation
(at least in social terms - see Chapter 1) but it is
the distributive nature of resource allocation within our chosen environmental milieux which is of most
concern.

Within this framework it is necessary to accept that
resource allocation is frequently performed in ways
which have spatial consequences, even though spatial
variations in need are not specifically considered.
More important, however is that certain social
groups enjoy powers of decision-making which dominate both the consumption and production of social
well-being[73]. Kirby, in the urban context, provides
a neat summary of the core issues of social resource
allocation:

> The impacts, or social outcomes, of dif-
> ferential access to resources are of major
> importance in the understanding of social
> well-being. Frequently this access will
> be an extension of the normal distribution
> of power within the community. However,
> there are many cases, particularly when
> we extend the scale of analysis to include
> not only intra-urban but inter-urban or
> even regional examples, where groups are
> systematically deprived in a way that
> transcends economic cleavages. In these
> contexts, social status derived from

consumption constitutes an additional
dimension to differentiation resulting
from production.[74]

NOTES AND REFERENCES

1. R.L. Desatwick, The Expanding Role of the
    Human Resources Manager (American Management
    Associations, New York, 1979).

2. M. Blacksell and A. Gilg, The Countryside:
    Planning and Change (Allen and Unwin, London,
    1981): 23.

3. Idem, 114.

4. Idem, 120.

5. R. Dennis and H. Clout, A Social Geography of
    England and Wales (Pergamon, Oxford, 1980): 1.

6. E.N. Ward, Land Use Programs in Canada: Ontario
    (Lands Directorate, Environment Canada, Ottawa,
    1977): 183.

7. H.S. Perloff (ed), The Quality of the Urban
    Environment (John Hopkins Press, Baltimore,
    1969).

8. J.W. MacNeill, Environmental Management (Privy
    Council Office, Government of Canada, Ottawa,
    1971).

9. M.C. Whitby and K.G. Willis, Rural Resource
    Development: An Economic Approach (Methuen,
    London, 1978): 7.

10. R.G.F. Spitze, 'Adequacy in Rural Human Resource
    Development', in Iowa State University Center
    for Agricultural and Economical Development,
    Benefits and Burdens of Rural Development:
    Some Public Policy Viewpoints (Iowa State
    University Press), 1980).

11. See, for example, the work of I.M. Gilder,
    'Rural planning policies: an economic appraisal'
    Progress in Planning, 11 (1979): 213-271.

12. T. O'Riordan, Environmentalism (Pion, London, 1976).

13. Idem, 39.

14. See, for example, R. Peet, Radical Geography (Metheun, London, 1978).

15. Dennis and Clout, Social Geography (Note 5): 6.

16. R. Muir, 'Radical geography or new orthodoxy?', Area 10 (1978): 322-327.

17. M. Perelman, 'Marx, Malthus, and the concept of natural resource scarcity', Antipode 11, (1979): 80-90.

18. G.J. Lewis and D.J. Maund, 'The urbanisation of the countryside: a framework for analysis', Geografiska Annaler, 58B (1976): 17-27.

19. M.C. Maurel, 'L'amenagement rural en union sovietique', Information Geographie 43 (1979): 210-224; J. Pallot, 'Rural Settlement planning in the USSR', Soviet Studies 31 (1979),214-30.

20. N.D. Sauchenko, 'Commuting links at lower levels of rural settlement', Soviet Geography: Review and Translation 20 (1979): 297-304.

21. D. Todd, 'On urban spill-overs and rural trans-formation: a Canadian example', Regional Studies 13

22. A.G. Champion, 'Population trends in rural Britain', Population Trends 26 (1981): 20-23.

23. P. Adams, 'Changing attitudes: new role for rural areas?' Planning and Building Development 54 (1979): 5-8.

24. See, for example, T.R. Ford (ed), Rural USA: Persistence and Change (Iowa State University Press, Ames, 1978).

25. J.L. England, W.E. Gibbons and B.L. Johnson, 'Impact of a rural environment on values', Rural Sociology 44 (1979): 119-136.

26. M.L. Price and D.C. Clay, 'Structural disturb-ances in rural communities: some repercussions

of the migration turnaround in Michigan', <u>Rural Sociology</u> 45 (1980): 591-607.

27.   R. Kyllingstad, 'Bygdesamfunnet - del 1: modent for museum?' <u>Plan og Arbeid</u>, 3 (1980): 151-3.

28.   G.V. Mogensen, H. Morkeborg and J. Sundbo, 'Smabyer i landdistrikter', <u>Social forsknings-institut, Copenhagen, Publication</u> No.86 (1979).

29.   H. Newby, <u>Green and Pleasant Land</u>? (Penguin, Harmondsworth, 1980).

30.   See, for example, R.E. Pahl, <u>Urbs in Rure</u> (London School of Economics Geographical Papers No. 2, 1965).

31.   Newby, <u>Green and Pleasant Land</u> (Note 29): 154.

32.   H. Newby, 'Urbanisation and the rural class structure: reflections on a case study', <u>British Journal of Sociology</u> 30 (1979): 475-499.

33.   B.A. Chadwick and H.M. Baker, 'Rural Poverty' in Ford, <u>Rural USA</u> (Note 24).

34.   E. Weissman, 'Humanising human settlement' , in Habitat Conference Secretariat, <u>Aspects of Human Settlement Planning</u> (Pergamon, Oxford, 1978).

35.   D.S. Elgin and A. Mitchell, 'Voluntary simplicity: life-style of the future?', <u>Ekistics</u> 45 (1978): 207-212.

36.   J. Uhlmann, H. Hellberg and H.G. Von Rohr, <u>Bevolkenings-nd Aretsplatzbnahme ineripheren endlichen Regionen. Vionzepte und Marnahmen einer stabi lisiening - sonentierten Entwicklungssteuerung. Literaturanalyse</u> (Gesellschaft fur Wohnungs - und Siedlungswesen, Hamburg, 1979).

37.   I. Hodge and M. Whitby, <u>Rural Employment: Trends, Options, Choices</u> (Methuen, London, 1981): 3.

38.   Whitby and Willis, <u>Resource Development</u> (Note 9).

39.   Idem, 209.

40. S. Winyard, 'Low pay and farmworkers', in A. Walker (ed), Rural Poverty (Child Poverty Action Group), 1978).

41. A.W. Gilg, 'Planning for rural employment in a changed economy', The Planner, 66 (1980): 91-93.

42. R. Green, 'Planning the rural sub-regions', Countryside Planning Yearbook, 1 (1980): 131-67.

43. Gilg, 'Planning' (Note 41): 92.

44. H. Schatt, 'Raumplanerishce aspekre der dorfer-neverung durch flurbereinigung', Zeitschrift fur Kulturtechnik und Flurereinigung 19 (1979): 127-37; P.R. Sinclair, 'Bureaucratic agriculture: planned social change in the GDR', Sociologia Ruralis 19 (1979): 211-226.

45. D.M. Smith, Where the Grass is Greener: Living in an Unequal World (Penguin, Harmonds-worth, 1979).

46. B.K. Roberts, Rural Settlement in Britain (Hutchinson, London, 1979): 111

47. A. Blowers, 'The declining villages of County Durham' in Open University, Social Geography , (Open University Press, Bletchley, 1972).

48. Roberts, Rural Settlement (Note 46): 112.

49. J. Weller, 'Rural building resources', Archi-tects Journal, 5 April, 1978: 641-643.

50. Idem.

51. S.N. Stokes, 'Rural conservation', Environmental Comment, May 1980: 10-15.

52. See, for example, P.J. Cloke, Key Settlements in Rural Areas (Methuen, London, 1979).

53. Gilder, 'Rural planning' (Note 11).

54. See, for example, the work of A. Mayhew, 'Agrarian reform in West Germany', Transactions I.B.G. 52 (1971): 61-76 and A. Rogers, 'Migration and industrial development: the Southern Italian experience', Economic Geography 46 (1970): 111-135.

55. R.D. Keating, 'Rural planning - another view-
    point', Town Planning Quarterly 54 (1979), 5-8.

56. Standing Conference of Rural Community Councils,
    The Decline in Rural Services (National
    Council of Social Service, London, 1978).

57. G. Cooper, 'The village school', Town and
    Country Planning 48 (1979): 190-1; P. Jones,
    'Primary school provision in rural areas',
    The Planner 66 (1980): 4-6.

58. F. Clerk, 'What size for rural organisation?',
    Economie et Finances Agricoles, June 1979, 61-66.

59. D. Glendining, Why did they leave Eketahuna? ,
    (Wairarapa Education and Rural Services Commit-
    tee, Masterton, 1978).

60. R.G. Healey and J.L. Short, 'Rural land: market
    trends and planning implications', Journal,
    American Planning Association 45 (1979): 305-17.

61. See, for example, Walker, Rural Poverty (Note
    40); W.G. Runciman, Relative Deprivation and
    Social Justice, (Penguin, Harmondsworth, 1972);
    J.M. Shaw (ed) Rural Deprivation and Planning
    (Geobooks, Norwich, 1979); P. Knox and B. Cottam,
    'Rural deprivation in Scotland: a preliminary
    assessment', T.E.S.G. 72 (1981): 162-75;
    B.P. McLaughlin, 'Rural deprivation', Town and
    Country Planning 67 (1981): 31-3.

62. G.P. Wibberley, 'Mobility in the countryside',
    in R. Cresswell (ed), Rural Transport and
    Country Planning (Hill, Glasgow, 1978): 5.

63. Shaw, Rural Deprivation (Note 61).

64. Association of County Councils, Rural
    Deprivation (Association of County Councils,
    London, 1979): 2.

65. Shaw, Rural Deprivation (Note 61).

66. D. Barkin, 'Confronting the separation of town
    and country in Cuba', Antipode 12 (1980): 31-40.

67. Idem, 39.

68. P. Nolan and G. White, 'Socialist development

and rural inequality: the Chinese countryside in the 1970's', <u>Journal of Peasant Studies</u> 7 (1979): 3-48.

69. R.J. Fuchs and G.J. Demko, 'Geographic inequality under socialism', <u>Annals of the Association of American Geographers</u> 69 (1979): 304-318.

70. Smith, <u>Grass</u> (Note 45): 32-3.

71. W.R. Lassey, <u>Planning in Rural Environments</u> (McGraw-Hill, New York, 1977): 99.

72. P.J. Cloke, <u>An Introduction to Rural Settlement Planning</u> (Methuen, London, 1982): P.J. Cloke 'Rural Resource Evaluation and Management' in M. Pacione (ed) <u>Readings in Rural Geography</u> (Croom Helm, London, 1982).

73. H. Newby, C. Bell, D. Rose and P. Saunders, <u>Property, Paternalism and Power: Class and Control in Rural England</u> (Hutchinson, London, 1978).

74. A. Kirby, 'Public Resource Allocation: Spatial Inputs and Social Outcomes' in B. Goodall and A. Kirby (eds) <u>Resources and Planning</u> (Pergamon, Oxford, 1979): 348.

SECTION II

RESOURCE CONFLICTS

It was pointed out in the Introduction that the
countryside is a veritable battle-ground in the
allocation of resources (both natural and human)
between competing demands. Section I sought to
establish which are the more important natural and
human resource components which figure in such con-
conflicts, and this Section is devoted to the exploration of situations in which resource-using conflicts arise in the countryside in countries such as
Great Britain and the United States.

The theme of conflict in resource allocation in the
countryside centres on balancing the needs and goals
of different groups of people who seek to use the
countryside in the pursuit of different goals. Conflicts arise through forces inherent in resource
allocation, such as the pressures of local and central government influences, differences in viewpoints
and motivations between urban and rural populations,
and competition between rural resource users seeking
to meet what are often inherently incompatible goals.

Planning of resource allocation in the countryside
is often beset by three particular problems, which
form a recurrent theme throughout this section. The
first is the need to balance local needs and aspirations with wider national or even international objectives and strategies. The Common Agriculture
Policy of the European Community, for example, sometimes creates local problems in particular rural
areas at the expense of success at the broader
European scale. Some forms of land use (such as mineral extraction) are encouraged in particular locations where it is accepted that those activities promote adverse social or environmental impacts, because
of the need to reduce dependence on foreign imports

of raw materials (for strategic or economic reasons).

The second problem centres on the need to preserve
the countryside for its own merits, and not simply
as the 'poor cousin' of the cities. Many rural planning problems are often seen as less pressing and
less worthy of investment than urban problems such
as inner city decline. The problem also encompasses
the need to coordinate and control urban encroachment
into rural and peri-rural areas in both a physical
form (through suburbanisation and development on the
urban fringe) and through social and economic influences (such as via gentrification of villages).
The third problem area stems from a common preoccupation with 'physical planning' in rural areas, often
at the expense of more immediate concern with the
social fabric and economic vitality of the countryside. Human-scale problems of accessibility, service
and infrastructure provision, and availability of
suitable housing stock in rural areas for local
families often lie right at the very heart of many
conflicts, and they underline the need to take careful stock of the needs and aspirations of country
dwellers at all stages in the resource allocation
process.

These various themes within resource conflict are
examined and evaluated by examining the differing
nature and strength of conflict in different situations and involving different resources. It would
be impossible and unwieldy to include all possible
areas of conflict within the countryside, and a deliberate concentration on a series of representative
conflicts serves to highlight some of the more important and pressing social and environmental impacts.

The chosen conflicts centre upon resource extraction
(Chapter 6), recreation and preservation (Chapter 7),
the built environment (Chapter 8), farming and forestry (Chapter 9), and access within the countryside
(Chapter 10). This choice reflects a desire to highlight both human problems (in Chapters 8 and 10 more
overtly than in the others) and environmental issues
(more specifically within Chapters 6,7 and 9), and
the linking theme of conflict generation and identification runs throughout the individual chapters.

Chapter Six

RESOURCE EXTRACTION

> Not all quarrying is offensive, and a very
> large part of our quarrying industry need
> raise no serious problems; in many cases
> quarrying is an eminently suitable form of
> land use, providing useful employment and
> interfering with neither agriculture,
> scenery or development.[1]

6.1 EXTRACTION - CONFLICT AND PARADOX

Resource extraction has traditionally been a centre
of conflict within resource management because many
different interests are involved and much extractive
activity is destructive by its very nature.

The rich harvest of minerals and materials offered
by the natural environment (see Chapter 3.2) has
been exploited for thousands of years, but early
activities were often small in scale, localised in
character, and limited in impact. Within the present century, however, there has been a massive increase in mineral extraction in many countries; in
the United Kingdom, for example, an output of some
40×10^6 tonnes in 1922 rose markedly to over
254×10^6 tonnes in 1964, but progressive adoption
of mechanisation through this period saw a parallel
reduction in number of operating quarries from 6000
in 1922 to about 4000 in 1964[2].

Many of the conflicts arise because the use of non-
renewable mineral and material resources through
extraction affect other renewable and non-renewable
resources such as scenery (Chapter 4) and the availability of natural habitats (Chapter 3.4). Any
country with limited land area needs to ensure an
optimum mix of land uses, and Warren argues that

161

'it remains questionable whether a crowded mobile
society like that in Great Britain can afford the
room and the affront to amenity which even the most
cleverly disguised mining may constitute'[3]. The
conflicts relating to extractive activities in the
countryside are wide-ranging, in part because side
effects are created at each stage in the flow of
materials through the economic system (FIGURE 6.1).

Yet two paradoxes underline resource extraction in
the countryside. One is that extraction is closely
associated with the opportunities offered for human
resources; positive factors (benefits) include
employment potential and the promise of affluence
(see Chapter 5.4) whilst negative factors (costs)
include the threat of pollution, inconvenience,
danger and spoiled landscapes (see Chapter 6.3).

The second paradox centres upon the significance of
past extractive activities in shaping the present
physical and socio-economic environment of many areas
of the countryside. Indeed, the very character and
fabric of many areas today owe much to the distinguished history of mining and extraction in the past.
The Dartmoor National Park Authority, for example,
argue that 'extractive industries have always been
associated with the hills, and much of the industry's
past is now dignified in industrial archaeology'[4].
Similarly, the countryside around St. Austell in
Cornwall owes much to the legacy of over two centuries of china clay mining.[5]

There are three main areas of concern in evaluating
resource extraction in the countryside - the heavy
social and economic costs incurred, reduced environmental quality, and limited post-mining potential of
quarried areas. Each arises in part because the
environment at large is commonly viewed as a common
property, and the impacts are external to an individual mining operation. Benefits from extraction are
reaped by the mine owners and operators, and their
shareholders, whilst the socio-economic and environmental costs of the operations are often broadly
shared by the community at large[6]. Local environmental and social issues might thus come way down
the list of priorities in extraction.

The need thus arises for local and national government intervention (through legislation and via
planning systems) to ensure that such factors as
social and environmental impacts are given due

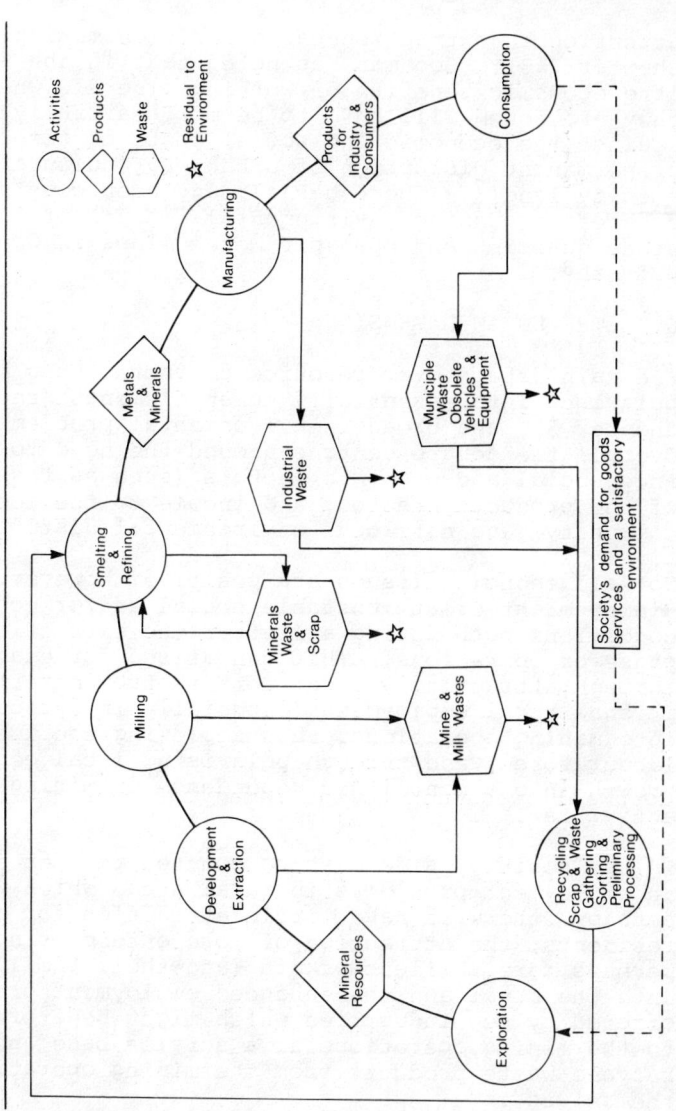

FIGURE 6.1 The Flow of Materials through the
            Economic System

Source: after D.B. Brooks, 'Conservation of miner-
         als and of the environment', in G.J.S. Govett
         and M.H. Govett (eds) World Mineral
         Supplies - Assessment and Perspective
         (Elsevier, Amsterdam, 1976).

attention in extraction-based decision making (see Chapter 2.3). Goodman has noted that in the future 'the economic benefits of working minerals wherever they are found will have to be more carefully weighed against the economic and social costs of temporary or permanent disruption of urban, agricultural or amenity land'[7]. There has already been considerable debate surrounding environmental impacts of large stone quarries and open pit metal mines in Great Britain[8].

6.2 THE HUMAN DIMENSION

The main debate over resource extraction can be polarised into essentially human elements (see Chapter 5), and broader environmental problems. Overall the debate centres around the need to balance social and economic factors (such as the value of the products created, and income to the local community) against local environmental disturbance.

Not all economic issues are positive, however. Mining might create unstable social and/or economic conditions both during and after the extraction phase of operations. This can arise, for example, through attracting younger workers from more traditional rural employment (especially in agriculture) into mining operations, thus depleting the local labour force, and through polarising local economic growth into a monolithic dependence on mining activities.

On the positive side must be counted the net increase in employment prospects in rural areas which would perhaps otherwise have little attraction for existing residents; the attraction of more enterprising and perhaps more skilled workers (and their families) into the area; and the enhanced employment prospects offered by new industries which might be attracted to the mining operations as a service base and to recycle waste products from the mining operations themselves[9].

Most forms of extraction encourage the growth of local service industries and infrastructure to service the needs of the extraction activities (see, for example, Figure 6.1). Aluminium mines, for example need locally available processing facilities for separation of ores, smelting, refining and eventual fabrication (casting, rolling and extrusion)[10]. This secondary economic activity might also affect other resource-using interests and activities in the local area through encouraging population migration, increasing local affluence, producing environmental side effects (such as pollution and wastes) and changing land uses and land values.

The regional multiplier effect of mining activities on the local economy can be very important. Long term or large scale extraction in an area often encourages the development of service industries, and the progressive increase in local affluence, coupled with migration of people into the area to work in extraction or service industries, stimulates local economic growth and investment. Economic activity thus widens from the original narrow base, and a cumulative process of building up the local economy and society can soon be triggered off.

The regional multiplier effect might be heralded as a boon in depressed rural areas, but the 'snowball' effect of changes in local social and economic structure may have serious impacts over the long term on community cohesion, social stability, population stability and the general socio-economic prosperity of the area. This becomes very self-evident if the extractive-base of the local economy collapses.

During the late nineteenth century Cornwall was one of the world's leading producers of tin, and thriving and prosperous mining towns encouraged large scale investment in new roads, railways and ports, and centres like Camborne and Redruth rose to prominence and affluence. Large scale mining of tin and copper ceased by the 1890's largely through shortage of capital to modernise; many mines failed, Cornish miners migrated to other mining areas at home and overseas, remaining folk suffered large scale unemployment. Warren concludes that 'West Cornwall retains in dereliction the material traces of its former greatness'[11].

6.3 THE ENVIRONMENTAL DIMENSION

Most vocal concern centres upon the environmental impacts of extraction, which are manifest in various ways.

Effects on Scenery

The most visible impact of resource extraction is
generally the open pit workings, waste tips, and
working sites, and the need is widely recognised to
protect and preserve landscape and scenic attractiveness (particularly in upland areas and areas used
extensively for outdoor informal recreation and
amenity uses - see Chapter 7). Thomas argues that
'clashes with amenity considerations are particularly
serious in slate, igneous rock and limestone quarrying. In the slate areas the excavations themselves
may not be objectionable if the main contour lines
are not broken, but the vast heaps of virtually sterile and intractable discarded slate are not a desirable landscape feature'[12].

Site configuration is important in influencing the
character and extent of visual intrusion, but the
architecture of plant and production units can be
equally important particularly where views are dominated by monocoloured stark shapes of sheds, silos
and plant. Careful and sensitive landscaping of
working areas both during and after use is thus a
key necessity in planning mine and excavation sites
so as to minimise effects on scenery. As noted
earlier, some resource extraction in the past has
actually enhanced scenic attractiveness, through
increasing diversity of landscape appearance or
through creating new landscape elements such as the
Norfolk Broads in East Anglia (by early peat digging).
Hutchinson[13] even welcomes 'landscapes of extraction',
dominated by pit heaps, quarries, gravel pits,
ridges of overburden and standing water bodies, as
interesting additions to some otherwise monotonous
landscapes.

On balance, nonetheless, effects on scenery are negative, particularly where extraction activities in-
trude into formerly natural habitats and unspoiled
scenery. Ratcliffe notes that 'from the amenity
angle, probably the most destructive effect of mineral exploitation is to 'wilderness character'[14]
(see Chapter 4.4).

Effects on Agricultural Potential

Good quality agricultural land is generally at a
premium (see Chapter 9) and so the requirement that
extraction should not trepass on such land can be
readily defended.

It is debatable in many cases, however, whether loss
of agricultural land in such conditions would of
necessity be permanent. Many open cast works have
been successfully restored to original ground level
after use, and with the replacement of top-soil,
re-seeding and drainage agricultural land of similar
if not better quality than the original can be
expected (se Section 6.5).

In yet other cases there is little realistic prospect of reclamation for agricultural use. Deep clay
pits often become waterlogged after extraction has
ceased, and in the absence of large amounts of natural soil for backfill such pits often have to be
backfilled with sanitary landfill (such as domestic
waste, building rubble etc.) which can pollute underlying groundwater reservoirs (see Chapter 3.3)
through infiltration and leaching from the fill material[15].

<u>Land Subsidence</u>

A marked impact of underground extraction is land
subsidence in the working areas which is common
especially where mining proceeds along several hori-
zontal seams simultaneously. Subsidence can damage
buildings, roads and engineering structures (such
as bridges and walls), and it can also produce land
drainage problems and safety hazards.

Coleman notes that slow surface subsidence occurred
widely under the concealed Kent Coalfield early in
the present century, but that it ceased within about
10 years after underground working stopped[16]. No
structural damage to buildings in the area was noted
but there was a significant loss of grazing land
occasioned through flooding of the low-lying subsided
land.

Wallwork has documented similar but more pronounced
subsidence in Cheshire triggered off by large scale
brine pumping since the last century[17] and damage
has included building subsidence, disruption of services and communications (such as piped water supply,
main drainage, and ruptured road' surfaces), and
deterioration of farmland in general and pasture in
particular through impairment of natural drainage
and subsequent land flooding.

Resource Extraction

Disposal of Solid Wastes

An inevitable consequence of large scale extraction
is the need to dispose of vast quantities of waste
material. The ratio of useable mineral products to
waste spoil is often extremely low; up to 95% of the
material removed from working china clay pits in
south west England is spoil, and between 90 and 95%
of slate rock is waste[18].

Wallwork points out that 'the existence side by side
of holes in the ground and waste heaps is a common
(enough) feature of many mining areas; the paradox
persists because of economic rather than technical
limitations'[19]. This is so particularly because of
the high costs of landscaping working sites and the
need to ensure ready access to all viable working
faces within a pit whilst that pit is operational
(thus partial backfilling with waste is often not
possible for logistical reasons).

Waste tips and spoil heaps generally reduce scenic
attractiveness, and they also add to the landtake
requirements of extraction operations. Problems of
accommodating vast quantities of mineral waste are
highlighted in Colorado in the United States, where
oil shale production has increased markedly in recent years. It has been estimated[20] that production
of one million barrels of oil per day would require
the processing of some 508×10^6 tonnes of oil shale
per year. This would yield in the order of 406×10^6
tonnes of spent shale, which would have to be accommodated locally because of the high transport costs
and bulky nature of the material.

Air and Water Pollution

The activities related to extraction operations
(ranging from blasting and cutting, through processing, purification and transport of the mineral
material and waste - see Figure 6.1) can induce
pollution of both air and water resources within
the extraction site and in surrounding areas. Water
pollution frequently arises from emission of the fine
solid matter from workings into streams, and the
transport and deposition downstream of this sediment.
For example, many of the streams draining from china-
clay working areas of Bodmin Moor, exhibit signs of
extremely high fine sediment loads and streams on
Dartmoor where gravels have been worked in the past
for alluvial tin, still preserve evidence of former
increases in coarse sediment load[21]. Particulate

168

sediment is complemented by the downwash of toxic heavy metals (especially lead and copper) in some mining areas. Vegetation of floodplain sites downstream from such workings is often markedly affected[22].

Acid mine drainage and the release of sewage from water treatment plants related to extraction operations can also produce problems of water pollution. Even small increases in the concentrations of some elements can trigger off marked impacts on aquatic ecosystems downstream; relatively small amounts of copper and zinc can have severe effects on fish populations even if the fish are able to survive successfully in such waters[23].

Air pollution is also common around extraction works, particularly if the operations involve blasting, extensive drilling, and/or the removal of fine unconsolidated material. Haythornthwaite noted substantial air pollution from the Hope Valley cement works in the Peak District during the 1950's, from dust and fumes emitted from chimneys on site[24]. The problem centred upon the conflict of installing taller chimneys which would more effectively disperse dust to the upper air (but add visual intrusion at the same time), or of continuing to suffer from the dust fallout but retain visual appeal.

Limestone dust creates particular problems when it falls on heathland soils, where fallout can measurably change species composition of grassland. Ecological and landscape effects on fallout are important from the point of view of rural resource management, but the human dimension is added via adverse effects of air pollution on manpower through health hazards.

Health Hazards

Occupational hazard through exposure to abnormally high concentrations of atmospheric dust and toxic materials provides only one aspect of the total health hazard from some extraction sites, and Goodman[25] stresses the need to consider broad health hazards to wildlife, crops, livestock and humans from locally increased concentrations of potentially toxic metals (such as lead, zinc and nickel) derived from wind and water borne mine dusts and smelter smoke.

Concern has been expressed over the possibility of inadvertent release of toxic and carcinogenic substances via air and water pollution, from large scale oil shale processing operations in Colorado, with possible impacts on the health of workers and local residents[26]. An above-average incidence of dust-related diseases such as silicosis and pneumoconiosis, associated with high concentrations of airborne dust in coal mining areas such as South Wales, is well established[27].

In recent years however, such medical problems have been reduced through the installation of dust extraction and dust-suppression equipment, and through more rigidly defined and enforced legislation and standards relating to working conditions and occupational exposure tolerance levels.

Effects on Nature Conservation

Many of the effects covered above are relevant to conservation of wildlife resources (see Chapter 3.4) but Ratcliffe isolates two specific dimensions to the problem[28]. The first is direct habitat destruction, such as occurs in the quarrying of important limestone areas (eg. limestone pavement areas around Morecambe Bay in north west England) and in the mining of ironstone. The second group of effects stem from pollution, and they reflect the production of chemical conditions unfavourable to both terrestrial and aquatic plants and animals (such as the effects of lead mining along the Rivers Ystwyth and Rheidol in central Wales).

Beneficial Impacts of Resource Extraction

The impacts outlined above reflect the essentially negative side to resource extraction, but a rational evaluation of such activities must also consider positive or beneficial aspects. These stem in part from direct enhancement of employment opportunities in rural areas (see Chapter 5.2) which would otherwise have net outmigration (especially of younger folk) and from the indirect regional multiplier effects of encouraging better social service provision (in terms of health care, education provision and transport and retail services)(see Chapter 5.4) and further expansion of the local economic activity base and employment potential through arrival of service and support industries (see Chapter 6.2).

But the benefits also encompass the increasing

diversity of local landscape and of habitats for
conservation of plant and animal species. It might,
indeed, be argued that a 'landscape of extraction',
properly tendered and maintained, adds diversity
which could serve to break up the monotony of some
landscapes. For example, many visitors to the
Dartmoor National Park are more interested in the
landscape of china clay working around Lee Moor, than
in the bleak moorland areas so characteristic of the
upland National Park.

Even within the city, extraction operations can add
variety to dreary scenes. Coleman[29] stresses the
compensating advantages of cement works in the Thames
valley, west of London, which offer a variety of
terrain and breathing space within an area of dense
urban settlement.

Diversity of habitats offered to plant and animal
species is an added benefit underlined by Kelcey and
others[30], who point out that extractive industries
often provide suitable conditions and opportunities
for many interesting plant species to colonise.
These include breeding sites for birds which nest in
areas devoid of vegetation; wetland habitats in un-
drained quarries for migrating wading birds; and the
varied microclimate and mosaic of habitat niches (including cliffs, screes, waste ground, old access
routes, salt-mine subsidences and flooded gravel
pits) offered in disused quarries.

6.4 PLANNING AND MINERAL WORKINGS

Mineral extraction tends to be an exclusive land use,
in the sense that it cannot readily be accommodated
alongside other land-using activities whilst extraction is in progress. As a dominant land use it tends
to be both destructive and exclusive for the life
time of extraction operations. Careful planning is
thus required to ensure that all available rural
resources are utilised in an optimum mix, with
extraction permitted wherever possible because of the
need for aggregates and mineral products in building
and in industry.

Conflict and Resolution

Overall the main need is to balance the national
need for sources of minerals, energy etc., with a
growing need to protect the environment and to preserve agricultural productivity at both national and

local levels.

Recent legislation has reflected this need to compromise. The major policy directive of the United States Surface Mining and Reclamation Act of 1977 is 'to ensure a fair and generally applicable set of standards for all mining operations'[31]. The district planning approach adopted widely in Eastern Europe for mining development (Figure 6.2) places absolute responsibility for the operations of mining activities on the state, and it demands complete district exploration of the possible resource base before development is allowed to proceed[32].

In Britain recent debate has centred around the role of central government in siting and planning mineral workings (particularly through the Department of Environment), and the extent to which policies adopted in this area conflict with those of other government departments (especially the Ministry of Agriculture, Fisheries and Food) concerned with the loss of high quality agricultural land[33]. The 1981 Town and Country Planning (Minerals) Act reflects this conflict within its three main functions[34], which are:

(a)   to improve provision for restoration and after-care (and to allow the planning authority to change the conditions attached to a mineral planning permission without compensation);

(b)   to allow the planning authority to suspend permission where working has ceased; and

(c)   to require the planning authority to review the planning situation in respect of mineral operations within their area.

National economic stability is a key ingredient in much of the debate surrounding the siting and development of mineral resource extraction operations. For example, Mills has pointed out that the British economy would suffer considerably if conservationists and environmentalists were to hamper the National Coal Board investment programme (which in times of economic expansion favours investment in new pits at Selby and the Vale of Belvoir)[35]. Moreover, Lucas argues that a ban on mining activities in national parks in the United Kingdom would soon lead to increased deficits in the national balance of payments, a reduced reliability of mineral supplies

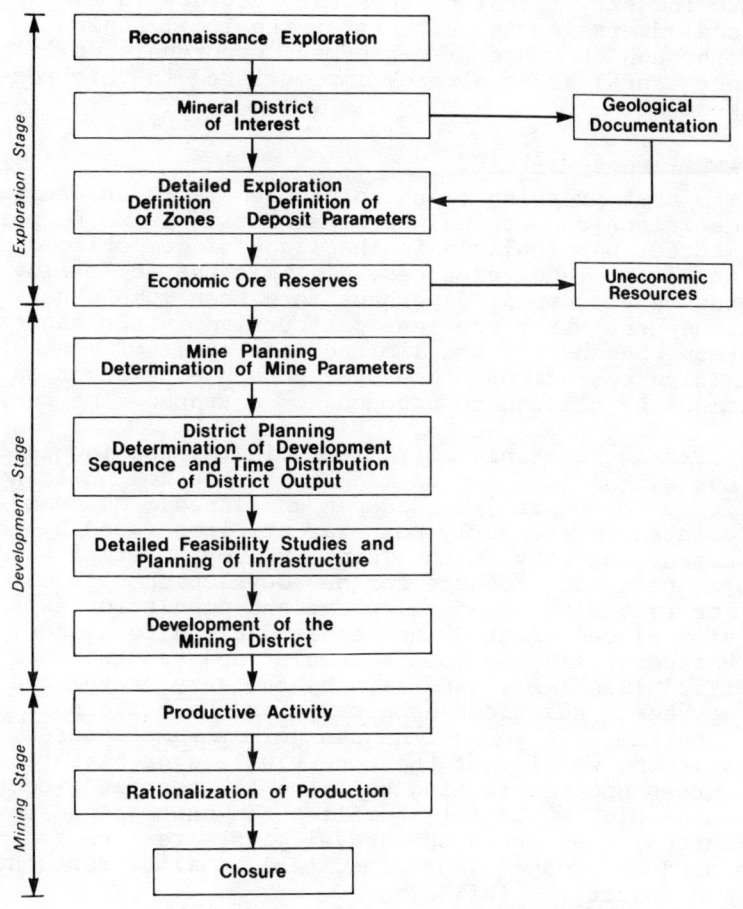

FIGURE 6.2   The Life Cycle of a Mining District,
             based on Eastern European Experience

Source: after J. Lajzerowicz and B.W. Mackenzie,
          'Planning the development of a mining dis-
          trict - an Eastern European approach',
          Transactions of the Canadian Institute of
          Mining and Metallurgy 74 (1971):   213-23.

to industry (vital to economic recovery in the 1980's)
and adverse social effects at the local scale
(through shortage of employment opportunities in remote rural areas already impoverished in this respect)[36].

Location and Zoning

The most pressing planning problem is to ensure wise
decisions concerning where extraction is to be permitted, particularly in the light of competing demands for land resources. In this respect mining
can be accommodated perhaps more than some other
land uses which are less destructive in the short
term, because of the limited life-cycle of most
mining operations. Wherever possible, extraction
might be allowed to proceed for a stated time period.

Building certainly sterilises mineral working land,
but worked land can be made available for building
if it is properly landscaped and zoned. Coloman[37]
pointed to the early post-war problems faced by the
cement industry in the Thames valley, west of London.
The post-war pressure for new developments to cater
for rehousing, re-development and population expansion placed great demand on land close to London.
Paradoxically the most suitable land was the Thames
floodplain land, underlain by the very gravel and
aggregate resources necessary for the building
programme. A zoned land use policy was favoured,
allowing working of the more viable aggregate resources and restricting building to specified locations which would not sterilise the underground resources; the worked out gravel pits were then restored to produce land of suitable quality residential
and industrial infilling.

In the United States and Canada, Sequential Land Use
policies (with related legal support) favour mining
in relation to other land uses[38]. Often a given
tract of land is dedicated to mining as a sole use
while mining is in progress; when mining ceases then
alternative or compatible post-use land uses are
sought. Policies thus favour extraction before land
subdivision and development, balancing the opportunities thus afforded to extract the minerals against
the social costs of disruption to the community of
deferred development. Mining would not be permitted
if it were possible to establish that there would be
an irreversible impact on wildlife; although the
problems of establishing what social costs would be

incurred, and of predicting effects on wildlife remain somewhat intractable.

6.5 EXTRACTION, RESTORATION AND REHABILITATION

The landscape legacy of extraction is commonly a landscape of neglect and decay, dominated by intrusive spoil heaps and artefacts (such as old colliery works, coke ovens, old factories and warehouse sites). Yet the structures provide both eyesores and fascinating industrial archaeology; Ratcliffe notes the paradox that 'when mineral working is long past (nature conservation and amenity interests) often wax enthusiastic about the fascinations of their wildlife, or the historical/antiquarian associations which tell the human story of bygone days. But when new workings are proposed or in action, there are often protests from the same interests at the desecration'[39].

These epitaphs of a once prosperous extractive economy provide planning problems because waste land is unacceptable in the face of pressures for development and after-use of worked-out land, and also because of public outrage at the loss of visual amenity during mining operations. However, much land can be restored to agricultural use after mineral working has ceased, and much abandoned but unrestored land may have high value for recreation, wildlife and amenity.

Forward Planning and After-Life Use

Restoration is often difficult and/or uneconomic in remote or upland areas. Even in accessible areas there are pressures and temptations not to foreclose on options to rework temporarily abandoned sites again in the future because of possible rises in mineral prices and growing national and international markets for many mineral resources (which might make extraction of presently unviable reserves more cost-effective in the future).

In the light of this uncertainty about after-use, Brooks[40] identifies three requirements on mining operations during the phase of mining. These are

(a) to plan to minimise the need for subsequent reclamation by careful location of access routes and careful placement of spoil or rock;

(b) to avoid dumping waste or building structures

on potential resources (because this would
otherwise sterilise them); and

(c)   to reduce the volume of waste to be dispersed
      during extraction by using it as roadfill or
      construction aggregate wherever possible, or
      by using it as underground fill or backfill
      while mining continues at the site.

Many quarry sites have valuable after-life uses for
tipping and dumping of waste material, often derived from nearby urban areas, as fill. Disused
quarries and mineral excavations close to urban
and industrial areas are being used increasingly for
the tipping of different kinds of waste - such as
sanitary landfill (domestic refuse), and highly
toxic chemical waste. For example, many former clay
pits near Peterborough have been infilled with power
station fly ash; and gravel pits along the Lea Valley
to the north east of London are used for refuse
disposal from the capital[41].

There are three broad aims behind land reclamation
after extractive use[42]:

(a)   to return land to original site conditions;
      if this is not possible, then restoration
      should aim to create new conditions that are
      both stable and compatible with the surround-
      ing area;

(b)   to ensure that a mine site is not a contin-
      uing souce of pollution or public danger, and

(c)   to ensure that 'restored land' is able to sus-
      tain similar biological and non-mineral
      economic productivity after use as it could
      pre-mining.

Open-Cast Working

Long term and widespread restoration schemes are
necessary in the wake of open cast coal mining.
Piercy[43] describes the first-year restoration sequence adopted in County Durham, which involves the
physical restoration of overburden after open cast
coal extraction has ceased, and treatment involving
grading, stone picking, and subsequent covering with
subsoil and topsoil. The scheme includes addition
of lime and fertilisers, seeding, tile drainage
after about three years, ploughing, reseeding with
permanent grass mixtures, and eventual handing back
of the reclaimed site to agriculture.

A similar success story of reclamation is reported
by Siviour[44] in the former ironstone quarrying area
of the Vale of Belvoir in the east Midlands. Here
strict restoration, partially financed by the Ironstone Restoration Fund, was implemented during the
1970's involving infilling, landscaping, tree-planting
to increase amenity value.

Within Great Britain one of the most successful
regional restoration schemes has taken place in the
Lower Swansea Valley[45], which has encouraged the re-
use of derelict urban land to revitalise the decaying inner city of Swansea, and involved large scale
community involvement in all phases of the scheme.
The area has a distinguished history of industrial
development since the 1730's evolving from copper
smelting, zinc smelting and more recently tin plate
and steel making. Reclamation began in 1966, with
grass planting experiments on waste tips, tree
planting on areas of eroded clays, and the wholesale
removal of unsafe and unsightly derelict buildings.
Unsightly tips were subsequently removed, with the
waste material used for filling and reclamation of
the low-lying marshland in the valley, which could
then be used for informal outdoor recreation. Some
50% of the original area of 323 half of derelict
buildings and tips had been cleared by 1976.

Sand and Gravel Workings

Restoration and rehabilitation following extraction
of sand and gravel resources represents one of the
more challenging problems in Great Britain. Many
gravel pits are located in valley bottoms, and with
land levels lowered between 4m and 6m during excavation the floors of most sand/gravel pits lie below
the local groundwater levels (so that most are
essentially 'wet pits'). Moreover, many are located
close to urban centres - partly because the most
valuable pits to work are those located close to
cities (because sand/gravel has high unit costs of
transport) but also because many cities are built on
good quality, low lying land in valley bottoms and
coastal estuaries, and these tend to be gravel-filled.

Many worked-out gravel pits are now landscaped after
closure. This sometimes involves provision of basic
facilities (such as access roads), and many pits
close to cities are ideally suited for outdoor
recreation and amenity uses. The Lea Valley Regional
Park scheme, north east of London offers an

Resource Extraction

interesting example of post-use development of worked-
out gravel pits. This is an area with over 2.84km^2
of flooded gravel pits, of which over 1.62km^2 are
now used by local sailing clubs and angling is
encouraged widely. Dunstan notes that 'future gravel
working in the valley will be phased as part of the
plan for the development of the Park, and should
result in a good deal more water for recreation'.[46]

Flooded worked-out gravel pits also offer valuable
potential as new wetland habitats for the conservation of breeding bird communities, especially for
migrating wading bird species[47]. Ratcliffe concludes
that 'the excavations produced by sand and gravel
extraction have.....proved to be the most positive
gains to the capital of wildlife habitat resulting
from mineral exploitation'[48].

6.6 CONCLUSIONS

There is little doubt that extraction creates a
variety of conflicts within the resource system of
the countryside. Indeed, Denisova concluded that
'mineral industries represent one of the most significant factors in human impact on the environment'
because of the direct impacts of extraction, coupled
with side effects in promoting population growth,
service industries and regional multiplier effects'[49].

It is clear that extractive industries provide the
mainstay of the rural economy in some areas, through
provision of employment prospects, a stable economic
base for the area, and a magnet with which to attract
other industrial and commercial enterprises.

In the light of this, planning for resource extraction is shrouded in conflict, concerning for example,
the scale of extractive industry and its destructive
characteristics in a rural area, and the needs of
people who depend on it (within and beyond the local
area) for employment and income. National scale
issues, such as the need for self-sufficiency in
mineral production and the need to expand production
of aggregates and other mineral resources, must also
be set against more local issues such as the visual
intrusion, noise, inconvenience and pollution impacts
of extractive operations.

As far back as 1944, Beaver saw the aims of planning,
in the context of mineral workings, as 'the formulation of principles, policies and detailed

178

programmes for the orderly and expeditious extraction of minerals in accordance with both local and national interests and in such a manner as to interfere as little as possible with other forms of land use'[50], and within six years he was to add that 'the problem is essentially one of conservation, for surface mineral working is a destructive activity unless some after-treatment of the site promises an eventual economic return'[51].

The evidence shows repeatedly that careful rehabilitation and after-use of excavation sites can provide valuable restored agricultural land, useful amenity and recreation facilities, and valuable habitats for the conservation of plant and animal species. This enhanced restoration has been encouraged in part because of the mounting pressure to ensure that the limited land resources of countries such as Great Britain are used in an optimum fashion, and in part because of mounting public awareness of the potential problems of extractive industries.

NOTES AND REFERENCES

1. S.H. Beaver, 'Minerals and planning', Geographical Journal 104 (1944): 169.

2. L.M. Dunstan, 'Some aspects of planning in relation to mineral resources', Cement, Lime and Gravel 41 (1966): 278-92.

3. K. Warren, Mineral Resources (Penguin, Harmondsworth, 1973).

4. Dartmoor National Park Authority, Dartmoor National Park Plan (Dartmoor National Park Authority, Exeter, 1977): 24.

5. P. Millbank, 'China clay waste - will Cornwall's scar ever heal?', Surveyor 150 (1977): 10-11, 14-15.

6. These are suggested by Sir Ronald Prain, quoted by Warren Mineral Resources (Note 3).

7. G.T. Goodman, 'Ecology and the problems of rehabilitating wastes from mineral extraction', Proceedings of the Royal Society of London A339 (1974): 373-87.

8. C.G. Down and J. Stocks, The environmental impact of large stone quarries and open pit non-ferrous metal mines in Britain. Department of Environment Transport Research Report 21, London (1975): 249pp.

9. See, for example, Dartmoor National Park Plan (Note 4).

10. D. Craig, 'The aluminium industry in Australia', Geographical Review 51 (1961): 21-46.

11. K. Warren, Mineral Resources (Note 3).

12. T.M. Thomas, 'Wales - land of mines and quarries' Geographical Review 46 (1956): 59-81.

13. J. Hutchinson, 'Land restoration in Britain - by nature and by man', Environmental Conservation 1 (1974): 37-41.

14. D.A. Ratcliffe, 'Ecological effects of mineral exploitation in the United Kingdom, and their significance to nature conservation', Proceedings of the Royal Society of London A339 (1974): 358.

15. E.A. Keller, Environmental Geology (Merrill, Columbus, 1976).

16. A. Coleman, 'Land reclamation at a Kentish colliery', Transactions of the Institute of British Geographers 21 (1955); 117-35.

17. These are described in K.L. Wallwork, 'Subsidence in the mid-Cheshire industrial area', Geographical Journal 122 (1956): 40-53, and K.L. Wallwork, 'Some problems of subsidence and land use in the mid-Cheshire industrial area', Geographical Journal 74 (1960): 191-9.

18. See, for example, M.J.G. Pounds , 'The china clay industry of southwest England', Economic Geography 28 (1952): 20-30, and T.M. Thomas, 'Wales' (Note 12).

19. K.L. Wallwork, 'Some problems' (Note 17): 195.

20. W.R. Chappell, 'Environmental and health consequences of oil shale production in the United States', Journal of the Geological Society of

<u>London</u> 137 (1980): 571-4.

21. See, for example, K.S. Richards, 'Channel
     adjustment to sediment pollution by the china
     clay industry in Cornwall, England', in D.D.
     Rhodes and G.P. Williams (editors) <u>Adjustments
     of the Fluvial System</u> (Kendall-Hunt, Dubuque,
     Ohio, 1979): 309-31, and C.C. Park, 'Tin
     streaming and channel changes - some preliminary
     observations from Dartmoor, England', <u>Catena</u> 6
     (1979): 235-44.

22. B.E. Davies, <u>Applied Trace Metals</u> (Wiley,
     London, 1980).

23. J.P. Sprague, P.F. Elson and R.L. Sanders, 'Sub-
     lethal copper-zinc pollution in a salmon river',
     <u>International Journal of Air and Water Pollution</u>
     9 (1965): 531-42.

24. G.G. Haythornthwaite, 'Cement works and the
     countryside', <u>Town and Country Planning</u> 21
     (1953): 500-5.

25. G.T. Goodman, 'Ecology' (Note 7).

26. W.R. Chappell, 'Environmental.....consequences'
     (Note 20).

27. Idem.

28. D.A. Ratcliffe, 'Ecological effects' (Note 14).

29. A. Coleman, 'Landscape and planning in relation
     to the cement industry', <u>Town Planning Review</u>
     25 (1954): 216-30.

30. See, for example, E.A. Greenwood and R.P.
     Gemmell, 'Derelict industrial land as a habitat
     for rare plants in south and west Lancashire',
     <u>Watsonia</u> 12 (1978): 33-40; and J.G. Kelcey,
     'Industrial development and wildlife conserv-
     ation', <u>Environmental Conservation</u> 2 (1975):
     99-108.

31. L. Bonnefoy, 'New standards for strip mining -
     social, economic and environmental costs now
     considered', <u>Natural Resources Journal</u> 18 (1978):
     909-12.

32. J. Lajzerowicz and B.W. Mackenzie, 'Planning

the development of a mining district - an
Eastern European approach', <u>Transactions of the
Canadian Institute of Mining and Metallurgy</u> 74
(1971): 213-23.

33. G.I. Fuller, 'Quarry resources and reserves -
the national framework', <u>Quarry Management and
Products</u> 8 (1981): 87-90.

34. J.R. Trustram Eve, 'The Town and Country Planning (Minerals) Act, 1981', <u>Journal of Planning
and Environmental Law</u> (December 1981): 857-63.

35. J. Mills, 'Mining and the environment', <u>Coal
and Energy Quarterly</u> 22 (1979): 2-7.

36. C.V. Lucas, 'The withdrawl of land from mining
- a study of the implications for the future',
<u>Minerals and the Environment</u> 3 (1981): 111-25.

37. A. Coleman, 'Landscape' (Note 29).

38. D.B. Brooks, 'Conservation of minerals and of
the environment', 287-314 in G.J.S. Govett and
M.H. Govett (eds) <u>World Mineral Supplies -
Assessment and Perspective</u> (Elsevier, Amsterdam,
1976).

39. D.A. Ratcliffe, 'Ecological effects' (Note 14):
357.

40. D.B. Brooks, 'Conservation' (Note 38).

41. J. Hutchinson, 'Land restoration' (Note 13).

42. D.B. Brooks, 'Conservation' (Note 38).

43. C.W. Piercy, 'Agriculture', 284-93 in J.C.
Dewdney (ed) <u>Durham County and City with Tee-
side</u> (British Association, London, 1970).

44. G.R. Siviour, 'Lost iron ore industry',
<u>Geographical Magazine</u> 50 (1978): 712-4.

45. H.F. Bishop and B.E. Hanna, 'Gravel mining and
land development can go hand in hand', <u>Civil
Engineering</u> 49 (1979): 65-7.

46. L.M. Dunston, 'Some aspects of planning'
(Note 2).

47.   A. Simmonds and S. Frost, 'Conservation recom-
      mendations for a sand quarry at Gwithian Beach,
      St. Ives, Cornwall', Landscape Research 3 (1978),
      17-8.

48.   D.A. Ratcliffe, 'Ecological effects' (Note 14):
      359.

49.   T.B. Denisova, 'The environmental impact of
      mineral industries', Soviet Geography 18 (1977):
      646-59.

50.   S.H. Beaver, 'Minerals and planning' (Note 1).

51.   S.W. Wooldridge and S.H. Beaver, 'The working
      of sand and gravel in Britain - a problem in
      land use' Geographical Journal 115 (1950): 42-54.

Chapter Seven

RECREATION AND PRESERVATION

7.1   RECREATION, LEISURE AND RESOURCE ALLOCATION

Social and economic changes in developed countries
since 1950 have increased the availability of
leisure time to the extent that recreation and
leisure now account for up to a third of many peoples'
available time.[1]

The Countryside Commission defines <u>recreation</u> as
'relaxation which requires little in the way of skill
or organisation, which lacks a competitive element,
and which requires a countryside location for its
full enjoyment'.[2] Whilst many recreational pursuits
can be carried out alongside (or even using) other
rural resource-using activities, recreation demands
careful consideration in resource allocation and
management because it constrains some types of
resource use and favours other.

However, clarification of the term 'recreation' is
required. Hockin, Goodall and Whittow[3] point out
that the 45 land-based recreational activities
recognised by the Sports Council in the UK can be
sub-divided into four groups:

(a)   overnight activities (such as camping and
      caravanning)

(b)   activities involving shooting (such as archery
      and various gun sports)

(c)   activities involving a significant element of
      organised competition (such as golf, skiing,
      motorcross and orienteering), and

(d)   activities involving little or no organised
      competition (such as angling, informal cycling,

184

horse-riding, rambling, picnicking and wildlife study).

Attention within this chapter will focus on the last group, although overnight activities are also appropriate and will be dealt with briefly.

Supply and Demand

There is widespread evidence of a marked increase in the number of visitors to the countryside in recent decades in countries like the UK and United States. Patmore isolates two important factors - a rapid increase in the amount of leisure time available to most people, and a marked rise in mobility made possible by rising car ownership (see Chapter 10.3).[4] These, coupled with increasing standards of living and changing attitudes to the countryside (see Chapter 12) have encouraged vast numbers of people into the countryside for informal recreation. This, in turn, has triggered off changes in the quality and quantity of the resource base which favoured recreational use in the first place, particularly in terms of landscape (see Chapter 4) and wildlife (see Chapter 3.4).

Mercer points out that 'recreation is the focal point of the evolution of an entirely new relationship between our cities and their surrounding areas'.[5] Like most forms of resource using activity, recreation can be visualised as an interaction between supply and demand. Supply of recreational opportunities will be influenced by both human and physical factors;[6] the former include historical evolution of land use in the area and patterns of resource management and allocation, while the latter include landscape attractiveness (see Chapter 4.3) and ecological stability of local wildlife habitats (see Chapter 3.4). Nolan[7] stresses that the potential of an area for tourism is determined by many factors, including location, existing recreational opportunities, carrying capacity, and degree of need. Demand, on the other hand, reflects factors such as population size, amount and timing of leisure enjoyed by that population, mobility, age and income structure, fashions and tastes in recreational pursuits and the opportunities available for recreation (ie supply)[8].

This balance between demand and supply is not static, however. Helleiner[9] isolates four likely future trends in patterns of recreational activities; a

likely increase in the amount of leisure time
available, a significant reduction in mobility
caused by energy shortages, a relatively unchanged
overall level of affluence and a reduction in the
amount of available recreational land through pressures from competing land uses (such as agriculture,
forestry (see Chapter 9) and mineral extraction (see
Chapter 6). Commentators on both sides of the
Atlantic foresee a growing influence of economic
factors on patterns of recreational activity, through
continued inflation and increasing fuel costs.[10]
Similarly there are signs that adventure sports (such
as mountain climbing and hang gliding) are becoming
more popular, and this is likely to continue so
through the 1980's.[11]

Overall it is likely that recreation will take place
in shorter periods of time, at frequent intervals,
in close proximity to consumers' homes (thus close
to major centres of population).[12] Such trends will
require careful planning to optimise consumer satisfaction and protection of the landscape and wildlife
resources so important to the countryside recreation
experience.

National versus Local Factors

Standard cost-benefit analysis of recreational land
use is extremely difficult because whilst costs can
be quantified in economic terms, benefits in this
context are non-utilitarian (see Chapter 2.4) and
therefore difficult to quantify in meaningful relative or absolute terms. Sinden and Worrell[13] explore the problems inherent in seeking to place
comparative values on non-market benefits such as
scenic beauty, wildlife preservation, and outdoor
recreation, and they conclude that each has no tangible market value, which makes it difficult to manipulate them in formal planning and decision-making
based on purely economic criteria.

At the regional or national scales, however, it is
necessary to evaluate recreation and tourism in
economic terms, particularly if heavy government
investment in infrastructure and recurrent costs of
recreation and tourism needs to be defended in monetary terms. The regional multiplier effect of
recreation and tourism is important, because of the
diverse nature of tourism-related employment and
establishments, but Baster[14] points out that a significant leakage of the economic benefits of tourism

often arises through tourist purchases of imported
goods.

At the national level, tourism and recreation are
clearly big business. It is estimated that some
£8,000 million is spent annually on tourism in
Britain, and that some 1.5 million jobs depend in
one way or another on the tourist industry.[15]

As with many of the conflicts in resource use in the
countryside, national and local views on the costs
and benefits of recreational land uses differ markedly. Naylor[16] points out that too much attention
is given to the few genuine instances of overcrowding of facilities and visitor pressure on certain
areas of the countryside, and not enough recognition
is given to attempts being made to combat this
pressure or the benefits which tourism brings by way
of holiday opportunities for a growing proportion of
the population.

Resource Use and Conflict Generation
Of all the resource-management conflicts in the
countryside, recreation offers perhaps the greatest
opportunities for multi-functional land use. Whilst
inevitably many forms of recreational activity are
compatible with others, some are not, and they have
to be specially sited.

However, most recreational pursuits have flexible
site requirements[17] which means that they could be
carried out in a variety of environments and habitats.
Similarly, most forms of recreation can be pursued
alongside many other resource using activities in
the countryside (FIGURE 7.1) so that in a few cases
does recreational land use need to be exclusive.
Indeed, the recreational potential of many other
rural land uses is implicit from other chapters in
this book - forestry land offers a range of recreational opportunities (see Chapter 9.6), flooded gravel
pits offer potential for sailing, angling, and
nature study (see Chapter 6.5) and many forms of
farming (especially in marginal upland and moorland
areas) are compatible with informal recreational use
and access provision for sensible numbers of
visitors (see Chapter 9.3)

Some resource-use conflicts are inevitable, however,
where recreational use of land is not fully compatible with other activities such as water supply -

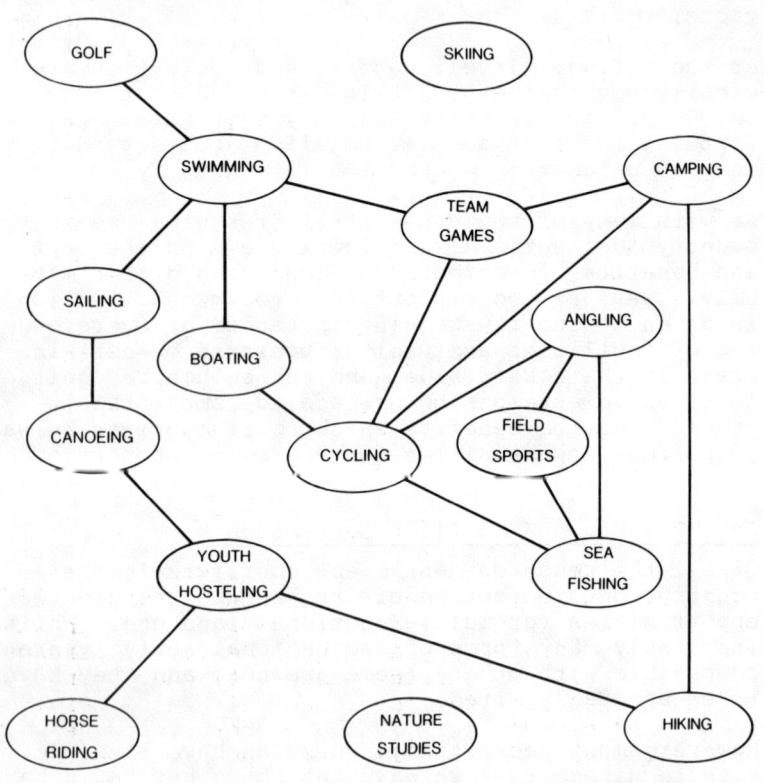

FIGURE 7.1 Compatible Recreational Activities in
the Countryside

The lines connect compatible activities.

Source: after R. Hockin, B. Goodall and J. Whittow,
The Site Requirements and Planning of
Outdoor Recreational Activities
(University of Reading, Geography Department
Geographical Papers 54, 1979).

where problems arise through litter, pollution,
accelerated erosion and other environmental impacts
of recreational land use.[18]. Conflicts also arise
where recreational activities are intensive, threat-
en the survival of tranquillity and serenity in the
countryside, or encourage the use of other destructive
activities. For example, the landscape of western

Canada is currently being threatened by the expansion
of transport corridors, the provision of intensive-
use recreation facilities, and increasing popularity
of all-terrain vehicles.[19]

Many of these sorts of conflict arise because of increasing use of the countryside for recreation.
Several factors underlie this trend, including changing attitudes towards landscape and the environment
and the rise of the amenity movement. Linton has
commented that 'for something more than a century
there have been people of sufficient sensibility to
set store by scenic variety or splendour, and of
sufficient wealth and leisure to travel in search of
them' so that increasingly 'the urban population of
Western Europe and eastern North America look to the
lakes, woods, hills and rivers relatively near to
their city homes for periods of rest, recreation and
refreshment'.[20]

Amenity

The elusive notion of amenity is of central importance. Gregory notes that amenity has become 'the
stuff of conflict between developers and their opponents, as the result of a growing preoccupation with
the quality of life',[21] although amenity is perhaps
a composite of three intertwined attitudes, concerned with public and environmental health, civic
beauty and pleasantness, and a concern to preserve
old buildings and established landscapes.

Hinton and Holford note that 'amenity is not a
single quality, it is a whole catalogue of values.
It includes the beauty that an artist sees and an
architect designs for; it is the pleasant and
familiar scene that history has evolved; in certain
circumstances it is even utility - the right thing
in the right place - shelter, warmth, light, clean
air.....'.[22]

The notion of amenity is, however, founded on a paradox. Growing affluence fuels a growing demand for
development and improvement of residential environments (such as post-war suburbia, village gentrification and growth of second home ownership in the
countryside - see Chapter 8) which encroach on the
countryside and reduce the land area available for
informal recreation. Yet the same affluence and
changes in lifestyle, aspirations and ideal quality
of life create a rise in demand for accessible areas

of countryside which can cater for informal recreational requirements, ideally in areas of heritage landscape (see Chapter 4) without visual intrusion, pollution or environmental damage.

Nonetheless some attempts to cater for the increased demand for recreational opportunities triggered off by rising affluence, changing life styles, and mounting interest in access and amenity in the countryside. For example, the amenity movement in Britain was an important catalyst for the 1949 National Parks and Access to the Countryside Act, which sought 'to make provision for National Parks and the establishment of a National Parks Commission; to confer on the Nature Conservancy and local authorities powers for the establishment and maintenance of nature reserves; to make further provision for the recording, creation maintenance and improvement of public paths, and for securing access to open country, and to amend the law relating to rights of way; to confer further powers for preserving and enhancing natural beauty; and for matters connected with the purposes aforesaid'[23] (see Chapter 4.2 and Chapter 10.3).

7.2 RECREATION USER PATTERNS

The distributions in time and space of recreational impacts on the environment and on other resource-using activities in the countryside will be heavily influenced by patterns of user hehaviour.

Satisfaction and Behaviour

The expectations of users will be an important influence on behaviour, despite the results of surveys by Groves and Kahalas[24] of recreation users in Pennsylvania which revealed low expectations within the population at large. Expectation, satisfaction and quality of recreation experience are closely inter-woven characteristics of the recreation activity, and they can markedly influence patterns of activity (in time and space). Pierce[25] used interviews to evaluate what satisfactions people felt they gained from their favourite free-time activity, and he found that respondents repeatedly rated intimacy, relaxation, achievement and power most highly. Five dimensions of satisfaction which might have high relevance to outdoor informal recreation (novelty, intellection, sociability, time-filling and constructiveness) received only moderate support, and transcendence and excitement gained only ephemeral support.

But the quality of the recreational experience means perhaps more than simply satisfaction with the activity itself. Recreation planners favour the view of outdoor recreation as a multi-phase experience, where different benefits are enjoyed from different stages in a recreational engagement.[26] These stages encompass anticipation (before the trip), travel-to (the journey to the countryside), on site (activities carried out there), travel-back (the journey home), and recollection (the memory of the event), so that overall assessment of the benefits of the recreational experience is extremely difficult.

User patterns might also be influenced by cultural factors. Robinson[27], for example, has detected close similarities in patterns of use of leisure time between Britons and Americans, but clear cross-national differences in recreational preferences. Americans appear to make greater use of their free time for attending religious services, adult education classes, playing sports, reading and free-time travel, whereas Britons favour listening to radios, records and tapes, frequenting pubs, walking and relaxing. Contemplative activities are more popular in Britain than in the United States, and so outdoor visits might be a more common occurrence in Britain.

Differences in user rates for National Parks between the two countries perhaps confirm this difference. In the late 1970's visitor levels in the Yosemite National Park in America stabilised at around 2.4 million visits per year, after a dramatic increase through the 1970's.[28] In contrast, in 1967 the much smaller Dartmoor National Park received an estimated 3 million visits (2.22 million of which were stopping visits).[29] Inevitably various factors additional to the cross-national differences in preferences underlie such differences in user levels, including the greater distances travelled in the United States, greater amounts of time spent in the Yosemite (about 32 hours on average) than in Dartmoor (about 3 hours) and in the North York Moors (day visits dominant), and differences in the range of recreational opportunities available in the different parks.

Crowding and Optimum levels of use

Informal recreation in the countryside will only be fully satisfactory to users if they derive optimum

satisfaction from their activities. A key component
of this satisfaction is the desire to enjoy tranquillity in the countryside as an antidote to the pressures of urban life.

Yet there is an inherent paradox in the way many
people look towards the countryside for recreation
and leisure; people want to escape to the countryside to be alone, but they also often want the feelings of security engendered from knowing that they
are sharing this feeling of solitude with a large
number of others at the same time (ie. 'solitude for
the masses'). Wilderness users differ in the sense
that the presence in a wilderness area of people
other than the individual, or his walking companions,
often serves to undermine the very sense of isolation
that attracts them there in the first place.

There will clearly be an optimum level of user for a
given recreational resource in the countryside, and
this level will differ between different resources,
different areas, and perhaps also different groups
of users (with different expectations and tolerance
limits). The concept of carrying capacity embodies
various criteria for defining 'optimum level of use',
and a wide variety of approaches for determining
appropriate carrying capacities for different types
of recreational resource have been evaluated.[30]

Two aspects of carrying capacity are important - a
perceptual dimension and an environmental dimension.

Perceptual carrying capacity: Defines the upper
limits to the number of people who can simultaneously use a given recreational resource or habitat without feeling or appearing crowded. Conflict among
users of outdoor recreation often arises when there
are too many people seeking to do too many incompatible things within a given area at the same time,
so that none of the participating individuals or
groups derives an acceptable level of satisfaction
from the experience.[31] Manning and Cialo[32] point
out the general assumption that visitor density and
user satisfaction are inversely correlated, but
they clarify this by observing that density has
little observable effect on levels of satisfaction
until it reaches a level where it is perceived as
crowding.

Crowding is difficult to define unambigously because
it depends closely on personal values and feelings.
The level at which crowding is perceived will depend
on the activities involved, the setting, and the
personal characteristics of the participants. Field
of vision will clearly be important, because visual
proximity is a key ingredient in perceptions of
crowding. Thus the perceptual carrying capacity of
habitats like upland forests, with low inter
visibility through screening,[33] will tend to be substantially higher than that in extensive open areas -
like at Ayers Rock in the Mount Olga National Park
in Australia[34] - where other people can be seen over
a much wider area.

Burton has demonstrated that individuals often react
to the problems of perceptual 'overcrowding' by
distributing themselves so as to avoid contact with
other groups as much as possible.[35] However, such
accommodation is only possible if alternative areas
are available within the recreational zone, and if
people are sufficiently aware of the presence of
others that they consciously modify their patterns
of behaviour and movement.

Environmental carrying capacity: Is a more tangible
concept. Burden and Randerson define carrying capacity as 'the maximum intensity of use an area will
continue to support under a particular management
regime without inducing a permanent change in the
biotic environment maintained by that management.'[36]
The environmental impacts of recreation are evaluated
more fully below and they stem largely from visitor
pressure via trampling.

Effects of trampling on soil (structure and stability),
vegetation (density, height, composition and cover),
footpath (path erosion) and landscape and scenic
quality, can be marked. In general the greater the
recreation use the more marked will be these effects,
so that an upper limit to the number of visitors who
can use a given site within a given amount of time,
without marked environmental impacts, can often be
determined.

However, the same area may have different carrying
capacities, depending on the overall objectives of
management.[37] Thus, for example, a low level of
recreational use might be tolerated if the objective
is to preserve a rare or sensitive species (such as

within a nature reserve), but a higher level might
be acceptable if the aim is to preserve a suitable
degree of flowering of ground species of plants.
Even higher levels of use are possible where the
objective is to encourage recreational use, and
complete grass cover is maintained by intensive
management involving artificial fertilisation,
seeding and watering.

Most attempts to define 'carrying capacity' marry
together the two ingredients of perceptual and
environmental tolerances, in recognising that both
affect attractiveness of a site for recreational use
but in different ways. Most concern over both perceptual and environmental carrying capacities has
been centred upon wilderness areas (see Chapter 3).

Wilderness Recreation

Crowding and perceptions of over-use create the most
serious conflicts within wilderness areas (see Chapter 4.4), where carrying capacities must be determined from both ecological and sociological criteria
(FIGURE 7.2). Lee[38] notes the conventional interpretation of wilderness recreation, that people seek
opportunities within wilderness areas to limit interaction with other visitors so as to achieve privacy
and solitude, but he also notes the paradox that all
visitors expect to be the sole users of the wilderness. Solitude for the masses seems an elusive goal,
because to some wilderness users any number of other
visitors at the same time is over-crowding. Equality of access opportunities to unspoiled areas (see
Chapter 10.4) varies considerably between different
groups within the overall population.

Wilderness in the United States has become a cherished element in the recreational landscape; Simmons
notes that

> from the status of an economic resource
> which had to be developed for gain by.
> felling, mining or farming, wilderness
> has now become to some a treasured rem-
> nant which must at all costs save national
> security be protected from such uses

but he adds that 'the difficulties associated with
their use may yet prove to be a greater despoiler
of true wilderness than the development interests
which opposed their reservation'[39].

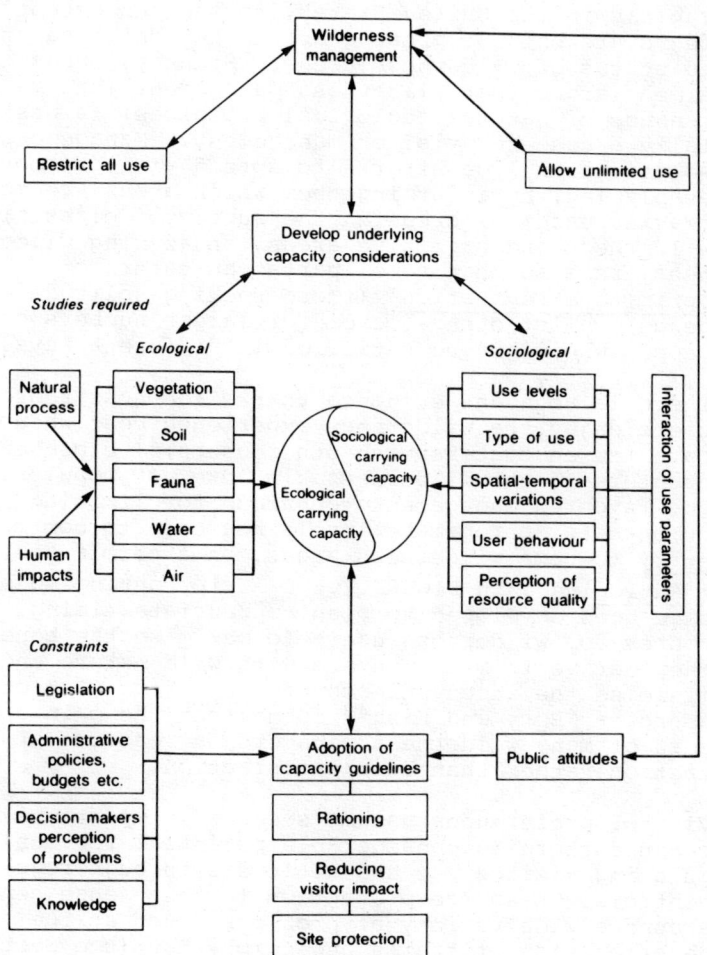

FIGURE 7.2   Conceptual Framework for Wilderness
              Carrying Capacity

Source: after B. Mitchell, Geography and Resource
           Analysis (Longman, London, 1979).

There is no doubt that wilderness use is rising rapidly in the United States, to such an extent that fears are being expressed about the continued unspoiled status of wilderness areas. Stankey, Lucas and Lime[40] argue that wilderness management (the maintenance of natural ecological processes) is essentially a case for visitor management. Management solutions include efforts to spread visitors more evenly (eg. by informing them which areas are most heavily used), increasing the supply of classified wilderness and primitive areas, and zoning wilderness areas so that some parts can cater for 'primitive recreation' (those seeking solitude and peace) whilst others cater for larger numbers of people who might be satisfied in different ways.

There is abundant evidence that wilderness recreation users enjoy the wilderness experience best when they have few encounters with other users;[41] close encounters of the wilderness kind are not popular. One favoured management technique for limiting user numbers to appropriate levels has been to control entry to some wilderness areas, on a permit basis ('Rationing', in FIGURE 7.2). Trip routing models have been developed to plan appropriate timings and routes for wilderness users to maximise the benefits they derive from encounters with wild nature and minimise the inconvenience of encounters with other users.[42] Bury and Fish[43] found that the main concern of many wilderness managers is resource protection rather than user satisfaction.

Visitor preferences assume secondary importance because there is considerable potential for manipulating visitor use and attitudes through regulatory controls. Resource protection in this sense centres around a wide variety of problems, such as the deterioration of trails and camp sites (see Section 7.5), regulating uses of vehicles and equipment, disaster control (such as forest fires), boundary designation, and resolution of conflicts between local uses (such as grazing and mining) and the wilderness ideal.[44]

One solution to the problems of over-crowding in wilderness areas lies in substitution of recreational opportunities elsewhere. Within the Brecon Beacons National Park in Wales, for example, the National Park Authority established a Country Park in part to attract recreational pressure away from an adjacent open moorland area where informal recreation'

threatens the wilderness value of the relatively
remote upland area. The wilderness areas (although
not formally called such) was zoned in the National
Park Plan for <u>suitable</u> recreational use by long
distance walkers and backpackers.[45]

Implicit within the notion of substitution in recreation planning is the assumption that alternative
sites or substitutes do, in fact, offer similar
opportunities for informal recreation, and that the
opportunities offered do promise to give similar (or
compatible) forms of enjoyment and benefit.[46] It is
likely that direct substitution of wilderness
opportunities (at least in Britain) is not really
possible, although certain of the benefits associated
with wilderness areas could be enjoyed in other parts
of the countryside such as a Forest Park and Country
Park.[47]

7.3 ACCESS, TRAVEL AND TRAFFIC

The theme of access to the countryside is explored
more fully in Chapter 10, but several important
points can be explored in this section. There are
various potential points of conflict between highway planning and recreation planning in the countryside, which arise from the simple fact that users
of recreational resources in the countryside generally have to travel from their homes in towns and
cities. The lack of co-ordination in planning for
tourist traffic is apparent in frustration and lack
of opportunities for users, long and tedious journeys
and congestion on rural roads at weekends and peak
holiday times.

Congestion and Access

Statham[48] reports, that the North York Moors
National Park attracts an average of 137,500 visitors
on a typical summer Sunday (about half of which stop
at least once). Most are day trippers, and congestion on roads is most marked at weekends, and in
particular during mid morning and late afternoon on
Sundays.

Congestion is also characteristic of the Dartmoor
National Park; surveys carried out in August 1969
show differences in traffic densities from over 30
moving cars per km (on major scenic routes and minor
linking roads) to none (on some of the inner roads).[49]
Clearly traffic and recreation management need to be

carefully harmonised to reduce delays, congestion,
and danger and also to optimise the benefits to users
of recreational activities.

In Britain the Countryside Commission has stressed
that 'highway planning.....has implications for recreation planning where accessibility to once remote
areas has improved. By the same measure, the planning of recreation schemes can influence the provision and management of new traffic routes'.[50]
Access to the countryside influences participation
rates in informal recreation, as well as levels of
satisfaction and enjoyment. Access problems are
most pronounced around major centres of population,
and on minor rural roads. Cracknell[51] describes
traffic surveys which indicate that at a distance of
about 30 km from large cities peak flow volumes of
visitors on Sundays may exceed those of the average
weekday; such surveys also indicate that recreation
traffic makes far greater use of minor road networks
than other kinds of traffic.

Traffic Management

Traffic management schemes are generally designed to
improve access, reduce congestion and delay, and
minimise adverse impacts of motor vehicles in the
countryside. Houghton-Evans and Miles[52] propose the
concept of an 'environmental capacity' for traffic
(comparable to carrying capacity for people). It
would take into account factors such as convenience,
pedestrian delays, noise, fumes, vibrations, visual
intrusion and impacts of vehicle encroachment on
footpaths and verges.

Such a concept has been used in a study of tourism
in Donegal which sought to define the optimum level
of traffic for major scenic routes.[53] Three possible
uses were envisaged for these results;

(a)   as a guide to the number of people who can be
      accommodated at a given facility without
      crowding;

(b)   to indicate levels of human use beyond which
      physical and ecological damage might occur to
      the facility;

(c)   as a guide to the scale of roads, car parks and
      related facilities which would be needed to
      provide convenient access to the recreational
      resources. The Donegal study has been critic-
      ised for failing to consider the comfort and

convenience of the motorist or define maximum
acceptable traffic volumes, and to examine flows in
areas with high pedestrian activity (with higher
danger), or traffic flow problems at bottlenecks or
junctions.[54]

Controlled access of vehicles is an alternative form
of traffic management. For example, in Britain,
the Forestry Commission has created a series of
scenic drives designed to attract car-borne visitors
away from vulnerable or more remote areas (such as
National Parks), and to ease pressure on narrow
country roads elsewhere in the countryside. These
scenic drives are roads designed or converted for
pleasure driving in areas of high scenic value,
within Forestry Commission land (see Chapter 9.6).
Two early drives were set up in Wales (at Dovey and
Gwydyr Forests) with one-way routes, controlled
entry points, car parks and picnic spots at specially
laid out areas, and sign-posted walks and nature
trails leading off the drives.[55] The entire scheme
is designed to encourage relaxed and safe driving
in scenic areas, with levels of use controlled to
minimise damage and crowding.

A comprehensive traffic and visitor management
scheme in the Goyt valley in the Peak District
National Park, includes the exclusion of cars from
the valley at weekends, with access provided by
minibus (see Chapter 10.4). This 'park and ride'
scheme became necessary after the opening of Errwood
Reservoir, which attracted large numbers of visitors
to watch sailing on the inland water. Miles points
out that this is

> an area of sensitive landscape and ecological
> interest under intense pressure from car-
> borne visitors attracted by water and open
> country; an area accessible from a nearby
> conurbation leading to conditions at cert-
> ain times which must detract from what it
> is the visitor came to see.[56]

The experimental traffic management scheme could be
introduced here because there are only three access
points to the valley (so that road closures could
be limited), there was no residential population in
the valley which would require exemption from the
scheme, and the area had already been designated as
an SSSI (which thus called for a sensitive approach

to traffic and visitor management). The success of
the scheme is clear, because some 82% of visitors
were in favour of a permanent Park and Ride scheme
in the Goyt Valley and similar areas elsewhere.[57]

7.4   RECREATION AND AGRICULTURE

Few parts of the countryside support recreation as a
single land use, so that recreation must be accommodated alongside other resource-using activities.

Conflict

Johnson[58] detects a growing conflict between those
who work on the land and those who want to play on
it, with agricultural land close to the urban fringe
(the most accessible thus most heavily used areas of
countryside) as the main battleground. The conflict
arises principally through the impact of visitors on
farm land and animals - such as trespassing, dumping
of rubbish, encouragement of pests, pollution and
litter, and harassment of stock (see Chapter 9.3).

Shoard[59] notes that such conflict stems from the current orthodoxy of recreation, which has three main
premises:

(a)   that recreation is an optional extra, not a
      need (thus equality of access to a range of
      recreational facilities is not seen as an aim
      worthy of active pursuit by local authorities),

(b)   the main issue in countryside recreation is
      protecting the countryside from people rather
      than opening it up for their enjoyment, and

(c)   virtually all opportunities for townspeople's
      informal recreation should be provided in towns.

Recreational use of agricultural land thus tends to
be ad hoc, unplanned and often unwelcomed. Whilst
many farmers are content to encourage sensible non-
consumptive use of their land by ramblers, the
damage to farm land, buildings, machinery, stock and
crops by a small minority of visitors can markedly
affect the economic viability of some farming
operations, especially in marginal areas. Phillips
and Roberts[60] reveal that damage to stone walls and
other structures can create very serious economic
problems for upland farmers whose net income may be
far below the wages of an industrial worker, and who
must rely on subsidy payments for hillsheep and

cattle paid by central government to secure their
livelihoods.

Attitude, Opposition and Assessment

The need to reconcile farming and recreation as users
of the countryside is widely recognised. However,
the farmer is often seen as the ultimate custodian
of the landscape, so the need to maintain a viable
farming community is as the principal priority. One
stated objective of the Yorkshire Dales National
Park Plan is 'to give every possible consideration to
the farmer and his agricultural methods, and planning should be so co-ordinated that the farmer does
not suffer any economic loss because of recreational
use and provision of facilities for public enjoyment,
as a result of National Park policy'.[61]

Farmers' attitudes towards recreational use of their
land inevitably reflect their assessments of the
balance between benefits and costs involved, and
there are signs that perceived economic benefits of
recreation are becoming more attractive to farmers,
who thus adopt a more positive view of recreation.
Kendall[62] interviewed a sample of farmers within the
Yorkshire Dales National Park in order to determine
their views on recreation, and he uncovered a growing feeling of concern and hostility amongst the
farmers because of damage caused by visitors on their
land. This included damage to structures (stone
walls, fences, stiles and gates) and to livestock
(sheep worrying, straying of livestock through broken
fences or gates left open) and crops (loss of hay
crops through trampling), as well as litter. However,
many farmers were not fully opposed to recreational
use of farmland because they saw the prospects of
financial returns from visitors via the sale of farm
produce and the provision of accommodation (as bed
and breakfast, or through letting of spare cottages,
or provision of camping and/or caravanning sites).

Keenleyside[63] foresees increasing hostility and conflict between farmers and countryside visitors in the
future, for various reasons. One is that farmers
are likely to have little time or money to spare for
the interests of other countryside resource users as
they are forced to increase their efficiency and
levels of productivity to keep up with rising costs
(see Chapter 9.2). In addition, recreational demand
continues to rise (see Section 7.2) yet suitable
areas within the countryside for recreation continue

201

to decline in extent (through development and land use changes).

It is also likely that more intensive farming methods will alter rural landscapes (see Chapter 9.2), and in doing so provide less opportunity for combining recreation with farming. A further factor is that the public is becoming more aware of the ways in which the countryside is used, and more articulate in its protests (see Chapter 12.1); conservation and land use are essentially political issues, and this is likely to remain the case in the future.

7.5 ENVIRONMENTAL IMPACTS OF RECREATION

Many conflicts between recreation and other resource-using in the countryside centre upon the effects of recreational use on environmental quality. These include the trampling of vegetation, compaction of soils, danger of forest fires, harassment or destruction of wildlife, pollution of lakes and rivers, and reduction of scenic quality through unsightly development.

The literature on the environmental impacts of informal recreation is wide ranging, and includes the impacts of trekking by horse and galloping in rural rides[64], and the impacts of visitor trampling on fragile habitats such as sand-dunes and beach areas[65]. Detailed studies are also available of the impacts of visitors on freshwater ecosystems and lakes, including the impacts of shore-based recreation and water-based activities (such as the effects of boats via wash, turbidity, propellor action and direct contact).[66]

Feedback

Recreation and environment are linked together by a series of feedback relationships (both positive and negative) involving soils and vegetation, so that excessive recreational use of an area can reduce environmental quality and hence diminish recreational potential, yet a tolerable level of use can enhance recreational potential. Goldsmith, Munton and Warren[67] illustrate the symbiotic link between people and vegetation in the Isles of Scilly (FIGURE 7.3). Visitors distribute themselves on areas of short grass sward rather than impenetrable bracken: in doing so they prevent invasion of bracken over the grassland by the impact of trampling.

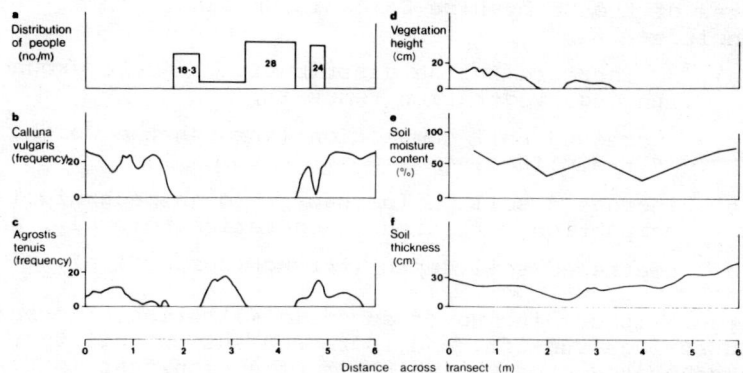

FIGURE 7.3 The Effect of Recreational Trampling on Vegetation and Soils

Source: after F.B. Goldsmith, R.J.C. Munton and A. Warren, 'The impact of recreation on the ecology and amenity of semi-natural areas: methods of investigation used on the Isles of Scilly', Biological Journal of the Linnean Society 2 (1970): 287-306.

People and soils are linked by a complex positive feedback. High visitor pressure increases trampling, which in turn increases soil erosion (via greater compaction, reduced infiltration, increased run-off and thus increased erosion). Extensive erosion reduces accessibility and limits the recreational attractiveness and suitability of the area.

Liddle[68] has reviewed the ecological effects of human trampling on soils and vegetation, and he notes the problems of attempting to derive suitable indicators of ecological carrying capacity. Experimental trampling plots, based on controlled intensity walking on a previously unworn area of a given habitat, have been used to determine site durability and to assess vulnerability of soils to damage from trampling.[69]

Soil Changes

Human trampling can have various impacts on soils. For example, Symonds[70] noted a regular pattern of

203

soil changes associated with trampling in a popular
area of the Derbyshire Dales in England. These
include

(a)   an increase in the distribution of bare ground
      (through vegetation removal);

(b)   increased soil compaction (through the weight
      of trampling);

(c)   increased soil pH (perhaps through mechanical
      compaction, or through vegetation removal), and

(d)   decreased soil depth (through compaction).

Other impacts include reduced infiltration, increased surface run-off, and increased susceptibility to
accelerated erosion (which is often manifest in
gully development on steep slopes, and in path
widening and deepening on more shallow slopes.

Footpaths

Footpaths of various forms are often provided in
popular areas to improve walking conditions and reduce the likelihood of widespread soil damage. The
evidence, however, suggests that many walkers prefer
to leave the paths provided for their use.

Bayfield[71] has observed a marked spread of walkers
around upland footpaths in Scotland, reflecting the
walkers' search for most convenient walking surfaces
when faced with unmanaged paths which vary in width,
surface roughness and wetness. He recorded a much
greater spread of walkers moving downhill than uphill; some 83% of those walking uphill on Cairngorm
were on or near the gravel path, whereas only 55%
walking downhill were. Overall, Bayfield noted 30%
of the visitors walking off the paths, in contrast
to the 5% which Picozzi[72] observed amongst walkers
in the Peak District National Park and the small
numbers observed by Bayfield himself[73] to leave a
woodland path where the path surface was easier to
walk on than the adjacent heather, grasses or
woodland.

Such studies of user behaviour are important in formulating realistic visitor management strategies for
heavily used areas of the countryside. The simplest
forms of visible management aim to improve the
attractiveness of existing paths for walking, through
a range of strategies such as placing boulders alongside paths, planting coarse vegetation, digging

skirting ditches and even erecting fences where appropriate. Management of footpaths and trails is an essential component of recreation management in the countryside, because the trails encourage increased access and use of an area, which in turn promotes vegetation changes and reduced wilderness quality (FIGURE 7.4).

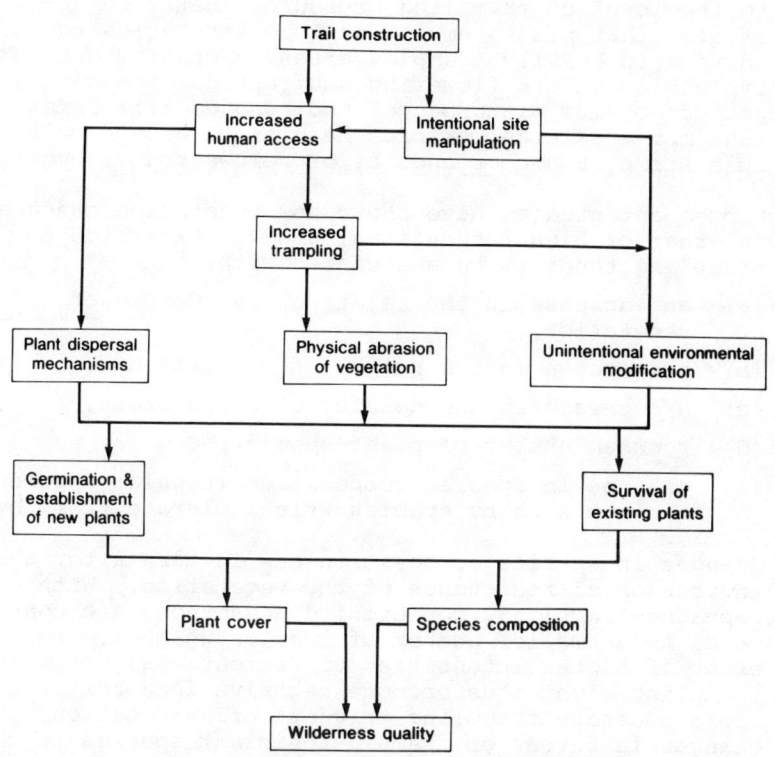

FIGURE 7.4   A Model of the Environmental Impacts of Trail Construction for Countryside Recreation

Source: after D.N. Cole, 'Estimating the susceptibility of wildland vegetation to trailside alteration', Journal of Applied Ecology 15 (1978): 282.

Vegetation Changes

Human trampling also triggers off changes in vegetation in areas heavily used for recreation (see
FIGURE 7.3). As early as 1935, Bates[74] established
that trampling has both direct mechanical effects on
vegetation, and indirect effects via soil changes.
He identified a common zonation of vegetation changes
associated with trampling, with bare ground in
areas with maximum recreational use and variations
in vegetation height and species composition related
to the level of trampling pressure. Bates demonstrated that plants employ various strategies to
survive in heavily trampled areas, such as short life
cycles (to ensure flowering and reproduction during
periods of low disturbance) and adopted life forms
(the more resistant species have flat leaves, multiple stems, and bear buds at or below ground level).

Subsequent studies have shown how vegetation changes
in areas of high recreational use[75]. Excessive
trampling tends to be associated with:

(a) an increase in the relative area devoid of
     vegetation,

(b) a decrease in the height of vegetation,

(c) a decrease in the density of grass stems,

(d) reduced number of plant species, and

(e) changes in species composition (regular species
     are replaced by species which tolerate trampling).

Changes in species composition can in turn alter the
environmental resistance of the vegetation. With
repeated trampling, competitive advantages are con-
veyed to a smaller number of species which are tolerant of higher intensities of recreational activity.
Trampling might thus promote negative feedback,
where moderate trampling triggers off vegetation
changes in favour of trample-resistant species at the
expense of sensitive ones; this newly-established
resistance increases the tolerance of the habitat of
sustained trampling, which in turn makes it more
attractive to walk on and therefore encourages
greater levels of recreational use.

Burden and Randerson notes that 'trampling acts both
directly upon the vegetation by bruising and crushing,
and indirectly by changing such soil characteristics
as air-filled pore-space and water content. These
soil changes in turn have an effect on the vegetation

in the long term. Vegetational changes appear, therefore, to be more sensitive indicators of the intensity of recreational use than soil characteristics
and are more easily measured.....'[76] The use of
vegetational indicators of recreational impacts
appears to be seductively attractive, yet results of
recent experiments by Quinn, Morgan and Smith[77]
reveal that by the time there is visual evidence of
declining plant cover, the critical period in which
soil erosion is initiated is already past.

Repair and Management

These environmental effects on soils and vegetation
require careful management if the landscape of the
countryside, which ultimately encourages and sus-
tains recreational interest, is not to be damaged
beyond repair.

Natural recovery of vegetation and habitat after
moderate recreation pressure is possible given sufficient recovery time free from trampling. For
example, Harrison[78] noted quite high recovery rates
in semi-natural grassland and heathland plots in
southern England after seasonal trampling. However,
many habitats such as steep slopes, peat and wetlands are slow to recover from even moderate trampling. Bell and Bliss[79] report extremely slow
recovery rates in an area of alpine flora in the
Olympic National Park in America, even after one
season of light use; they suggest that it could take
up to 1,000 years for natural regeneration of the
fragile ecosystem. The Kosciuska National Park in
Australia has required careful planning to repair
damage from trampling pressure and prevent further
environmental deterioration.[80]

Remedial measures include installation of cross
drains to divert water from tracks, stabilisation
of eroded areas, construction of wooden bridges and
elevated pathways across fragile bog surfaces, and
transplanting of native species from stable areas
to assist in recolonisation of denuded areas.

British experience. In Britain there have been
orchestrated demands for more positive planning of
countryside recreation facilities and opportunities
and concern has been expressed over increasing recreational impacts on landscapes of high scenic and
amenity value, such as the Pennine Way and summit of
Snowdonia.[81] The Countryside Commission has

introduced harmonised management schemes in an
attempt to resolve such conflicts in resource use.
Upland Management Experiments[82] were first introduced in the Lake District and Snowdonia National
Parks in 1969.

The Tarn Hows visitor management scheme experimental
restoration project, in the English Lake District is
typical of the experiments. Visitor pressure on the
National Trust site was mounting by the early 1970's
and consultants were called in to advise on management options to reduce soil erosion.[83] Various options such as the installation of hard path surfaces
were considered, but the most feasible solutions lie
in modifying patterns of visitor use by various
schemes such as closing or relocating car parks,
advising visitors on best routes (through-way mark-
ing of walks), and encouraging visitors to ascend
the steeper slopes and descend the shallower ones
(which would be less damaging). A study of the possibility of introducing tariffs for entry (to encourage longer visits and alter patterns of disper-
sion around Tarn Hows) was also proposed.

Similar management problems have been experienced on
the chalk downland surrounding Box Hill in Surrey,
another National Trust site within 30km of London,
which receives up to 6,000 visitors on a typical
summer day. Continued intensive wear of the grassland habitat by trampling has completely destroyed
the vegetation cover in some areas, and triggered[84]
off erosion of the shallow soils on chalk slopes.
Once gullying is initiated on the chalk paths,
natural processes of overland flow and erosion concentrate in the shallow gullies and broaden them out
considerably; accelerated erosion follows, landscape
quality declines, and suitability for walking and
ease of access are reduced accordingly.

Various schemes were introduced to repair the damage,
such as infilling of the gullies, restoration of the
surfaces after backfilling with spoil, and reveget-
ation to stabilise the surface, discourage further
use by visitors, and restore visual continuity to the
landscape.[85]

Management Objectives. Brotherton has stressed that
'the extent to which it will be possible to solve
the problems of excessive wear and tear by increased
management effort within a site without discouraging
total usage has yet to be determined. Management

will need to be effective yet unobtrusive'.[86] Ultimately the most appropriate type of management will depend on long-term objectives for the site in question.

If the objective is to maintain botanical richness of vegetation, recreation management should aim to direct people away from vulnerable areas by closing worn footpaths, allowing access to more tolerant areas and channelling people away from sensitive or ecologically important flora and habitats. If, on the other hand, the main objective is to provide facilities for outdoor recreation, management policies should seek to disperse people over as wide an area as possible so that no one part is damaged too much. Results from many botanical studies reveal in fact that most grass swards increase in species diversity with slight visitor pressure.[87] Other suitable management options include seeding (especially with species known to be resistant to trampling), and fertiliser applications designed to encourage colonisation by more resistant species.

7.6   RECREATION AND CONSERVATION

The association between recreation and conservation in the countryside is symbiotic. The use of a habitat for recreation often promotes changes in the character of soils and vegetation and these can markedly reduce the conservation value of the habitat (see Section 7.5). Yet habitats with high conservation value, high ecological diversity or rare or particularly attractive species (such as orchids) often attract large numbers of visitors (see Chapter 3.4). The association also reflects mounting public interest in amenity, access to unspoiled landscapes and conservation of the environment.

Non-Consumptive Uses of Wildlife

More[88] distinguishes two broad categories of non-consumptive wildlife use:

(i) primary non-consumptive uses - such as general wildlife observation, bird watching, bird feeding, wildlife and bird photography and

(ii) secondary non-consumptive uses - such as nature walks, membership of animal-related organisations, ownership of wildlife pets, and visits to zoos.

Consumptive uses of wildlife for recreation (such as

hunting, fishing and shooting of game animals and
birds) can benefit nature conservation, such as
thorough culling of over-crowded herds, or eradic-
ation of pests or predators. Similarly some land
management schemes orientated around consumptive use
of wildlife, such as heather moorland burning to
encourage young succulent growth of shoots as food
and shelter for young grouse can also benefit nature
conservation because they prevent rapid secondary
succession, increases ecological diversity and thereby increase wildlife value.[89] On balance, however,
consumptive uses of wildlife are detrimental to
nature conservation, as well as antagonistic to many
people's moral views.

There is a clear demand for the conservation of wildlife in the countryside. Despite protection offered
by special status designations such as National Parks
and National Nature Reserves and protection for
listed species given under legislation (such as the
1981 Wildlife and Countryside Act), Nevard and
Penfold[90] argue that there is still an unsatisfied
demand for nature conservation in Britain which probably occurs elsewhere as well. Studies of rates of
participation in non-consumptive recreation suggest
that since individuals invest considerable scarce
time and income in visits to open spaces to watch or
photograph wildlife, enjoyment of such activities is
closely influenced by factors such as the variety of
species available to watch, and the extent of natural
habitat and unspoiled environment in which to watch
them[91].

Nature Reserves and Recreation

A key element in the association between conservation
and recreation is the use of special wildlife resources, nature reserves and nature trails, for
recreation. Chanter and Owen[92] suggest that many
visitors to nature reserves fail to derive maximum
satisfaction from their visits, and Bull[93] stresses
the need to recognise wildlife interest as an important leisure activity in its own right so that greater
provision for public access to most nature reserves
might be encouraged.

Nature Reserve provision. Nature reserves established primarily for conservation reasons might also
prove popular as recreational resources, and aid the
conservation case by increasing public understanding
of the aims and practices of wildlife conservation.

Indeed, there is evidence to suggest that many
visitors to nature reserves remain unaware of the
prime reasons for creating the reserves. Kinoulty[94]
found that 48% of a sample of visitors to High
Salvington Bird Sanctuary near Worthing in west
Sussex were not aware that it was a bird sanctuary;
only 5 of the 77 people interviewed went specifically to watch birds, yet 39 went to go for a walk
and 64 were attracted more by the pleasant environment than by the prospect of bird watching.

The establishment and management of nature reserves
must recognise the recreational potential offered by
the protected sites. Whilst only 15% of the visitors
to Bridestones Nature Reserve in the North York Moors
National Park who were interviewed by Usher et al[95]
cited 'natural history' as the principal reason for
their visit, most visitors were sensitive to the need
to cater for wildlife as much as possible in planning
and managing the reserve. A follow-up study[96] examined whether visitors' views altered after a picnic
site and a sign-posted nature trail were created at
the reserve, and their results were encouraging.

The first survey had uncovered a demand by visitors to
the reserve for structural improvement, which would
enhance the conservation facilities (such as hides
and better footpaths), and for facilities (such as
toilets and a tea room) which would be detrimental
to conservation and the tranquillity of the area.
The follow-up survey revealed that the structural
improvements, which did not affect the conservation
potential of the habitat, had reduced visitor demand
for the incompatible developments.

Recreation and Wildlife. The most detailed studies
of the recreation - conservation association of
nature reserves have been carried out in the Dalby
Forest Area of the North York Moors National Park by
Everett.[97] He evaluated the basis of visitors'
interest in and understanding of wildlife in the
area using formal interviews and questionnaires.
Part of the study focussed on the benefits visitors
felt they gained from being in contact with wildlife
during their visit; his results suggest that emotional benefits (cited by up to 74% of visitors) far
outweigh physical (8%) or aesthetic (35% or less)
benefits, and he concluded that

the interviewees' interest in wildlife was
made up of an appreciation of the aesthetic,

emotive and psychological elements of wildlife, as well as a purely active pursuit in
nature study. These attributes of wildlife
are all aspects which should be taken into
consideration when assessing the role of
wildlife in the recreational qualities of an
area.[98]

A second focal point was the wildlife preferences
shown by visitors; of 200 species mentioned in interviews, visitors expressed most interest in seeing
roe deer, badgers, foxes, squirrels, rabbits,
pheasants, woodpeckers, kingfishers and adders, although what they actually did see during the visit
was often somewhat different.[99] The study also
looked at the overall levels of interest shown by
visitors in the wildlife of the Forest Area, and in
the factors which control these. Interest in wildlife was found to be greatest amongst higher income
levels, older visitors, members of wildlife organisations, and those who visited the Forest Area more
frequently.[100]

The results of Everett's studies underline the need
for greater efforts to inform visitors to the countryside of what they are seeing, and about the importance of the wildlife they are in contact with. Thus
there arises the need for sensitive siting and design
of outdoor facilities, especially those orientated
around countryside interpretation.

Countryside Interpretation. Pennyfeather[101] identifies three basic objectives within countryside
interpretation:

(a) to foster greater respect for the countryside,
     encourage protection and highlight the need for
     conservation,

(b) to increase enjoyment, by increasing awareness
     of opportunities available within the area, and

(c) to provide an effective tool of countryside
     management, to influence visitor behaviour and
     movement and thus promote resource protection
     at the local level (for example by steering
     visitors away from fragile habitats).

Interpretation is an important element in management
schemes for informal outdoor education because it
encourages visitors to respect the countryside,
appreciate the wildlife and management problems of

the area, and recognise the possible impacts of
their presence on wildlife and landscape in that
area. The ultimate goal is to nurture a conservation
mentality in the visitor; Pennyfeather coins the
maxim 'through interpretation, understanding;
through understanding, appreciation; through
appreciation, protection.'[102]
Interpretative strategies and facilities need to be
carefully devised to ensure that they meet the needs
and objectives of both visitor use and recreational
management (FIGURE 7.5).

One tool of countryside interpretation is the provision of facilities such as display boards, guided
walks, information leaflets and specially designed
visitor centres.[103] For example the Sherwood Forest
Visitor Centre, in Sherwood Country Park in Nottinghamshire, attracts some 250,000 visitors per year
because of its association with Robin Hood and
Sherwood Forest.[104] The Centre has separate buildings to cater for different services, such as an
exhibition area, auditorium, shops, refreshments and
toilets. Interpretative facilities focus on four
themes related to 'Man in the Forest'-the medieval
forest; destruction of the forest; the Great Estates;
and exploitation and conservation of the Forest in
modern times.

Nature trails represent another common interpretative
facility designed specifically to encourage a greater
awareness of wildlife and its problems amongst users
of countryside recreational resources. As with interpretation in general, a number of objectives can
be met by nature trails, including interpretation
of the countryside for visitors; education of school
parties and other groups or individuals seeking information about the countryside and its ecology;
provision of publicity for particular aspects of the
work of the promoting agency; and providing a recreational facility in its own right.[105]

Nature on its own might not provide a strong magnet
to attract visitors to nature trails, however, because results of surveys by Bayfield and Barrow[106]
reveal much lower levels of use on trails where no
additional attractions (such as visitor centre) were
present, and they suggest that only about 25% of
users of nature trails see use of the trail as the
main reason for their visit.

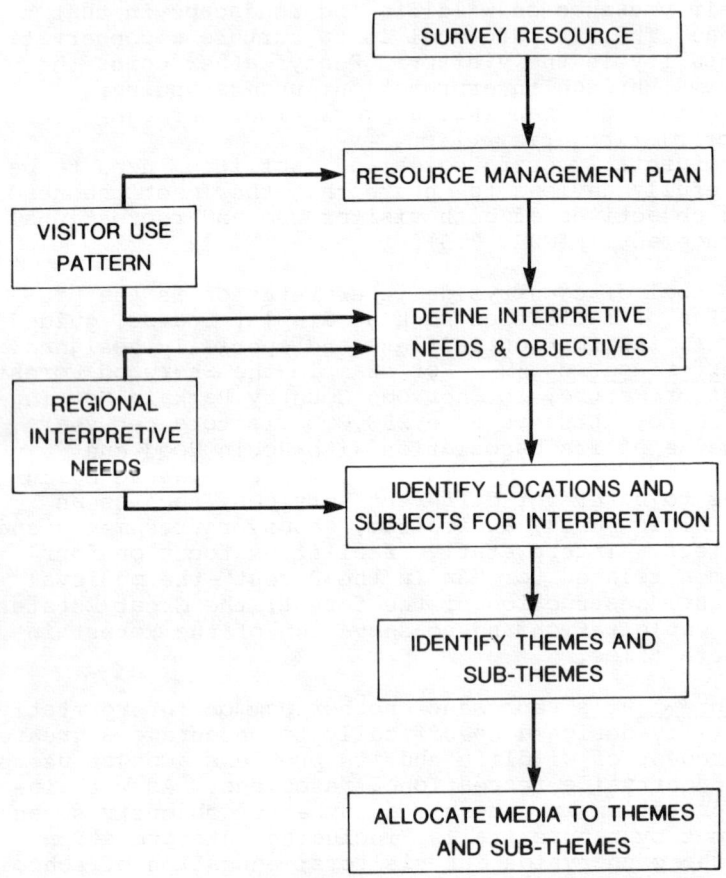

FIGURE 7.5 The Principles of Regional Countryside
            Interpretation

Source: after D. Aldridge, Principles of Country-
         side Interpretation and Interpretative
         Planning (HMSO, London, 1975).

7.7 CONCLUSIONS

This chapter has explored various dimensions of the
conflicts surrounding recreational use of the countryside. These include the problems of defining
optimum levels of use of recreational resources,

related problems of access, traffic and recreational
trip patterns, and the environmental impacts of recreation in the countryside (particularly the effects
of trampling on soils and vegetation).

As a resource use in the countryside recreation in-
teracts with agriculture and nature conservation by
exploiting the opportunities they afford for non-
consumptive use of wildlife and in turn by affecting
these resource using activities.

In Britain, the Countryside Recreation Management
Association has formulated a series of objectives
for countryside recreation.[107] These include the
need to continue to strive for equitable distribution of benefits and costs of tourism; the need to
respect the local resource base; the need to link
tourist developments to perceived needs within conservation; and the need to encourage tourism to
finance conservation. The association between protection of the countryside resource base, and exploitation of these resources within recreation, is
widely recognised. The Countryside Commission, for
example, claim that whilst they 'aim to promote the
rapid provision of well-designed facilities and
services where they are most needed to enable the
public to enjoy the countryside, they are equally
concerned to secure the conservation and enhancement
of the beauty of the countryside'.[108]

Similarly, Revelle outlines growing awareness of the
precarious position of National Parks in the United
States; he notes that

> although these treasures of the continent
> area, in part, sites for active recreation,
> skiing, mountain climbing, fishing and
> camping, they are in essence great natural
> wonders, things of joy and beauty, places
> for an individual to lose himself in con-
> templation. While their values cannot be
> enhanced by human action, they can easily
> be destroyed by it.[109]

The need for careful integration of recreation and
other uses of the countryside (including conservation)
is thus paramount. From the human point of view
also, the need to ensure that as many sectors of
society have fair access to the countryside for recreation is paramount. This important theme will be
considered in Chapter 10.

NOTES AND REFERENCES

1. M. Chubb and H. Chubb, One Third of our Time?
    An Introduction to Recreation Behaviour and
    Resources (Wiley, London, 1981).

2. Countryside Commission, Countryside Recreation
    Glossary (Countryside Commission, London, 1970).

3. R. Hockin, B. Goodall and J. Whittow, The Site
    Requirements and Planning of Outdoor Recreation
    Activities, University of Reading Geographical
    Papers 54 (1978): 52pp.

4. J.A. Patmore, Land and Leisure (David and
    Charles, Newton Abbot, 1970).

5. D.C. Mercer, 'The geography of leisure - a con-
    temporary growth point', Geography 55 (1970):
    261-73.

6. Idem.

7. H.J. Nolan, 'A booming recreation resource'
    Parks and Recreation 14 (1979): 21-3.

8. Mercer, The geography (Note 5).

9. F. Helleiner, 'Recreation and leisure-time
    patterns', Ontario Geography 16 (1980): 47-55.

10. C.S. Van Doren, 'Outdoor recreation trends in
    the 1980's; implications for society', Journal
    of Travel Research 19 (1981): 3-10.

11. D. Dunn, 'Leisure', New Society 37 (1976):
    22-3.

12. Helleiner, Recreation (Note 9).

13. J.A. Sinden and A.C. Worrell, Unpriced Values
    (Wiley, London, 1979).

14. J. Baster, 'Input-output analysis of tourism
    benefits - lessons from Scotland', International
    Journal of Tourism Management 1 (1980): 99-108.

15. H. Naylor, The Contribution of Tourism to the
    Quality of Life in Britain (The Tourism Society,
    London, 1980).

16. Idem.

17. Hockin et al, Site Requirements (Note 3).

18. See, for example, K. Smith, 'Recreation and water supply - the example of Longendale', Town and Country Planning 45 (1977): 494-9.

19. D. Thompson and M. Nelischer, 'Oska ka Asusteki - changing landscapes and changing attitudes', Landscape Planning 6 (1979): 127-49.

20. D.L. Linton, 'The assessment of scenery as a natural resource', Scottish Geographical Magazine 84 (1968): 219-38.

21. R.G. Gregory, The Price of Amenity (Macmillan, London, 1971).

22. C. Hinton and W. Holford, Preserving Amenities (Central Electricity Generating Board, London, 1959).

23. National Parks and Access to the Countryside Act, 1949 (HMSO, London, 1949).

24. D.L. Groves and H. Kahalas, 'Recreational expectations', Regional Studies 10 (1976): 193-200.

25. R.C. Pierce, 'Dimensions of leisure 1. Satisfaction', Journal of Leisure Research 12 (1980): 5-19.

26. See, for example, W.E. Hammitt, 'Outdoor recreation - is it a multi- purpose experience?', Journal of Leisure Research 12 (1980): 107-15.

27. J.P. Robinson, 'British-American differences in the use of time', Loisir et Societe 3 (1980): 281-97.

28. J.E. Van Wagendonk, 'Visitor use patterns in Yosemite National Park', Journal of Travel Research 19 (1980): 12-7.

29. C. Board et al, 'Leisure and the countryside - the example of the Dartmoor National Park', 129-52 in M. Chisholm (editor) Resources for Britain's Future (David and Charles, Newton Abbot; 1974): and D.C. Statham, Patterns of

Informal Recreation in the North York Moors
National Park (North York Moors National Park,
Helsley, 1981).

30. See, for example, A.C. Fisher and J.V. Krutilla,
'Determination of optimal capacity of resource-
based recreational facilities', _Natural Resour-_
ces Journal 12 (1972): 417-44; and R. Jackson
et al, 'Carrying capacity and lake recreation
planning - a case study of north central Sas-
katchewan, Canada', _Town Planning Review_ 47
(1976): 359-73.

31. G.R. Jacob and R.M. Schreyer, 'Conflict in outdoor recreation - a theoretical perspective',
Journal of Leisure Research 12 (1980): 368-80.

32. R.E. Manning and C.P. Cialo,'Recreation density
and user satisfaction - a further exploration
of the satisfaction model', _Journal of Leisure_
Research 12 (1980): 329-45.

33. See, for example, D. Small, Recreational potential of the upland forests, _Forestry Commis-_
sion Occasional Paper 6 (1980): 135-59.

34. J.A. Sinden, 'Carrying capacity as a planning
concept for national parks - available or
desirable capacity?', _Landscape Planning_ 2
(1976): 243-7.

35. R.J.C. Burton, 'A new approach to perceptual
capacity - some results of the Cannock Chase
research project', _Recreation News Supplement_
10 (1973): 25.

36. R.F. Burden and P.F. Randerson, 'Quantitative
studies of the effects of human trampling on
vegetation as an aid to the management of semi-
natural areas', _Journal of Applied Ecology_ 9
(1972): 439-58.

37. Idem.

38. R.G. Lee, 'Alone with others - the paradox of
privacy in wilderness', _Leisure Sciences_ 1
(1977): 3-20.

39. I.G. Simmons, 'Wilderness in the mid-twentieth
century United States', _Town Planning Review_ 36
(1966): 249-56.

Recreation

40. G.H. Stankey, R.C. Lucas and D.W. Lime, 'Crowding in Parks and Wilderness', Design and Environment, Fall (1976): 1-4.

41. See, for example, R.C. Lucas, 'Wilderness perception and use - the example of the Boundary Waters Canoe Area', Natural Resources Journal 3 (1964): 394-411; and C.J. Cicchetti and V.K. Smith, 'Congestion, quality deterioration and optimal use - wilderness recreation in the Spanish Peak primitive area', Social Science Research 2 (1973).

42. H.C. Romesburg, 'Scheduling models for wilderness recreation', Journal of Environmental Management 2 (1974): 159-77.

43. R.L. Bury and C.B. Fish, 'Controlling wilderness recreation - what managers think and do', Journal of Soil and Water Conservation 35 (1980): 90-3.

44. V.B. Godin and R.E. Leonard, 'Management problems in designated wilderness areas', Journal of Soil and Water Conservation 34 (1979): 141-3.

45. P.J. Cloke and C.C. Park, 'Country Parks in National Parks - a case study of Craig-y-Nos in the Brecon Beacons, Wales', Journal of Environmental Management 12 (1981): 173-85.

46. See, for example, G. Romsa, 'A method of deriving outdoor recreational activity packages', Journal of Leisure Research 5 (1973): 34-46; and J. Hendee and R. Burdge, 'The substitutability concept - implications for recreational research and management', Journal of Leisure Research 6 (1974): 137-62.

47. C.C. Park, 'Wilderness and the substitution of informal recreational opportunities - a case study of British attitudes', The Manchester Geographer 2 (1981): 54-62.

48. Statham, Patterns (Note 29).

49. Board et al, Leisure (Note 29).

50. Countryside Recreation Research Advisory Group, The Design of Surveys of Leisure and Recreation Traffic (Countryside Commission, London, 1971).

51. B. Cracknell, 'Accessibility to the countryside as a factor in planning for leisure', Regional Studies 1 (1967): 147-61.

52. W. Houghton-Evans and J.C. Miles, 'Environmental capacity in rural recreation areas', Journal of the Town Planning Institute 56 (1970): 423-7.

53. An Foras Forbartha Teoranta, Planning for Amenity and Tourism (The Government for Ireland, Dublin, 1966).

54. Houghton-Evans and Miles, Environmental capacity (Note 52).

55. Countryside Commission, Scenic Drive Survey - Dovey and Gwydyr Forests, July 1969 (Countryside Commission, London, 1970).

56. J.C. Miles, The Goyt Valley Traffic Experiment (Countryside Commission, London, 1972).

57. Idem.

58. G. Johnson, 'Conflict in the countryside', Farmers Weekly 94 (1981): 92-7.

59. M. Shoard, 'Recreation - the key to the survival of England's countryside', 58-73 in M. MacEwan (editor) Future Landscapes (Chatto and Windus, London, 1976).

60. A. Phillips and M. Roberts, 'The recreation and amenity value of the countryside', Journal of Agricultural Economics 24 (1973): 85-102.

61. Yorkshire Dales National Park Authority, The Yorkshire Dales National Park Plan (Yorkshire Dales National Park Authority, Northallerton, 1977).

62. D. Kendall, 'The impact of recreation on the farming community in the Yorkshire Dales National Park - an evaluation of the conflicts and benefits', 30-43 in J.C. Cooper (editor) Recreation and the Environment - some geographical perspectives (Department of Geography, Kingston Polytechnic, Kingston, 1980).

63. C.B. Keenleyside, Farming, Landscape and Recreation (Countryside Commission, London, 1971).

64. See, for example, J. Cook-McGuail, 'Effects of hikers and horses on mountain trails', <u>Journal of Environmental Management</u> 6 (1978): 209-12.

65. See, for example, M.B. Usher, M. Pitt and G. De Boer, 'Recreational pressure in the summer months on a nature reserve on the Yorkshire Coast', <u>Environmental Conservation</u> 1 (1974): 41-9; and R.W.G. Carter, 'Recreational pressure and environmental change in a small beach-dune complex at Tyrella, County Down', <u>Irish Journal of Environmental Science</u> 1 (1981): 62-70.

66. See, for example, J. Tivy and J. Rees, 'Recreational impact on Scottish lochshore wetlands', <u>Journal of Biogeography</u> 5 (1978): 93-108; and M.J. Liddle and H.R.A. Scorgie, 'The effects of recreation on freshwater plants and animals; a review', <u>Biological Conservation</u> 17 (1980): 183-206.

67. F.B. Goldsmith, R.J.C. Munton and A. Warren, The impact of recreation on the ecology and amenity of semi-natural areas; methods of investigation used on the Isles of Scilly', <u>Biological Journal of the Linnean Society</u> 2 (1978): 287-306.

68. M.J. Liddle, 'A selective review of the ecological effects of human trampling on natural ecosystems', <u>Biological Conservation</u> 7 (1975): 17-36.

69. See, for example, T.A. Cieslinski and J.A. Wagar, <u>Predicting the durability of forest recreation sites in northern Utah</u> (USDA Forest Service Research Note, Washington, 1970); and M.J. Liddle, Selective review (Note 68).

70. A. Symonds, 'The effect of public pressure on the soil and vegetation of Thorpe Cloud, Dovedale', 13-30 in J.C. Cooper (editor) <u>Recreation and the Environment - some geographical perspectives</u> (Kingston Polytechnic School of Geography Occasional Paper 8; 1980).

71. N.G. Bayfield, 'Use and deterioration of some Scottish hillpaths', <u>Journal of Applied Ecology</u> 10 (1973): 635-44.

72. N. Picozzi, 'Breeding performance and shooting

bags of red grouse in relation to public access in the Peak District National Park, England', Biological Conservation 3 (1971): 211-5.

73. N.G. Bayfield, 'A simple method of detecting variations in walker pressure laterally across paths', Journal of Applied Ecology 8 (1971): 533-5.

74. G.H. Bates, 'The vegetation of footpaths, side-walks, cart-tracks and gateways', Journal of Ecology 23 (1935): 470-87; and G.H. Bates, 'Life forms of pasture plants in relation to treading', Journal of Ecology 26 (1938): 452-4.

75. See, for example, G.P. O'Hare, 'A review of studies of recreational impact in the Peak District National Park', North Staffs Journal of Field Studies 18 (1978): 21-30; and F.B. Goldsmith, 'The ecological effects of visitors in the countryside', in A. Warren and F.B. Goldsmith (editors) Conservation in Practice (Wiley, London, 1974).

76. Burden and Randerson, Quantitative Studies (Note 36).

77. N.W. Quinn, R.P.C. Morgan and A.J. Smith, 'Simulation of soil erosion induced by human trampling', Journal of Environmental Management 10 (1980): 155-65.

78. C. Harrison, 'Recovery of lowland grassland and heathland in southern England from disturbance by seasonal trampling', Biological Conservation 19 (1981): 119-30.

79. K.A. Bell and L.C. Bliss, 'Alpine disturbance studies - Olympic National Park, U.S.A.', Biological Conservation 5 (1973): 25-32.

80. I.J. Edwards, 'The ecological impacts of ped-estrian traffic on alpine vegetation in Kosciusko National Park', Australian Forestry 40 (1977): 108-20; and P.A. Keane, 'Current trends in soil conservation - erosion and walking tracks in the Alps', Journal of the Soil Conservation Service of New South Wales 35 (1979): 30.

81. See, for example, Countryside Commission,

Pennine Way Survey (Countryside Commission,
London, 1973); and Countryside Commission,
Snowdon Summit Report (Countryside Commission,
London, 1975).

82. See, for example, Countryside Commission,
Upland Management Experiment (Countryside
Commission, London, 1974); and S. Bucknell,
'Experiments in landscape management', The
Planner 63 (1977): 70-2.

83. G.C. Barrow, D.I. Brotherton and D.C. Maurice,
'Tarn Hows experimental restoration project',
Recreation News Supplement 9 (1973); 13-8.

84. D.T. Streeter, 'The effects of public pressure
on the vegetation of chalk downland at Box Hill,
Surrey', 459-68 in E. Duffey and A.S. Watt (eds)
The Scientific Management of Animal and Plant
Communities for Conservation (Blackwell, Oxford,
1971).

85. D.T. Streeter, 'Gully restoration on Box Hill',
Countryside Recreation Review 2 (1977): 38-40.

86. D.I. Brotherton, 'Conservation and recreation -
the challenge to management', 17-28 in R.D. Hay
and T.D. Davies (eds) Science Technology and
Environmental Management (Saxon House, Chiches-
ter, 1975).

87. E. Duffey, M.G. Morris, J. Sheail, L.K. Ward,
D.A. Watts and T.C.E. Wells, Grassland Ecology
and Wildlife Management (Chapman and Hall,
London, 1974).

88. T.A. More, The demand for non-consumptive wildlife uses - a review of the literature (USDA
Forest Service General Report NE52, 1979).

89. C.C. Park, Ecology and Environmental Management
(Butterworth, London, 1981).

90. T.D. Nevard and J.B. Penfold, 'Wildlife conservation in Britain - the unsatisfied demand',
Biological Conservation 14 (1978): 25-44.

91. M.J. Hay and K.E. McConnell, 'An analysis of
participation in non-consumptive recreation',
Land Economics 55 (1979): 460-71.

Recreation

92. D.O. Chanter and D.F. Owen, 'Nature reserves -
     a customer satisfaction index', Oikos 27 (1976):
     165-7.

93. C. Bull, 'Wildlife conservation and leisure
     provision', Ecos 1 (1980); 7-13.

94. D.M.L. Kinoulty, Recreation in the High Salving-
     ton Bird Sanctuary, Worthing. Unpublished B.A.
     dissertation, St. Davids University College,
     Lampeter (1979).

95. M.B. Usher, A.E. Taylor and D. Darlington, 'A
     survey of visitors' reactions on two Naturalists'
     Trust nature reserves in Yorkshire, England',
     Biological Conservation 2 (1970): 285-91.

96. M.B. Usher and A.K. Miller, 'Development of a
     nature reserve as an area of conservational and
     recreational interest', Biological Conservation
     2 (1975): 202-4.

97. R.D. Everett, Conservational Evaluation and
     Recreational Importance of Wildlife within a
     Forested Area. Unpublished D. Phil. thesis,
     University of York (1978).

98. R.D. Everett, 'A method of investigating the
     importance of wildlife to countryside visitors'
     Environmental Conservation 4 (1977): 227-31.

99. R.D. Everett, 'The wildlife preferences shown
     by countryside visitors', Biological Conserv-
     ation 14 (1978): 75-84.

100. R.D. Everett, 'Varying interest in wildlife
     with different characteristics of countryside
     visitors', Environmental Conservation 6 (1979):
     33-43.

101. K.R. Pennyfeather, 'Countryside interpretation
     - its nature and trends', Recreation News Sup-
     plement 12 (1975): 18-21.

102. Pennyfeather, Countryside (Note 101): 21.

103. See, for example, D. Aldridge, Principles of
     Countryside Interpretation and Interpretative
     Planning (HMSO, London, 1975).

104. G. Taylor, 'Sherwood Forest Visitor Centre',

Countryside Recreation Review 2 (1977): 17-22.

105. N.G. Bayfield and G.C. Barrow, 'The use and attraction of nature trails in upland Britain', Biological Conservation 9 (1976): 267-92.

106. Idem.

107. Countryside Recreation Management Association, Tourism and Countryside Conservation (Losehill Hall Study Centre, Castleton; 1980).

108. Countryside Commission, Grants to local authorities and other public bodies for conservation and recreation in the countryside (Countryside Commission, London, 1974).

109. R. Revelle, 'Outdoor recreation in a hyperproductive society', Daedalus 96 (1966): 1172-91.

Chapter Eight

THE BUILT ENVIRONMENT

                    Nothing but a hovel now
                    Between moorland and meadow,
                    Once the owners saw in you
                    A comely cottage, bright, new
                    Now roof, rafters, ridge-pole, all
                    Broken down by a broken wall.
                              Dafydd Ap Gwilym (1340-1370)

8.1 CONFLICT AND CHANGE

The analysis of social resources in rural areas in
Chapter 5 established settlements as a secondary
resource on which the primary resource of population
depends and to which access to the tertiary resources
of life-style requirements is allocated. The rural
built environment may thus be viewed as a kind of
fulcrum for a resource perspective of human elements
in the countryside. Although it is people which are
the most important commodity therein, the conflicts
and incompatabilities between different types of
rural resources often revolve around the role of
settlements in the rural environment.

Chapter 5 also suggested that rural settlements
have historically been subject to the ebb and flow
of growth and decline (eg. the desertion of medieval
villages - see FIGURE 5.1). The spectre of settlement decline in 14th century Wales suggested in the
quote above has often been repeated in subsequent
times and it is important that this historical context be stressed in any analysis of resource conflicts connected with the built environment in rural
areas.

Darley[1] argues that it is only recently that society

has become sufficiently conceited to discard the age-old lessons of scale, organic proportion and eschewing fashionable whims when dealing with rural settlements. She maintains that

> Despite the great upheavals of history - medieval plague, the Enclosures and the Agricultural Revolution in particular - the recuperative powers of rural communities have always been extraordinary. In answer to prevailing conditions, settlements achieved balance, in structure, function and pattern.[2]

The issue raised here, then, is whether concern for the future of rural settlements and their inhabitants as a result of twentieth century socio-economic change constitutes either:

(i) an arrogance and conceit in believing that society has the collective wisdom to counteract the apparently cyclical process of growth and decline, or

(ii) an appreciation that modern changes are more fundamental, widespread and faster-acting than previously, especially when seen in relation to the general acceptability of social goals involving equality and equity of opportunity.

Decisions taken by both private- and public-sector agencies serving rural areas will tend to reflect one or other of these interpretations. The issue is further complicated because rural areas do not demonstrate ubiquity of response to structural change, but rather suffer differentially due to spatial diseconomies. In broad terms, for example, Moss's[3] examination of rural problems in European countries led to a three-fold categorisation of rural areas:

Grade 1 - expanding areas. With adequate population size, public and private investment, diversity of employment opportunity, social facilities, access and transport, all leading to a stable social and economic foundation.

Grade 2 - static areas. With adequate population size to attract reasonable public investment and social provision but little private investment beyond existing commercial or industrial activities.

Hence less stability is attained.

Grade 3 - declining areas. With outflow of population and employment, insufficient public service
investment and little in the way of private sector
investment. Such areas are socially and economically unstable and inhabitants are often forced to
travel unreasonable distances to gain access to a
full range of life-style opportunities.

It should be stressed that these area types do not
conform to a simplistic continuum distribution with
increasing distance from urban centres (see Chapter
1.3) Rather, they are interspersed to a complex
degree so that area-based policies are difficult to
enact successful.

The main thrust of this chapter, therefore, is to
ascertain whether to the rural built environment
changes are being engineered or indeed modified del-
iberately through the actions and decisions of
governments or private-sector institutions, and
whether the outcomes of these processes discriminate
against any particular part of the social resource
base of rural areas. A convenient starting point
for this task is the isolation of the two principal
elements of change affecting rural settlements.

Contraction

Functional Obsolescence. Although cross-cultural
comparisons are often simplistic and less than explanatory, there does appear to have been a consistent trend in westernised rural areas whereby rural
settlements founded to service primary industries
such as agriculture have suffered an erosion of their
traditional functions due to decreasing demands for
labour (see Chapter 9.2) and increasing demands for
economies of scale in service provision (see Chapter
10.2). These mechanisms are most evident in Moss's
Grade 3 area but are also in operation throughout
the rural settlement structure.

The potential consequences are outlined by Amiran
in the case of Israel:

> The result is a decreasing importance of
> the service functions of the traditional
> central place in the rural settlement
> fabric, ie. the obsolescence and conse-
> quently regression of many a small town

.....As this situation approaches, and the
process will most probably intensify during
the twenty-first century, our settlement
structure based on villages as its main
element will become obsolete. Agricultural
villages will in future be accessories to the
settlement fabric only, whereas towns with
inhabitants engaged in non-agricultural
occupations will form its basic element.[4]

The forces which sponsor this obsolescence of rural
settlements are often subdivided into 'natural' and
'planned'. The notion of 'natural' contraction is,
however a false one. The mechanisation of agriculture, for example, is founded on individual and
collective decisions to substitute capital for
labour in search of operating efficiency and profit
(see Chapter 9.2). If however, efficiency and profit
were measured in terms of the value to society of
full employment rather than economic gain accruing
to entrepreneurial classes, then this seemingly
natural trend may not have occurred. The decline of
the agricultural labour force should thus be viewed
as consequent on the planned decisions both of the
private sector landowner and of the public sector
agencies who offer grant-aid for mechanisation.

As an aside, it is significant that the 'natural
progression' to a rustproof automobile has not
occurred, not because of technological deficiencies,
but because maximum profit for entrepreneurs accrues
from a regular replacement of new automobiles for
rusty ones. Natural change, then, is not inevitable,
but responds to the economic planning of decision-
makers in society.

Service Provision. A similar viewpoint may be adopted in the explanation of the movement of rural
service functions up the settlement hierarchy.
Several North American researchers in the 1960's[5]
explained the decline of small rural towns in terms
of a search for economies of scale in service provision. Again, the preference for servicing points
in larger, more urban, settlements can be diagnosed
as a planned reaction to a declining clientele in
rural settlements and as a search for scale economies
leading to profit maximisation on behalf of the
entrepreneur.

Alongside this trend of service supply decisions, the
increases in personal mobility among rural population

have meant that demand decisions have also favoured
the lower costs of services in centralised locations.
These changes have been summarised and to some extent
legitimised by a general recognition that <u>thresholds</u>
for vital rural facilities are constantly increasing.

Green and Ayton in Britain came to the conclusion
that:

> If it is accepted that methods of retailing
> are changing in favour of larger catchment
> populations, that some degree of competition
> is desirable, and that a chemist is a neces-
> sity, the minimum population to support an
> acceptable range of retail shopping may be
> 8000 or even more. From this it appears
> that most community services need between
> 5000 and 8000 people to support them.[6]

<u>Planning Policies.</u> Once these private sector dec-
isions had started the contraction of small rural
settlements, it has often been the case that government planning processes have exterminated the trend.[7]

In Britain, the need to regroup the rural population
was argued by Peake[8] as early as 1918 and most county
development plans in the 1950's and 1960's adopted
an approach involving the concentration of new investment into 'key' centres in the rural settlement
hierarchy.[9] In some cases these resource concentration policies merely reflected the private sector
trend of favouring larger settlements. Elsewhere,
there was a definite motive of rationalising a
seemingly outdated settlement pattern, as is suggested by Green's [10] hypothetical plan in FIGURE 8.1.
In-built prejudice against new development in small
unselected villages thus became mainstream in British rural settlement planning.

Moreover, similar policies have also been adopted
elsewhere with various levels of severity. Mizgajski[11] has reported on the formation of large vigorous rural service centres in Poland, brought about
through processes of centrally planned resource
rationalisation. In similar vein, the Khruschev
administration in the USSR sought to rehouse the
Soviet rural population in purpose built '<u>agrotowns</u>'
and in 1959 the production of long term development
plans for each agricultural district led to the
categorisation of rural settlements into <u>perspekhvnyi</u>
('perspective' settlements) which were to receive
further growth, and <u>neperspekhvnyi</u> ('non-perspective'

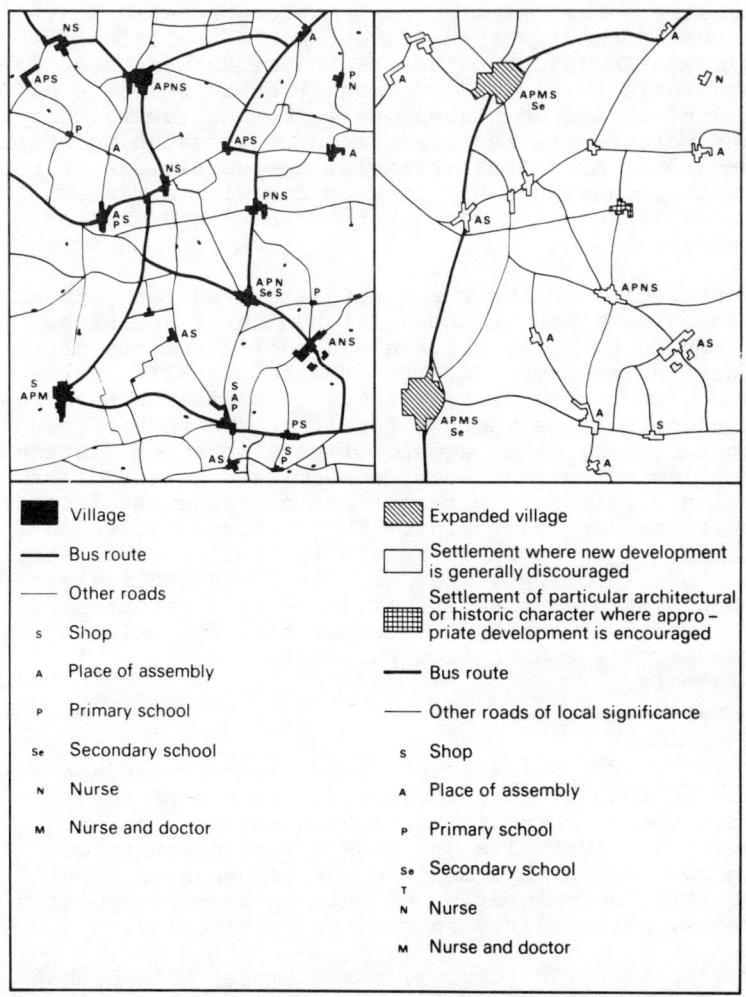

Village

Bus route

Other roads

s   Shop

A   Place of assembly

P   Primary school

Se   Secondary school

N   Nurse

M   Nurse and doctor

Expanded village

Settlement where new development is generally discouraged

Settlement of particular architectural or historic character where appropriate development is encouraged

Bus route

Other roads of local significance

s   Shop

A   Place of assembly

P   Primary school

Se   Secondary school

T
N   Nurse

M   Nurse and doctor

FIGURE 8.1   <u>Green's Model for Planned Concentration of Settlement and Facilities</u>

Source: after R.J. Green, 'The remote countryside - plan for contraction', <u>Planning Outlook</u> 1 (1966):   17-37.

settlements) where no investment would be sanctioned[12].

The resettlement programme in Newfoundland[13] serves
to stress that similar contraction processes have
occurred under very different socio- political regimes. In 1953 considerable payments were made
available to aid whole communities to relocate close
to the expanding highway network, and several small
and more remote settlements were evacuated under this
program. As a final example, the settlement of new
Dutch polderlands has taken place with a pattern of
a few large settlements rather than many smaller
ones.[14]

Contraction of the rural settlement pattern, then,
has taken place because of fundamental decisions
taken in both the private and public sectors of society and economy. It has occurred in all rural
areas to some extent, although its effects have been
hidden in areas where concomitant growth has been
sponsored by other agents of rural change. In theory,
settlement rationalisation permits a better distribution of life-style resources to residents of centres
selected for investment. What, though, of those inhabitants who wish to remain in smaller rural settlements? In effect, they are discriminated against
both by the contraction of life-style resources (see
Chapter 5.4) and by the competition for existing
resources stemming from particular groups of in-
migrants.

Resurgence

Rural in-Migration. The early 1970's witnessed a
marked reduction in the attractiveness of the
traditional metropolitan concentrations in North
America, Australia and many European countries.[15]
In most areas this decline was accompanied by a
positive net-migration balance in non-metropolitan
areas, particularly in remoter rural areas.

The British 1981 Census, for example, showed that
local authority districts categorised as 'remoter,
largely rural, districts' were the only areas to
maintain their rate of population growth during the
1970's. In fact this rate increased slightly over
that of the previous decade from 9.7 to 10.3%, the
significance of which is stressed by Champion:

> Not only was this positive shift contrary
> to the national trend towards slower growth,
> the national mean fell from 5.7 to 0.5 per
> cent between the two intercensal periods,

but it made this category nearly the fastest-growing type in the country - outdone only by districts that include new towns.[16]

Similar phenomena have been recorded in the USA, where non-metropolitan growth has not been limited to short distance overspill from major urban areas, but rather has also occurred in previously remote and unpressured rural regions.[17] Some explanation of these trends in the American context has been offered by Fuguitt, Voss and Doherty[18]. They stress that declining agricultural employment has been counteracted in some areas by an increase in energy development, service employment or expanded recreational opportunities. Moreover there has been an apparent lessening in the significance of economic motivations for migration. In particular, the growth of net migration of older people is instrumental in this trend, since such migrants are seeking not enhanced employment opportunities but rather a place to live out and enjoy their post-retirement years.

Quality of life, and quality of environment appear to be increasingly important factors in the rural in-migration process. Parallel concentrations of retirement age population have been noted in Britain,[19] and in some areas their significance has been so great that the term 'geriatrification' has been coined to describe the influx. Furthermore, in those rural settlements of the highest environmental quality, in-migration has often been dominated by a 'geriatrification' trend whereby affluent sectors of society have tended to purchase their rural idyll, and have often priced local people out of the housing market as a result.[20]

New Villages. Another indicator of the resurgence movement is the planned establishment of new villages such as those at New Ash Green in Kent, and Bar Hill in Cambridgeshire. As yet, this element of repopulation is miniscule compared with the scale of major socio-economic trends in the countryside, and has taken place mainly in pressured rather than remote rural areas. There is, however, a strong ideological and 'folk-culture' support for the new village idea, which may thus have an important role to play in the future of some rural areas.[21]

Ebb and Flow. Rural settlements in the western world have thus been subject to major socio-economic trends

over the last 30 or 40 years. Such changes conform
to an historical pattern of ebb and flow, but as
modern society feels the need to manage resources
more firmly and responsibly than ever before, the
health of individual settlements and their residents
has assumed significant political importance. In
some settlements, the results of contraction dominate. Elsewhere resurgence has selectively replaced
out-migrants to establish a rather distributional
stability in environmentally attractive locations.
In other places again, settlement growth has completely outstripped the underlying processes of contraction.

This situation of conflict and change forms an un-
certain backcloth for three crucial resource issues,
which are addressed individually in the rest of this
chapter:

(i) to what extent should the physical fabric of
      rural settlements be conserved?

(ii) how far should rural settlement management be
      dominated by the need to preserve surrounding
      landscape resources?

(iii) should built environment resources be sub-
      jugated to the maintenance of an adequate res-
      ource base in rural settlements?

8.2 RURAL SETTLEMENTS AND CONSERVATION

The first of these issues encompasses a major conflict between different perspectives on rural
resources. The rural built environment consists
both of a physical fabric, which itself constitutes
a resource in society's eyes, and of a social fabric,
representing the framework for a life-style within
the rural environment. As a physical resource,
settlements are prized and cherished as an essential
part of a nation's heritage, and their conservation
is often inherently accepted within the ethics of
resource management.

Much has been written on the subject of planning for
conservation[22], and so discussion here will be limited to a synopsis of salient evidence connected with
the concept, practice and outcomes of rural settlement conservation. These issues are by no means
modern ones. Haines points out:

    There has always been conservation and

planning on some scale or we should have no
buildings from the past in any of our towns.
But in previous generations these were matters which were settled by discussion among
the people concerned at local level, and by
their own feeling for the town. Now, however,
planning and conservation have become industries detached from the mainstream of
life. Although those concerned are trying
to do their best, their outlook in many
cases is too theoretical and governed more
by a reverence for the past than by the necessity to plan for the future.[23]

The Conservation Ethic

The conservation ethic has always been one to attract a depth of sentiment, either supportive or
adverse.

Pro-Conservation. Until recently, most emotion
(both public and private) has been automatically in
favour of conserving the rural built environment.
Middleton's insistence that 'there are 10,000 villages and hamlets in Great Britain and they surely
constitute, collectively, a major national asset to
be guarded and cherished at all costs'[24] is reasonably indicative of the ingrained belief that rural
settlements should be preserved, or at least conserved, as of right. There have in fact, been few
voices of protest against this ethic.

Debate. Eversley[25], however, substitutes quantity
of support with quality of argument in this respect.
He suggests that the conservationist movement has
become overemotional to the extent that 'the desire
to conserve every scrap of existing fabric has now
become absolute.'[26] Such emotion has led to an un-
willingness to compare the value of preserved buildings with that which might accrue from new development. His analogue question - 'the house is on fire,
which would you save, the Baby or the Rembrandt?'
highlights the potential dangers of shifting new
development in favour of the benighted preservation
of antiquity.

In short, Eversley accuses the conservation ethic
of elitism whereby a small minority of self-appointed
arbiters of taste dictate the life-style of the majority. His final verdict on the matter is clear:

> Conservation should not be the minority,
> as long as it is not a social goal in
> itself. Conservationists, by their ex-
> cesses, by their indiscriminate attacks
> on all forms of development, by their
> assertions of the right to preserve
> every structure just as it was, by their
> demand to divert public funds on a large
> scale away from demolition and re-build-
> ing into the freezing of the status quo,
> are losing the right to be heard.[27]

These comments remain unacceptable to most decision-
makers, particularly in the rural environment.
Cantell's[28] rejection of Eversley's argument stresses
the need to fulfil the duty of 'handing on our heritage', not only to future generations, but also as
a boost to tourism and recreation. Moreover, he
emphasises that:

> Things that remain the same and express
> stability are cherished in a time of rapid
> change. The continued existence of familiar
> surrounding may satisfy a psychological
> need which, even if irrational, is nonetheless
> real.'[29]

Conservation for Who? This argument would have
greater force of relevance if it took account of
whose psychological need was being satisfied. Does
conservation of rural settlements lead to exclusiv-
ity, upward price spirals, gentrification, and satisfaction only for the affluent resident and the visitor, or can conservation be carried out in a balanced way so as to achieve an equity of opportunity to
live in the conserved environment? These questions
are often overlooked.

For example, McNair-Wilson's passionate description
of the smothering of traditional rural architecture
singularly avoids the issue of 'conservation for
who?':

> at a time when any broken-down country
> cottage as long as it is old, is snapped
> up almost the moment it goes on the
> market - there is clearly an enormous
> demand for traditional English rural arch-
> itecture including thatched roofs. In
> other words the suburban houses are not
> the preferred style, only that which is

available for a house-hungry population.
If this is true I find it incomprehensible
that, as a nation, we are so unconcerned
about the architectural quality of our
villages - something which, to their un-
dying credit, the great landowners cared
about deeply and still do.[30]

With attitudes such as these, rural settlement conservation can be seen to involve the preservation of
archaic life-styles (dominated by the 'great landowners'?) and the diminution of the opportunities
for non-affluent groups to obtain housing in the
rural environment. Thatched roofs may be attractive,
but they are also costly, and to impose expensive
style in villages is to produce a distributional outcome for home-seekers of different affluence levels.

The issues raised both for and against the conservation ethic demonstrate the need for a balance
between preservation of rural buildings as a visual
resource, and preservation of opportunities for
people of any class or income to live in rural settlements. At present, the balance in ethic may be
tipped too far towards physical rather than human
resources, although in practice the implementation
of conservation has often been ineffective in the
achievement of commonly accepted goals.

This suggested imbalance may be seen in the ground
rules for conservation established by Nuttgens[31]
(TABLE 8.1). Only rule 8 and to some extent rule 9
give any attention to the social use of rural settlement resources and clearly these ground rules, if
followed to the letter, could present severe problems
for the concept of equity of opportunity for living
in a rural environment.

Conservation Practice

In Britain two major mechanisms have been adopted
for rural settlement conservation.

Listed Buildings. The conservation ethic discussed
above is directly related to the perceived need for
a retention of old buildings in the settlementscape.
It is hardly surprising, therefore, that the first
attempt to enact this ethic was aimed at such
buildings.

The Historic Buildings and Ancient Monuments Act of

TABLE 8.1 Ground Rules for Conservation (after Nuttgens)

1. Conservation depends on the study and discovery of the pattern of a place, its pattern of growth, its style.

2. The major physical component of a place is housing.

3. Conservation involves the elimination of accretions as well as the making of additions.

4. Conservation involves the management of transport and traffic.

5. The use of old buildings is fundamental to conservation.

6. The essence of integrated conservation is the use of old landscapes.

7. Conservation requires a policy for the design of new buildings.

8. Use and appearance are linked; it is the correspondence of the two that ultimately creates an architecture or an environment which is both aesthetically satisfying or practically sound.

9. Conservation should reflect the progressive integration of urban and rural environments.

10. Conservation must in the end require that places be self-conserving.

1953 established Historic Buildings Councils which were to advise on the listing of buildings of architecture and historic importance and on grant aid for the repair and maintenance of outstanding examples. The actual listing of buildings is carried out by local authorities (empowered by the 1947, 1962 and 1968 Town and Country Planning Acts) within a three grade system:

Grade 1. buildings of outstanding interest (nationally important)
Grade 2. buildings of special interest (regionally important)
Grade 3. buildings of local importance.

Grades 1 and 2 are subject to Town and Country Planning Legislation which does not allow alterations to

the structure of buildings without permission, and
which makes some grants available for the restoration of buildings. Grade 3 buildings are not considered sufficiently important to be placed on the
statutory list, but are earmarked for local planned
preservation.

This build-up of legislation has created a situation
whereby the preservation of listed buildings is to a
reasonable degree assured. Nevertheless, many commentators are critical of the listed building concept
as an agent of settlement conservation. Chitham[32]
identifies three problems. First, conservation issues have been identified with delays and complications in the development control process because
developers have repeatedly challenged the control
system by applying to demolish listed buildings.
Second, the architectural profession has been more
geared towards new construction than to concepts of
repair, rehabilitation, conversion and alteration
of listed buildings. At the rural settlement level,
such tasks are costly due to diseconomies of scale,
and in any case the lack of adequate financial provision to underwrite listed building legislation has
gravely impaired its success as a positive conservation measure. Third, the same range of controls
have been exerted on a very wide range of buildings
with varied age, type, structure and state of repair.

These broad criticisms of listed building conservation are effectively placed into the rural context
by Furness[33], who suggests that the architectural
problems outlined by Chitham are of less significance
than the practical problems of enacting this particular vehicle of conservation. She uses evidence from
a survey by North Norfolk District Council to show
that approximately ten times as many buildings which
are eligible for listing in this predominantly rural
area are actually listed by the local authority.
Part of the reason for this apparent underlisting is
that the surveys undertaken in the 1950's to indicate suitable listed buildings have not been repeated
in many of the rural settlements in the area.

Furness argues that the original surveys missed out
on much that would have been worth conserving:

> The little village of Upper Sheringham, for
> instance, could have been a little gem had
> it been statutorily protected. Now most
> of the flint and brick buildings, which had

until recently survived largely unaltered
since the seventeenth century, have been
seriously defaced by unsympathetic
modernisation.[34]

Conservation Areas. From the point of view of physical resource conservation in rural settlements,
current listed building activity thus appears under-
financed and lacking in breadth of attention. In
addition it became evident during the 1960's that a
building or group of buildings could only be appreciated and conserved within a given setting, and this
realisation led to the Civil Amenities Act of 1967
which made provision for the designation of special
policy areas as Conservation Areas. These zones
were to have five broad objectives (TABLE 8.2) but it

TABLE 8.2   Conservation Area Objectives[35]

1. The safeguarding of listed buildings and other buildings
   contributing to the character of the area, both by
   statutory powers and by the use of grants and loans for
   improvements to or repair and maintenance of important
   buildings.

2. A closer control over new development by insisting on
   detailed designs or sketches before any decision is
   given; particular attention will be given to materials
   and colours, building lines and height.

3. A more critical assessment of existing development,
   including advertisements and 'permitted development'.

4. A greater attention to details - street furniture, signs,
   poles, wires and lighting can all detract from the
   appearance of an area; statutory undertakers, local
   authorities and developers will be encouraged to give
   priority to minimizing clutter and unsightliness.

5. Local effort and initiative from individuals or local
   societies must be encouraged.

---

is clear that some aims have proved easier to fulfil
than others.

For example Circular 53/67 from the Department of the
Environment advises a two-stage approach to the enactment of Conservation Areas:

(i) designation - demarcation of the boundary and

identification of special buildings

(ii) <u>detailed planning</u> - both for development control and for positive enhancement schemes in
the area.

With some notable exceptions, local authorities have
been zealous in designation, slow in the provision
of development control details and positively sloth-
ful in the encouragement of enhancement.[36]
Estimates for 1981 suggest that more than 6000 Conservation Areas have been designated, or are in the
process of being designated in England and Wales.

Indeed individual county structure plans have acknowledged the continuous need to enact the conservation
ethic. The Kent plan suggests a wide framework for
implementation:

> When considering the visual quality of the
> smaller county towns in Kent, in conjunction
> with the visual quality of villages, it is
> possible to define broadly areas, which prima
> facie, could be regarded as areas of import-
> ance to conservation insofar as they contain
> concentration of pleasant country towns and
> villages.[37]

Thus, in addition to a full quota of Conservation
Areas, the plan nominates 62 'Villages of Special
Overall Character' where any permitted new development would be restricted to infill of existing gaps
within settlements, and would be required to be of a
high standard of design. This pattern is repeated
throughout Britain within structure plans and local
plans.

<u>International</u>. Conservation of rural settlements is
by no means restricted to Britain. Indeed McNair-
Wilson bemoans the fact that:

> The West Germans maintain a rural style,
> as do the Austrians and the Swiss. Yet
> Britain, with a Department devoted to the
> environment, appears not to care whether
> country housing looks as if it belonged
> to the landscape or the suburbs of an
> industrial city.[38]

Space does not permit a full review of conservation
practice overseas, but several informative accounts

are available elsewhere. For example, Hendry[39]
reviews the distinct differences between Northern
Ireland and the rest of the United Kingdom even
though conservation is sought through similar legislation; Binney[40] provides evidence of successful conservation of buildings in Bavaria; Masson[41] looks at
a case study settlement in Italy in relation to the
scheduling and preservation of Piccoli Centri Storici;
and Skovgaard[42] analyses the preservation of historic
and architectural heritage in Denmark.

What is clear is that in all nations where heritage
is cherished the management of rural settlements is
strongly influenced and in some cases dominated by
the perceived need to conserve and preserve the
physical fabric of the built environment.

Outcomes of Conservation

It has been noted above that considerable potential
for conflict exists between the physical resource
value and the social resource value of rural settlements. For example it has been argued that in the
British context, conservation legislation has been
used as a convenient and logically plausible method
of restricting the scale and type of new housing
development in particular settlements.[43]

One reason for this trend is that typical residents
of rural Conservation Areas tend to conform to the
environmentalist ethic:

> Very often local residents of their elected
> representatives are the initiators of moves
> to achieve Conservation Area status, a fact
> which suggests both that they are unwilling
> to sanction any significant development in
> the area and that they are willing to under-
> go the financial implications which can
> accompany house-ownership in this type of
> area.[44]

Such attitudes can thus be self-perpetuating if
Conservation Area status becomes a convenient peg on
which to hang planning refusals for 'unwanted development, which will usually be of the cheaper and
visually less attractive type. If artificial restrictions are placed on the housing market in such
settlements, it is to be expected that existing
housing stock will become increasingly desirable, and
thus the subject of extreme competition from affluent

external groups. This process has already in some
places led to an exacerbated rate of gentrification
to the detriment of the housing opportunities enjoyed
by disadvantaged local people.

This rather bleak outlook should be treated with some
caution, in view of the circularity of argument involved. Conservation Areas, by their very nature,
are attractive places in which to live, and their
environmental quality will place a premium on house
prices whether or not they happen to be subject to a
particular planning designation. It could be, then,
that gentrification processes would occur in these
conditions anyway, and that Conservation Area status
does not necessarily induce a state of deprivation
for local, less affluent, residents.

There is, however, some evidence to suggest that
designation does sponsor status and a sentiment of
future environmental protection. Cantell, in a paper
supporting the work achieved by Conservation Areas
concedes that: 'Even designation alone achieves
something. Confidence is engendered in the future of
the area, which encourages people to invest in and
care for the fabric.'[45]

There is a strong likelihood that an ability to invest in and care for the fabric of these preserved
rural settlements will depend on social status,
wealth and income, and that Conservation Area policy
will thus, sooner or later, lead to discriminatory
outcomes. This is not to say that all British rural
Conservation Areas or indeed similar protected zones
elsewhere are demonstrating these phenomena at
present.

Generalisations concerning social manoevrability are
always hazardous because of the wide variety of
settlements and communities which are affected by
protective zoning policies. Nevertheless it is clear
that in some of the worst instances, local people
who wish to remain local are being prevented from
entering on open housing market because of powerful
external competition, and are thus either forced
into a clearly segregated 'unconserved' part of the
settlement, or are compelled to move to another
settlement where they can afford the price demanded
for housing opportunities.

What is needed, therefore is some small-scale, inexpensive and mixed tenure residential development in

all rural settlements (including specially designated
areas). This requirement will, however, be a long
time in coming so long as decision-makers' attitudes
remain fixed. Baldwin highlights this problem:

> Conservation, preservation and local
> authority committees and officers are in-
> creasingly drawn from those with high
> incomes, greater personal mobility and
> with interests which revere traditional
> farms and land use, old styles of archi-
> tecture and rural craft occupations.[46]

Until the needs of local rural people are permitted
due emphasis within planning policy, the conflict
between physical and social resource perspectives in
rural settlements is likely to continue.

8.3 RURAL SETTLEMENTS IN A CONSERVED LANDSCAPE

It is clear that conflict exists between the wish to
conserve the physical fabric of buildings and settlements and the need to ensure that the opportunity to
live in such places does not become the sole domain
of the affluent. There is, however, a further string
to the conservation bow which also appears to act
against the provision of social opportunities in
rural settlements.

In addition to settlement conservation for its own
sake, other policies concerned more with landscape
conservation have also served to oppose social development in rural settlements. Villages and rural
towns are viewed as an integral element in rural
landscape heritage (see Chapter 4) and so any attempt
to preserve or conserve landscape inevitably includes
measures to control unsympathetic growth in settlements.

In fact, the multiplicity of conservation policy impact on rural settlements is complex in its extent
and its outcome, but from the point of view of social
planning, such policies have been seen as a major
source of disadvantage:

> Countryside planning in Britain may be
> likened to an onion. In order to get
> to the heart of it you have to peel off
> layer after layer of policy.....
> National Parks, AsONB, AsGLV, green belts,
> conservation areas, and various copycat

policies all represent layers of policy which
in some circumstances are capable of producing gross inequalities of socio-economic
opportunity in their attempts to conserve the
rural heritage.[47]

The rural built environment, therefore, appears to
harbour wider resource conflicts than those relating
simply to the physical and social value of buildings.
Rural settlements are fundamental to the concepts
of landscape (see Chapter 4) and landscape management,
and the requirements for a conserved landscape inevitably reflect on settlement management. A brief
analysis of the potential outcome of these conflicts
is attempted here in the British context, although
some details of the potential for opposing resource
perceptions in designated landscapes areas of
Europe and other western nations have begun to appear
elsewhere.[48]

Landscape Conservation Zones. The trade-off between
physical conservation of settlements and their socio-
economic health has become increasingly important
for British rural planners. In general, it has become expected that specially designated landscape
conservation zones in the countryside will restrict
the growth and life of any rural settlements falling
within them, with a result similar to that discussed
in Section 8.2 where settlement conservation for the
affluent minority was found to be a central theme.
Nevertheless, there is some evidence to suggest that
this assumption may be overemphasised. Blacksell
and Gilg note that:

> One of the more curious features of develop-
> ment control in rural areas is the small
> number of special controls in National Parks,
> Areas of Outstanding Natural Beauty and other
> protected landscapes. Despite the fact that
> nearly 50% of the land area of England and
> Wales has now been designated under one or
> other of these protection orders and the
> strictures about the need for high standards
> of development control in the official guid-
> ance to local authorities, there are few
> extra powers available.[49]

Evaluation of this set of resource conflicts, then,
hinges on the question of whether development control
is more strictly interpreted in landscape conservation zones, and if so, whether the effects of these

controls are distributional. Evidence on these
matters is patchy[50], and it deals with National Parks,
Designated Landscape Areas and Green Belts.

National Parks

There are currently ten national parks in England and
Wales covering 9% of the total land area. In the
late 1970's each national park authority was required
to produce a National Park Plan, and these have highlighted the conflicts between issues of conservation,
recreation and local needs within these areas.

Local Needs. It is clear from these plans that
'local needs' is likely to be the objective to which
least importance is attached in the resolution of
these conflicts. The plan for Exmoor, for example,
stresses this point: 'It must be recognised, however, that to make the interests of local people
the first objective of the NPA (National Park
Authority) would be to defeat the purpose of the
National Park.'[51]

Given this ordering of priorities, it might be expected that rural settlements and communities in
national parks will be subject to specific pressures
arising from high levels of residential popularity
and very restricted planning policy and practice.
This expectation appears to have been ratified by
some of the available evidence. The Lake District
Special Planning Board, for example, claims that:

> The popularity of the Lake District as a
> holiday and retirement area has put ex-
> ceptional pressures upon the housing
> market.....there is bound to be concern
> when people with local employment or
> local affinities find themselves unable
> to compete with other purchasers for local
> housing.[52]

This idea of national park-specific pressures on
local communities finds wide support elsewhere.[53]

An alternative view has been expressed by the Peak
Park Joint Planning Board[54] which suggests that
evidence supporting claims that local people were
being priced out of the Peak District due to extreme
competition for houses by persons from outside was
not convincing. Indeed, a recent government-spon-
sored report by the Tourism and Recreation Research

Unit[55] on the role of rural communities within national parks advocates greater emphasis on tourism
as an economic prop to the parks' population.

Research findings on the structures of development
control in national park settlements is also mixed.
The Brecon Beacons plan[56] adopts a control policy
based on the edict that 'acceptance of the philosophy
of national parks must presume a stringent control of
development.' Accordingly the national park authority has made heavy use of Conservation Area designations to control development in certain rural
settlements and has imposed strict conditions on new
housing development elsewhere in the park, which have
tended to steer developers towards the building of
larger, more attractive and more profitable dwellings.
These guidelines represent the norm in most national
parks, yet Blacksell and Gilg[57] provide interesting
case study evidence to show that housing growth in
the declining settlements of Exmoor has been encouraged by the same county council (Devon) which has
restricted development in the more pressured situation of Dartmoor.

Implications. Two general conclusions may be reached
concerning the conflicts relating to settlement resources in national parks.

First, development trends in national parks up to
the late 1970's can be seen to be little different
at aggregate level than those in undesignated rural
areas. Pressured settlements within the parks have
received similar planning strictures as commuter
areas outside, and remoter areas show little difference in policy implementation than that in operation outside the park boundary. In some cases,
therefore, park-specific restrictions have resulted
in no discernible additional pressures on national
park communities. What this has meant, in effect, is
that the supposedly strict development controls in
national parks have proved incapable of restricting
speculative commuter, retirement and holiday-oriented
housing development in areas of pressure. As a consequence neither conservation nor social resource
objectives have been satisfied.

Second, a review of the national park plans and
accompanying structure plans and local plans[58],
reveals that a much stricter framework of development control in national parks is intended for the
1980's. Less loopholes appear to remain for any

housing development in these areas which is not
warranted by local needs. Conversely, planning
authorities appear increasingly aware of the potential social difficulties resulting from the restriction of settlement growth and have given higher priority to the provision of specific opportunities for
local communities.

Although on the surface these trends give grounds
for hope, there is still a high probability of conflict between strict control on development and allowing opportunities for social development. It
remains to be seen whether conservation objectives
will permit the extension of local opportunities for
non-affluent groups or whether it will be the gentry
who will continue to thrive in this environment of
policy incongruity.

Designated Landscape Areas

Over 40% of England and Wales is now covered by
landscape designations other than national parks.
Areas of Outstanding Beauty (AsONB), Areas of Great
Landscape Value (AsGLV), Coastal Preservation Areas
(CPAs) and the like have proliferated to the extent
that they represent at least as much of a threat to
the social welfare of rural communities as the more
highly publicised national parks. Generally, development control policies in these areas has been similar to that in national parks. The Devon County
Council Structure Plan[59] includes a typical policy
which gives particular weight to the scale of development, its siting, layout and relationship with
existing development, its design appearance and the
materials to be used in construction.

If such policies are fully implemented over 40% of
England and Wales, then their effects could be substantial. Once again, however, evaluation of the
resource conflicts involved here depends on whether
any problems encountered through over zealous controls or pressure on the housing market are policy-
induced or policy-independent.

In 1978, the Countryside Commission[60] reported on the
future of AsONB and in doing so sparked off considerable debate over the usage of landscape designations
in general. A summary of the replies to this report
is also available[61] and a useful catalogue of the
socio-economic implications of designated areas has

been produced by the Standing Conference of Rural Community Councils.[62]

Key Themes. From this considerable body of evidence, several themes emerge. Although it is not easy to differentiate between trends due to designation and those which would have happened anyway, it does appear that AsONB status has not so far restricted the granting of planning permissions any further than would be expected in a similar but undesignated rural area (see Chapter 11). This finding may appear surprising but Anderson[63] suggests that this similarity is due to the general strictness and effectiveness of restrictive policies throughout rural areas rather than to any laxity of implementation within AsONB.

Although planning permissions and refusals do not directly mirror AONB or AGLV status, considerable pressure is exerted by planners through attaching planning conditions to permissions for development. By imposing conditions on the materials, cladding and colours used in new buildings, an inevitable price premium occurs resulting in the construction of larger and more expensive dwellings. Thus although different areas of landscape designation will naturally reflect different patterns of migration, demand and development, it does appear that AONB or AGLV status can locally exacerbate difficulties caused by other external pressures even if such status does not itself cause these problems. It certainly seems to be the case that dwelling prices in designated areas are above average.

Given this situation, further restrictions (whether by type or number) on housing development in these areas in the name of landscape conservation will inevitably exaggerate the expense of entering the housing market unless specific measures are taken to satisfy the housing needs of local groups of less affluent people.

Green Belts

One final landscape category which can be seen to place differential resource values on the rural built environment is that of green belts. Although generally studied in their wider role of urban growth barriers,[64] green belts can also be viewed as yet another policy stratum which is capable of polarising socio-economic opportunities in rural settlements.

Gregory[65] has charted the combination of restricted
new growth and severe pressure on the housing market
in green belts which in tandem can lead to the occurrence of gentrification processes. For the non-
affluent groups that remain, life-style opportunities
have been subject to decline. Buckinghamshire County
Council, for example, acknowledge that: 'Limited
growth, however, has rarely made it easier to provide the necessary services and has consequently
placed more people at a disadvantage.'[66]

Practical Considerations. In recognition of these
trends, county structure plans have sought to improve green belt performance in two ways.[67] First,
county authorities have sought to extend the designation of green belt status by some 5180km^2 to a
total of 20,720km^2. This trend represents an attempt
by local authorities to extend the role of green
belts so as to include, for example, the conservation
of environmental resources. Also apparent is the
desire for stricter controls on development within
the expanded green belts.

Second, authorities have sought to cater for local
housing needs within these overall restrictive strategies. Rather as in the case of national parks,
rural planners are attempting both to tighten up
policies of control and to relax these controls so
as to provide much needed local opportunities.
Achieving a balance between tighter overall controls
and a flexibility to permit local needs development
will be extremely difficult. If this balance is
tipped towards provision for local needs, green belt
restrictions could eventually become far more lax
than during the development plan era, and conservation objectives would suffer. 'Local needs' policies could, on the other hand, be used to limit both
the role and the occupancy of any permitted development and thereby restrict green belt controls even
further than before.

As is usual in these cases, insufficient research
evidence is available to evaluate whether the social
resources inherent in green belt settlements will be
given greater emphasis under these new policies.
Healey, Evans and Terry[68] suggest that local needs
policies will allow more development within green
belts than initially envisaged, but at present the
anticipation of significant socially-oriented advances in these areas is rather more hopeful than
realistic.

Distributional Implications. In attempting to anal-
yse the conflicts between preserving the built environment as part of the cherished rural landscape,
and carefully developing rural settlements so that
the needs of local, non-affluent groups can be
realised, a careful balancing act is required. Too
much conservation of physical resources leads to
the distributional outset of opportunity deprivation
among certain groups of rural people. Too much uncaring development in villages can result in the
destruction of the rural milieux which after all
represents the alternative living environment which
is the real reason for providing equity of housing
opportunity in the first place.

The foregoing analysis has uncovered some warnings
for the evaluation of these various resources. Although it appears that conservation has taken priority over social equity in the specially protected
areas of Britain, it is nevertheless tempting and
very easy to overemphasise the direct links between
designation and outcome. It would be much more cir-
cumspent to suggest that links of this nature are
not proven by the current state of research, and
therefore to restrict criticism of these zones to
the fact that they represent yet another hurdle which
has to be overcome by the non-affluent, low-opportunity local population groups in rural areas. These
are the very groups who are already structurally deprived and who already have the greatest difficulty
in securing life-style opportunities without these
additional hurdles.

Clearly then, if settlement and landscape protection
policies are to continue in use, supplementary policies are required to deal with these distributional
outcomes.

8.4   RURAL SETTLEMENTS AND SOCIAL RESOURCES

Thus far, this chapter has suggested that rural
settlements are subject to historical cycles of
growth and decline, but that the intervention of
planned resource management has skewed these 'natural
processes'. Not only has the rationalisation of
public and private sector facilities been encouraged,
but it is also the case that concurrent conservation
policies aimed at both the built and the unbuilt
environments have been instrumental in producing
differential opportunities to live and work in rural

settlements according to affluence.

In order to act as an equitable social resource, rural settlements therefore appear to be in need of specific management to ensure that various opportunities remain open within them. Issues of <u>access</u> to various services and facilities are dealt with in Chapter 10, but some fundamental resources are required in situ as an integral part of the built environment framework.

Rural Housing

The most obvious tertiary resource (see Chapter 5) within rural settlements is that of housing. Sections 8.2 and 8.3 have demonstrated that the balance of housing resources is often opposed by the resource concentration ethic. Any planning process in the developed world will thus be faced with a dilemma of housing resource management.

For example the local plan for the village of Antwerp in Jefferson County, New York State[69] lists eight objectives for residential planning which are not fully compatible:

1. To preserve and improve residential character and dwelling conditions.

2. To encourage quality subdivision development that will not be a detriment to the village tax base or natural environment.

3. To locate new residences in areas which can be served most conveniently by public facilities and utilities.

4. To provide for a variety of housing types in the community to meet the needs of individuals and families.

5. To conserve residential values by excluding commercial, industrial, and agricultural uses from residential areas.

6. Locate residences outside of nature areas where they could be endangered by physical forces and processes.

7. To protect the scenic, natural and recreational resources of the village environs.

8. To have reasonable but firm controls regarding mobile homes, both permanent and seasonal.

Although planning systems differ from nation to nation, and the balance of housing pressures is often unique to individual settlements, this range of issues presented for a small American village has universal relevance in any society where public and private sectors co-operate in providing rural homes. The resolution of these issues in accordance with objectives of equality or equity will depend on the emphasis given to the social aims of objective 4 as opposed to the economic administrative and conservation oriented aims of the remaining seven.

The mutual comparability of non-social objectives often tends to predetermine the conflict resolution process unless specific measures are undertaken to safeguard the meeting of housing needs from all sectors of the rural community.

Problems and policies of rural housing have received detailed attention elsewhere, but in reviewing housing as a rural resource, several salient features should be borne in mind. First, housing plays several roles in society. Dunn et al[70] suggest three:

(i) a house as a <u>home</u>, catering for needs of shelter and of adequate accommodation

(ii) housing as <u>wealth</u>, particularly invested wealth, and

(iii) housing as a <u>positional good</u>, a key symbol of success in an acquisive society.

The equitable management of housing resources will encounter differential requirements from these three roles: Dunn et al stress that 'For some households the achievement of the first role is a difficult enough goal; for others the motivation has long involved more than merely the need for shelter'.[71]

This differentiation between role-seekers has been seen to be caused largely by an 'ability to pay' for rural housing, which in turn is linked in with the location and wages of employment. Shucksmith gives a lucid summary of these divisions:

> The essence of the housing problem in
> rural areas is that those who work there
> tend to receive low incomes, and are thus
> unable to compete with the more affluent
> 'adventitious' purchasers from elsewhere
> in a market where supply is restricted.[72]

253

It does appear therefore that the 'wealth' and 'positional good' roles for rural housing tend to be easily accommodated within the market system, but the 'home' role as demanded by low income local families requires intervention of some kind from planners and resource managers. Phillips and Williams[73] suggest that the public sector can often provide the only source of housing for these groups, and they stress that rationalisation of public housing can be detrimental to these specific needs.

Finally, it is clear that there is no shortage of initiative and possible resource compromises available in the quest to secure adequate rural housing for local groups. Both Clark[74] and Winter[75] (see TABLE 8.3) have produced blueprints for primary and secondary action to provide housing for local people. The degree to which these alternative proposals can be successfully implemented depends largely on the political will of decision-makers to acknowledge the social resource role of the rural built environment.

If the conservation of the physical fabric of rural settlements maintains its exalted position in rural resource management, then there will always be a strong probability that strict controls on new development will result in disadvantage for local low-income groups. If, however, conservation objectives can be made sufficiently flexible as to incorporate some of the more radical and unconventional low-cost housing schemes suggested in TABLE 8.3, then a more equitable juxtaposition of physical and social resources in rural settlements may be achieved.

Rural Industry and Employment

Although development constraint in the name of conservation has largely been aimed at housing, industrial and other employment providing enterprises have also been viewed as inappropriate within the rural settlement context. Given the continuing need for jobs in the countryside, the pernicious effects of over strict planning controls are often highlighted as a major obstacle for social resource management.

For example, the Rural Advisory Committee of the National Council for Voluntary Organisations in Britain clearly states this case:

> We believe there is a need for more flexible attitudes among planning authorities towards

TABLE 8.3   Action on homes for locals

Primary

More council housing

Flexible planning permission in case of local need

North Wiltshire scheme

Conversion of council dwellings

Shell homes

Increased parish council involvement

Housing advice

Sale of plots to local people in need

Increased grants and loans to those in housing need

Secondary

Starter homes

Building for sale

Housing Association development

Equity sharing schemes

Purchase of dwellings

Co-operative and self-build schemes

the conversion of agricultural and other buildings into factories, workshops and other economic activity; to the location of factories and workshops in smaller rural settlements; and to the continued activity and even expansion of 'non-conforming users'. In their early days, few small businesses can afford to pay substantial capital costs or rent for premises; and over-rigid planning attitudes can effectively stifle enterprise.[76]

As with the question of providing a suitable mix of housing in rural settlements, it would be foolish to suggest that a change in planning controls could by itself encourage the build-up of employment facilities. Flexibility of development control has to

work hand-in-hand with measures of public sector
encouragement if the physical/social resource mix in
rural settlements is to be achieved in this respect.
Such encouragement might take the form of direct
efforts of job creation, particularly through the
development of industrial estates, advance factories
and rural workshops.

There are perhaps some lessons to be learned here
from the example of Israel's industrial villages[77]
where some rural settlements are now entirely supported by co-operative industrial employment at
village level. Once again the conservation-develop-
ment balance has to be maintained in heritage-
conscious nations, but it does appear that any present imbalance occurs on the side of socially required
development in conserved environments.

The Rural Community

Other types of building have engendered less discard
of resource perception in rural environments.
Churches, schools, village halls, pubs and shops
somehow assume a conforming quality within the built
environment, often because of their age, but sometimes because they fit the expected pattern of land
use even though they themselves might not always be
perceived as intrinsically attractive. Often with
these facilities social deprivation occurs because
of issues other than clashes with the conservation
ethic.

The broad trend of contraction due to economies of
scale was discussed in Section 8.1, and village services have often fallen into disuse as a result of
this external decision-making.

In 1974, Devon County Council[78] undertook a detailed
survey of the structure of the communities in Rural
Devon. It was concluded that a 'thriving rural community' should possess the following facilities and
services:

1. public utilities - mains water, electricity
   and sewerage;

2. social facilities - primary school, places of
   worship, village hall, and possibly a doctors'
   surgery;

3. shops, for day-to-day needs, and post office;

4. employment either in the village or conveniently

situated nearby.

Clearly, the built environment in Britain and other developed countries is changing rapidly due to structural and conservation pressures[79] to the extent that positive socially-oriented intervention is required to replace the essential social resource base in rural settlements. Such action can either operate by ensuring the provision of suitable buildings as dwellings, services and so on in the settlement concerned or by a partial surrogation of some life-style opportunities by providing access to those located elsewhere.

The equity of rural living will eventually depend on the balancing of these resource perspectives.

NOTES AND REFERENCES

1.   G. Darley, 'Rural settlement - rural resettlement: the future', Built Environment, 4 (1978) 229-310.

2.   Idem, 301.

3.   G. Moss, Reviving Rural Europe (Council of Europe, Strasbourg, 1980).

4.   D.H.K. Amiran, 'The settlement structure in rural areas: implications of functional changes in planning', Norske Geografiske Tidskrift, 27 (1973): 3.

5.   For example, G. Hodge, 'Do villages grow? - some perspectives and predictions', Rural Sociology, 31 (1966): 183-96; G.V. Fuguitt, 'The growth and decline of small towns as a probability process', American Sociological Review, 30 (1965): 403-411; M. Clawson, 'Factors and forces affecting the optimum future, rural settlement pattern in the United States,' Economic Geography, 42 (1966): 283-93.

6.   R.J. Green and J.B. Ayton, 'Changes in the pattern of rural settlement'. Paper presented to the Town Planning Institute Research Conference, 1967: p4.

7.   For a full discussion of this theme see
        P.J. Cloke, An Introduction to Rural Settle-
        ment Planning (Methuen, London, 1983).

8.   H.Peake, 'The regrouping of rural population',
        Town Planning Review, 7 (1916-18):   243-50.

9.   Development plan policies are reviewed by
        B.J. Woodruffe, Rural Settlement Policies and
        Plans (Oxford University Press, Oxford, 1976);
        P.J. Cloke, Key Settlements in Rural Areas ,
        (Methuen, London, 1979); P.J. Cloke, Intro-
        duction (Note 7).

10.   R.J. Green, 'The remote countryside: a plan
        for contraction', Planning Outlook 1 (1966):
        17-37.

11.   A. Mizgajski, 'Przyrodnicze warunki rosbudowy
        wybranych osad rozwojowych w Wielkopolsce,'
        Badania Fizjograficzne nad Polska Zachodnia,
        Seria A Geografia Fizyczna 31 (1978):   126-142.

12.   J. Pallot, 'Some preliminary thoughts on Soviet
        rural settlement planning', School of Geog-
        raphy, University of Leeds (1977).

13.   K. Hoggard, 'Resettlement in Newfoundland',
        Geography 64 (1979):   215-8.

14.   J.P. Thijsse, 'Second thoughts about a rural
        pattern for the future in the Netherlands',
        Papers and Proceedings of the Regional Science
        Association 20 (1968):   69-75.

15.   A.G. Champion, 'Rural-urban contrasts in British pop-
        ulation change'. Paper presented to the Institute of
        British Geographers Annual Conference, 1982.

16.   A.G. Champion, 'Population trends in rural
        Britain', Population Trends, 26 (1981):   20.

17.   See, for example, P.A. Morrison and J.P. Wheel-
        er, 'Rural renaissance in America?, Population
        Bulletin 31 (1976):   1-27; D.R. Vining and
        T. Konhily, 'Population dispersal from major
        metropolitan regions: an international com-
        parison', International Regional Science
        Review 3 (1978):   49-73.

18.   G.V. Fuguitt, P.R. Voss and J.C. Doherty,
        Growth and Change in Rural America (Urban Land

Institute, Washington, 1979).

19.   See, for example, Association of County
       Councils, Rural Deprivation (Association of
       County Councils, London, 1979).

20.   D.M. Shucksmith, No Homes for Locals? (Gower,
       Farnborough, 1981).

21.   Darley, Rural settlement (Note 1).

22.   See, for example, D. Lowenthal and M. Binney
       (eds), Our Past Before Us: Why do we save it?
       (Temple Smith, London, 1981); R. Kain (ed)
       Planning for Conservation (Mansell, London,
       1981).

23.   G.H. Baines, Whose Countryside? (Dent, London,
       1973): 96.

24.   M. Middleton, 'The conservation of village
       values', The Village, 28 (1973): 10.

25.   D. Eversley, 'Conservation for the minority?',
       Built Environment, January (1974), 14-15.

26.   Idem, 14.

27.   Idem, 15.

28.   T. Cantell, 'Why we need to conserve our archi-
       tectural heritage', County Council Gazette, 67
       (1975): 276-9.

29.   Idem, 277.

30.   M. McNair-Wilson, 'Traditional charms of rural
       architecture being smothered', Surveyor, 147
       (1976): 30.

31.   P. Nuttgens, 'Conservation: from continual
       change to changing continuity', Journal of the
       Royal Town Planning Institute, 61 (1975):
       255-257.

32.   R. Chitham, 'A new look at listing', Architects'
       Journal, 30 March (1977): 588-590.

33.   M. Furness, 'Rural neglect', Architects'
       Journal, 11 April (1979): 736-737.

34.   Idem, 737.

35.   B.J. Woodruffe, Rural Settlement (Note 9):   58.

36.   R. Wools, 'Conservation in the counties',
      Building Design, 424 (1978):   8-9.

37.   Kent County Council, Structure Plan: Conserv-
      ation and Character of the Built Environment
      (Kent County Council, Maidstone, 1975):   11.

38.   McNair-Wilson, Traditional charms (Note 30): 30.

39.   J. Hendry, 'Conservation in Northern Ireland',
      Town Planning Review, 48 (1977):   373-388.

40.   M. Binney, 'Conservation in Bavaria', Country
      Life, March 8 (1979):   622-624.

41.   G. Masson, 'Albori: contrasts in conservation
      in Italy', Architectural Review, 161 (1977):
      186-188.

42.   J.A. Skorgaard, 'Conservation planning in
      Denmark', Town Planning Review, 49 (1978):
      519-539.

43.   P.J. Cloke, Introduction (Note 7).

44.   Idem.

45.   T. Cantell, 'Caring for character', Country
      Life, March 22 (1979):   808.

46.   P.N. Baldwin, 'Countryside renewal II', The
      Architect and Surveyor, 17 (1972):   10.

47.   P.J. Cloke, Introduction (Note 7).

48.   See, for example, 'Land Management and Con-
      servation', Report on the European Conference
      at Losehill Hall, April 7-11, 1980; and Inter-
      national Union for Nature Conservation, United
      Nations List of National Parks and Equivalent
      Reserves (Bowker, London, 1980).

49.   M. Blacksell and A. Gilg, The Countryside:
      Planning and Change, (Allen and Unwin, London,
      1981).

50.   For a more detailed review of this evidence see

P.J. Cloke, Introduction (Note 7).

51. Exmoor National Park Committee, Exmoor National Park Plan, (The Committee, Dulverton, 1977): 51.

52. Lake District Special Planning Board, Lake District National Plan (The Board, Kendal, 1979): 3.

53. For example the Peak District study carried out by S.F. Penfold, Housing Problems of Local People in Rural Pressure Areas, (Department of Town and Country Planning, University of Sheffield, 1974).

54. Peak Park Joint Planning Board, Peak District National Park Plan, (The Board, Bakewell, 1976).

55. Tourism and Recreation Research Unit, The Economy of Rural Communities in the National Parks of England and Wales, (The Unit, Edinburgh, 1981).

56. Brecon Beacons National Park Committee, Brecon Beacons National Park Plan, (The Committee, Brecon, 1977).

57. Blacksell and Gilg, The Countryside, (Note 49).

58. See P.J. Cloke, Introduction (Note 7).

59. Devon County Council, County Structure Plan: Written Statement (The Council, Exeter, 1979).

60. Countryside Commission, Areas of Outstanding Natural Beauty: An Analysis, (The Commission, Cheltenham, 1978).

61. Countryside Commission, Areas of Outstanding Natural Beauty: An Analysis of the Comments Received in Reponse to the Countryside Commission's Discussion Paper CCP 116 (The Commission, Cheltenham, 1980).

62. Standing Conference of Rural Community Councils, Whose Countryside? (national Council for Voluntary Organisations, London, 1979).

63. M.A. Anderson, 'Planning policies and development control in the Sussex Downs AONB', Town Planning Review, 52, (1981): 5-25.

64. See P. Hall, R. Thomas, H. Gracey and R. Drewett, The Containment of Urban England, (Allen & Unwin, London, 1973): D. Thomas, London's Green Belt (Faber and Faber, London, 1970).

65. D. Gregory, 'Green Belt Policy and the Conurbation' in F.E. Joyce (ed) Metropolitan Development and Change: The West Midlands - A Policy Review (Teakfield, London, 1973).

66. Buckinghamshire County Council, County Structure Plan: Report of Survey (The Council, Buckingham, 1976): 271.

67. See M.J. Elson, 'Structure plan policies for presumed rural areas', Countryside Planning Yearbook 2, (1981), 49-70.

68. P. Healey, S. Evans, and S. Terry, The Implementation of Selective Restraint Policy: Approaches to Land Release for Local Needs, (Department of Town Planning, Oxford Polytechnic, 1980).

69. Jefferson County Planning Board, The Village of Antwerp: Comprehensive Plan (The Board, Watertown N.Y., 1978).

70. M. Dunn, M. Rawson and A. Rogers, Rural Housing: Competition and Choice (Allen and Unwin, London, 1981).

71. Idem, 247.

72. M. Shucksmith, No Homes for Locals? (Gower, Farnborough, 1981): 11.

73. D.R. Phillips and A.M. Williams, Rural Housing and the Public Sector, (Gower, Farnborough, 1982)

74. D. Clark, Rural Housing Initiatives (National Council for Voluntary Organisations, London, 1981).

75. H. Winter, Homes for Locals (Community Council of Devon, Exeter, 1980).

76. Rural Advisory Committee, National Council for Voluntary Organisations, Jobs in the Countryside: Prospects for Rural Employment (The

Council, London, 1980): 19.

77.   F. Meissner and W. Ruby, 'New industrial vil-
       lages in Israel', _Ekistics_ 43 (1978): 43-7.

78.   Devon County Council, _First Review of the_
       Development Plan (The Council, Exeter, 1974):
       45.

79.   See Standing Conference of Rural Community
       Councils, _The Decline in Rural Services_ (Nat-
       ional Council of Social Service, London, 1978).

Chapter Nine

FARMING AND FORESTRY

9.1 INTRODUCTION

Agriculture can create conflicts within the countryside in a variety of ways, such as through pollution
stemming from the disposal of agricultural waste
products, destruction of important wildlife habitats,
and impacts on landscape beauty, despite claims that
farmers are the real custodians of the landscape.

MacEwan[1] identifies a broad change in attitude in
recent years, with an increasing number of farmers
expressing concern for landscape and wildlife, and
the acceptance by many conservationists that landscape can best be protected by a prosperous farming
community. This suggests that compromise, co-existence and harmonisations of interests between conservation, forestry and agriculture might be both
possible and viable. A prosperous farming community
can (and, indeed, often does) destroy landscape to
achieve posterity, but farmers cannot be expected to
maintain landscape entirely out of their own pockets.

Farming represents without doubt the most widespread
element in rural resource use. In England and Wales
overall, farmers affect roughly 80% of the land surface directly, although the area of agricultural
land has contracted particularly since the 1950's.
Some $97.2 \times 10^3 km^2$ are farmed in England alone, which
yields roughly 90% of the total arable output of the
UK, and some 2/3 of the output of livestock and livestock products[2].

Continuity and Change

Farming, like all rural land uses, represents an
inherently dynamic resource using system, and there

is mounting evidence from many countries that established rural traditions and lifestyles have been markedly eroded and modified particularly within recent decades.

One catalyst for recent changes in farming practices has been the need to foresee future demand and to make adjustments with a suitably long lead time. Schmidt[3] describes the need to adapt farming practices in Australia to accommodate a growing demand for animal products and foodstuffs, a reduction in the rate of growth of agricultural production, and an increase in farming costs (through increases in costs of fertilisers, and increased shipping costs). In Britain, the very unsettled social, economic and political climate of post-war reconstruction and recovery made it expedient to maintain a health home production of food. The Scott Committee, set up to examine the implications of land use changes in rural areas in Britain during the Second World War, stressed the importance of home-based agricultural production to enhance strategic security. It also foresaw an amenity/preservation problem in post-war rural Britain in concluding that 'even where there are no economic, social or strategic reasons for the maintenance of agriculture, the cheapest way, indeed the only way, of preserving the countryside in anything like its traditional aspect would be to farm it.'[4]

Even at the world-wide scale, the need for agricultural development to proceed broader economic development is widely stressed. Global estimates of the annual increases in food production required to meet rising demand between 1980 and 2000 A.D. are between 3 and 4% and Wittner[5] suggests that up to 25% of this could be met by expansion of arable areas worked (the rest from intensification).

Post-War Changes. The post-war period has witnessed a renaissance in farming in many countries, and the arrival and rapid dissemination of agricultural technology, and the parallel evolution of new farming life-styles and patterns of behaviour have served to visibly transform many rural landscapes. Two dominant changes have been increased mechanisation in farming, and an allied increase in capital investment and requirement for capital support within agriculture. Beresford[6] argues that these have transformed the farmer from peasant into capitalist and the farm worker from labourer into craftsman. These changes,

in turn, have served as catalysts for other more
wide-ranging social changes within the farming
community (see Section 9.2).

For England and Wales overall, Cornwallis[7] identifies
two basic ingredients of recent (post 1950) changes
- a contraction of the area under agriculture and a
fundamental change in farming practices. The latter
includes the replacement of rotational systems in
lowland Britain by arable cropping with cereals
(especially barley, in monoculture) dominant. There
has also been a reduction in the area of permanent
grassland, drainage of wetland areas and extensive
removal of hedgerows, felling of field-boundary copses and filling of farm ponds.

Moore[8] sees three broad phases of change since 1920.
Between the wars the main features of change in
Britain included large scale scrub removal, extensive
field drainage, and the turning over of many fields
to grass lay. The period between 1950 and 1970 was
to witness extensive hedge removal (especially on
farms with arable or mixed farming) and exponential
increases in the use of chemicals (such as pesticides)
within agriculture. Since the early 1970's food
production in Britain has increased at about 2.5%
per year, and this has been accompanied by a marked
emphasis on sugar beet (made possible by intensive
cultivation and use of pesticides) and dairy farming
(made possible by improvement of pasture through
ploughing, reseeding, improved drainage, increased
use of fertilisers and herbicides).

Modernisation and Improved Efficiency

The agricultural landscape represents a palimpsest
of elements from different periods. Farming in many
countries has evolved from a simple rustic pursuit
into highly organised business enterprises.

Modernisation. Agricultural modernisation in most
developed countries implies increasing productivity,
declining farm-based employment, and increased
mechanisation. For example, between 1961 and 1970
the agricultural labour force in Southern Italy fell
by 4.3% per year, whilst labour productivity rose by
some 8.2% per year; in the United States labour productivity tripled between 1920 and 1960, yet the
number of male farmworkers declined by 39% over the
same period; in Japan labour productivity grew by
5.5% per year on average between 1950 and 1965, but
there was an annual decline in the number of actively

engaged agricultural workers of about 2.5%[9]. In America farming is now seen as a capital intensive and debt-laden industry (in fact, the largest and most successful industry in the United States), and farmers are becoming very vulnerable to high interest rates and small price falls. Problems triggered off by modernisation include the decreasing number of small farms, high land prices (which make it difficult for young folk to enter farming), and high prices which hurt farmers because they stimulate the search for synthetic substitutes[10].

<u>Efficiency</u>. Farming and agricultural supply industries in the United Kingdom are relatively efficient in comparison with other European countries, although productivity is higher overall in the Netherlands, Belgium and Denmark.[11] Without doubt this efficiency reflects increased mechanisation within British agriculture in the post war period. In 1938 there were an estimated 50,000 tractors and about 50 combine harvesters in use in England and Wales; by 1970 these had expanded to 413,180 and 56,670 respectively. This enhanced efficiency and improved productivity yields economic returns for the agricultural industry at large, and for the more successful and entrepreneurial farmers individually.

However the break-down and replacement of traditional agricultural values and practices have triggered off sweeping changes in the appearance of farming landscapes. Traditionally rustic areas, such as the Outer Hebrides and western Ireland[12], have preserved timeless landscapes where small family farms survive from one generation to the next; where cattle, sheep, hay making and potato cultivation are staple ingredients in the farming way of life, and peat is cut locally for domestic fuel.

Modernisation and mechanisation of farming practices, coupled with increased speculative and institutional purchasing of land and EEC farming policies which favour farm amalgamation, all threaten the survival of the traditional rural way of life, and the landscapes which are so inherently a product of this.

Debate over the benefits of large scale agricultural mechanisation and modernisation also highlights the implications of energy usage within farming systems. Energy budgeting of farming systems tends to highlight the relatively high energy usage and low biological efficiency of intensive agricultural production[13].

Loss of Agricultural Land

In the twentieth century in Britain as elsewhere,
the total area of agricultural land has reduced
through retreat from the margins (leaving marginal
upland areas abandoned or worked at low levels of
productivity) and from increasing competition within
from other land uses[14] (FIGURE 9.1) Land losses have

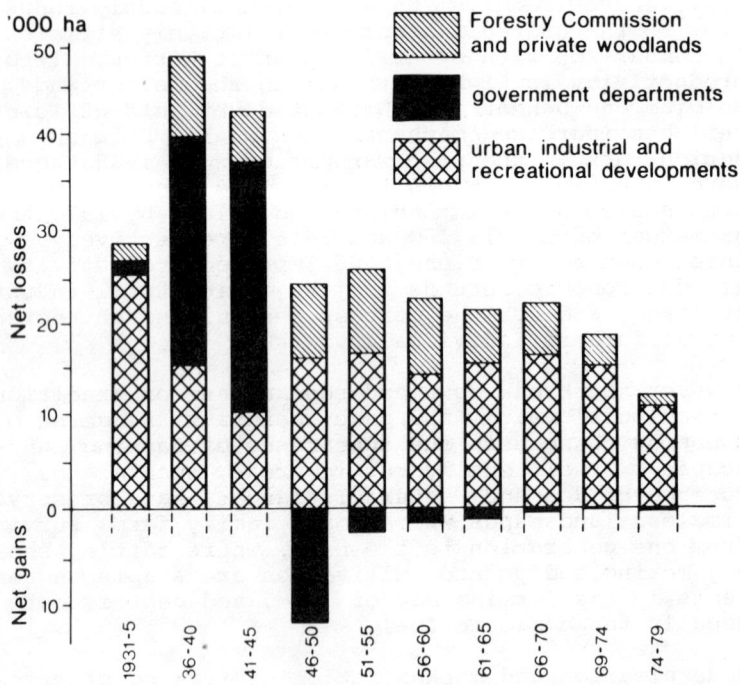

FIGURE 9.1   The Transfer of Agricultural Land in
             England and Wales to Urban and Other
             Uses, 1931-1979.

Note: 1ha = 0.001 km^2

Source: after M. Parry, 'The changing use of land',
         in R.J. Johnston and J.C. Doornkamp (eds)
         The Changing Geography of the United Kingdom
         (Methuen, London, 1982): 27.

been to a large extent compensated for by large scale
increases in output per unit area of land through
mechanisation and intensification.

Similar trends are witnessed in the United States,
where the land areas occupied by cropland, pasture
and range, and forest land each decreased by roughly
1% between 1969 and 1974, during which time 'special
uses' of land (including military and recreational
uses) increased by 6% overall[15].

Land conversion to other uses poses a series of problems for overall resource use in the countryside[16],
for three particular reasons:

Permanence. Land conversion from agriculture is
generally permanent, so that once farming land has
been converted (eg. to urban land use) it is unlikely
ever to return to agricultural use again. One notable exception is conversion to mining/quarrying
(see Chapter 6.5), where careful after-use restoration and landscaping can recreate fertile and productive agricultural land - sometimes of higher quality than the original.

Sterilisation. Direct effects of change are amplified through the blighting or sterilisation of
farming land adjacent to the area of urban growth,
and of such land pending development or a radical
change in long term land use. Such changes arise
when high quality farming land is purchased by spec-
ulators who view the land as a financial investment
in tangible resources, rather than a productive asset
in its own right.

Amplification. Conversion of agricultural land to
urban or suburban use is affected by yet further
amplification through the need to provide infrastructure for the urban area, so that land use changes are more extensive than simply the land lost
directly to housing. Ripple effects on land use are
created through the need to provide services such as
new water resource reservoirs (see Chapter 3.3), new
amenity and recreation areas close to the populations
(see Chapter 7.1) new industrial areas for employment
and new roads for access.

Whilst controversy surrounds the interpretation of
available data on land use changes in Britain[17],
there is widespread agreement that substantial
amounts of high quality land have been lost from

agriculture in the post-war period. Tarrant[18]
quotes average land losses in England and Wales of
around 150km^2 per year since 1945, and he predicts
future losses in the order of 182 to 192 km^2 per
year (ie. a loss of about 1% of agricultural land
per decade). Moreover, the rates of loss vary
considerably between different parts of the country:
the greatest losses occur in the south and east of
England, where urban and suburban developments have
been more widespread and continous, but also where
higher quality farm land is to be found.

Parry[19] detects four main components in the pattern
of changing land use in the United Kingdom in the
post-war period (see FIGURE 9.1):

(a) the growth and changing composition of urban
    areas,

(b) changes in the agricultural sector (particularly
    between roughland and improved land, tillage and
    pasture),

(c) the extension of forest and woodland, and

(d) growing competition for rural land from quasi-
    urban uses (such as recreation and water-
    gathering).

Without doubt the growth of urban areas, and the suburbanisation of the more accessible countryside (see
Chapter 8.1) have contributed heavily to the loss of
farming land, although the impact of such changes has
been markedly uneven across the country[20]. Best[21]
predicts that by 2000 AD urban land will probably
take up about 14% of the land surface area of
Britain, and he argues that if growth continues, by
the year 2300 all land not now protected in some way
for amenity and/or agriculture could be used up for
urban programmes. The direct loss of land for such
development inevitably creates many problems for the
farming community and for food production.

But the problem is amplified because land conversion
or transfer to other uses tends to differentially
favour high quality farm land[22]. This has been the
case, for example, with recent land conversion in
the Grampian and Highlands regions of Scotland,
where agricultural land-blight and massive rates of
land transfer from agriculture have occurred since
1969 as a result of oil-related developments along
the east coast. A disproportionately high amount
of the land lost falls within the higher land

capability classes.[23]

Land loss from agricultural use is clearly occurring widely, and much of it is taking place on above-quality farmland. However, from the point of view of resource management in rural areas, changes in farming practices, along with structural changes in agriculture, and the impacts of these on the farming landscape, pose greater problems and offer more pressing threats to other rural resource users.

9.2 THE CHANGING FARMING ENVIRONMENT

Structural changes in agriculture

Structural changes in farming in the post-war era reflect the search for more efficient and more productive approaches to agriculture. These changes, which have triggered off changes in the size of many farming holdings, in land ownership and in holding patterns, also reflect changing attitudes within the farming community. Intensification of both husbandry and cropping, along with increasing mechanisation within agriculture, have brought about a decline in the total area of agricultural land since 1950 in Great Britain (see Section 9.1) and a parallel decline in agricultural employment.[24]

The trend towards more mechanised, specialised and sophisticated methods of farming is evident in many different countries. In Sweden, for example, the number of farms fell during the 1970's from about 200,000 to below 80,000 and surplus agricultural housing was used either for retired farmers or for people working in neighbouring towns.[25] In Canada, many farmers left the dairy farming industry in Quebec between 1971 and 1976 and a growing number increased their reliance on off-farm work to supplement regular farm incomes.[26] Danish agriculture has also witnessed important structural changes since 1945, with a tendency towards fewer farms, simplified production programmes, reduced use of farm labour, and increased mechanisation.[27]

Bracey[28] charts the declining numbers of farm workers in Britain since 1950, and the steady rise in average farm sizes over the same period; in 1951 there was one agricultural worker per 0.18 km^2, in 1956, one per 0.23 km^2, in 1964, one per 0.30 km^2 and by 1969, one per 0.39 km^2. During the 1960's there were on average of about 25,000 regular employees leaving farming each year.

In short farms in Britain were becoming fewer, larger, more technologically efficient, and more productive.

Farmers' goals and aspirations

One important catalyst for recent structural changes has been changing attitudes and values within the farming community. Whilst agricultural decision-making reflects the interplay between many different factors such as physical, economic and social constraints on the individual farmer, it is possible to identify three ways in which farmers' goals might be motivated[29]:

(a) he will aim to achieve physical well-being; that is, he will aim to provide for both present and future needs of himself and his dependents, and to safeguard a certain amount of leisure time,

(b) he will aim to achieve social recognition by gaining status, respect and influence within the community in which he lives, and

(c) he will conform to some sense of ideology, based on personal notions of what is right and what is wrong. These might influence his decisions and mould his patterns of behaviour as much as more conscious 'economic' and 'social' objectives.

Clearly the social context of farming plays a central role in determining attitude, values and aspirations, and these in turn influence decision-making and patterns of behaviour. Newby et al[30] paint a broad picture of the sociological setting for farmers and landowners within modern Britain, and they stress both the economic importance of modern mechanised farming and the potentially significant power of the farming lobby. The farming lobby can be a well orchestrated and highly motivated pressure group in campaigning for their rights to use the countryside for food production when rural resource use conflicts arise.

The Small Farmer

There is a widespread agreement that an agrarian structure based mainly on traditional small farming units is neither efficient nor suitably productive to meet the needs of society in the 1980's. But many small farmers are entangled in a web of shortages which make it impossible for them to become large farmers. Hirsch and Maunder describe this catch-22 situation:

> Good management is absent because the conditions do not exist in which good management can flourish, as too much labour and equipment is combined with too little land. This inefficient use of resources cannot supply the material and social needs of the present number of small scale farmers and their families.[31]

Faced with such problems, the small farmer has four main options. First, groups of small farmers can work together, with informal mutual aid and common use of some means of production (such as machinery). An alternative is to enlarge the farm by acquiring additional land from other farmers. Option three is to continue to farm existing land, but on a part-time basis, and to work for the bulk of the income in employment outside agriculture. The final option is to leave farming altogether, and to sell or lease the farm to other farmers. But entrepreneurial potential is often limited in the small farmer, and such options are frequently not even perceived, let alone carefully evaluated by the small farmer faced with financial problems.

Certain sociological characteristics are shared by many small farmers, which favour persistence of traditional practices and ideas[32]. Small farmers tend to be older than most other farmers, so they have less opportunity to obtain capital for expansion, and they are less willing than some to innovate. Small farmers tend also to have relatively limited aspirations beyond the desire to remain independent, although there is little evidence to support the view that small farmers are inefficient through choice, or that they like their low incomes and insecurity. They also tend to share conservative outlooks, to that they readily reject new management methods. Finally, the small farmer has little time spare in which to search for information about markets or new developments, or to take advantage of farming advisory services.

Thus 'small is beautiful' for many small farmers through necessity rather than choice - the treadmill of survival ensures that they continue but that they change little in the face of difficult times.

Farm amalgamation

Whilst forces such as these affect the small farmer, they are not typical of farming at large: average farm sizes have increased in recent years, whilst the number of active agricultural holdings has declined accordingly. The mean size of farm holding in Scotland grew from 0.4 km^2 in 1960 and 0.54 km^2 in 1975.[33]

Changes in farm size in south west England also reflect the dynamics of amalgamation; Edwards[34] notes that some 46% of a random sample of 125 farms in central Somerset surveyed in 1963 and 1976 had increased in size over that period, 20% had decreased and some 11% had disappeared altogether (the rest showed no change).

Such trends highlight the tendency for small farms to grow by amalgamation, which has several advantages for the farming community[35]:

(a) small farms generally provide only meagre incomes so that amalgamation might serve to boost income levels and reduce the number of impoverished farmers,

(b) the land vacated by farms which go out of business can be added to the holding of another small farmer, and thus facilitate expansion of his operation,

(c) small farms (below 900 standard man days of workload) tend to be very inefficient users of agricultural resources, so that amalgamation boosts efficiency overall, and

(d) amalgamation helps to maintain income prospects of farmers in relation to other sectors of society.

Land Ownership

Changes in land ownership is another dimension to the recent structural changes within agriculture. Lee[36] argues that some 43% of the medium to high quality potential cropland in the United States has at least one ownership obstacle which prevents ready development, and in Britain also the pattern of ownership can exert considerable influence of all agriculture decision-making.

One notable change in Britain has been the switch

from tenanted to owner-occupied farming: most farms were tenanted before 1914, yet by 1976 over 50% were owner-occupied.[37] Miles stressed that 'whoever owns the land has responsibilities towards it which entail continually investing capital in its permanent equipment in order to enable profitable occupation to persist, a need to conserve the countryside and to look after the well-being of those who live in it.'[38] Traditional farmers are true entrepreneurs who resent policies which seek to curtail their independence, so that conflicts often arise between farmers and other resource user groups in the countryside. Such conflicts commonly arise between farming and the amenity lobby (see Chapter 7), landscape interests, and nature conservation groups. Wibberley[39] points out that farmers and landowners are often quite free to ravage the landscape unchecked, because agriculture lies beyond the jurisdiction of most planning legislation.

One group who tend to exploit this planning loop-hole are the institutional landlords (such as pension funds) which bitterly oppose any interference, are indifferent to landscape and wildlife interests, and are motivated simply by the prospect of financial gain. Any long-term interest in the survival of farming communities, in long-term stability and preservation of farming landscapes, and in long-term sustainable management of the agricultural land resource is usually beyond their immediate interest.

Coppock[40] interprets the growth in owner occupation in farming in England and Wales as a reflection of three trends; the break up of large agricultural estates and the sale of constituent farms to sitting tenants, difficulties for new farmers of securing tenancies (so they tend to purchase their own farm), and a growing interest in part-time and hobby farming. Part-time and hobby farming are becoming increasingly common.[41] Ashton and Cracknell[42] identified 180,000 part-time holdings throughout England and Wales in 1960, of which 48,000 provide less than 25 man days of work per year.

Grant support for agricultural improvement

One of the more paradoxical aspects of post-war rural planning has been the extent to which conflicts of interest between different government departments can be reflected in grant support and subsidy schemes. It is in the role of arbitrator in conflicts between farming and conservation that formal planning plays its largest part.

Leonard[43] sees intervention and planning in agriculture as a mechanism for ensuring compromise between polarised viewpoints, in the sense that management agreements, conservation grants and so on represent attempts to counteract the primary effects of
agricultural policy without actually modifying that
policy. At the same time, he underlines the waste-
fulness of present arrangements in Britain whereby
one government department awards grants for 'improvement' schemes which might damage landscape (such as
land drainage), whilst another department offers
grants to conserve landscape.

One example of such conflicting policies arises in
the 1968 Countryside Act[44], which contains two conflicting provisions. Section 37 of the Act requires
the Countryside Commission and all public authorities
to have due regard to the needs of agriculture and
forestry, yet there is the reciprocal obligation in
Section 11 on the same authorities to have regard to
the desirability of conserving the natural beauty
and amenity of the countryside.

The paradox is clear, yet in most cases in Britain
of such conflicting viewpoints, it is the farming
view which emerges triumphant. MacEwan bemoans the
fact that the Ministry of Agriculture pays grant
subsidies 'as of right, regardless it seems of the
landscape quality, the agricultural potential or the
farmers' capabilities. The answer is to be found in
the Ministry's subservience to the farming lobby, and
to its inability to escape from the fetters of its
own compartmentalised thinking'[45]. Such matters
point to the need for a more formally integrated
land-use policy, which will be explored in greater
detail in Chapter 12.

Problems of upland farming

Upland and marginal farming areas highlight the
dynamics of agricultural systems because these are
the areas of expansion during times of economic boom
and population expansion, and contraction during
times of economic depression or population contraction. The upland and marginal areas thus offer a
mosaic of worked and abandoned farmland[46] as fitting
testimony in the rural landscape to the fluctuating
fortunes of farming enterprises.

<u>Decline</u>. The upland economy was once able to support
large populations, and it played an important role in
the Industrial Revolution by providing food, materials, manufactured goods and manpower for expanding
industries in the lowlands. Collins[47] argues that
the modern economic history of the uplands is dominated by backwash effects of the Industrial Revolution on the hinterland economy, and by the inherently harsh physical environment of upland areas (which
means that upland agriculture has always been less
productive than elsewhere).

From the 1880's onwards the upland economy began to
decline, and there was large scale rural depopulation
from the uplands encouraged by push factors of population pressure, land hunger, under employment and
declining non-farming industries, and pull factors
of higher wages and better standards of living in
the lowlands.

<u>Revival</u>. Recent attempts to revive upland areas
through agricultural investment have been frustrated
largely by the inherently low physical productivity
of marginal hill land, and by its inherent tendency
to run to waste. The two main forms of incentive
offered to upland farmers in Great Britain are the
grant aiding of improvement (such as cultivation,
re-seeding and enclosure), and the provision of hill
cow and sheep subsidies under the 1946 Hill Farming
Act to encourage farmers to make full use of under-
grazed hill land during summer months[48].

Neither scheme is cost-effective in terms of productivity and efficiency of upland farms, but they offer
essential support for hill farmers which serves to
keep hill communities alive and to maintain hill
landscapes. This subsidised perpetuation of inherently uneconomic ways of farming does at least go
some way towards ensuring that upland landscapes are
not fossilised. A 1974 survey of upland farm landscapes by the Countryside Commission[49] noted widespread loss of stone barns and tree cover in recent
years, along with decay of and declining numbers of
walls, hedgerows and fields in marginal areas where
upland farms are less prosperous.

The amenity value of upland and marginal areas must
not be overlooked - these are, after all, amongst
the most scenic (Chapter 4) and highly valued areas
for recreational use (Chapter 7). A 1975 Ministry
of Agriculture White Paper on <u>Food From Our Own</u>

Resources stressed that 'the continuing improvement of grazing and hill land can contribute to a better looking as well as to a more productive countryside',[50] and it pointed out that enclosure of upland areas both alters landscape appearance and deprives the public of access to open areas. The White Paper also underlined the need to preserve moorland landscapes for the enjoyment of a large number of visitors (such areas as the Exmoor, Dartmoor, North York Moors National Parks), although recent surveys have revealed large scale intrusion into and improvement of moorland habitats in some upland farming areas[51].

9.3 LANDSCAPE, AMENITY AND AGRICULTURE

The Landscape Custodian

The farmer has traditionally been seen as the effective custodian of the landscape in the countryside, yet most farmers' motives and aspirations centre upon commercial success in their operations. Questions of protecting or even enhancing farming landscape quality, of opening up some farmland for recreational use and for amenity gain, and of adopting farming techniques which benefit wildlife and contribute to nature conservation objectives, are often addressed after the problems of commercial success have been accommodated.

Yet many agree with Ward[52] who identifies three broad objectives to the wise use of farming resources. These are:

(a) to ensure regular and reliable income from the farming business,

(b) to develop non-agricultural features of the farm in a creative way, and

(c) to adopt conservation measures particularly where these can have direct benefits to agricultural productivity (such as the management of 'non-productive' areas such as woodland, watercourses and lakes, in order to provide secondary income via shooting, fishing, etc).

One of the best orchestrated areas of conflict within agricultural use of the countryside is the changing nature of the farming landscape, particularly in the context of visual appearance and amenity potential[53]. Modernisation of farming practices, and of the agricultural fabric, which Weller sees as 'perhaps the greatest change in the social fabric of Britain since the breakdown of the feudal system'[54], has involved reorganisation of field and farm road layouts, centralisation of buildings, change of use and redundancy of old farm buildings as well as adoption of the technology of the late twentieth century (such as improvements in fertilisation and land drainage).

The New Agricultural Landscape

Concern has centred on increasing monolithic appearance of farming landscapes in Britain in the wake of disappearance of hedgerows and increased mechanisation. The decline in landscape diversity has occurred in part through loss of particular features such as paddocks, water-meadows, hedgerows and small mosaic patchworks of old and irregularly shaped field systems[55].

The net effect has been a gradual but progressive change in farming landscapes away from those which most closely reflect English landscape tastes, which Lowenthal and Prince see as 'landscapes compartmentalised into small scenes furnished with belfried church towers, half-timbered thatched cottages, rutted lanes, rookeried elms, lichgates and stiles'[56]

In the early 1970's the Countryside Commission sponsored a study of the impact of modern farming on lowland landscapes in England and Wales. The New Agricultural Landscapes[57] study concluded that such landscapes would continue to decline without changes in policy which at present stress maximisation of food production largely at the expense of other objectives. It also concluded that new landscapes, 'no less interesting than the old', could be created by landowners (on land surplus to present day agricultural production), by public authorities (on publicly owned land), and by strengthening farm, parish and other boundary hedges.

The study stressed that 'these new landscapes would differ critically from those which are already evolving because there would be a conspicuous input of new features; they would not, in other words, be the accidental product of modern farming'. Proposals for public authorities include the need to plant more trees, and to enter into management agreements with farmers to encourage planting, and government is advised to play an active role by attaching landscape considerations to agricultural grants, or

offering tax incentives for landscape conservation
works carried out.

Hedgerow Removal

One of the most characteristic elements in the farming landscape of Britain is the hedgerow boundary
between fields. Hedgerows and small fields are a
product of special economic circumstances which no
longer prevail today.[59] These include abundant cheap
labour, large seasonal variations in work load, and
poorly developed agricultural technology with relatively primitive equipment for ground preparation,
planting and harvesting.

Most English fields date from about 1750 to 1850,
which can be seen as a 'Golden Age' in country landscaping[60]. Decline in agricultural prosperity after
about 1850 led to reduced standards of living for
many rural landowners, cultivation was reduced, and
much of the farming landscape was neglected.

Modernisation, mechanisation and changing farming
practices have led to wholesale destruction and removal of old hedgerows in many parts of lowland
Britain, particularly in the post war period. Large
expanses of hedgerow were removed in Norfolk between
1946 and 1970[61], and Allen[62] estimates that hedgerow
clearance since 1950 has proceeded at a rate of
between 112,000 and 160,000 km per decade (most within eastern counties).

There is no doubt that 'the enlargement of fields to
accommodate large scale machinery can give an appre-
ciable saving in costs that can easily repay the
costs of changing field boundaries'[63], although the
valuable roles played by hedgerows are commonly overlooked. These benefit both the farmer and the conservationist. The former enjoys hedgerows because
they provide long-term boundaries to properties,
prevent livestock from straying and/or damaging
growing crops, act as a shelterbelt for both livestock and crops, and reduce soil erosion by both
wind and water. Conservationists benefit from
hedgerows because they offer shelter and habitats
for birds and wildlife, provide corridors for dis-
persion of plant and animal species within intensively managed agricultural landscapes, and provides
valued aesthetic features within the landscape.

Direct impacts of hedgerow removal thus include the

replacement of diverse farming landscapes (with mosaic patches of fields and boundaries) by monotonous landscapes with large stretches of open field and the reduction in wildlife habitat for birds, animals and plants. Moreover, the shelter effect is reduced and accelerated soil erosion often quickly follows (leading to declining soil fertility and reduced productivity).

9.4 NATURE CONSERVATION AND AGRICULTURE

The controversy surrounding many agricultural improvement schemes (such as land drainage, ploughing of old meadows, and removal of internal field hedgerows) reflects mounting interest in the association between nature conservation and agriculture[65]. Recent changes in farming practices include replacement of rotational systems in lowland Britain by arable cropping reduction in permanent grassland, drainage of wetland habitats, and removal of hedges.

Mabey points out that 'almost all farmland is now cultivated (in the sense of being ploughed or chemically treated) and even 'permanent' pasture is ploughed and re-seeded every few years to maintain its productivity. Habitats with long histories of unchanged status are becoming scarce. Those that do remain are shrunk and isolated, and the less mobile plants and animals have become stranded, with little hope of being naturally replenished from outside populations'.[66]

Loss of Habitat

Modern farming practices seek efficiency in various ways, one of which is to maximise productive use of available farmland. Traditional farming tended to be an extensive form of land use, but modernisation has led to intensification and the removal of many characteristic landscape features (FIGURE 9.2). Farm ponds and ditches have been filled in, hedgerows and farmland trees have been cleared and uprooted, old pastures have been converted to grass leys, and old fields have been sprayed with weedkillers and artificial fertilisers to improve productivity and maintain fertility in the face of recurrent intensive cropping practices.[67]

Such visible changes have been complemented by the progressive disappearance of old elements of the traditional farming landscape such as water meadows,

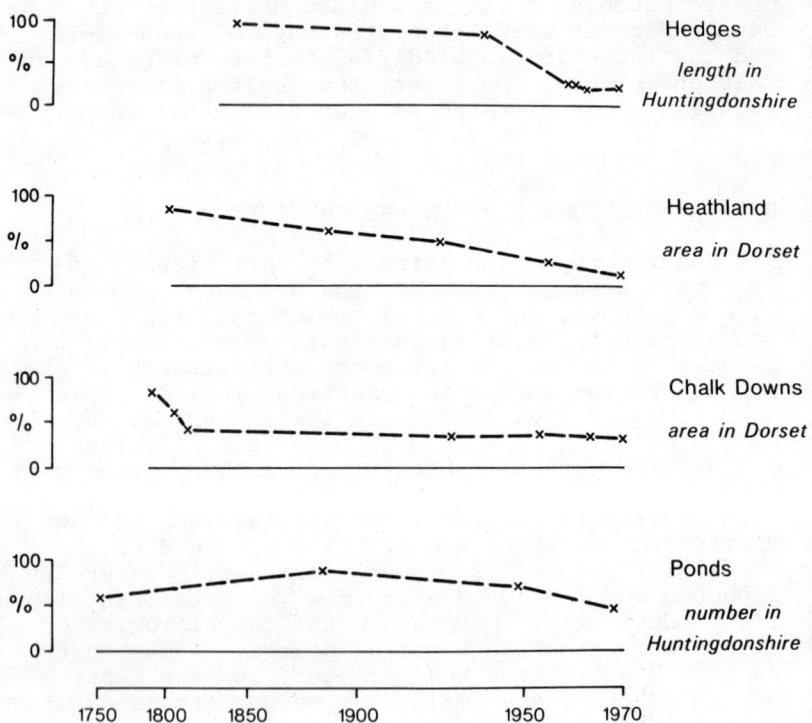

FIGURE 9.2   Loss of Wildlife Habitats in Lowland
England since 1750.

Source: after Nature Conservancy Council, Nature
Conservation and Agriculture (Nature
Conservancy Council, London, 1977).

sheep walks, dairy pastures, and extensive rough
grazing on heathland, moorland, salt marsh and fen-
land. Such features added diversity to the rural
scene, but they also created a diversity of habitats
which favoured certain plant and animal species
which could happily co-exist alongside the less
intensive agriculture. Hedgerows offered habitats
and safe corridors for the spread and movement of
plants and animals; farm ponds and ditches offered

refuges and habitats for wetland species; old meadows which had escaped artificial fertilisers and chemical additives offered habitats for plants and animals.

One habitat markedly affected by recent farming practices (particularly expansion of cereal production since 1950) has been the ploughing up of old chalk downland. Only 433 of 13.16 x 10^3km^2 of chalk soils in England remained as downland in 1966, although it is argued that since the Ministry of Agriculture withdrew ploughing grants for the lowlands in 1972 the greatest threat to remaining chalk downland is aerial spraying of fertilisers and weedkillers.[68]

The Nature Conservancy Council has predicted that a policy of complete modernisation would require the conversion of all old pastures to grass leys, spraying of all fields with weedkillers and artificial fertilisers, treatment or filling in of all ponds and ditches, and clearance of all hedges and field trees.[69] The survey estimated that because of these habitat losses, up to 8¼% of all birds and 100% of all butterfly species commonly found in farming landscapes would be lost, no dragonfly species would be left, and only about 6 mammal species capable of surviving in open grassland and arable prairies would survive.

Agriculture affects nature conservation in two basic ways - by changing habitats and by reductions in the spatial distribution of plant and animal species (although the two are closely related). Moore concluded that 'nearly all the habitats which are most important to wildlife, notably ancient woodlands, lowland heaths, marshes, bogs and unimproved pastures and meadows, have declined in area'[70] in Great Britain within the last two decades. Habitat loss can in turn lead to local extinction of species. The shrinking distribution and local disappearance from many areas of the Pasque Flower (<u>Pulsatilla vulgaris</u>) in the wake of increased ploughing of chalk and limestone areas in lowland England provides a clear example of such induced extinction.[71]

Options for Conservation

Such changes in farming landscapes highlight the need to reconcile nature conservation with modern agriculture, particularly in terms of protecting

wildlife on farmland. Compromise is without doubt
better than conflict: two options are to physically
separate the areas where each is carried out, or to
modify the intensity of farming techniques so that
they are no longer so destructive to wildlife.[72]

Complete isolation and protection of certain cherished habitats might ultimately become an inevitable
requirement, but modification of farming practices
probably holds more potential for conservation in
general. The Nature Conservancy Council recommended
that the farming community refrains from reclaiming
the last remnants of good wildlife habitats on farms
and also that it seek extra-production by more intensive and efficient farming on the presently
cropped area.[73]

The success of changes in farming practices designed
to facilitate nature conservation on farmland depends
heavily on the attitudes of the farmers involved.
Their attitudes, values and priorities inevitably
in part reflect many factors such as their background,
farm size and tenure arrangements and it is generally
assumed that most farmers regard wildlife with indifference if not hostility.

Such a view is not fully realistic, however. A
Ministry of Agriculture survey in the mid-1970's
showed that whilst 13% of farmers who were interviewed intended to remove semi-natural habitats from
their farms a further 13% intended to either improve
or even create habitats (both for field sporting
purposes and for wildlife conservation).[74] Newby
studied the attitude to conservation of farmers in
East Anglia and found that 87% expressed views
sympathetic to nature conservation; 20% were prepared
to accept that there is some justification in frequently voiced criticisms of farmers for destroying
habitats in agricultural areas.[75]

9.5   WOODLANDS AND FORESTRY

Ancient Woodland

Woodland has traditionally been an important component of the landscape of rural areas in many
countries. The Domesday Book of 1086 records woodland present in at least 60% of parishes and villages
in England, and archeological and palaeo-environment-
al evidence (such as fossil pollen grains and wood
fragments preserved in peats) indicates a wide dis-

distribution of woodland during prehistoric times.[76]
Trees and woodland communities have played an important part in the evolving political economy and human
ecology of rural areas, and in the past agriculture
and the use of wood for fuel, timber, grazing etc.
were closely entwined as land uses.

Ancient woodland has declined in distribution and
extent throughout the present century because of
changes in farm management, intake of land for
development and building, and changes in rural land
use (particularly coniferisation in upland areas of
Great Britain). Ancient woodland is important for
wildlife conservation because of its age and stability, its lack of intensive management, and its inherent naturalness. It is a characteristic feature
of much of the English countryside,[77] yet its disappearance through clearance or conversion to conifer plantation has been matched by an increase in
the total areas covered by trees.

Woodland Decline

Contemporary woodland in Great Britain differs from
historic woodland in distribution and composition.
The distribution of woodland has shrunken markedly
in the last century but the composition of the
remnant woodlands has also altered in terms of species richness and composition, habitat diversity and
inherent conservation value.

Rackham[78] notes that traditional woodland (the 'wild-
wood') in England comprised six broad communities.
Most were old woods, comprising ash, maple, hazel
coppices with oak timber trees, but a variant occurred on waterlogged soils (aspen groves). Third were
the ash swamp communities, and these were complemented by younger woodlands which grew up along abandoned fields, adjacent to major areas of woodland.
Last were patches of elm scattered through the 'wild-
wood'. Recent surveys highlight the extent changes
in traditional woodland habitats such as these.
Harding[79], for example, records the clearance of 17%
of old woodland in West Cambridgeshire between 1946
and 1973 (mostly in the early post-war period) or
since 1960, with most turned over to agriculture.

Three main factors account for much of the recent
woodland decline in Great Britain;

Old Age. Part of the marked decline in non-commercial

woodland in Britain since about 1900 can be attributed to the fact that a great many native trees are
extremely old. Many date from the period of widespread tree planting during the enclosure movement
of 1700-1870, and old age encourages both natural
death by die-back, and also death through reduced
resistance to disease, drought, pollution and other
environmental stresses.[80]

Disease. The appearance of much of the British
countryside has also been affected by loss of trees
through various forms of disease. The most notable
has been the rapid and widespread dissemination of
Dutch Elm Disease, which killed over 9 million elms
in lowland Britain between about 1968 and 1976, but
other outbreaks have included beech bark disease,
ash decline, top-dying of Norway Spruce, die-back
of London Plane and disease in Weeping Willows.[81]

Extensive surgery and felling of diseased trees, and
replanting for amenity and landscape purposes have
alleviated many of the most readily apparent impacts
of such devastations in the woodland landscape, but
recovery through replanting is a long term solution
which might take several generations to witness to
its best advantage.

Land Management. Land management has encouraged
woodland clearance and felling for a variety of
reasons. One has been clearance of deciduous woodland by farmers who decide to convert old woodland
patches on their farm into productive agricultural
use, motivated both by rising land values and a
growing need to increase agricultural output (which
would thus provide further income for re-investment).
Thus many small woodland plots and field-corner copses have been felled in recent years. A second has
been the wholesale removal of hedgerows between
fields, to enlarge field sizes and so accommodate
larger modern farm machinery (see Section 9.3). The
benefits from removing unwanted internal hedges include extra workable land, savings on hedge trimming
and maintenance, increased machine operating efficiency and savings on wasted overlap of distributed
seed and fertilisers[82]. The costs of such hedge
removal however, include loss of windbreaks, increased erosion, reduced natural habitats, monotony
of landscape appearance and loss of cultural heritage[83]

In addition, land management practices often have
inadvertent effects on remnant trees.[84] These include

deep ploughing and improved land drainage (which lower local water tables and can lead to tree die-back); increased exposure if adjacent protective woodland is removed; grazing of stock between trees (which can reduce natural regeneration); and the use of mechanical hedge-trimmers and modern hedge-management techniques (such as spraying with herbi-cides and pesticides).

There have been many calls for more attention to be devoted to evaluating the broader benefits and val-ues of small woodlands. Crowe[85], for example, stresses values such as visual qualities of wooded landscapes, opportunities for recreational and amen-ity use of small woodlands, and the use of woodlands as reservoirs for wild plants and animals within intensively farmed areas of the countryside.

Forestry plantation and commercial woodland

One paradox of the woodland landscape is that the contraction in distribution of natural woodland has been accompanied by an increase in the total area of land covered by trees (see FIGURE 9.3). Forest plantation has increased markedly in many countries

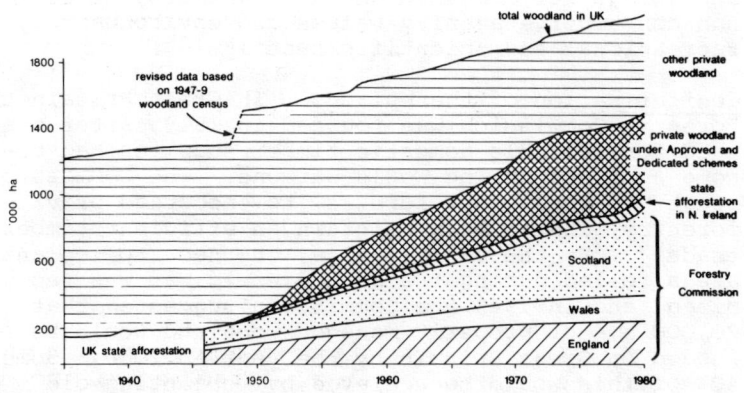

FIGURE 9.3   Changes in the Area under Woodland in the United Kingdom, 1935-1980.

Source: after M. Parry, 'The changing use of land', in R.J. Johnson and J.C. Doornkamp (eds) The Changing Geography of the United Kingdom (Methuen, London, 1982): 33.

since 1900, in response to various needs such as the desire to increase regular supplies of wood (for commercial and strategic use), the quest to bring marginal moorland into productive use, and the amenity planting of some areas of upland. Not all forest land is commercially run, but the days of large scale planting for estate landscaping purposes are long since passed.[86] Neither is all forest land state-owned. Harou[87] estimates that about 60% of the forest area of the European Community is privately owned, and since the average size of holding (4.5ha, ie. 0.045 km^2) is extremely small fragmentation of holdings poses serious obstacles to effective forest management and regular wood supply.

Forest land differs from natural woodland largely in terms of management. Thus although forests are man-made habitats, they can materially add to the amenity, landscape and conservation potential of the countryside if such objectives are included in the management plan. Smith and Lessard note that in general, forestry 'has as its objective the growing of trees and the management of forest resources for the present and potential contributions to the economic, social and physiological well-being of society. These contributions include wood, water and forage for domestic and wild animals, as well as non-consumptive amenity values and environmental, recreational and scientific benefits'[88].

Coniferisation of the Uplands. In Great Britain the Forestry Commission was founded in 1919, after the need for reliable domestic timber supplies had become apparent during World War One. The Commission sought to create new forests, to encourage private forestry, and to help maintain an efficient timber trade[89]. By the early 1940's, the need to replant areas felled during the Second World War was recognised, and in 1943 the Commission suggested that 20,000 km^2 of properly managed woodland would be needed in Great Britain by the year AD 2000. Some 40% of this would be achieved by replanting old woodland areas, and 60% by planting on new land (for which the Forestry Commission purchased felled woodland, moorland and mountain land from private owners).

The availability at viable prices of large tracts of poor quality, marginal upland has encouraged recent extension of forestry activities into upland Britain. Upland planting has also been encouraged by growing industrial and commercial demand for softwoods.

Poor quality upland is not suitable for growing hardwoods, and so the Forestry Commission and commercial
forestry enterprises have concentrated on planting
conifers over extensive tracts of marginal upland.

The conferisation of upland Britain has fuelled a
vociferous and increasingly polarised debate between
those who favour such use of the uplands and those
who argue that it is unproductive, unwise and unwanted. The arguments in favour of conifers include
the need to meet demand for softwood, the need to use
non-farming land for forestry as far as possible
(which means land unsuitable for growing hardwoods
without excessive investment in land improvement),
the desire to revitalise ailing rural economies in
remote moorland areas, and the relatively rapid return on investment from the fast growing conifer
species. Doyle[90] argues that up to 20,000 km^2 of
hill-land could be released for forestry before the
year 2000, mainly in Scotland and Wales, without
jeopardising land requirements for either agriculture
or urban expansion.

Opponents to conifer planting in the uplands stress
that conifers are alien to the present British landscape and therefore conifer plantations look incon-
gruous (because of their mono-species structure, and
green appearance throughout the year). Efficient
forestry practice and optimum use of available land
demand that plantations adopt geometrical shapes
with straight edges and sharp corners which give a
synthetic appearance of regularity to the landscape
of conifer forests. Moreover much conifer forestry
is not compatible with amenity use of the uplands
because access through closely spaced conifer trees
is difficult, and open access to commercial forests
is often denied because of increased fire-risk and
damage potential to the trees. Conifer plantations
also have less inherent value for wildlife than
natural decidous woodlands (especially mixed woodlands with varied habitats and thus greater nature
conservation potential).

The landscape argument has attracted much attention,
although concern over forestry landscapes is far
from new. Wordsworth commented on forestry plantations in the English Lake District that 'their
sombre uniformity, the hard edges where they meet
the natural hillsides, and the general air of regimentation are always out of harmony with the landscape of this country'.[91] The Forestry Commission,

sensitive to the charge that regimented conifer
plantations detract from landscape quality, has
established a series of principles to be followed in
new planting which are designed to reduce such visual impacts.[92] These include the need to vary planting schemes as much as possible to improve landscape
diversity; the desire to follow layouts of natural
communities as much as possible; schemes to cater
for seasonal successions of colour; incorporation of
lines of movement for people, vehicles and wildlife;
and inclusion of natural features such as rock faces
and water as much as possible into planting and landscaping schemes.

The Commission sees one of its principal objectives
as 'to perpetuate the predominantly broadleaved
character of the typical southern lowland landscape,
while giving conifers an appropriate place there,
which is widely accepted. In the uplands, where often only conifers can be grown, it seeks effective
landscaping at every opportunity'.[93]

9.6   RECREATION POTENTIAL OF FORESTS

A second area of conflict centres around the use of
forest areas for outdoor informal recreation.
Amenity use of forest and woodland habitats reflects
a broadening of the objectives of the Forestry
Commission from its original narrow focus on simply
growing trees, towards making forest environmental
accessible for public access.

The Commission established its first National Forest
Park near Loch Lomond in Scotland in 1936, and since
then others have been opened in areas like Snowdonia,
Forest of Dean and at the Border Forest Park. These
are all areas of high scenic value, made open for
recreational uses compatible with the requirements
of timber production[94]. Unobtrusive facilities like
camp sites, forest trails, information centres and
landscaped car parks are often provided to enhance
recreational prospects within such forest areas.
Studies of visitor patterns in the Forest of Dean
Forest Park[95] show that visitor use is affected by
many factors such as the socio-economic characteristics of the trippers, accessibility and attraction
of different areas within the forest park, and geographical location (in relation to centres of population).

Recreational use of forest areas in Britain lags

some way behind the carefully managed recreational
systems developed in American forests, where wilderness users are permitted access in limited numbers
so as not to exceed the environmental and perceptual
carrying capacities of the forest areas (see Chapter
7). However, many of the major forests in Britain
lie within ready access from centres of population
(FIGURE 9.4), so that more recreation-orientated
forest management may be worthwhile as a long-term
objective.

Whilst more forest areas are managed to allow simultaneous achievement of several objectives (such as
timber production, controlled access for visitors,
and nature conservation in places), land use planning
conflicts can arise where a forest resource is expected to cater for non-compatible resource-users.
However, as Hyde stresses, 'we can reasonably assert
that among all forest users, only a few compete with
timber production to an extent that it is important
(for our analysis). Besides timber, the usual
classes of forest use are recreation, forage, fish
and wildlife, water and wilderness. Only (i) dispersed recreation, including some hunting, fishing
and hiking, and (ii) other wilderness uses perhaps
including biological reserves, compete with timber
production. These uses cannot exist jointly with
timber production on the same forestland base'[96].

In member countries of the European Community there
is agreement that a common forestry policy is required to foster closer integration between forestry
and other rural resource using activities[97]. In some
parts of Great Britain afforestation has been actively encouraged. This has been the case in Northern
Ireland since 1970, for example, where incentives
have included the need for strategic timber reserves,
the need to reduce imports of timber, the need to
utilise upland areas, and the need to reduce rural
unemployment[98]. In the United Kingdom as a whole,
however, there is a real possibility that forest expansion could lead to reduced agricultural output by
encroachment of forest onto good quality farmland.
Benson[99] argues that such a conflict should be avoided by policies which integrate agriculture and
forestry, and by improvement of rough pasture.

9.7 NATURE CONSERVATION AND FORESTS

One of the more important conflicts within forest
management centres on the value of forest areas as

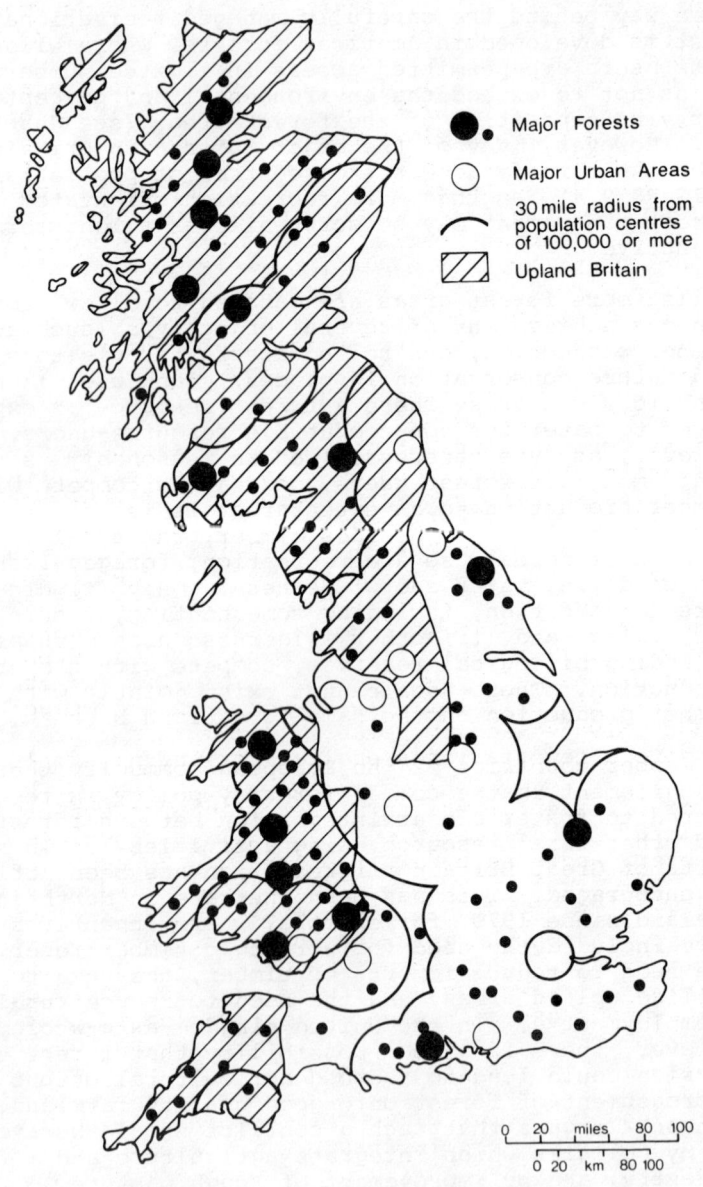

FIGURE 9.4 Location of Major Forest Areas and Urban
Centres in Great Britain
Note: 30ml = 48 km.
Source: after R.M. Sidaway, 'Public pressure on the
countryside', Forestry 44 (1971)

habitats for wildlife, and on the nature conservation
potential of different forest practices.

The Forestry Commission recognises the significance
of such issues, in pronouncing that 'the importance
of forests as natural wildlife reservoirs places
upon the Commission a special responsibility for
following enlightened conservation management policies, one it gladly accepts. The type and intensity
of such management varies from forest to forest,
though there are virtually none of the Commission's
forests which are unfit to serve as refuges for wildlife. It is the Commission's aim to improve forests
as wildlife habitats and to integrate balanced conservation and wood production in a pattern of good
land use and sound management'[100].

Whilst coniferous plantation is of less value to conservation than deciduous woodland, because of its
ecological monotony, every patch of forest or woodland has at least some potential as a habitat for
wildlife and a refuge for some of the species whose
habitats have been lost to intensive agriculture.
Mabey suggests that whilst careful woodland management is required to ensure that habitat diversity
(vital for enhancing wildlife conservation potential)
is maintained, 'any wood, once it has been established, is a better wildlife prospect than a grubbed-out
and cultivated memory, even if all it does initially
is give a few starlings shelter for the night.'[101]

Reconciliation of the interests of nature conservation and timber production is not always possible,
however, and Gane underlines the need to adopt careful definitions of management objectives to solve
possible conflicts of land use.[102] There are doubtless some sites in which the national interest is
best served by putting nature conservation first and
forestry interests second. For example, some lowland heaths are sufficiently interesting in ecological terms to justify their retention as heathland
instead of conversion to pine plantations. In other
areas (such as most woodland in lowland Britain),
forestry objectives might take precedence, even
though conservation interests aim to influence
forestry practices in favour of wildlife.

NOTES AND REFERENCES

1. M. MacEwan, 'The unknown future', 13-25 in
   M. MacEwan (ed) Future Landscapes (Chatto and
   Windus, London, 1976).

2. T. Beresford, 'Agriculture in a time of inflation', 86-102 in M. MacEwan (ed) Future Landscapes (Chatto and Windus, London, 1976).

3. H.C. Schmidt, 'Food and agriculture - a scenario
   for the eighties', Trends, Australia 11 (1980):
   1-5.

4. The Scott Committee, The Report of the Committee
   on Land Utilisation in Rural Areas, Cmd 678
   (HMSO, London, 1942).

5. S.H. Wittner, 'Agriculture in the 21st century',
   450-95 in Proceedings of the Agricultural Sector
   Symposium, Jan 7-11 (1980), World Bank,
   Washington.

6. Beresford, Agriculture (Note 2).

7. R.K. Cornwallis, 'Farming and wildlife conservation in England and Wales', Biological
   Conservation 1 (1969): 142-7.

8. N.W. Moore, 'Agriculture and nature conservation',
   Bulletin of the British Ecological Society 8
   (1977): 2-4.

9. K. Marsden, 'Technological change in agriculture,
   employment and overall development strategy',
   1-18 in International Labour Office, Mechanisation and Employment in Agriculture (International
   Labour Office, Geneva, 1973).

10. See, for example, Anon, 'World champions - a
    survey of American farming', Economist 274 (1980):
    20-22; and T. Alexander, 'Free the farm half
    million', Fortune 104 (1981): 116-29.

11. Anon, The Efficiency of British Agriculture,
    University of Reading Centre for Agricultural
    Strategy Report 7 (1976): 116pp.

12. See, for example, D.L. Waldron, 'Connemara's
    traditional ways are threatened', Geographical
    Magazine 53 (1981): 822-31; and C.C. Park,

'Timeless Hebrides face the future', Geographical Magazine (April 1981): 437-42.

13. See, for example, K.L. Blaxter, 'The energetics of British agriculture', Biologist 22 (1975): 14-8; and I.G. Simmons, 'Ecological-functional approaches to agriculture in geographical contexts', Geography 65 (1980): 305-16.

14. Summarised by J.R. Tarrant, Agricultural Geography (Davis and Charles, Newton Abbot, 1974).

15. H.T. Frey, Major Uses of Land in the United States 1974 (Agricultural Economic Report, Washington, 1979).

16. L.D. Stamp, The Land of Britain - its use and misuse (Longman, London, 1950).

17. See, for example, A. Coleman, 'The second land use survey - progress and prospect', Geographical Journal 127 (1961): 168-86; J.T. Coppock and A. Coleman, 'Land use and conservation', Geographical Journal 136 (1970): 190-210; R.H. Best, 'Recent changes and future prospects in land use in England and Wales', Geographical Journal 131 (1965): 1-12; and R.H. Best and J.T. Coppock, The Changing Use of Land in Britain (Longman, London; 1962).

18. Tarrant, Agricultural Geography (Note 14).

19. M. Parry, 'The changing use of land' 13-36 in R.J. Johnston and J.C. Doornkamp (eds) The Changing Geography of the United Kingdom (Methuen, London, 1982).

20. See, for example, R.H. Best, 'Extent of urban growth and agricultural displacement in post-war Britain', Urban Studies 5 (1968); 1-23; R.H. Best and A.G. Champion, 'Regional conversion of agricultural land to urban use in England and Wales, 1945-67', Transactions of the Institute of British Geographers 40) (1970): 15-32.

21. R.H. Best, 'The extent and growth of urban land', The Planner 62 (1976): 8-11.

22. G.S. Swinnerton, 'Land quality and land use in England and Wales', Landscape Research News 1 (1976): 10-2.

23. J.S. Smith, 'Land transfers from farming in
    Grampian and Highland, 1969-80', Scottish
    Geographical Magazine 87 (1981): 169-74.

24. J.T. Coppock, An Agricultural Atlas of England
    and Wales (Faber and Faber, London, 1976).

25. T.W. Freeman, Geography and Planning (Hutchinson,
    London, 1974).

26. F.L. Tung and D. McClatchy, 'Structural adjust-
    ment in the Quebec dairy farm sector, 1971-76',
    Canadian Farm Economics 15 (1980): 13-21.

27. J. Floystrop-Jensen and B. Dyreborg-Carlsen,
    'Factors influencing ownership, tenancy, mobil-
    ity and use of farmland in Denmark', Information
    on Agriculture 17 (1981): 145pp.

28. H. Bracey, People and the Countryside (Routledge,
    London, 1970)

29. T.P. Bayliss-Smith, The Ecology of Agricultural
    Systems (Cambridge University Press, London, 1982)
    see also B.W. Ilbery, 'Agricultural decision-
    making; a behavioural perspective', Progress in
    Human Geography 2 (1978): 448-66.

30. H. Newby, C. Bell, D. Rose and P. Saunders,
    Property, Paternalism and Power - Class and
    Control in Rural England (Hutchinson, London,
    1978).

31. G.P. Hirsch and A.H. Maunder, Farm Amalgamation
    in Western Europe (Saxon House, Westmead, 1978).

32. This is summarised in W.B. Morgan and R.J.C.
    Munton, Agricultural Geography (Methuen, London,
    1971): 63-4.

33. G. Clark, 'Farm amalgamations in Scotland',
    Scottish Geographical Magazine (1979): 93-107;
    see also E.L. Naylor, 'Farm structure policy in
    north east Scotland', Scottish Journal of
    Political Economy 28 (1981): 266-72.

34. C.J.W. Edwards, 'Changing farm size and land
    occupancy in central Somerset, a note', Journal
    of Agricultural Economics 31 (1980); 249-51;
    see also E.T. Davies, 'Some aspects of the
    changing structure of farming in Cornwall and

Devon, 1957-1977', Farm Business Review 6 (1980) 20-8.

35. Clark, Farm amalgamations (Note 33).

36. L.K. Lee, 'Cropland availability - the landowner factor', Journal of Soil and Water Conservation 36 (1981): 135-7.

37. C.W.N. Miles, 'Land management and land use' 74-85 in M. MacEwan (ed) Future Landscapes (Chatto and Windus, London, 1976).

38. Idem.

39. G.P. Wibberley, 'The proper use of Britain's rural land', The Planner (1974): 35.

40. Coppock, Agricultural Atlas (Note 24).

41. J.W. Aitcheson and P. Aubrey, 'Part-time farming in Wales - a typological study', Transactions of the Institute of British Geographers 7 (1982) 88-97; see also A.M. Blair, 'Urban influences on farming in Essex', Geoforum 11 (1980): 371-84.

42. J. Ashton and B.E. Cracknell, 'Agricultural holdings and farm business structure in England and Wales', Journal of Agricultural Economies 14 (1961): 472-98.

43. P. Leonard, 'Agriculture in the National Parks of England and Wales - a conservation viewpoint' Landscape Planning 7 (1980): 369-86.

44. G. Sinclair, 'Open landscapes and hill farming', 103-18 in M. MacEwan (ed) Future Landscapes (Chatto and Windus, London, 1976).

45. MacEwan, Unknown future (Note 1): 19.

46. M.L. Parry, 'Abandoned farmland in upland Britain - reconnaissance survey in southern Scotland', Geographical Journal 142 (1976); 101-10.

47. E.J.T. Collins, The Economy of Upland Britain 1750-1950; an illustrated review, University of Reading Centre for Agricultural Strategy Paper (1976): 116pp.

48. Sinclair, Open landscapes (Note 44).

49. H. Moggridge, S. Wright and J. Medland, 'The future of upland farm landscapes in England and Wales', Landscape Research 2 (1976): 11-2.

50. MacEwan, Unknown future (Note 1).

51. M. Parry, A. Bruce and C. Harkness, 'The plight of British moorlands', New Scientist 90 (1981): 550-1.

52. P. Ward, 'Conservation and the farmer', Agricultural Progress 51 (1976); 159-61.

53. P.L. Leonard and R.D. Cobham, 'The farming landscapes of England and Wales - a changing scene', Landscape Planning 4 (1977): 205-36.

54. J. Weller, Modern Agriculture and Rural Planning (Architectural Press, London, 1967).

55. See, for example, T. Aldous, 'New landscapes for old', New Scientist 72 (1976): 206-7; and C. Taylor, Fields in the Landscape (Dent, London, 1975).

56. D. Lowenthal and H.C. Prince, 'English landscape tastes', Geographical Review 55 (1965): 160.

57. R. Westmancott and T. Worthington, New Agricultural Landscapes (Countryside Commission, London, 1974); Countryside Commission, New Agricultural Landscapes - a discussion paper (Countryside Commission, London, 1974); and Countryside Commission, New Agricultural Landscapes - issues, objectives and action (Countryside Commission, London, 1976).

58. F. Sturrock and J. Cathie, Farm modernisation and the countryside, University of Cambridge Department of Land Economy Occasional Paper 12 (1970).

59. G.R. Allen, 'The scope of rural life: the influence of agriculture in the 1970's, unpublished paper cited by H. Clout, Rural Geography (Pergamon Press, Oxford, 1972).

60. Sturrock and Cathie, Farm modernisation (Note 58).

61. W.W. Baird and J.R. Tarrant, Hedgerow destruction in Norfolk 1946-70, (University of East Anglia, Norwich, 1973).

62. See, for example, G.R. Allen, The scope of rural life (Note 59); M.D. Hooper, 'Hedgebank removal', Biologist 21 (1974): 81-6; and E.K. Teather, 'The hedgerow - an analysis of a changing landscape feature', Geography 55 (1970): 146-55.

63. Sturrock and Cathie, Farm modernisation (Note 58).

64. Suggested by Clout, Rural Geography (Note 59).

65. See, for example, D. Barbour (ed) Farming and Wildlife - a Study in Compromise (Royal Society for the Protection of Birds, Sandy, 1970); J. Davidson and R. Lloyd (eds) Conservation and Agriculture (Wiley, London, 1977); J.G. Hawkes (ed) Conservation and Agriculture (Duckworth, London, 1978); and K. Mellanby, Farming and Wildlife (Collins, London, 1981).

66. R. Mabey, The Common Ground (Arrow, London, 1980): 116.

67. J.R. Dalton, 'Conservation and farm management policies', Agricultural Progress 51 (1976): 155-8; and G. Harvey, 'Neighbours with nature', Farmers Weekly 85 (1976): 49-61.

68. See, for example, J.W. Blackwood and C.R. Tubbs, 'A quantitative study of chalk grassland in England', Biological Conservation 3 (1970): 20-25; and R. Mabey, The Common Ground (Note 66); 132.

69. Nature Conservancy Council, Nature Conservation and Agriculture (Nature Conservancy Council, London, 1977).

70. N. Moore, 'Conservation and agriculture', Naturopa 27 (1977): 19-23).

71. T.C.E. Wells, 'Land use changes affecting Pulsatilla vulgaris in England', Biological Conservation 1 (1968): 37-44.

72. See, for example, R.D. Hodges, 'A case for

biological agriculture', Ecologist Quarterly 2
(1978): 123-42; and K. Mellanby, 'Protecting
wildlife on farmland', Biologist 27 (1980):
171-3.

73.   Nature Conservancy Council, Nature Conservation
(Note 69).

74.   Ministry of Agriculture, Fisheries and Food,
Wildlife conservation in semi-natural habitats
on farms - a survey of farmer attitudes and
intentions in England and Wales (HMSO, London,
1976).

75.   Newby et al, Property (Note 30).

76.   H.C. Darby, Domesday England (Cambridge University Press, London, 1977).

77.   See, for example, O. Rackham, Trees and Woodland in the British Landscape (Dent, London,
1977); and O. Rackham, Ancient Woodland - its
history, vegetation and uses in England
(Arnold, London, 1980).

78.   Rackham, Trees (Note 77).

79.   P.T. Harding, 'Changes in the woodlands of
West Cambridgeshire, with special reference to
the period 1946-73', Nature in Cambridgeshire
18 (1975): 23-32.

80.   Such issues are noted in C.C. Park, Ecology
and Environmental Management (Butterworths,
London, 1981).

81.   P. Jones, 'The spread of Dutch Elm Disease',
Town and Country Planning 45 (1977): 482-5;
and J. Elkington, 'A treeless Britain?',
New Scientist 78 (1978): 72-4.

82.   Council for the Protection of Rural England,
Loss of cover - through removal of hedgerows
and trees (CPRE, London, 1971).

83.   J.M. Caborn, 'The agronomic and biological significance of hedgerows', Outlook on Agriculture
6 (1971): 279-84; and F. Terrasson and
G. Tendron, 'The case for hedgerows', Ecologist
11 (1981): 210-6.

84. Nature Conservancy Council, Tree Planting and Wildlife Conservation (Nature Conservancy Council, London, 1974).

85. S. Crowe, 'The value of small woodlands to landscape and society', Parks 4 (1979): 5-7.

86. See, for example, J.M. Lindsay, 'The commercial use of highland woodland 1750-1830; a reconsideration', Scottish Geographical Magazine 92 (1976): 30-40; and P.E. O'Sullivan, 'Land use changes in the Forest of Abernethy, Invernesshire (1750-1900 AD)', Scottish Geographical Magazine 89 (1973): 95-106.

87. P.A. Harou, 'Forest ownership in the European Community', Journal of Forestry 79 (1981); 298, 307-9.

88. J.H.G. Smith and G. Lessard, Forest Resources Research in Canada (Science Council, Ottawa, 1971).

89. This history is traced by N.D.G. James, A History of English Forestry (Blackwell, London, 1981); and R.O. Miles, Forestry in the English Landscape (Faber, London, 1967).

90. C. Doyle, 'The land use jigsaw - land for forestry in the future', Quarterly Journal of Forestry 72 (1977); 129-39.

91. Cited by W. Rollinson, A History of Man in the Lake District (Dent, London, 1968).

92. This is summarised by A. Gilg, Countryside Planning (Methuen, London, 1980); see also B.M.S. Dunlop, 'The regimentation of our native pinewoods', Scottish Forestry 2 (1975): 111-9; J.E. Garfitt, 'Irregular silviculture in the service of amenity', Quarterly Journal of Forestry 71 (1977): 82-5; and A. Grainger, 'The shape of woods to come', New Scientist 91 (1981): 26-8.

93. Forestry Commission, The Forestry Commission's Objectives (Forestry Commission, London; 1975).

94. Clout, Rural Geography (Note 59).

95. R.J. Colenutt and R.M. Sidaway, Forest of Dean

<u>Visitor Survey</u> (Forestry Commission, London, 1973).

96.   W.F. Hyde, <u>Timber Supply, Land Allocation and Economic Efficiency</u> (Johns Hopkins University Press, Baltimore, 1980).

97.   J.P. Trower, 'Towards a forestry policy for Europe', <u>Quarterly Journal of Forestry</u> 70 (1976): 197-9.

98.   D.N. Wilcock, 'Afforestation in Northern Ireland since 1970', <u>Irish Geography</u> 11 (1979): 166-71.

99.   J. Benson (ed), <u>Strategy for the UK Forest Industry</u>, University of Reading Centre for Agricultural Strategy Report 6 (1980): 347pp.

100. Forestry Commission, <u>Objectives</u> (Note 93).

101. Mabey, <u>Common Ground</u> (Note 66): 66.

102. M. Gane, 'Nature conservation in relation to a national forest policy', <u>Forestry</u> 49 (1976): 91-8.

Chapter Ten

ACCESS

10.1 ACCESS AND SOCIAL RESOURCES

> The reasons why someone or something may
> be 'inaccessible' or 'difficult to get at'
> may be quite varied. An aloof boss may
> be located in the next room and yet be
> inaccessible because of the bureaucratic
> paraphenalia with which he surrounds him-
> self. A well-paid job, a pretty girl or
> a desirable residence may each be located
> only five minutes away and yet effectively
> inaccessible because one's inadequate
> skills, social talents or income effect-
> ively place them out of bounds.[1]

Malcolm Moseley's tongue in cheek comment on the
nature of social inaccessibility appears in his
seminal work <u>Accessibility: The Rural Challenge</u>. It
has become increasingly apparent over the last decade
that <u>access</u> to rural resources, even more than the
local-scale presence or absence of the resources
themselves, has become the crucial challenge in rural
resource management.

A case was made in Chapter 5 that the primary social
resource of rural people, and their secondary resource expressions of community and labour, depend in
turn on a series of tertiary resources comprising
various life-style requirements such as services,
housing and income. Furthermore, it can be argued
that the successful upkeep of primary and secondary
social resources revolves around the maintenance of
access to tertiary resources within a dynamic rural
environment.

Definitions

There has been a wealth of recent studies[2] demonstrating the changing nature of access and mobility
in rural areas. These terms have been the subject
of some confusion in the past but now have widely
accepted meanings and definitions:

(i) Accessibility is simply 'the ability of people
     to reach to be reached by the services or
     activities they require'[3]. Any changes in the
     characteristics of rural people, rural services
     and facilities, and the links between them will
     create a need for accessibility management in
     the countryside.

(ii) Mobility is 'the ability of people to move
     about'[4] and this can be measured by (a) the
     number and nature of trips actually travelled
     (whether on foot or using a vehicle) and (b)
     the ease of movement experienced by the in-
     dividual according to personal and socio-
     economic criteria (such as age, or disability)
     and transport criteria (such as availability
     of and ability to use private or public trans-
     port). Again, changes in actual movements of
     people in rural areas and changes in their
     personal constraints on movement will form
     important considerations in the wider question
     of accessibility management.

Recent Trends

Recent changes in the modern countryside have markedly affected the rural people themselves, their potential and actual trip-making capacities, the services and facilities they rely on, and the access
links available to them. The traditional wisdom of
rural population distributions is represented by a
spatial bifurcation between 'remoter' areas experi-
encing long-term and irretrievable depopulation
through extensive out-migration, and 'pressured'
areas where ex-urban in-migrants consistently swell
the indigenous population (see Chapter 1.4).
Although a glance at the extensive indicators of
change in rural U.S.A.[5] would have heralded a breakdown of this wisdom, the 1981 Census in the U.K.
still managed to surprise rural commentators with its
revelations of widespread reversals of depopulation
trends in remoter rural areas, and a deceleration of
growth in some pressured areas[6] (see FIGURE 10.1)

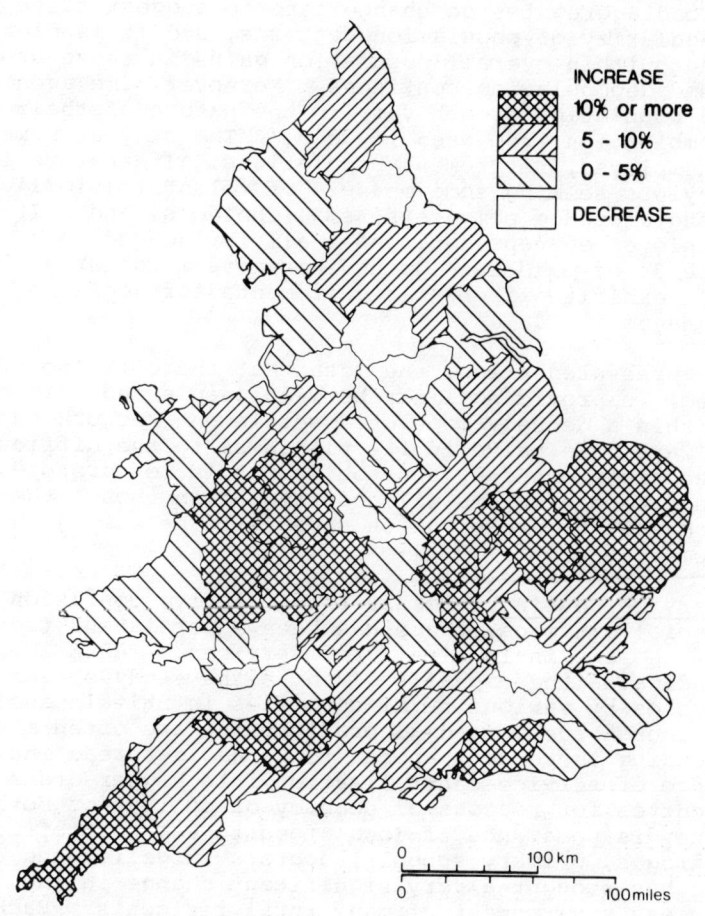

FIGURE 10.1 <u>Percentage Population Change in England and Wales, 1971-81</u>.

Source: after A.W. Gilg, 'Population and employment', in M. Pacione (ed) <u>Progress in Rural Geography</u> (Croom Helm, London, 1983).

Thus the expectation that access management in upland areas was solely concerned with a shrinking and increasingly socially polarised clientele has encountered an unexpected U-turn. Some care is needed in

the interpretation of these phenomena. Firstly,
broad aggregates of change tend to suggest false
regularity of population patterns, and it is clear
that within overall population gains in these areas,
some depopulation continues. Moreover, the agents
of population growth vary in the nature of their
combination from area to area.[7] The stay-at home
unemployed, retirement populations, alternative life-
stylers seeking some measure of voluntary simplicity,
long-distance commuters, small holders, and self-
employed entrepreneurs have all influenced the
trends of population gains in remote rural areas and
all exhibit different requirements for accessibility
management.

In pressured areas, the idea that there is 'no problem' in providing links between people and services
within a densely populated settlement network has
always been naive in its blindness to the difficulties experienced by non-mobile population groups[8],
and these problems will continue even though the
pressure of urbanisation appears to be easing in
some cases.

<u>Service Decline</u>. Amidst this relative confusion of
social dynamics, there has been a persistent trend
of decline in in situ rural services. TABLE 10.1
indicates the emphasis given to the study of service
losses by various rural countries in Britain and
although such broad generalisations are often misleading there does appear to be a widespread incidence of service centralisation into higher order
centres for reasons of economy or policy, or both.
The disappearance of local foodstores, post offices,
garages, primary schools, doctors surgeries and so
on has wrought a very significant change in the
access environment of many rural residents. Packman
and Wallace's[9] survey of service losses in Norfolk
and Suffolk underlines both the magnitude of the
problem and the range of settlement sizes affected
by it (TABLE 10.2).

Without adequate access to tertiary social resources
in distant locations, certain groups of rural residents are starved of essential life-style requirements (see Chapter 5.4) often necessitating an unwanted migration to centres of higher facility nour-
ishment. Moreover, those services and amenities
deemed 'not essential' are also affected. The
ability of rural children to participate in extra-
curricular educational activities, the ability of

TABLE 10.1 Some Surveys of Service Losses in Rural Counties in Britain[9]

COUNTY	DATE	TITLE	DATA SOURCES
The South-West	Aug 1978	The Decline of Rural Services	Various
Dorset	Dec 1979	1979 Village Facilities	Questionnaire to Parish Councils
Cheshire	Jan 1980	Rural Communities Study	Survey of Parish Councils
Devon	Feb 1980	Community Facilities in Rural Areas 1979	Parish Clerks and service agencies
Nottinghamshire	Feb 1980	Village Services: Time for Decision	Parish Councils
Suffolk	Mar 1980	The Future for Suffolk Villages	Parish Council Questionnaire
Gloucestershire	Apr 1980	Rural Community Services and Facilities – an explicit role for the County Council	Not known
Gwynedd	Sept 1980	Service Provision in Rural Gwynedd	Community Council questionnaire and service agencies
Avon	Feb 1981	Village Life in Avon	Household survey in four villages
Lincolnshire	Mar 1981	Rural Facilities Survey 1980	Parish Council and Women's Institutes
Cambridgeshire	Nov 1981	Not known	Not known
Norfolk	Dec 1981	Services in Rural Norfolk 1950-80	1950 Questionnaire survey of parish clerks: 1980 various sources

Access

TABLE 10.2 Service Losses in Norfolk and Suffolk[9]

		0-100	101-200	201-300	301-400	401-500	501-600	601-800	801-1000	1000+	TOTAL
						Parish Population					
NORFOLK 1951-1980											
Number of parishes in 1951		33	66	93	80	52	45	57	31	78	535
Food shop		1	19	36	48	37	30	31	19	49	270
Post Office		–	15	16	12	3	7	5	5	7	70
Doctor's surgery		–	–	2	4	5	3	13	10	24	61
Primary School		2	16	29	29	11	7	1	3	11	109
SUFFOLK (a) 1961-1971 (b) 1971-1978											
Number of parishes	1961	53	99	68	45	46	10	33	16	30	400
	1971	53	91	69	44	37	20	34	14	38	400
General store	(a)	1	7	9	8	12	1	6	–	5	48
	(b)	3	14	12	7	6	3	12	6	8	71
Post Office	(a)	–	6	5	1	2	1	1	–	1	16
	(b)	2	9	10	2	1	1	1	–	1	27
Public House	(a)	–	15	7	9	5	2	7	2	3	50
	(b)	–	5	5	3	3	1	1	1	7	26
Garage	(a)	–	3	1	1	2	–	4	–	1	11
	(b)	–	3	5	3	5	1	3	–	2	22

rural dwellers to visit patients in hospital, and
the ability of the young to enjoy the social and
cultural life offered by urban centres in the evenings or at weekends are all dependent on the degree
to which either personal or public access management
can respond to the ever greater distances and friction imposed between rural people and the resources
they need.

If the planned rationalisation of rural people and
services could be carried out in conjunction with
planned access provision to compensate for additional
distance and friction, then access conflicts in the
socio-economic rural environment would not be the
important issue that they undoubtedly are. As it is,
population and service dynamics have been superimposed on changes in vehicle ownership and public
transport services. It is these interactive changes
which have produced access conflicts, and these in
turn have disadvantaged particular groups of rural
residents in both social and spatial terms[10]. Only
against the background of this disadvantage can the
inherent difficulties in managing rural access be
understood.

Social Inaccessibility

Vehicle Ownership. Vehicle ownership levels in rural Britain have continued to exhibit above-average
increases despite the rising costs of new cars and
increasing fuel prices. Banister reports that 'in
rural areas, about 80 per cent of households own at
least one car, and the total level of vehicle ownership is much higher if bicycles and motorcycles are
included'[11]. Moreover, Rhys and Buxton[12] have shown
a positive correlation between car ownership levels
and mean household income per county and a negative
correlation between ownership levels and population
density per county. Low income families are therefore susceptible to 'reluctant' car ownership in
rural areas in contrast to their urban counterparts.

To a large extent high levels of vehicle ownership
reflect the ideal solution to the increasing distances and friction involved in access to rural
social resources. The car offers a flexible and
fast method of transport, to be preferred (all other
things being equal) to the more rigid access response
of public transport.

In two important respects, however, all other things
are not equal. The other side of the 80% car

ownership coin is a 20% level of non-car ownership.
Moreover the ownership of one car in a household
does not ensure access to the car for all members of
that household throughout the day (particularly if
the main wage earner uses the vehicle for a journey
to work). So, once source of inequality hidden within high rates of car ownership is differential access
to the car itself. Although many rural <u>households</u>
are in a position to purchase private accessibility
to shrinking resources through the ownership of at
least two vehicles, significant minorities of <u>indiv-
iduals</u> in rural areas might be termed 'non-mobile'
and thereby be subject to access deficiencies unless
other means of linking them with vital services and
activities are organised.

The second hidden inequality occurs in the inter-
relationships between private and public transport.
A viable hypothesis might suggest that these socially
uneven increases in car ownership tend to undermine
the provision of both public transport services and
other village services which become ever more costly
and unviable through lack of use.

British concerns over these forms of disadvantage to
minority groups are mirrored elsewhere in the developed world. For example Paaswell points out that in
the U.S. context 'Transportation must be conceived
as a public service, to be affordable by all.....
The largest group without access to the car are the
poor. Rising fares, declining public transportation
service, and increasing separation of both employment
and shipping from residence do not help them'.[13]
Heinze et al, in a Lower Saxony case study in Federal
Germany, conclude that'even more attention should be
paid to constitutional and social aspects of supply-
ing marginal groups with public transport, than has
been the case in the past'.[14]

<u>Affected Groups</u>. Social inaccessibility is experi-
enced by particular target groups, typically the
elderly, low income groups, housewives and young
people. Elderly groups are obvious consumers of
mobility deprivation in rural areas. For reasons of
health and low income the proportion of car-owning
elderly households tends to be low: it has been
calculated at around 30%[15] or 35%[16]. Moseley paints
an all-too-familiar picture of problems associated
with retirement:

an elderly couple in their sixties retire

to a rural area with a car and the money
to run it. Then inflation or the physical
disability or death of the driver robs the
couple, or the surviving member, of the use
of the car. Quite quickly what was an
attractive rural environment becomes a
liability and the house-price gradient
which originally attracted the couple from
their high-value urban or suburban home,
now inhibits their return or the return of
the surviving member. A social problem
ensues.[17]

Detailed studies in Britain have highlighted both
the difficulties experienced by the carless elderly
even when rural public transport is available[18], and
the isolation which results from being unable to
make or receive social visits which would be considered normal in urban environments.[19] In short, the
elderly are the most significant disadvantaged group
in the countryside and are the most frequent victims
of the conflicts which arise in the management of
access to rural resources.

Even disabled people, whose need for access in rural
areas appears paramount, are in one sense in a more
favoured position than the elderly because of special
mobility allowances offered by central and local
government.[20] However Gant and Smith's[21] study of
the elderly and disabled in the Cotswolds suggests
that deprivation has markedly differing impacts within these two generic groupings of rural population.

Rural housewives have also been identified as a group
susceptible to access problems. Surveys in East
Anglia[22] suggest that only 31% of housewives had a
car available for their use, and over half of these
women did not hold a current drivers licence. In
these cases the spatial concentration of pre-school
and primary education facilities, food stores and
health care facilities all present considerable
access problems to the economically inactive mother
reliant on public transport (such as it is) or on
usage of other people's private transport. Young
people, too, are similarly deprived of opportunities
for educational, cultural or social trips, especially
in the evenings and at weekends.

Inaccessibility in rural areas, then, is socially
divisive. Certain non-mobile groups (albeit minorities of the total population) are unable for various

reasons to buy their own accessibility through end-
less availability and usage of personal private
transport. Even where public transport is available,
the burdens of cost and inflexibility imposed upon
users may be such that accessibility is still not
achieved for individuals within these groups. It is
certainly the case that where public transport is
lacking, severe problems can ensue for the non-mobile
minority. Such variations in the public provision
of access suggest that spatial manifestations of inaccessibility also occur.

Spatial Inaccessibility

Conflicts over access to social resources in the
countryside have a spatial element, which results
from the distribution of public transport services.
Even within Britain, the pattern of services varies
considerably but the pattern of service deficiency
in FIGURE 10.2 is reasonably typical of many counties
encompassing remoter rural areas.

A special report on minimum levels of service for
rural public transport[23] suggests a revealing list
of potential responses to a situation of transport
service reductions:

- an increase in walking distances to transport
  services
- a greater dependence on obtaining lifts from
  those with cars
- a greater reliance on (more expensive) local
  and mobile facilities
- increases in car ownership, including the
  purchase of second cars by households
- loss of employment and reduced activity levels
- an increased sense of isolation amongst those
  living in rural communities
- increased migration out of rural areas by those
  without cars.

It would be a distortion of reality to ignore the
high incidence of adaptation in unserviced areas
through both a willingness to walk considerable distances and a highly complex series of lift-giving
and car-sharing strategies. Conversely it would be
unwise not to appreciate the significance of the
last three reactive options in this list, including
the forced out-migration of non-mobile and low income groups.

Two factors reduce the impact of spatial views of spatial inaccessibility in resource terms.

Topography and Isolation. First, the cross-cultural problems of comparing situations

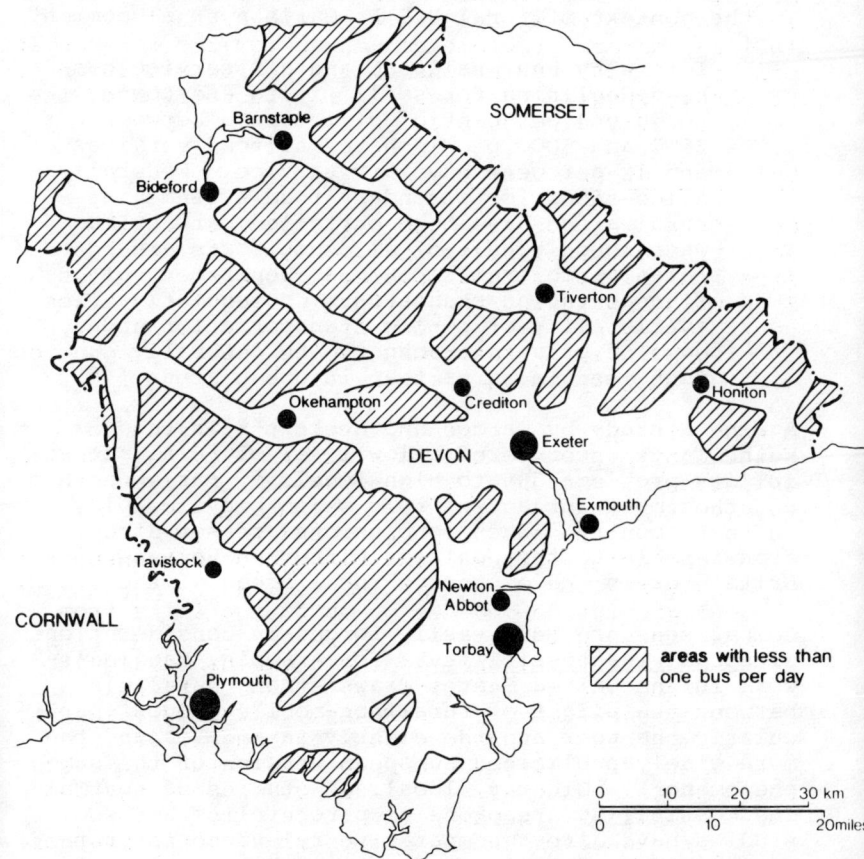

FIGURE 10.2   Devon County Council Transport Policies and Programmes

Source: after D. Awdas, 'Rural transport co-ordin-ation', in R. Cresswell (ed) Rural Transport and Country Planning (Leonard Hill, London, 1978).

even within the developed world are sigɪɪɪcantly

constrained both by physical topography and isolation and by policy-making perceptions. For example, the scale differences between the U.K. examples given above and the overview of transportation in rural U.S.A. are self-evident.

In the context of rural U.S.A., Carlson et al comment that:

> Intercity bus, railroad and air service has been declining for small cities and towns. Roughly 4 per cent of cities with between 2500 and 5000 people have railroad services and 12 per cent have air service. Federal allocations for secondary road systems in rural areas have been curtailed, at a time when roughly half of all such roads are rated 'intolerable' by U.S. Department of Transportation standards. Consequently availability of public transportation and ease of private transport are generally much less in rural than in urban areas.'[24].

Again, a study by Garden and Hoebert[25] in the Netherlands encountered a low level of rural access-ibility problems due to high levels of car ownership and the important access role which bicycles play in that country. Such conclusions are not directly transferable to the position either in upland Britain or in the expansive rural areas of the U.S.A.

Comparisons are more easily forged in considerations of social inaccessibility. For example, Maggied's[26] work in the United States draws strong parallels between the plight of rural non-mobile groups (parti-cularly the poor and the elderly in America and the more widely publicised European version of the same phenomenon). Clearly, localised studies of spatial inaccessibility are prone to parochialism but some studies have direct comparative relevance for rural researchers and policy-makers in other countries. One example is a study of Jefferson County in New York State, U.S.A.[27], which showed that 26.2 per cent of the population can be classified as 'trans-portation disadvantaged' (residents who cannot drive or do not have access to an automobile) and that these elderly, handicapped and low income groups form the focus for transport management policies.

Social Emphasis. A second factor which devalues studies of spatial accessibility is that they are but one element in the wider areas of concern arising

from a focus on disadvantaged social groups experi-
encing access deficiencies. Moseley[28] argues
strongly that an <u>area</u> focus for access studies is insufficient because of the wide variations in mobility
and access deprivation to be found side by side in
the same village. Similarly a <u>household</u> focus is
inadequate because of within - family variations.
Even if bus services exist, and by definition spatial
access is 'available', there are those groups who cannot afford to <u>use</u> these services. It is therefore
paramount that the management of access to rural
social resources takes account of social inaccessibility, over and above spatial inaccessibility.

10.2   MANAGEMENT RESPONSES TO SOCIAL ACCESS
       DIFFICULTIES

The accessibility difficulties noted above have been
widely publicised and tacitly accepted by the bureau-
cracies and political groups within government in
Britain.[29] Their collective response has been substantial, but has suffered from symptoms of gross
variation in the localised interpretation of management requirements.

First of all by regarding resources access defici-
ences as a 'rural transport problem', there has been
an assumption that solutions can be implemented
through which the 'problem' can be made to disappear.
Blowers argues that this perception has resulted in
'a tendency to focus on short term incremental
changes to the transport system to improve mobility,
rather than to pursue longer term strategies which
relate transport planning to rural development
policy to improve accessibility'.[30]

<u>Problems and Policy Responses</u>

The old-style keynotes of problems with transport
<u>capacity</u> and <u>finance</u> should according to this anal-
ysis, be overhauled with a recognition that the
'problem' is one of <u>access distribution</u>. Management
responses, therefore might be expected to tackle the
inflexibility of access supply to meet the scatter
and variety of access demand from rural people, particularly the non-mobile groups. Any such redirection
of response, however, will inevitably encounter inequalities between rural areas of inter-agency co-
ordination, historical circumstance and political
willingness to act.

To some extent, the progress exhibited by legislation and formal planning processes connected with
rural accessibility does give credence to this perceived drift of emphasis in management response.
David Banister's[31] very useful summary of policy
changes (TABLE 10.3) charts the steps which have
been taken to address rural transport 'problems'.
For example, the 1968 Act established a system of
50% grant aid for loss-making bus services and paved
the way for the use of school buses by the fare-
paying public. Legislation in 1972 required non-
metropolitan county councils to review their use of
transport subsidies and their objectives in meeting
the needs of rural residents in a yearly Transport
Policy and Programme (TPP). Section 203 of the Act
specifically stressed that county authorities should
provide 'a co-ordinated and efficient system of
public passenger transport to meet the county's needs'

The 1978 Act invited county councils to increase
their bids for central revenue in connection with
rural transport subsidy (only 50% of counties did
so, and almost all of these received high revenue).
It further strengthened written policy statements on
these issues by requiring of each county an annual
Public Passenger Transport Plan (PTP) in which 'needs'
and 'responses' were to be correlated. Finally (to
date) the 1980 Act's move to deregulate public transport services gave some flexibility to unconventional transport schemes.

Access Standards. This impressive list of central
policy responses appears to offer tremendous scope
for increasingly equitable and efficient management
of rural access conflicts. It is in the implementation of these measures, however, that considerable
spatial and political variations have occurred.
Much of this variation centres on a dilemma over
which level of government (central or local) should
lay down guidelines and minimum standards (if any)
for access provision. In a situation where rural
public transport is now expected to meet the 'needs'
of rural residents, the expression of these needs is
of crucial importance.

The view from some local authorities is predictably
straightforward. John Barrow, County Planning Officer for Oxfordshire, states that 'The application of
standards and the imposition of centrally derived
solutions must be avoided..... Planning must involve
finding new solutions concerned with matters of

TABLE 10.3   Principal Transport Policy Changes and their Impact on Rural Areas[31]

	Date	Recommendations and Actions
Jack Committee's Report on Rural Bus Services	1961	Selective direct financial assistance to unremunerative services
Beeching Report on the Re-shaping of British Railways	1963	Closure of 5000 km of rural railways
Series of surveys in six areas	1963	To examine the problems of and the demand for rural transport services
Transport Act	1968	System of direct grants with central government paying half where the services covered half its operating costs. Revenue grants to cover losses on un-remunerative rail services. National Bus Company set up. School service contracts could now exceed fare-paying passengers if there is excess capacity. Fuel tax rebates increased. New bus grants introduced. Concessionary fares.
Local Government Act	1972	Co-ordinating function for the county councils through the Transport Policies and Programmes. County Councils to administer the distribution of the Transport Supplementary Grant.
Passenger Vehicle (Experimental Areas) Act	1977	Relaxation of the licensing laws in certain areas so that innovative services could be introduced.
	1977	Rural Transport Experiments set up in four 'deep' rural areas.
Transport Act	1978	Country Public Transport Plans to co-ordinate passenger transport to meet the 'needs' of the public. Guidelines set for concessionary fares. Minibuses (8-16 seats) exempt from Public Service Vehicle Licences and Road Service Licences, provided that the drivers were from approved voluntary organisations. Traffic commissioners permitted to introduce short-term Road Service Licences. Car sharing allowed for payment.
Transport Act	1980	Major changes in bus licensing – deregulation. Small vehicles (fewer than 8 seats) no longer classified as Public Service Vehicles. Express services (min. journey length over 30 miles) no longer required Road Service Licences. Road Service Licences 'create a presumption in favour of the applicant'. Trial Areas can be designated where there are no Road Service Licences.

organisation and relationships; derived from political guidance and based on a philosophy of decentralising decisions where they are responsive to local initiatives and needs'[32] (our italics).

Yet other viewpoints from within local authorities suggest that localisation of standards in meeting rural transport needs is prone to the subjective political decisions of resource allocation at that level. Knight, for example, goes as far as to suggest that 'had the county councils been given a completely free hand in choosing between public transport and highways, the national rural public transport network would have suffered even further deprivations than it has in fact experienced'.[33]

Both of these viewpoints encompass part of the truth. The Oxfordshire 'localisation' attitude has in fact received a bad press. It has been portrayed as having made 'no real mention of "needs" in their PTP since local people are expected to identify their own particular transport problems and priorities.'[34] Oxfordshire has been branded as the county which organises and operates its bus services to the best practicable level without subsidy by the authority.[35]

A more sympathetic critique of the county's efforts, however, might stress that the reason for Oxfordshire's rejection of nationwide standards of rural transport is because it would stifle local initiative at the district and parish level.[36]

So, does a reluctance to adopt standards reflect a denigration of local authority duties by counties using a least-cost approach, or does it reveal a desire to prevent the blocking of grass roots initiatives? In real terms only evidence of the outcomes of such policies will decide between political tub-thumping and a desire to provide access in rural areas. It is certainly true that counties such as Cheshire[37] have managed to produce county-wide access standards; in the Cheshire case to the effect that all villages (note not residents) should be within one mile of a public transport service giving daily access to schools and weekly access to shops and hospitals.

Financial Viability. The recent trend is to vary standards within counties so that financial 'realism' can be accepted as a limiting factor on standards that can be adopted. It would seem, therefore, that

if the imposition of national standards imposes unacceptable or unwanted financial strains on individual counties by directing them to spend more on
rural transport than they otherwise would have done,
the counties will inevitably reply with a 'put up or
shut up' attitude towards central government financial aid in this area.

A very useful contribution to this debate has come
from the Peat, Marwick, Mitchell and Co. report on
minimum public transport service levels[38] which produced several revealing findings concerning the
attitudes of local authorities to access provision.
First, the report suggests that access management by
counties has suffered from tunnel-vision in that by
and large the emphasis has been on short-term mobil-
ity/transport relationships rather than on longer-
term and wider links between locational policies and
transport objectives in rural areas. Moreover, the
criteria for decision-making within this short-term
context also appear to leave something to be desired.
The report suggests that in many instances the decision on whether or not to provide financial support
for a particular bus service is largely a matter of
the political judgement of elected members or
officers.

Although apparently democratic, this approach if used
without the aid of decision criteria will inevitably
produce inconsistencies in decision-making. Where
such criteria are adopted, however, they often rely
on a minimum revenue/cost ratio and pay little heed
to the needs which are being catered for. Even in
situations where needs are taken into account, their
measurement tends to be in terms of the size of population which justifies services and not the structure
of that population in terms of non-mobile groups.

Although this situation has improved since this report's publication in 1977, the central issues of
access management remain largely unaltered. Provision should be based on the needs of non-mobile
groups; need should be carefully measured (using
relevant criteria) rather than nonchalantly judged;
and financial decisions to support access services
should not be left entirely to the free choice of
those whose ideological inclination is to spend as
little as possible on social provision for minorities.

With the inherent conservatism of most shire county
councillors, all three of these proposals appear

unlikely to be adopted and implemented. Yet it is
against this background of political decision-making
that management responses should be viewed.

Experimental Transport Schemes for Providing Access

FIGURE 10.3 shows the options available to policy-
makers who are searching for the means to improve
rural accessibility. As stressed throughout this
chapter, the traditional perception of planners has
been of a 'rural transport problem' and it is therefore not surprising that a 'rural transport solution'
has been the principal adopted option.

With the increasing urgency of expenditure reduction
by local authorities coupled with both the realisation that full access provision implies impossibly
high subsidies of stage bus services, and the natural
predilection of conservative councillors for the
'self-help' approach, the rural transport solution
has inevitably turned to the panacea of unconventional transport schemes. Even though some interest
groups insist that 'the country would miss the bus'[39],
interest has inexorably focussed on smaller vehicles
to meet the needs of rural access.

Experimental schemes have been detailed elsewhere[40]
and are summarised only in the barest outline here:

Commercial midibus/minibus. This type of scheme
comes closest to the conventional rural bus service,
the main difference being in the size of the vehicle
used by the operators. Smaller vehicles, such as
that utilised by the Huntingdonshire Area Midibus
Scheme, are manoeuvrable, inexpensive to purchase
and achieve good relative fuel economy. But they
incur high relative labour costs and they cannot be
used in situations where high peaks in demand are
experienced. If used conventionally on scheduled
services, they reflect most of the problems of larger
rural stage buses.

Demand Responsive Bus Services. One potential method
of overcoming the phenomenon of little used buses on
scheduled routes is to inject some form of demand -
responsiveness into services. Dial-a-ride services
have been prescribed in this context, whereby a door-
to-door service to fit the individual bus user's request might be initiated as in some urban areas in
Britain and North America.

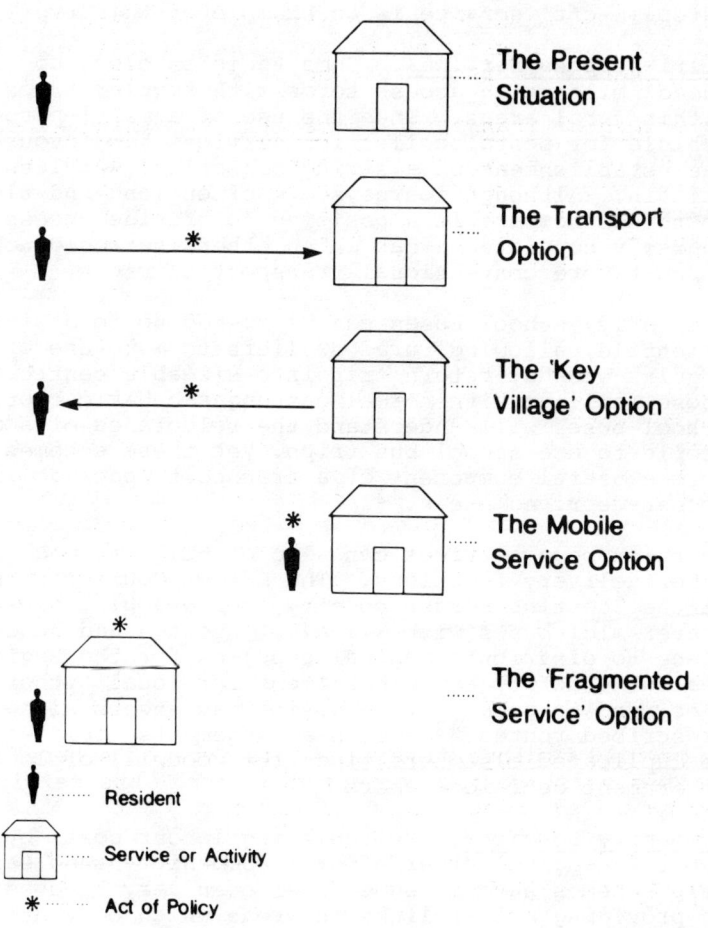

The Present
Situation

The Transport
Option

The 'Key
Village' Option

The Mobile
Service Option

The 'Fragmented
Service' Option

.... Resident

.... Service or Activity

* ...... Act of Policy

FIGURE 10.3 <u>The Rural Accessibility Policy Options</u>

Source: after M.J. Moseley, <u>Assessibility: The
          Rural Challenge</u> (Methuen, London, 1979): 116.

Dial-a-ride potential has not been fully tested in
rural areas, perhaps because of long journey times
and expensive control facilities inherent in the
scheme. There have, however, been experiments in
fixed route services into town but flexible routing
on the return journey to allow passengers to be
dropped off at their homes. The Hertfordshire

'drop-me-off' service is an example of this type.[41]

Multi-purpose Services. Some vehicles clock up
'dead' mileage in access terms with regular trips
within rural areas. Thus the use of a multi-purpose
vehicle for postal collection services has favoured
the establishment of a string of postbus services in
Britain. Although journeys are often long and slow,
postbuses now are in a position to provide access in
sparsely populated areas which otherwise would not
support more conventional transport services.

Similarly, school buses can be opened up to a wider
clientele, allowing rural dwellers to make use of a
regular weekday return trip into sizeable centre.
Those familiar with normal passenger behaviour on
school buses will understand the reluctance of some
people to use school bus trips, yet these schemes can
form a useful component of a transport 'package' for
access-deprived areas.[42]

Multi-purpose services can also be built around
other delivery functions. The Border Courier scheme
in the Scottish Border country, for example, uses 13
seater midi-buses with 3.1 m^3 of storage and goods
space to distribute medical supplies for the Regional
Health Authority and other items for local authorities, and to pick up fare paying passengers along
prescribed routes.[43] Such arrangements could well
be duplicated elsewhere given the goodwill of local
government decision-makers.

Community Services. By replacing labour costs by
substituting volunteer effort, community-based self-
help schemes have in some cases been very successful
in providing access links in areas which conventional
services fail to cater for. A range of vehicles have
been used in such schemes. In examples such as the
Coleridge Community Bus in the South Hams of Devon,
a community committee has been able to organise not
only the purchase of a minibus (often with substantial help from the local authority) but also the
training of a volunteer pool of local people as PSV-
tested drivers for the vehicle. With these resources
the community is able to run and administer its own
scheduled services into the local town.

More often, self-help is harnessed in the form of
voluntary car schemes in which a rota of local
drivers is drawn up by organisations such as the WI,
the WRVS and the Red Cross. Representatives of these

organisations act as central clearing-houses for non-mobile rural residents wishing to use one of the 'on duty' cars to make a particular trip.

As with all self-help projects, the distribution of expertise and enthusiasm in rural areas (prime factors in the initiation of these types of service) are un-evenly distributed, and so community self-help transport programmes have proved to be of partial but not universal benefit.

<u>Hire Services</u>. Rather than encumber themselves with the financial liability of purchasing community vehicles, some local groups have used commercially hired minibuses to operate typically a weekly shop-ping trip into a nearby town. The National Consumer Council[44] have earmarked these schemes as among the most successful of the unconventional range. More-over it has been suggested by Watts[45] that the use of shared hire-cars in rural areas can be as cost-effect-ive as any other means of unconventional transport. Once again, however, a high degree of administration and motivation is required to bring these potential schemes into viable operation.

The current situation of access management through unconventional transport schemes in Britain is one of relative stagnation after an exciting initial burst of activity. Some of the mechanisms above have been the subject of sporadic experimentation, while others (for example postbuses) have been adopt-ed more widely. Stagnation has come about because we are still in the stage of experiments which have not been co-ordinated into a comprehensive package of schemes for all rural areas with an access need.

<u>Rutex</u>. A significant step along that path was re-presented by the government-sponsored series of <u>rural transport experiments</u> (RUTEX) undertaken in four rural localities in Britain. In each study area an assessment of travel needs was made, and suitable sites and routes were identified for experimental schemes (TABLE 10.4). Moreover these schemes were implemented and co-ordinated by local working groups, with financial resources being made available where required, to underwrite RUTEX inspired innovations.

Many of the individual RUTEX projects have now been adopted as permanent facets of the local access net-work and their administration has been taken over by local groups. The idea of overall co-ordination,

323

TABLE 10.4 Basis of four RUTEX schemes in rural Britain[46]

DEVON STUDY AREA (four schemes)

(i) Shared hire-cars operating feeder services to local
        centres, to longer distance bus services and to the
        Exeter-Barnstaple railway.
(ii)   A feeder service using private cars authorised to charge
        fares.
(iii)   A community minibus, driven by full-trained volunteers.
(iv)   A special zone designated under the Experimental Areas
        Bill where motorists would be authorised to make private
        arrangements to give lifts for payment on a regular
        basis provided there was no public advertisement.

NORTH YORKSHIRE STUDY AREA (five schemes)

(i) A variable-route, prebookable, professionally driven bus
        service providing garden-gate pick-up and set-down
        facilities for people.
(ii)   A shared hire-car service taking people into the town of
        Masham for shopping, business and bus connections.
(iii)   A hospital transport scheme to provide a way for those
        in remote places to get to hospitals in Northallerton.
(iv)   A scheme using private cars authorised to charge fares,
        giving easier access to facilities in Old Catterick and
        Bedale, and access to long-distance coaches at Leeming Bar
(v)   Another private car scheme, serving four parishes to the
        north west of Northallerton.

SCOTTISH STUDY AREA (four schemes)

(i) A hospital transport scheme giving representative rural
        zones of South Ayrshire a direct link to five major
        hospitals.
(ii)   A shared hire-car service, serving a sparsely populated
        area for shopping, business and bus connections.
(iii)   A link between Dalmellington and Cumnock to give better
        access facilities in the two terminal towns.
(iv)   A variable-route professionally driven minibus providing
        connections with longer distance buses and linked with
        a post bus route.

WELSH STUDY AREA (three schemes)

(i) A scheme involving private cars authorised to charge fares
(ii)   A voluntary emergency car service, operating throughout th
        study area, to meet urgent transport needs (eg hospital
        visits) for people who have no other means of transport.
(iii)   A post bus system.

however, lapsed as the experiments came to a close,
and the RUTEX programme has been valuable in highlighting both the potential benefits to be gained
from co-ordinated access schemes, and the inevitable
patchiness of initiative when co-ordination is absent.

Co-ordination. The situation is thus one of a wealth
of ideas (many successfully experimented with) but
no universal drive to administer and finance a co-
ordinated set of schemes in all rural areas. Two
main approaches are currently being pursued to trans-
cend this stagnant state involving co-ordination by
local authorities and central government.

The co-ordinating role of local authorities has been
pioneered by East Sussex County Council in their
study of the Lewes area.[47] The aim of this study was
to integrate together all transport elements (conventional and unconventional) into a satisfactory
overall framework - 'satisfactory' being defined as
'one that is realistic to the practical world'.[48]
The adopted methodology is outlined in FIGURE 10.4.
The study claims to have formulated a basis for
identifying both the needs which are unfulfilled
because of gaps in the conventional bus network, and
various methods of providing for these needs:

> practicable alternatives for each situation
> must be examined and specifically costed.
> The county council would generally have to
> provide financial support for such provision
> and this can be assessed in forms of £ per
> trip for the need categories concerned[49].

This latter commitment to funding is important, because it begins to suggest that the dual criteria of
administrative co-ordination and finance might be
met (if only partially) under the auspices of county
councils.

The second approach to the problem of co-ordination
is for central government to institute a permanent
co-ordination initiative at the local level.
Moseley is critical of the restricted role available
to Transport Co-ordinating Officers employed by
county councils whose work (often through no fault
of the individual) 'tends to be passive and piecemeal
in that they tend to respond to proposed service
modifications and to try to co-ordinate timetables
rather than to devise and implement a comprehensive
strategy'.[50]

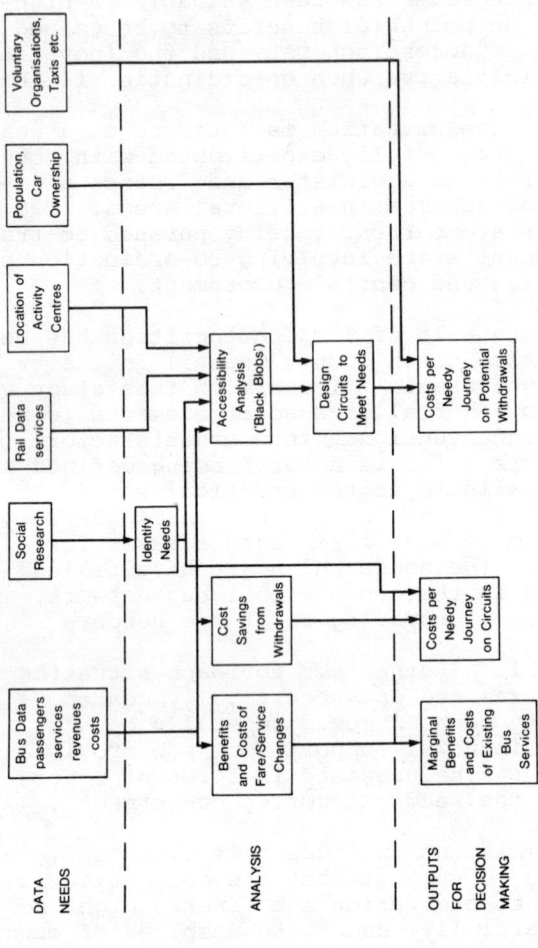

FIGURE 10.4 Methodology Adopted in the East Sussex County Council Transport Study

Source: after G. Searle, Co-ordinating Public Transport in Rural Counties – Summary of the Lewes Study Approach (Department of Transport, London, 1982): 8.

A clearer emphasis on access rather than transport from central government would make the local officers' task less restricted and more rewarding in terms of rural community benefit. Whether inside or outside the local authority bureaucracy, a rural access co-ordinator in each rural area, and sponsored by central state funding, might be in a better position to achieve this access management required in rural areas.

In the United States, for example, the <u>Federal Surface Transportation Assistance Act</u> of 1978 set up the so-called 'Section 18 Program', which:

(i) designates a Section 18 Co-ordinator in each non-urbanised county whose task it is; to be·· come familiar with the county's transportation needs and resources; to prepare a Service Plan for new access schemes; to act as local contact person both with rural residents (particularly the non-mobile in need of assistance from the scheme) and with the State Department of Transportation; and to co-ordinate the selection and utilisation of Section 18 funds in the county.

(ii) allocates grant aid for both capital and oper-ating assistance for the acquisition or oper-ation of buses, vans, and other equipment need-ed for transport operations. The program covers 80% of the cost of capital facilities and vehicle acquisition and 50% of net operat-ing deficit, the residual to come from non-federal sources.

The Section 18 Program clearly demonstrates that central government initiative can be crucial in the establishment of co-ordination and finance for local rural access schemes.

A cautionary note should be sounded before moving on to non-transport schemes for providing access. Even if local management, co-ordination and finance is established for a comprehensive package of rural access, rural people still have to be convinced of the worth of the exercise. The Development Board for Rural Wales (now Mid Wales Development) recently offered financial and administrative aid to any com-munity council within its area for the establishment of a community minibus service. Despite the gener-osity of the offer, and wide advocacy on the part of the Board, not one council took up the offer.

Unconventional access schemes are not universal; they need to be carefully tailored to the needs and aspirations of local non-mobile groups; and perhaps they need to be imposed over the apathy of the majority of residents for the sake of the non-mobile minority.

Non-Transport Schemes for Providing Access

Brief mention should be made of other options for the management of access which deal with the 'person' and 'activity' factors in the person-link-activity equation. Figure 10.3 outlines the various combinations of resource allocation and access management which might be directed towards increasing the access of non-mobile groups.

Resource Concentration. One way of approaching the conflicts inherent in rural access is to work towards a rationalisation of the rural settlement pattern so that people and activities can be channelled into planned 'resource centres'. This theme has been detailed elsewhere[51], but it is clear that post-war planning in Britain has been directed towards the establishment of so-called 'key settlements' wherein the development of new housing and employment is matched with statutory and private sector service provision.

It is equally clear that this policy trend has emerged because local authorities have sought a strategy which offers administrative pragmatism and economic expediency, rather than because of a deliberate and well planned attempt to improve rural access for non-mobile groups. Indeed, one of the marked failings of key settlement strategies is that they have focussed their concentration on building up the key settlements themselves to the exclusion of ensuring that access links between hinterland villages and the planned centre are provided as an integral part of the key settlement policy.

Nevertheless, the structure plan policies pertaining to rural areas continue to reflect a belief in the long-term goal of settlement rationalisation[52], and the overwhelming majority of professional planners in Britain recognise this policy mechanism as being the most efficient and (in the long term) beneficial strategy for improving rural living conditions. The

widely-believed inevitability of this approach is
reinforced by reviews of similar policies in western
and eastern Europe, and other parts of the developed
world, where despite widely differing scales of rural
area and types of political economy, a basic predilection for rural resource concentration prevails.[53]

Resource Dispersal. The reverse of resource concentration - broadly but often in an ill-defined manner
termed 'resource dispersal'[54] - suggests an option of
taking the services and activities to the people in
rural areas. In fact this is not one option, but
several.

It has been argued[55] that every rural settlement
should have as of right a basic group of services
including a shop/post office, a school, a pub and a
regular public transport service. This list of
seemingly 'essential' services in each settlement
has shrunk from those optimistically presented in the
post-war development plan manifestos which would
have included a doctors surgery, a church, local
employment and even possibly a chemist as essential
items.

The fact that the common perception of just what is
an essential in situ service seems to have shrunk
has been interpreted in two ways: First, as a signal
of increasingly general recognition that resource
dispersal on a wide scale is totally impracticable
given current levels of financial resources in rural
areas; and, second, that traditional means of dis-
persing services in permanent fixed buildings with
a profit-making rationale are indeed impracticable,
but that a similar result may be achieved through
other means.

Two 'unconventional' programmes for resource dispersal have been openly discussed over the last few
years involving mobile services and information
technology.

The idea of mobile services is not a new one, but
has conventionally been restricted to the retail
sector in Britain as a whole, although rural Scotland
also has a tradition of mobile banks. Given the
dual management resources of finance and administration (mentioned above) it would be reasonable to
endorse Moseley's plea for a weekly market of mobile
services for each rural community. A range of
services and facilities - post office (with its

banking, pension and social security roles), doctor, dentist, information centre, shops, professional services, playbus and so on - might thus be congregated within reach of non-mobile groups on a regular basis. Moreover, this access to services might be enhanced by the increased use of peripatetic doctors, teachers, clergy and other important personnel.

The role of the postman has been one fruitful area of experimentation in this field:

> As perhaps the last public persons to operate on a wide scale in the rural areas and being in regular contact with the whole community, they can serve as a lifeline between the housebound and the world at large. They can inform the appropriate authorities when needs develop, provide a small-scale door-to-door post office, collect and deliver pensions, collect prescriptions and deliver medicines and in extreme circumstances take emergency action.[57]

There are already over 150 schemes whereby rural postmen and postwomen will respond to a special card in the window of a householder who needs help of some kind.

The second 'unconventional' means of achieving resource dispersal is through the widespread use of information technology. Already, shopping-by-computer experiments are commonplace in urban areas, and given sufficient initiative and financial and administrative support, rural areas would appear to be fertile ground for the use of machine access. The village shop, for example, could become a kind of local resource centre where a terminal could be placed giving local residents direct access to wholesale distribution centres for food and other items. The shop would also act as a receiving centre for the delivery of ordered goods, which would then be collected by the customer. It has even been suggested that computer diagnosis of illness (it works on Volkswagens so why not on people!) is a practicable proposition, and the role of information technology in education programmes, information access and so on, is obvious.

Neither the mobile service market, nor the information technology system of distribution have been subject to the kind of experimentation which has

been levelled at unconventional transport services.
As yet the 'easy option' (or perhaps the least
expensive) has been to redistribute transport subsidies into low-cost and politically high-profile
and safe schemes connected with vehicles. Nevertheless there does appear to be significant scope for
the improvement of rural access through the mobili-
sation of services and facilities in one way or
another.

Distributional Implications. The conflicts inherent
in providing access to social resources in rural
areas can be ameliorated by positive forms of planning, including a sympathetic distribution of finance and administrative capability. It is paramount,
however, that the distributive nature of these amel-
iorations is understood and accounted for in the
resource allocation process.

For example, even if a package of unconventional
transport schemes is established in a well co-ordinated programme for all rural areas (something which
at present seems unlikely to occur) it should be
remembered that the use of transport incurs payment
of fares and that low income groups may have difficulty in using the access provided. In short, just
because a service is provided it should not be assumed that all population groups will automatically be
able to use it. Similarly, information technology
schemes might require input points such as telephones,
televisions and special attachments all of which are
least likely to be afforded by the most disadvantaged
groups in rural society.

Such possible outcomes could mean that unless use is
made of income redistribution or access/mobility
allowances to rectify these positions of disadvantage,
solving one set of conflicts concerned with access to
rural resources might only lead to the exacerbation
of existing conflicts within the primary rural social
resource - that is rural people. They might even
result in a series of new conflicts as the disadvantaged become more isolated in their ability to make
use of seemingly 'problem-solving' resource management techniques.

10.3 ACCESS AND LANDSCAPE RESOURCES

Strong parallels exist between the conflicts arising
from inaccessibility to social resources and those
relating to inaccessibility to landscape resources.

Although no conclusive proof has been found of a direct relationship between access to countryside recreation and high levels of mental health (the reverse has, however been strongly suggested[58]), it would appear a reasonable socio-political require-ment that such access should be made available to all those who require it. As with the question of social access, considerable shortfalls occur between this hypothetical requirement and the actual manage-ment of landscape resources.

Access to Landscape

Access to landscape resources occurs at two scales - to the countryside, and within the countryside. Of relatively minor although increasingly significant importance is the issue of journeys from urban resi-dential areas to rural recreation areas (see Chapter 7.2). Cracknell[59] has suggested that the location of metropolitan residential growth in Britain should take account of the ease of access to the countryside for the increasingly numerous urban residents. This explicit recognition of access problems has never been seriously taken up by urban planners, and indeed the expanding motorway networks have been seen as a considerable amelioration of any access deficiency.[60]

Moreover, with recent trends towards a return migr-ation to rural areas by population groups seeking an ex-urban lifestyle (see Chapter 1.4) it might appear that the requirement of equal access to rural land-scape resources has been achieved. Some families' acccess is, however, more equal than others in that the costs of car ownership or long journeys by public transport still effectively preclude certain of the disadvantaged groups discussed above from regular utilisation of prime landscape resources for sustain-ed recreation.

Following the general (if false) assumption that everyone is capable of getting to rural landscapes, much more management attention has been focussed on opening up access within the countryside. To a great extent, provision of access for recreation has been granted as a secondary objective to the desig-nation of high-value areas for landscape conservation (see Chapter 4). Some newly developing nations such as South Africa and parts of Asia have followed the American model of setting aside vast tracts of un-developed land which would be publicly owned and rig-idly protected.[61] Such designated areas of

'wilderness' tend to fence in extensive roadless
zones and so public access provision has been built
on minimal infrastructural foundations and favours
the hardy and athletic recreationalist keen both on
walking, and a prolonged exposure to the outdoor
life (see Chapter 4.4 and Chapter 7.2). Elsewhere,
for example in England and Wales and other European
nations, protected areas have remained in private
ownership and agricultural and forestry enterprises
have continued to mould the 'protected' landscape.

In England and Wales, the 1949 National Parks and
Access to the Countryside Act made only limited
funds available for recreational facilities, despite
the grandiose nature of its title. It did, however,
make it possible to secure general access for recreation to open country and it also led to a cataloguing of existing public rights of way. Marion
Shoard[62] has argued that access powers accruing from
the 1949 Act and the 1968 Countryside Act in England
and Wales have been little applied and often ill-
understood.

Although local authorities are empowered to make
open country available to public access, the definition of 'open country' specifically excludes the
majority of rural land, for example:

(a)   agricultural land, except rough grazing land
(b)   nature reserves
(c)   land covered by buildings
(d)   parks, gardens and pleasure grounds
(e)   quarries, railway land, golf courses, race-
       courses and aerodromes
(f)   land covered by works used for a statutory
       undertaking
(g)   land which is being developed
(h)   land to which common land legislation applies.

Access Agreements. In permitted 'open country' areas
local authorities can make agreements with landowners to ensure that the public can wander freely
over that land - a much more flexible arrangement
than with footpath right of way which does not grant
the public any right to linger on the path during
their permitted journeys to and fro. Where agreement
is not forthcoming, the authorities can make an order
and in the last resort may secure access through
compulsory purchase. All of these actions entail
compensation payments to landowners, and authorities
in turn may be reimbursed to the tune of 75% by the

Countryside Commission.

For various political and financial reasons, the access agreement mechanism in Britain has been less than fully successful. Gibbs and Whitby[63] found that up to 1973 only 98 access areas covering 353km^2 had been developed, with 80% of these being within national parks, and 56% within one park - the Peak District. MacEwen and MacEwen note

> The consequence of this limited use of
> the Act was .....to save public money,
> to exacerbate conflicts with landowners
> and farmers and to diminish the role of
> the national park authorities. For it
> was only in these access areas that the
> authorities could provide wardens to help
> visitors, repair damage, make byelaws
> about behaviour, or pay compensation.
> The 1949 Act enabled the NPAs to duck the
> job of managing the open country in the
> interests of all its users.[64]

Access by footpath, however, with the long history of pressure group activity in its favour, is now highly developed to the extent that footpaths exist in Britain in greater number than anywhere in the world; with a network of well over 190,000 km[65].

Access Disadvantage

This combination of plentiful access <u>routes</u> but restricted numbers of access <u>zones</u> in the rural landscape was important during the leisure boom starting in the early 1950's, because the greatly increased recreational pressures on the countryside were channelled towards areas which either were perceived as being of high landscape quality or as having a well-defined recreational role. As a result, the idea that recreational use of rural landscape resources was a <u>problem</u> became ensconced in the minds of managers and decision-makers.

It is undoubtedly true that in some cases, an excess of recreational traffic[66] and people[67] did prove problematic in terms of congestion and over-use of physical resources in the countryside (see Chapter 7.3). It is equally valid to suggest, however, that (as is often the case in establishing parameters for resource management when the specific is easily translated into the universal) specific instances of

conflict between landscape resource access and landscape resources themselves became viewed in the
decision-making psyche as universal.

As a consequence, a general solution of reducing
access was sought to this perceived problem. Marion
Shoard argues that 'public bodies have tended to
dissuade people from making trips into the most
beautiful areas of our countryside: they have sought
to protect the countryside and rural interests from
townspeople rather than open it up to them for their
enjoyment'.[68]

<u>Access Apartheid</u>. Acknowledging the danger of falsely
universal conclusions (as mentioned above) there
does nevertheless appear to have been a general tendency towards restricting recreational use of countryside resources so that conservation objectives can be
achieved. Once again, however, the deliberate denial
of access, or the tacit acceptance of landowner
rights and privileges (which often amounts to the
same conclusion) does result in distributional consequences.

Just as lack of access to social resources caused
disproportionate disbenefits to groups of non-mobile
populations in rural areas, so lack of access to
landscape resources also allocates disadvantage
unevenly. Shoard[69] labels this phenomenon as <u>access</u>
<u>apartheid</u>, and highlights the fact that important
potential areas for recreational access - woods and
parks used for the rearing and shooting of pheasant,
and rivers, streams and lakes used solely for angling
- are currently the reserve of the nobility and
gentry alone.

Underlying the accusation of access apartheid is the
realisation that many rural local authorities are
dominated by landowners and others with conservative
viewpoints who would thus be likely to proliferate
existing access inequalities by mirroring the concerns of the farmer and conservationist rather than
those of the recreationalist. Access disadvantage
occurs, however, in a wider fashion than the woods
and rivers issue suggests.

If opened up areas of countryside are difficult to
get to, either in terms of distance and cost or in
terms of other impediments such as the imposition
of a long walk rather than providing transport-home
access to a site of scenic beauty, then particular

groups like low income groups and the elderly and
the handicapped will receive disproportionate disadvantage. The conflicts relating to managing access
to landscape resources are therefore both crucial to
the fulfilment of welfare criteria in resource management, and closely parallel to those identified in the
case of access to social resources.

One further conflict serves to complicate the issue
of landscape access. By restricting access, decision-
makers not only limit the distributive nature of access benefits amongst urban populations, but they
also serve to tamper with the life-styles of those
rural residents who depend on a substantial contribution from tourism and recreation to the local
rural economy. This dilemma serves only to re-em-
phasise the importance of a proper balance between
permitting and restricting access to areas of
countryside (see Chapter 7).

Access Policies in National Parks

The resource base which is represented by rural
landscapes was described in Chapter 4. It is worthwhile at this juncture, however, to review the attitudes towards access of decision-makers in argu-
ably the most environment-conscious and recreation-
ally magnetic areas of the countryside: namely the
national parks. These vulnerable yet environmentally (and to some extent administratively) elite
areas highlight both the problems of access management and the potentially innovative resolutions of
these problems.

Once again it should be stressed that management
strategies in national parks worldwide are entirely
subject to the political climate and will of decision-
making in both the national and local state. A case
in point is that of Alaska's national parks, where
the passage of the Alaska National Interest Lands
Conservation Act by the US Congress in 1980, granted
'permanent' protection to $417 \times 10^3 km^2$ land (including five new national parks).[70] The change of
central administration to that heeded by President
Reagan has, however, been marked with an increased
emphasis on the development of oil and gas in Alaska
and so the previous 'permanent' protection is already
being eroded by legislation to reduce the size of
areas covered by the 1980 Act.

Political conflicts between conservation and mineral

resource use have tended to squeeze out any demands for large-scale recreational access in American national parks. Simmons notes that 'many NPs..... are, gradually, to be reorganised so that developed areas for visitor's needs are to be at the edge of or outside the park; the possibility of banning cars and using shuttle minibuses or other public transport has also been studied.'[71]

If the vast state-owned national parks to be found in the USA and elsewhere (for example New Zealand) have been founded on the principle of access restriction, the very different context of the UK parks, which are predominantly privately owned and are criss-crossed with public highways, has sponsored a more obvious management dilemma. Dennier[72] pinpoints this conflict by demonstrating that while 'Sandford and the Government have given conservation the edge over recreation' it is still the case that 'visitors continue to flock to the Parks in search of both informal and active recreation.'[73] Access deprivation in English and Welsh national parks is thus brought about by partial exclusion techniques.

In their analysis of national parks in England and Wales, MacEwen and MacEwen outline three main arms of a general recreation strategy:[74]

Management schemes for honeypot areas. The aim here is to channel the car-borne hordes of recreation-seekers into locations of mass attraction, where adequate facilities, such as car parking, toilets, picnic sites and information services, can be provided. A dual motive underlies this arm of the strategy. Well-organised honeypots not only round visitors up into 'manageable' and robust sites, but also serve to attract pressure away from more vulnerable locations.

The use of Craig-y-Nos country park in the Brecon Beacons for this purpose (see Chapter 7.1) is an example of this dual role in reasonably effective operation.[75] The question here is whether sections of the recreational public are being unknowingly duped into visiting sites given the official blessing of national park authorities, or whether they would in any case seek out such sites as being the ones where maximum enjoyment value can be achieved. On the answer to this as yet unanswered question lies the moral burden of access restriction.

Protection of remote and fragile areas. By various
means (such as carefully structured countryside interpretation strategies)(see Chapter 7.6), restricting roadside parking or use of some roads (see
Chapter 7.3) and not improving access to particular
sites (except perhaps via a long walk), authorities
have sought to preserve the remoteness and the resource
quality of sensitive landscape areas. There is an
inherent judgement here that particular zones can
only be conserved by discouraging their recreational
use and thus restricting their accessibility to most
age and fitness groups.

Indeed there have been moves, beginning with the
Countryside Review Committee's proposals in the
1960's, to ensure much stricter preservation of the
remote heathlands within national parks - in effect
creating parks within parks. Tinker's[76] proposal
for super-elite 'wilderness areas' was taken up by
the 1974 Sandford Committee which recommended the
establishment of 'national heritage areas' in national parks, where access by vehicle would be strictly
limited. In short:

> It seems a general trend which will become
> ever more apparent in the next decade, that
> identification of the vulnerable places,
> be they scenic, cultural or biotic, is
> going to occur and that as their true value
> is realised, most civilised nations will
> not stop at some form of rationing of
> visitor numbers in order to ensure the un-
> impaired perpetuation of the resource.[77]

Once again, the acceptability of this genre of
resource management is dependent on the degree to
which restricted access can be translated as access
apartheid whereby groups with impaired mobility or
low-level socio-economic accessibility characteristics
are debarred from elite landscape resources.

Integrated management of recreation, traffic and
public transport. The objective of this third
strategic policy is to attempt a channelling of
recreation traffic onto suitable roads in suitable
areas, and to transfer some accessibility to recreation sites from private behicles to public transport
services. The Goyt Valley Scheme in the Peak
District National Park (Chapter 7.3) is a typical
example.

It is suggested in the British case that such
measures have been more effective as a publicity
exercise than in practice[78], although any failure is
due less to a lack of enthusiasm on the part of park
planners than to the lack of power and finance for
access projects and the severe difficulties encountered in separating the British public from their cars.

Faced with this three-pronged strategy, it is the
proportion of effort and priority allocated to each
element that is all-important in evaluating policies
in access terms. Two examples from national park
plans serve to illustrate the relative priorities
currently adopted by park authorities.

The Dartmoor Plan. The Dartmoor plan[79] isolates
seven landscape resource types, each with its own
management objectives (TABLE 10.5).

TABLE 10.5 Landscape Resource Types Adopted in the Dartmoor
National Park Plan[79]

I   Towns and Villages: to accept appropriate settlements
       as 'visitor service centres', but to maintain visitor
       access and car parking so as to maintain the initial
       attraction and diminish impact upon the community itself.

II   Fringe Farmland: to maintain and improve the footpath
       net, and channel visitors to appropriate enclaves of
       woodland and heath so as to diminish the effect upon
       farming efficiency; otherwise to discourage intensive
       recreational use.

III   Moorland/Valley Farmland Mix: to maintain the apparent
       logic of the relationship of man to landscape here, and
       accept and encourage the concentration of recreational
       activity to appropriate sites; to manage such sites
       positively.

IV   High Farmland: to recognise a low capacity for recrea-
       tion, and discourage any intensive recreational use.

V   High Moorland: to recognise the rarity of the experi-
       ence offered here, to protect it and its availability,
       to encourage informal use on foot, and discourage
       vehicles; to monitor, and if necessary control, the
       level of use in remote parts of this landscape type.

VI   Major Wooded Valleys: to investigate the potential for
       raising the level of use within the capacity of the tree

cover to conceal it from outside, bearing in mind the
constraints of nature conservation, potential erosion
of surface, vandalism and woodland management.

VII   Major Conifer Plantations: to investigate the potential
       for increasing recreational use within the constraints
       of forest and water management.

FIGURE 4.3 shows the landscape mosaic of these land-use categories within the Dartmoor National Park.

The access related policies stand out sharply:
  I   to manipulate visitor access

  II   channel visitors to appropriate enclaves.....
       otherwise to discourage intensive recreational
       use

  III accept and encourage the concentration of
       recreational activity

  IV   to discourage any intensive recreational use

  V   to encourage informal use on foot and dis-
       courage motor vehicles

  VI   potential raising of use within capacity

  VII potential increasing of use within constraints.

An idea of the relative spatial distribution of dis-
couragement and encouragement of access is given by
FIGURE 10.5 which highlights the degree of honeypot
strategy adopted in the national park plan (see also
Figure 4.3). As if to reinforce the point, TABLE
10.6 demonstrates the park authority's management
targets for immediate action (listed in terms of
priority). First and second in priority in the list
are the strategies of concentrating recreation
into heavily used sites, and reducing access on high
moorland which to most visitors typifies the landscape resources of Dartmoor National Park. The
authority concedes that 'other needs will require
action' (perhaps special access provision for disadvantaged groups or even to the general public to
a wider variety of resource types are relevant here?)
but it stresses that 'the emphasis in a climate of
severely limited resources must be on the central
themes of re-locating demand into appropriate areas
and sites, and managing that demand to achieve a
National Park which is as tidy, enjoyable and uncontentious as possible.'[80]

Given the political and administrative complexities

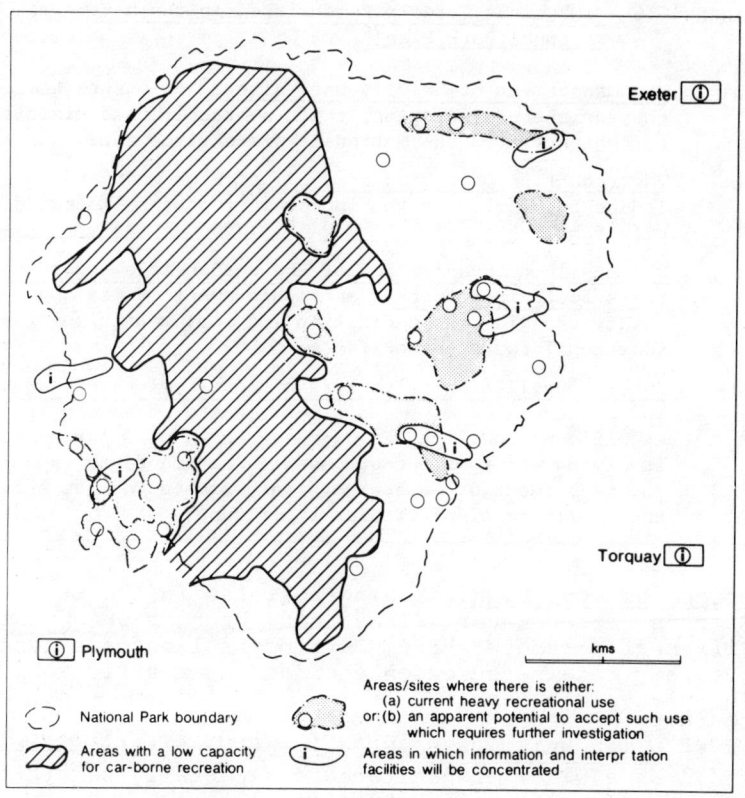

FIGURE 10.5 <u>Dartmoor National Park Plan - Proposed</u>
<u>Strategy for Recreation and Information</u>

Source: after Dartmoor National Park Authority,
          <u>Dartmoor National Park Plan</u> (Exeter, Dart-
          moor National Park Authority, 1977):   38.

inherent in the organisation of national park authorities and the implementation of their policies,
perhaps the issue of <u>access apartheid</u> may be deemed
as 'uncontentious' although a resource management
approach attaching significant weight to social
resources leads directly to a questionning of that
judgement.

TABLE 10.6   Management Targets Established in the Dartmoor
              National Park Plan[79]

(a)   The management of heavily-used sites: to ensure that
       they neither deteriorate, their attractiveness diminish,
       nor detract from the National Park environment.

(b)   The reduction of vehicular use: of High Moorland
       landscape, including the improvement of the 'moorgate'
       situation.

(c)   The sensible organisation of the road/bridleway/green
       track/footpath network: and achievement of its appro-
       priate use (ie. the definition and implementation of a
       functional route network).

(d)   The reconciliation of factors of access, local interest
       and conservation at other sites: where these are in
       significant conflict. Management and Access Agreements
       involving works on the ground will be necessary, and
       the management of waterside sites which do not come under
       above will be of particular importance.

Brecon Beacons Plan. Zoning policies in the Brecon
Beacons National Park Plan[81] have been drawn up using
different parameters from Dartmoor's landscape types,
but they retain the essence of access restriction.
The plan nominates:

(i) vulnerable areas where remote qualities or value
       as a wildlife habitat are especially sensitive
       to increases in recreational use,

(ii) pressure areas where an increase in recreation-
       al use is likely to make seriously worse exist-
       ing problems, and

(iii) zones of special management opportunity where
       there is either an immediate need to relieve
       existing problems such as those faced by
       pressure areas, or where a situation is favour-
       able for the development of new or improved
       facilities.

Again, policy priorities are important in assessing
the access ramifications of these strategies. The
plan makes clear that there is a presumption against
any developments which would increase visitor pressure in vulnerable or pressure areas,[82] and that
designation of zones of special management opportunity does not necessarily imply an intensification of
recreation activity. It should be stressed that the

Brecon Beacons is noted as one of the more accessible national park locations where remote landscape qualities may be enjoyed, at least by car-borne visitors. Nevertheless the main tenor of management policies suggests that these access opportunities are certainly not advertised (and could be said to be disguised) in the information and interpretative services offered by the park authority, so as to channel visitor pressure into acceptable sites.

As in all the national parks, these manipulations of perceived access opportunities for recreationalists are not adequately counterbalanced by specific access provision schemes either into high quality but restricted sites, or more generally for disadvantaged population groups. It would seem that the third of the three strategic arms of recreation management - the integrated management of recreation, traffic and public transport - receives the least priority within national park plans. Although it is common for a road hierarchy such as that for the Brecon Beacons (TABLE 10.7) to be established, these classifications tend more towards access restriction than provision. Moreover, although authorities have been energetic and innovative in their study of potential public transport schemes within national parks, the cost of subsidies and the inter-organisational difficulties of implementation have prevented a widespread take-up of this access option. As with rural planning in general, it is far easier to operate a control function than to attract financial resources and co-ordinate decision-making agencies so as to bring about a more positive form of planning and management.

Two major inconsistencies are highlighted in the access policies to be found within national park plans. First, access provision is tied to two societal groups - the car-borne visitor in honeypot areas, and the physically fit and energetic long-distance walker in more remote areas. There is, however, considerable evidence to suggest that a large and growing middle group exists which requires greater access to landscape resources outside honeypot locations.[84] Second, recreational use of park zones is usually limited to its capacity whereby the quality of landscape resources is not impaired (ie. the environmental carrying capacity - see Chapter 7.2). This tendency is contradicted by the fact that most remoter zones within park designations are restricted to a very low level of recreation activity, despite the fact that their carrying capacity might

TABLE 10.7 <u>Brecon Beacons National Park Road Hierarchy</u>[81]

Road Category	Function
Strategic Roads	To accommodate movement of national/ regional traffic between main manufacturing and consuming centres, conurbations and holiday areas of Wales.
National Park Primary Roads	Lying mainly within the National Park these roads serve as good scenic routes for recreational traffic and connect: - larger, more important settlements within (or just outside) the National Park, - strategic routes - tourist centres.
National Park Secondary Roads	To carry recreation traffic to specific destinations or along scenic routes and/or act as local distributors.
National Park Minor Roads	Provide access to farms, dwellings and small settlements. In practice some of these roads carry a certain amount of recreational traffic.
Restricted Roads and Tracks (R.U.P.P.s and/ or 'green lanes')	For mainly foot or bridleway use, but where motor vehicle rights of way exist or are alleged to exist.

indicate potential for increased use without spoilation of the resource.

MacEwen and MacEwen point the way to a more equitable
form of access management:

> Improved access, restraints on the private
> car, the promotion of shared forms of trans-
> port and the provision of inexpensive
> accommodation would have a double pay-off.
> If combined with social policies to benefit
> those who are disadvantaged socially and
> geographically it would encourage the active
> enjoyment of 'the living landscape behind
> the new', particularly for those who have
> no ready access to cars[85]

It is to these types of management tools that attention is now turned.

10.4 IMPROVING ACCESS TO LANDSCAPE RESOURCES

Any critique of discriminatory access policies should be set alongside those positive attempts to improve access provision in countryside areas. These schemes relate to access within landscapes, and access for non-mobile groups.

Access Within Landscapes

The relative paucity of negotiated access agreements, particularly outside the national parks was identified in Section 10.3 Yet increased success in providing for such agreements remains one important target for access management policies. Within the national parks, some emphasis is placed on extending the area of landscape covered by agreements, but authorities such as the Peak District Board have been honest in their recognition that the intransigence of farmers and landowners presents an often insuperable barrier to a significant increase in negotiated agreements.[86]

Indeed, it is significant that park authorities have over recent years turned to the alternative of purchasing land so as to manage access on it, rather than concluding agreements with existing landowners.[87]

Land purchase on a large scale remains, however, outside the scope of all but the largest authorities and is in any case prone to the ravages of land speculation by private sector entrepreneurs in protected landscape areas.[88]

<u>Farms and Farm Trails</u>. A more successful source of co-operative effort has been the opening up of farms and farmland for public recreation on specific open days (see Chapter 7.4). An initiative by the Countryside Commission[89] led to an experimental opening up of farms to visitors with the aim of increasing the visitor's enjoyment of farmed countryside, increasing the public's understanding of farming and the countryside, and reducing conflict between farmers and visitors. The success of these schemes led to the recommendation that the Countryside Committees of County Councils should encourage farm open days as a regular feature of the recreation calendar.

Nevertheless, Tinley's[90] review of similar schemes in

345

Western Europe suggests that a more significant take-off of open farm projects will only be achieved by gaining the financial support of the national agricultural organisations and the larger farmers' co-operatives.

A more permanent feature of extended recreational access is the farm trail which again offers educational value as well as a recreation experience. As with open days, these facilities are not yet sufficiently widespread to make more than a token impact on the overall access situation, but there is clearly scope for increasing the stock although again the major private sector decision-makers remain to be convinced of the worth of the idea. As Beynon suggests, 'existing farm trails demonstrate that there is scope for farm trails on both private and publicly owned farms, but perhaps the most immediate opportunities are available on farms owned by county councils, MAFF, agricultural colleges or on some of the 950 or so farms owned by the National Trust.'[91]

Footpaths. Farm trails are usually accompanied by a significant level of visitor services and are thus the product of considerable effort of preparation and upkeep. Footpaths, however, require less upkeep and considerable success has been achieved both in opening up the countryside through the network of footpaths, and in the proper way-marking of important routes.[92]

The spatial distribution of this success is understandably patchy. A recent report on national parks[93] denotes considerable achievements in this respect:

> The attention given to footpath maintenance in the National Parks is generally at a much higher level than elsewhere reflecting the public's use of the network and the problems posed for local farmers. For example, it is the practice in both Yorkshire National Parks to assist farmers financially with footpath maintenance by the provision of gates and stiles and repair of surfaces.[94]

In less elite sections of landscape, only the eternal vigilance of watchdog environmental groups has prevented the widespread decay of the footpath network.[95] Nevertheless, in comparison to the situation in the U.S.A. where there are less than 1600 km of trails for each million population[96], the

346

British system of footpaths continues to present a
high level of access to those whose recreational
aspirations and freedom of mobility permit their
usage of these paths.

Scenic Routes. For those who are happy to spend
most of their recreation time seated in their car,
the opening up of scenic routes and drives has
boosted access to areas not previously perceived by
decision-makers as desirable for recreation use.
The work of the Forestry Commission in conjunction
with other agencies has been very fruitful in the
establishment of such routes in forest areas (see
for example, Chapter 9.6). There is, however, a
danger that scenic routes will become very much part
of honeypot management strategies (see Section 10.3),
and rather than being used to extend access into the
countryside, they could become devices to restrict
access elsewhere.

For example the national park plan for the North
York Moors firmly places certain fears and hopes
alonside the establishment of scenic routes: 'by
establishing recognised scenic routes, the National
Park Committee can influence recreational pressures
through guiding traffic on to the most suitable
routes. However, there is some danger that instead
of redistributing visitors already in the Park, such
routes may attract additional people.'[97] In other
words, scenic routes are part of the road hierarchy
management plans to divert traffic from vulnerable
areas (and thus restrict access in those locations)
rather than being management tools to extend access
- hence the expressed horror of potentially attracting additional rather than redirected recreation to
these routes.

All in all, it would appear that the best methods of
widening access in the countryside revolve around
land ownership by public authorities and other agencies such as the National Trust. Ownership permits
proper management which in turn legitimises access
extension within the overall honeypot strategy.
Other schemes discussed above rely on landowner co-
operation or compensation, and thus far these
attributes have been difficult to achieve despite
the best endeavours of public authorities.

Even where successful co-operation is achieved, the
resulting access links again fall under the umbrella
of the overall strategy of recreation concentration,

and the degree of publicity and information given to the rising public (see Chapter 7.6) concerning newly accessible sites and routes will vary according to whether visitor pressure is desired or not.

Access for Non-Mobile Groups

Recreation managers have actively pursued the possibility of providing access to landscape resources in the countryside by means of public transport schemes. Such projects perform a three-fold function:

(i) as a means by which non-mobile groups can gain access to recreation areas,

(ii) as an alternative to which habitual car-borne visitors might be attracted, or in some cases persuaded by stronger means, and

(iii) as a supplement to the accessibility of local residents within countryside areas.

Innovation. Some national parks have again led the way in this policy areas. The Goyt Valley park-and-ride scheme in the Peak District (see Chapter 7.3) pioneered this approach, as part of a traffic management scheme in a particularly pressured yet sensitive area. The Peak Park Board have since been active in promoting 'Peak Pathfinders' bus services in areas where previously there was inadequate public transport services to villages and attractive scenic areas.[98] These services have provided an alternative to car transport, and have proved popular with walkers, family groups, local people and bike-and-riders.

Similar services have been adopted by other national parks, and are mirrored by some private sector initiatives such as the longstanding Mountain Goat minibus services in the Lake District. In the Yorkshire Dales, imaginative use has been made of the 'Dales Rail' railway route which runs through the park, and has been connected with local bus services and special recreation facilities at or near the stations within countryside areas.[99]

Despite these innovative achievements, the practical result in access terms is a few scattered schemes, rather than a comprehensive package of conventional and unconventional services (much as has happened in the case of providing access to social resources - see Section 10.2). Some indication of why this is

so may be found in the North York Moors National
Park Plan where, despite feasibility studies, re-
creation-oriented bus services were found not to be
worth pursuing in current circumstances: 'the main
disadvantages were found to be cost, the danger of
weakening the revenues to existing services by competition, and the likelihood of the new services
making a negligible contribution to the achievement
of the Park's statutory aims.'[100]

This last reason appears crucial. In terms of the
general allocation of priorities and resources within recreation management, the counterbalancing of
access restriction by schemes which extend the access
of those who have to , or who wish to use public
transport services receives only secondary consideration - and a poor second at that.

Public transport experiments to provide access to
recreational opportunity in the countryside are not
limited to the national parks. Surrey County
Council, for example, launched its 'Ramblers Bus'
services in 1977, linking Dorking with the deep
countryside of the North Weald and Surrey Hills.
This service has been well used by walkers and family groups, and due to effective advertising and
information services it does not run at a loss.

Shoard argues enthusiastically in favour of a widespread replication of such services:

> But even if some of the services that may be
> developed do use money, and there is an argu-
> ment for keeping fares down so that low-in-
> come groups are able to use these buses - the
> price would be low compared with what little
> money has been spent each year since the war
> on countryside recreation provision of use
> only to the car-owning members of the community
> who need least help.[101]

Disadvantaged Groups. There certainly does appear
to be a case for allocating greater priority to the
task of providing access to countryside recreation
for non-mobile and other disadvantaged groups.

In North America, there is a long and creditable
history of special schemes to provide recreation
opportunities to handicapped people.[102] Projects
such as Riding for the Disabled, and specific
locally-organised ventures have created a similar

framework of access to countryside recreation for
disabled people in Britain. Although nothing that
is achieved in this specialised management area can
ever be sufficient to compensate for the obvious
needs of these groups, it is fair to say that their
needs are visible and therefore perhaps able to
catch the eye of politicians and decision-makers
who effectively control the allocation of access to
countryside recreation resources.

There are, however, social groups whose needs are
far less visible, though equally pressing. Some are
catered for by society's administrative pigeon-holes.
School age children, for example, are often granted
irregular opportunities to use outdoor activity
centres and to make field visits and so on through
the auspices of the education services.

But what of low-income, non-mobile, elderly and
other groups whose need for access to countryside
resources does not diminish because of their disadvantaged position? Access policies tend to assume
that all potential clients have the use of a car,
prefer to congregate together in popular and well-
managed honeypots, and are capable of obtaining for
themselves sufficient information concerning the
landscape resources offered by entire areas of
countryside (such as the national parks) rather than
being restricted in awareness to a cognition of those
sites which are advertised by the authorities
concerned.

All three of these presumptions may to a large
measure be true, but there is mounting evidence to
suggest that management strategies based on these
precepts will further disadvantage significant minority groups in society who do not have the affluence,
mobility or knowledge to fit the presumptive mould.
As with the question of access to social resources,
we may have reached the stage where a low cost package of co-ordinated conventional and unconventional
schemes are a vital supplement to existing policies
if a welfare input to resource management is to be
realistically upheld.

NOTES AND REFERENCES

1.   M.J. Moseley, <u>Accessibility: The Rural
     Challenge</u> (Methuen, London, 1979)

2.   See, for example, D.J. Banister, <u>Transport
     Mobility and Deprivation in Inter-Urban Areas</u>
     (Saxon House, Farnborough, 1980); R. Cresswell
     (ed), <u>Rural Transport and Country Planning</u>
     (Hill, Glasgow, 1978); D.J. Banister and P.
     Hall (eds), <u>Transport and Public Policy Plan-
     ning</u> (Mansell, London, 1981); M.J. Moseley,
     R.G. Harman, O.B. Coles and M.B. Spencer,
     <u>Rural Transport and Accessibility</u> (University
     of East Anglia, Norwich, 1977); Moseley,
     <u>Accessibility: The Rural Challenge</u> (Note 1).

3.   M.J. Moseley, 'The supply of rural (in)access-
     ibility', in Banister and Hall (Note 2): 183.

4.   D.J. Banister, 'Transport and Accessibility',
     in M. Pacione (ed), <u>Progress in Rural Geog-
     raphy</u> (Croom Helm, London, 1983).

5.   B.J.L. Berry, <u>Urbanisation and Counterurban-
     isation</u> (Sage, London, 1976); J.P. Wheeler and
     P.A. Morrison, 'Rural reconnaissance in
     America?', <u>Population Bulletin</u> 31 (1976): 1-27.

6.   See A.G. Champion, 'Population trends in rural
     Britain', <u>Population Trends</u> 26 (1981): 20-23;
     A.W. Gilg, 'Population and Employment', in
     Pacione (Note 4); and W. Randolph and S. Robert,
     'Population redistribution in Great Britain',
     <u>Town and Country Planning</u>, September (1981):
     227-31.

7.   See P.J.Cloke, <u>An Introduction to Rural
     Settlement Planning</u> (Methuen, London, 1983):
     Chapter 12.

8.   G.P. Wibberley, 'Mobility and the Countryside',
     in Cresswell (Note 2).

9.   J. Packman and D. Wallace, 'Rural Services in
     Norfolk and Suffolk: The Management of Change'
     in M.J. Moseley (ed) <u>Power, Planning and People
     in Rural East Anglia</u> (University of East Anglia,
     Norwich, 1982).

10. D. Radford, 'Accessibility as a Consumer Standard in Rural Areas', in Welsh Office, Rural Transport: A Symposium (Welsh Office, Cardiff, 1979).

11. Banister, Transport (Note 4): 134.

12. D.G. Rhys and M.J. Buxton, 'Car ownership and the rural transport problem', Journal of the Chartered Institute of Transport, 36 (1974): 109-12.

13. R.E. Paaswell, 'Problems of the carless in the United Kingdom and the United States', Transportation 2 (1973): 370.

14. G.W. Heinze, D. Herbst and U. Schuhle, 'Travel behaviour in rural areas: a German case study', International Journal of Transport Economics 9 (1982): 203.

15. National Consumer Council, Rural Rides (National Consumer Council, London, 1978).

16. Moseley, Accessibility (Note 1).

17. Idem, 46.

18. J. Garden (ed) Solving the Transport Problems of the Elderly: The Use of Resources (Department of Adult Education, University of Keele, 1978).

19. M. Hillman, I. Henderson and A. Whalley, Transport Realities and Planning Policy (Political and Economic Planning Broadsheet 567, London, 1976).

20. Many rural local authorities do not offer concessionary fares to pensioners. For a debate on these issues see J. Garden, 'The Mobility of the Elderly and Disabled in Great Britain: An Overview', in N. Ashford and W. Bell (eds) Mobility for the Elderly and Handicapped (Loughborough University, Loughborough, 1978).

21. R. Gant and J. Smith, 'Spatial mobility problems of the elderly and disabled in the Cotswolds' Paper presented to the British-Dutch Symposium on Living Conditions in Peri-Urban and Remoter

Rural Areas in North-West Europe, University of East Anglia, 1982.

22. Moseley et al, Rural Transport (see Note 2).

23. Peat, Marwick, Mitchell and Co., Minimum Level of Service for Rural Public Transport (National Bus Company, London, 1977): 64.

24. J.E. Carlson, M.L. Lassey and W.R. Lassey, Rural Society and Environment in America (McGraw-Hill, New York, 1981): 366.

25. J. Garden and M. Hoebert, 'The importance of public transport to life in small villages - a study in progress', Paper presented to the PTRC Annual Conference, University of Warwick, 1981.

26. H.S. Maggied, Transportation for the Poor: Research in Rural Mobility (Kluwer-Nijhoff, Boston, 1981).

27. Jefferson County, Countrywide Public Transportation Service Plan (Jefferson County Section 18 Co-ordination office, Watertown NY, 1980).

28. Moseley, Accessibility (Note 1).

29. See, for example, The Labour Party, Out of Town, Out of Mind (The Labour Party, London, 1981).

30. A. Blowers, 'Future Rural Transport and Development Policy', in Cresswell (Note 2).

31. Banister, Transport (Note 4): 140.

32. J.F. Barrow, 'Public Transport - A Key Issue in County Plan-Making', in Cresswell (Note 2): 15-16.

33. V.A. Knight, 'Priorities in Transport Policies and Programmes (TPPs)', in Cresswell (Note 2): 117-8.

34. Banister, Transport (Note 4): 138.

35. A. Blowers, Future Road Transport (Note 30): 47.

36. P.D. Ennor 'Public transport in rural areas: a review', in Transport and Road Research

Laboratory, Symposium on Unconventional Bus Services (TRRL, Crowthorne, 1976).

37. W. Lea and N. Archibald, Passenger Transport Co-ordination: A Shire County's Approach, (Cheshire County Council, Cheshire, 1976).

38. Peat, et al, Minimum Level (See Note 23).

39. Rural Voice and Bus and Coach Council, The Country Would Miss the Bus (Rural Voice and Bus Coach Council, London, 1983).

40. See, for example, Moseley, Accessibility (Note 1).

41. Hertfordshire County Council, Public Transport for Rural Communities (Hertfordshire CC, Hertford, 1975).

42. This is the case in the Dinefurr Rutex Scheme: see Transport and Road Research Laboratory, Rural Transport Experiments: The Welsh Schemes (TRRL, Crowthorne, 1979).

43. Borders Regional Council, Border Courier Service: Final Monitoring Report (Borders Regional Council, Newtown St. Boswells, 1981); P. Gregory, 'Providing public transport in sparsely populated areas', Surveyor 153 (1979): 13-14.

44. National Consumer Council, Rural Rides (Note 15)

45. P.F. Watts, 'Rural shared hire-cars: a comparative assessment of their potential', In Transport and Road Research Laboratory, The Rural Transport Experiments (TRRL, Crawthorne, 1979).

46. D.C. Milefanti, 'Government Rural Transport Experiments 1977', in Cresswell (Note 2); individual RUTEX schemes are reported by the Transport and Road Research Laboratory, Crowthorne.

47. G. Searle, Co-ordinating Public Transport in Rural Counties: Summary of the Lewes Study Approach (Department of Transport, London, 1982)

48. Idem, 3.

49. Idem, 22.

50. Moseley, Accessibility (Note 1): 173.

51. P.J. Cloke, Key Settlements in Rural Areas (Methuen, London, 1979).

52. P.J. Cloke and D.P. Shaw 'Rural settlement policies in structure plans', Town Planning Review 54 (1983): 338-54.

53. Cloke, Introduction (Note 7).

54. P.J. Cloke, 'Planners' attitudes to resource concentration and dispersal in rural areas', Planning Outlook 25 (1982), 16-21.

55. T. Hancock, 'Planning and Community clusters', Town and Country Planning 44 (1976): 264-8; D.G. Venner, 'The Village has a Future', The Village 31 (1976), 39-41.

56. Moseley, Accessibility (Note 1).

57. The Labour Party, Out of Town (Note 29): 24.

58. H.J. Gans, 'Outdoor Recreation and Mental Health', in D.W. Fisher, J.E. Lewis and G.B. Priddle (eds) Land and Leisure: Concepts and Methods in Outdoor Recreation (Maaroufa Press, Chicago, 1974).

59. B. Cracknell, 'Accessibility to the countryside as a factor in planning for leisure'. Regional Studies 1 (1967), 147-161.

60. R. Jackson, 'Motorways and National Parks in Britain', Area 4 (1970): 26-28.

61. M.F. Tanner, 'Recreation', in M. Pacione (ed) Progress in Rural Geography (Croom Helm, London, 1983).

62. M. Shoard, 'Opening the countryside to the people', Journal of Planning and Environment Law May (1974) 266-271.

63. R.S. Gibbs and M.C. Whitby, Local Authority Expenditure on Access Land (Agricultural Adjustment Unit, University of Newcastle-upon-Tyne, 1975).

64. A. MacEwen and M. MacEwen, <u>National Parks:
    Conservation or Cosmetics?</u> (Allen and Unwin,
    London, 1982): 20.

65. See Chapter 8 of P. Clarke, B. Jackman and
    D. Mercer (eds) <u>The Sunday Times Book of the
    Countryside</u> (Sunday Times, London, 1980).

66. See, for example, Clwyd County Council,
    <u>Recreational Traffic in Clwyd</u> (Clwyd C.C.,
    Mold, 1976).

67. The surveys incorporated in all National Park
    Plans highlight sensitive areas within each of
    the parks.

68. M. Shoard, <u>The Theft of the Countryside</u> (Temple
    Smith, London, 1980): 226.

69. Idem: 230.

70. T. Swem and R. Cahn, 'The politics of parks in
    Alaska', <u>Ambio</u> 12 (1983) 14-19.

71. I.G. Simmons, <u>Rural Recreation in the Indust-
    rial World</u> (Edward Arnold, London, 1975): 185.

72. D.A. Dennier, 'National Park Plans: A Review
    Article,' <u>Town Planning Review</u>, 49 (1978):
    175-183.

73. Idem: 178.

74. MacEwen and MacEwen, <u>National Parks</u> (Note 64).

75. P.J. Cloke and C.C. Park, 'Country Parks in
    National Parks: A Case Study of Craig-y-Nos
    in the Brecon Beacons, Wales', <u>Journal of
    Environmental Management</u> 12 (1981): 173-185.

76. J. Tinker, 'Do we need wilderness areas?' <u>New
    Scientist</u> (4 November, 1973).

77. Simmons, <u>Rural Recreation</u> (Note 71): 245.

78. MacEwen and MacEwen, <u>National Parks</u> (Note 64).

79. Dartmoor National Park Authority, <u>Dartmoor
    National Park Plan</u> (DNPA, Exeter, 1977).

80. Idem: 40.

81. Brecon Beacons National Park Committee,
    National Park Plan, (BBNPC, Brecon, 1977).

82. Idem, Paragraph C4.11.

83. Idem, Paragraph C.4.10.

84. See MacEwen and MacEwen, National Parks (Note
    64): Chapter 6.

85. Idem: 149.

86. See, for example, Peak Park Joint Planning
    Board, National Park Plan (PPJPB, Blackwell,
    1978).

87. Gibbs and Whitby, Access Land (Note 63).

88. Countryside Commission, 'Minister supports
    park policies' National Park News, Winter
    (1980): 79-80.

89. Dartington Amenity Research Trust, Farm Open
    Days (DART, Darlington, 1974).

90. H. Tinley, 'Bridging the gap between town and
    country', Farmers Weekly (March 2nd, 1979):
    21-27.

91. J. Beynon, 'Farm trails in the countryside',
    The Planner 61 (1975): 56.

92. Countryside Commission, Waymarking for Footpath
    and Bridleway (HMSO, London, 1974).

93. Association of County Councils, National Parks:
    An Appraisal of Some Current Issues (ACC,
    London, 1982).

94. Idem, paragraph 38.

95. C. Speakman, 'Rights of way', Vole 2 (1979):
    31-32.

96. Outdoor Recreation Action, 'America's trails'
    Outdoor Recreation Action (Winter, 1976): 1-9.

97. North York Moors National Park Committee,
    National Park Plan (NYMNPC, York, 1977): 66.

98. Peak Park Joint Planning Board, Additional

Survey Report (PPJPB, Bakewell, 1977).

99.   Countryside Commission, Dales Rail (Country-
      side Commission, Cheltenham, 1979).

100. North York Moors National Park Committee,
      National Park Plan (see Note 97):   67.

101. Shoard, Theft (Note 68):   229.

102. R. Duffy, 'Outdoor recreation for people with
      special needs' Environment Views May/June
      (1983):   17-20; Outdoor Recreation Action 45
      (1977), special issue on 'Recreation for
      Special People'.

SECTION III

MANAGEMENT THEMES FOR RURAL RESOURCES

This section seeks to integrate the various strands
of thought developed in Sections I and II into a
number of related themes for resource management in
the countryside. The aim of this section is to
illustrate the need for co-ordinated management of
rural resources in the light of the various types of
conflict detailed in Section II, and to evaluate some
existing approaches to resource allocation in the
countryside. Selected examples are used to highlight the difficulties of simultaneously attempting
to accommodate all environmental and human elements
in rural decision making, and a recurrent theme is
the conservatism and parochialism of most central
government agencies charged with rural decision-
making in countries like Great Britain.

Chapter 11 focusses on the different mechanism which
are available for countryside management through
planning. The adopted planning systems in various
parts of the world are viewed as constrained by the
political and ideological characteristics of the host
society. Most commonly, planning has been by agreement or control, being thus susceptible to the
barriers of power (thereby blocking agreement or at
least dictating the terms for it) and negativism
(leaving few options for positive planning within
the control mechanism). The protectionist policy of
setting aside some parts of the countryside under
special area designations is examined, particularly
in the context of imposing unrealistic constraints
on the life styles and socio-economic opportunities
available to those who live and work in the countryside.

Planning by direct development and through the co-
ordination of external decision-making agencies is

also discussed, with particular emphasis being given to the fragmentation of public sector agencies entrusted with sectoral decisions and actions in situations where unification of decision-making powers would upset the carefully preserved status quo of societal continuity. The themes of equity and deprivation are woven throughout this chapter, as is the conflict between the planning objectives favouring resource conservation and positive provision of opportunities in cases of disadvantage.

Chapter 12 concentrates on integrated approaches to rural planning, and it seeks to establish the need (as yet unfulfilled) for more creative approaches to management which create opportunities for all countryside users. In particular, the question of the need for more fully integrated land use strategies in a country with strictly limited availability of land and resources is addressed, with specific reference to debates about dissonance and compartmentalised thinking and policy formulation within central government. Sectoral approaches to rural planning serve more to accentuate many conflicts than to resolve resource-using conflicts, and the chapter examines the evidence in favour of new initiatives on multi-purpose use of the countryside in Britain.

Structural inertia within both local and national government planning systems, coupled with sectoral decision-making and lack of open dialogue about wider issues in countryside use and management emerge as priority areas for future investigation, and it is concluded that rural resource allocation and management is as yet in its infancy. Whilst it alone cannot provide a panacea for the future, resource management offers a useful vehicle for identification and resolution of planning conflicts within the countryside.

Chapter Eleven

COUNTRYSIDE MANAGEMENT BY PLANNING

11.1 THE PLANNING MACHINERY

> The rationale of rural planning systems
> lies in the inability of society to
> secure a coherent and stable pattern of
> land use in rural area in such a way as
> to produce the most life-enhancing pat-
> tern of activity for the community as a
> whole.[1]

> Somehow, the blood and the fire have
> gone out of British planning. It isn't
> that the planning machine has shut down
> - far from it.....What has gone is not
> the substance, but the spirit.[2]

These two expressed views neatly summarise both the
allotted and the growing disatisfaction which occurs
when performance is measured against these demanding
goals. Section B of this book has detailed many of
the resource conflicts - both physical and social -
which represent a rich habitat for countryside
management by planning. Yet these very conflicts
have severely interrupted the rationalist planning
model of coherent and stable land use leading to
life-enhancing social patterns which Robins speaks of.

Where, then, has planning gone wrong? To what extent
have the planning techniques adopted in rural areas
been inappropriate for the objectives required of
them?

Questions such as these have prompted a lengthy and
often spurious debate over the future of planning.
Some of the pros and cons are summarised in the work
of Jones (TABLE 11.1). His conclusion is damning:

Planning policy in Britain is ill-conceived and poorly administered. The aims of it are obscure, and there is little evidence that they are achieved even where they can be discerned.[3]

TABLE 11.1   PLANNING - The case for and the case against[4]

FOR

(a)   Planning prevents harm done by profiteering
(b)   Planning prevents chaos
(c)   Planning allows a city to protect its basic identity ('but what about the countryside' - authors insertion)
(d)   Planning policy puts the community first
(e)   Planning enables people collectively to control their environment
(f)   Property values are preserved by planning restraints

AGAINST

(a)   Planning inhibits enterprise
(b)   Planning has created a bureaucratic nightmare
(c)   Planning policy freezes development
(d)   Planning creates a false market
(e)   Planning policy encourages the politics of influence
(f)   Urban planning causes higher prices for goods and services (again 'what about the countryside' - authors insertion)
(g)   Planners do not have the superior knowledge required

Planning-related professions have naturally sought to disarm much of this criticism. The Royal Institution of Chartered Surveyors[5], for example, considers much criticism of planning to be ill-informed, contradictory and universalist, even though it admits to some problems of slow response, lack of objectivity, and lack of a proper balance between competing needs within the planning system. The Royal Town Planning Institute[6] has also addressed these issues, and having done so suggests that criticisms often do not prove to be specific to the statutory planning system itself, but rather reflect the whole style of a complex modern bureaucracy where planning is dispersed among many different agencies. Often, the reaction to adverse analysis of planning has been a defensive justification of the record so far. A typical assertion is that 'it is ridiculous to assume that the relatively high standard of physical environment enjoyed in many areas would have been achieved without planning control.'[7]

The sterility of this in-house debate is evident when it is realised that considerable difficulties have been experienced in evaluating the relationship between changing circumstances and planning policies in rural areas. The Martin and Voorhees report[8] on rural settlement policies, for example, stresses the difficulties of discernment between 'natural' and 'planned' phenomena. Quite simply, it is difficult to ascertain what would have happened if no planning or different forms of planning had taken place over a period of time in rural areas. A further problem arises in discovering the exact details and political motivation of planning policy.

Only recently have rural researchers fully acknowledged that over-emphasis on <u>written</u> policy statements is often misleading since these statements do not represent an accurate reflection of planning intentions or outcomes. Recognition of these deficiencies has been reflected by a rejection of rational decision-making models by current planning theorists[9] and has led to a redirection of research towards the shadowy area of the mechanisms through which policies are prepared and implemented in rural areas.[10]

An understanding of policy formation is important in the evaluation of two very different explanations of the failure of planning in rural areas:[11]

(i) Suitable <u>planning policies</u> are being formulated for rural areas, but their impact is being significantly diluted by difficulties of implementation;

(ii) The <u>policy-implementation dichotomy</u> falsely represents the complex procedures of rural planning which are currently structured in such a way as to preclude positive attempts to redress disadvantage.

The second explanation appears to be gaining ground. Cherry[12] points out that planning defects derive as much from political defects as from professional and technical factors. Local politics are currently volatile and lacking in concensus for reform, largely because of the increasingly significant role played by

ideological factors in policy formulation[13] and also
because in a climate of expenditure reduction. Dis-
putes over the allocation of resources are often more
acrimonious. If the political nature of statutory
planning processes does preclude the more 'positive'
aspects of planning, then our expectations of what
planning can do to resolve the conflicts outlined
in Section B of this book have been set too high.

Traditional analysis of the statutory planning
machinery in Britain emphasises two major focal areas
in which rural decision-making has been found want-
ing[14]. First, it has been suggested that the level
of powers and resources available to decision-makers
has been deficient for the task in hand. Secondly,
there are perceived problems in achieving a consistency in the decisions made by various participant
organisations and agencies each with its own jealous-
ly guarded policy objectives, need-assessments and
investment programmes. Even the planning function
is divided between district and county authorities
thus leaving a situation ripe for divide-and-rule
tactics from the central state which is able to
allocate and reallocate roles and powers between
these two agencies almost at will.

By adopting a political economy perspective, the
limitations arising from these focal areas can be
readily appreciated. The work of Hanrahan and Cloke[15]
has emphasised that rural planning and policy-making,
being aspects of state activity, are automatically
caught up in the state's role of preserving its own
structure and managing the conflicts ensuing from
that structure. In terms of social resources therefore, far from spawning resource reallocation towards
deprived groups, the state on the whole will maintain
the inequalities on which it is built. The local
state will be severely restricted in its range of
policy options both by central state activity, and by
the devolution of decision-making powers to other
public-sector agencies and to the private sector.

It is against this background that countryside management by planning should be judged. The interactions
of the central state, the local state and the private
sector are often such that planning options are
limited to different reactions to circumstances and
events rather than permitting more positive resource
allocating techniques to be utilised. Minay[16] has
outlined four views of planning which highlight the
gaps between planning action and reaction.

(i) <u>Planning as a response to private action</u>
where planning implementation involves a
reactive control over the initiatives of
private and public sector developers.

(ii) <u>Planning as co-ordination</u> - involves the identification of areas where policy incompatibility
is problematic and the encouragement of
greater conformity by various decision-makers.

(iii) <u>Planning as the positive promotion of environmental change</u> - in which planners seek to
mobilise resources (controlled invariably by
others) with which to institute changes in the
rural environment which would not occur without
such intervention.

(iv) <u>Planning as resource management</u> - suggests that
planning might act as a management system at
least for physical and landscape resources, and
maybe for the total resource base of society.
Planning would thus represent the actual process of resource allocation - an unrealistic
concept both because a large proportion of
resources belong to the private sector (and
currently evade public sector control) and
because even within the public sector, the
competition for resources is a national one,
and thus a reallocation of resources within
society as a whole would be required to counter
resource deprivation in the countryside.

Of these four schemes, the limitations highlighted
by a political economy perspective suggest that (i)
is the realistic task for statutory planning; (ii)
may be sought after but only partially achieved;
(iii) will suffer because available resources are
only a drop in the ocean, and the state's unspoken
role of preserving societal status-quo will deter
the allocation of further finance for this purpose;
and (iv) is a revolutionary pipe-dream, impossible
to fulfil within the statutory planning system as
it stands. It is, therefore, more realistic to
evaluate current rural planning practices against
this background of <u>institutional limitation</u> than to
subscribe to the more common yardstick of whether
planning meets its own hypothetical and untenable
goals.

11.2 PLANNING BY DEVELOPMENT CONTROL

The statutory system in the United Kingdom has often

been portrayed as the pinnacle of legislative excellence in planning. Although such accolades may be viewed as a little uncritical[17], the fact remains that the techniques available to British Planners are the envy of the world. The core of these techniques is <u>development control</u>, with which planners can refuse, accept or modify applications for development which are placed before them. A developer must obtain planning permission from the local authority before 'the carrying out of building, engineering, mining or other operations in, on, over or under land, or the making of any material change in the use of any buildings or other land'.[18] An idea of the processes involved in obtaining planning permission may be gained from FIGURE 11.1.

This seemingly comprehensive requirement for permission is, in fact, counterbalanced by a number of exemptions:

(i) <u>The Use Classes Order</u> - prescribes various classes of building, and allows for change <u>within</u> classes, but not <u>between</u> classes, outside of the planning permission procedure. Some of the more commonly encountered classes are shown in TABLE 11.2, and it has been pointed out in this context that:

'a change of use from a solicitors office to an insurance office does not require planning permission and that the change from a clerical outfitters shop to a sex shop is similarly outside the planners remit.'[19]

Several small-scale changes to the rural built environment are therefore exempt from development control because of the Use Classes Order.

(ii) <u>The General Development Order</u> - places outside the statutory system those changes of land use solely connected with agriculture and forestry. Again changes of use within these categories are exempt, but the use of agricultural land, for example, for housing development would require planning permission before the changeover occurred. The Order similarly ensures that agricultural buildings (other than dwellings) not exceeding 465 square metres in ground area or 12 metres in

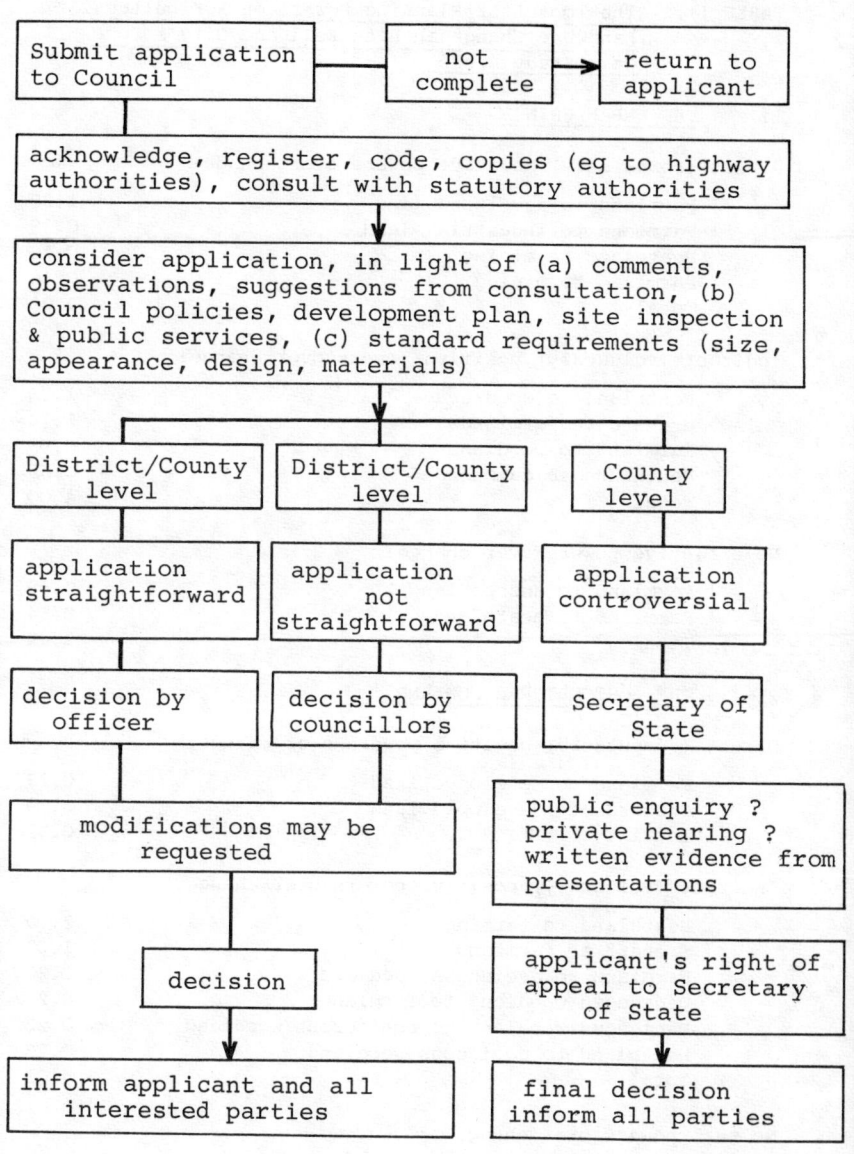

FIGURE II.I <u>Main stages in the progress of a</u>
<u>planning application</u>

TABLE 11.2   The Impact of Planning Powers on Agricultural
             Land Use Change in Blacksell and Gilg's Four
             Case Study Areas

1.   THE URBAN FRINGE

Direct (compulsory) negative powers over change: km^2

         Farmland to developed land   1.29
         Farmland to industrial land   0.39
         Heathland to mining   0.16
         Farmland to mining   0.16
         Total   2.06

Indirect (voluntary) positive powers over change:

         Heathland to woodland   1.26
         Orchard to farmland   1.14
         Farmland to woodland   0.95
         Heathland to farmland   0.65
         Total   4.00

No effective powers over change.

         Farmland to unused land   0.88
         Farmland to heathland   0.54
         Total   1.42

2.   THE AGRICULTURAL LOWLAND

Direct (compulsory) negative powers over change:

         Farmland to developed land   0.23
         Orchards to developed land   0.09
         Total   0.32

Indirect (voluntary) positive powers over change:

         Heathland to farming   2.09
         Orchard to farmland   1.02
         Farmland to deciduous woodland   0.26
         Deciduous woodland to farmland   0.21
         Deciduous woodland to coniferous woodland   0.22
         Heathland to deciduous woodland   0.23
         Total   4.03

No real powers over change:

         Farmland to unused land   0.26
         Parkland to farmland   0.21
         Farmland to parkland   0.16
         Orchard to deciduous woodland   0.11
         Developed land to farmland   0.10
         Total   0.84

TABLE 11.2 (continued)

3.   THE HILLS

Direct (compulsory) negative powers over change:	km^2
Farmland to developed land	0.52
Total	0.52

Indirect (voluntary) positive powers over change:	
Heathland to farmland	4.73
Heathland to deciduous woodland	2.25
Heathland to coniferous woodland	1.61
Deciduous woodland to coniferous woodland	0.88
Farmland to deciduous woodland	0.44
Farmland to coniferous woodland	0.32
Total	10.23

No real powers over change:	
Farmland to heathland	1.87
Farmland to unused land	0.31
Total	2.18

4.   THE UPLANDS

Direct (compulsory) negative powers over change:	
Farmland to developed land	0.23
Heathland to developed land	0.15
Total	0.38

Indirect (voluntary) positive powers over change:	
Heathland to farmland	5.74
Heathland to deciduous woodland	0.61
Farmland to deciduous woodland	0.21
Heathland to coniferous woodland	0.19
Total	6.75

No real powers over change:	
Farmland to heathland	1.24
Farmland to unused land	0.68
Total	1.92

Source: Blacksell and Gilg (Note 33): 60, 74, 81-2, 95.

---

height do not require planning permission.
Also included under the Order are various
developments by public authorities and

nationalised industries.

It will be seen from the effects of these two Orders that development control is geared principally towards controlling the nature and growth of the built environment while it is relatively important in its dealings with the extensive land uses of the countryside. Two sets of problems occur, therefore, in the relationship between rural management by planning through development control and the resource bases, both social and physical, as outlined in Section A. First, problems exist in the use and mis-use of planned control procedures where they apply; and secondly, a different set of difficulties arise from the absence of control procedures over agriculture and forestry. Particular examples of both problem types are examined here in order to explore the ramifications of control exerted and control exempted.

Development Control and Rural Housing

Through the development control function, local authorities have the power to exert considerable influence over the design, scale and location of housing development. In design terms, the authority is itself subject to central government regulations and standards regarding light, space and curtilage requirements, but in addition it imposes a value judgement as to whether any planned dwellings are compatible with the existing building stock.

Perhaps more important in the analysis of the ramifications of development control for rural housing are the considerations of scale and location. Under the 1968 Town and County Planning Act, county councils are required to produce structure plans[20] which amongst other tasks set out the broad preference for the location of new houses in rural areas. While it would be erroneous to typify all structure plan policies with one example,[21] the policies for housing in Salop rural settlements serve to spotlight some of the issues under consideration at the structure plan level.[22]

First, the county council sets out its role as one of retaining overall control of the number of houses built in the rural area so as to ensure that its strategic policies on the scale and location of development in the county as a whole are safeguarded. Second, it proposes that large-scale development (where needed) should be restricted to so-called 'main villages'[23] where services, facilities and access to employment will also be concentrated. Outside of these elite growth locations, the county's policy is to ensure that, subject to certain safeguards, small scale infilling should normally be allowed in most villages. Third, this package of location strategies is handed down to district council authorities for application to the local scene. The county plan states that:

> Sufficient discretion has been left with district planning authorities to enable them in the preparation of local plans and in the exercise of their development control powers to relate the location of future housing development in rural Shropshire to local circumstances.[24]

Just to be on the safe side however, the county offer some guidelines to be used by district councils in the exercise of their control powers. They are to ensure that priority is given to:

(i) the supply of adequate housing for the local needs of people who work in the area or have strong ties with it;

(ii) the provision of houses suitable for the young and the elderly; and

(iii) the location of housing so as to provide additional support to existing services and facilities - especially primary schools and rural transport services.

District councils will all receive a broadly equivalent (although not necessarily parallel) package of economic, social and political guidelines for the use of their control over new housing. They in turn produce a local plan which details their marriage of strategic policy and local circumstances.

More guidelines are introduced at this stage. Bassetlow District Council[25] (Nottinghamshire), for example, suggest five factors for the location of residential land within their rural area:

(i) the need to achieve reasonable accessibility to employment opportunities and existing community facilities;

(ii) the awareness that it would be unrealistic to bolster those settlements long characterised by small scale and remoteness, and therefore the need to concentrate residential expansion in selected villages;

(iii) the desirability of providing a reasonable choice of housing land;

(iv) the need to safeguard village form and character; and

(v) the need to restrain unnecessary development in the countryside, in deference to factor (i) above, and in the interest of maintaining unspoilt landscapes and preserving good quality agricultural land.

Consideration of these factors led the district council to apportion the great majority of housing land between three <u>primary growth villages</u> and nine <u>secondary growth villages.</u>

The stage is thus set for <u>development control</u> to take place, but it is apposite here to take heed of the warnings in Section II.1 of this Chapter regarding the misleading nature of written policy statements. What appears at first sight to be a workable partnership between strategic policy and local detail so as to ensure the fulfilments of both social and economic planning goals, in practice falls foul of several difficulties before development control procedures can logically enact foregoing policies. Considerable friction has arisen between the two tiers of planning.[26] Despite the fact that district councils participate in the evaluation of draft county structure plans, and that district council local plans require the blessing of the county council to prove their strategic compatibility, there often remains the situation that the political ideologies of the two councils concerned may be sufficiently different for them to conflict over precise planning goals, methods and distributions.[27]

In practice, then, the written policy statements may be over-ridden by prevailing political views within the district council, and it will be these views which flavour development control decisions. Indeed, Healey et al's[28] investigation of development plans and policy implementation concluded that 'the decisions of development interests and planning authoritie were not <u>plan-based</u> so much as based on the <u>policy stance</u> of each authority.'[29]

The conclusion from this brief procedural review is that development control is first restricted by local and central state requirements, then subjected to politicisation which can be warped by inter-agency friction, and finally is put into practice by individuals (albeit professional planners) who are subject to their own behavioural quirks and organisational role-playing.[30]

Small wonder, than, that there is significant evidence which suggests a considerable gap between stated policy intentions for rural housing, and what actually happens. Development control is by nature a reactive process, dependent on a steady flow of 'appropriate' applications from private sector developers. Thus in rural areas under pressure of urbanisation, development control has some chance of success, but where there is no such pressure for development, little can be done by statutory planners to stimulate it. Moreover, private sector developers are governed by the profit motive which often leads to them wishing to build large, expensive dwellings rather than the smaller cheaper variety which might be considered as 'appropriate' for the needs of local low income families.

So both the flow and the appropriate nature of development applications are subject to extreme locational and market variations. Thus in situations of low pressure for growth and planning restriction on more than a few dwellings in any location, development control exists like a stranded whale, unable to promote housing growth and unable to prevent the use of existing quotas for affluent in-migrants rather than the local disadvantaged.

It would be false to suggest that rural management by planning control has been a failure. The enactment of restrictive key settlement policies, whereby the bulk of estate-type housing has been channelled into selected growth centres, has not only prevented undue sporadic development in the countryside, but also has indirectly sponsored the increased provision of infrastructural services such as sewerage systems[31]. In general, the control system has managed to guide development into suitable key locations, although this generalisation tends to overshadow a significant diversity of achievement in this respect.

The Martin and Voorhees report on settlement policies reinforces this view. They conclude that:

> The key settlements which function as
> central places are relatively few, and
> they are those which had a good range of
> facilities and were central places prior
> to designation. Again, key settlement
> policy has worked best when it has been
> reinforcing past trends. No cases were
> found where key settlement policy was
> able to reverse the trends and establish
> a new central village by injecting new
> community facilities.[32]

It does appear, therefore, that planning by development control is <u>per se</u> an inadequate method of
achieving planning aims under certain conditions.
Blacksell and Gilg's[33] work in Devon illustrates
this point. In their Dartmoor case study area which
included three key settlements only 22.0 per cent
of planning permission between 1964 and 1974 were
granted in these key locations. 33.9 per cent of
permission was given in other villages and a very
high figure of 44.1 per cent was granted in the open
countryside. This unexpected pattern is accounted
for by heavy pressure for housing both from the area's
agricultural population and from commuters to nearby
urban areas.

Fundamentally, these data demonstrate a clear conflict between the objectives of Devon's key settlement policy and these demands for development.
Development control procedures in this and other
cases have therefore bowed to the inevitable changes
to stated policy caused by the pressures and political influence stemming from strong and affluent
housing markets. Unfortunately, the need for low-
cost housing does not generate equal pressure and
influence, so that disadvantage within rural housing
is often perpetuated by the very planning processes
which seek to reduce it (see Chapter 8).

Two significant attempts have been made to augment
rural planning's use of <u>control mechanisms</u>. In an
attempt to ensure that all future housing is channelled towards people with a local need, the Lake
District Planning Board have pioneered the use of
Section 52 Agreements to limit the sale of new houses
to specific client types. The policy statement for
Eden District details this approach:

> Whatever planning consent is sought for a
> new dwelling, or for the conversion of a

building not previously in residential use,
the application will be considered firstly
in relation to widely used land-use guidelines. If the proposal meets these criteria,
consent will be given subject to the signing
of an agreement under Section 52 of the 1971
Town and Country Planning Act, that the
dwelling will be occupied full-time by some-
one who is employed, to be employed or was
employed locally.[34]

Planning permission conditions have previously been
used in respect of new dwellings for farmworkers,
but this extension of their usage has led to a
vigorous debate led by Clark[35] and Shucksmith[36] as
to the advantages and disadvantages of this form of
rural resource management. In general, although
seeking a laudable outcome, the use of Section 52
agreements in this context is likely to become a
most unwieldy instrument, not least because of monitoring problems, and because pressure from in-migrants
for housing will inevitably be transferred to existing dwellings.

The problem also remains that planners have little
control over the type of house built, and this alone
may filter out the most disadvantaged local home-
seekers on the grounds of size and expense.

The second modification of development control procedures has resulted from a Conservative central
government and its ideological wish to speed up the
planning decision process in order to assist the
private sector. Circular 22/80 from the Department
of the Environment makes several firm requests to
local authorities regarding their development control
guidelines:

> Local Planning Authorities are asked therefore
> to pay greater regard to time and efficiency;
> to adopt a more positive attitude to planning
> applications; to facilitate development; and
> always to grant planning permission, having
> regard to all material considerations, unless
> there are sound and clear-cut reasons for re-
> fusal. They are asked to ensure that their
> planning policies and practices create the
> right conditions to enable the house building
> industry to meet the public's need for
> housing.[37]

Planning

Herrington's[38] study of planning appeals in
Leicestershire following this circular makes two
disturbing claims. The first is that:

>The decisions which were made in the
>examples studied pre-empt local settlement
>planning and contradict other planning
>desiderata offered by the Local Plan
>approach, notably the opportunity to
>implement the Structure Plan in a logical
>manner with reference to alternative sites,
>to balance housing provision with related
>local policies for infrastructure and
>services; and most importantly, to permit
>public comment on proposals for the use
>of land.

Herrington's second main claim is that:

>The scale of the alteration in growth
>proposed (more than 2000 dwellings)
>exacerbates the political problem
>facing District Planners when they have
>to explain (reluctantly) to local com-
>munities why it is that they will be
>receiving additional development beyond
>that implied by rural settlement policy
>and perhaps beyond that being contem-
>plated in their own Local Plan.[39]

Circular 22/80 appears to reinforce the view that
any tinkering with devleopment control procedures
will inevitably have ideological motives and political outcomes. In this case, central state
intervention has served to reduce the ability of
planners to hold to their policy objectives,
whilst substantially easing the problems of private
sector developers wishing to pursue their profit
motives or meet the public's need for housing
(whichever view you care to adopt). By the same
token, the use of Section 52 Agreements, although
not achieving the redistributive aim of re-allocat-
ing housing resources to needy rural people, can be
viewed as over-restrictive of the freedom of individuals and developers.

Development control appears capable of acting as a
coarse-grained sieve for housing, allocation in
rural areas, but attempts to modify the technique
to first-tune the system for socio-political objectives of redressing disadvantage appear doomed to

376

failure. Such goals are more likely to be met by positive development planning., working alongside reactive development control (see Section II.3).

Development Control and Agriculture

It is the lack of control powers which has fuelled a debate concerning the relationships between planning and agriculture. Because no development control over agricultural land use practices exists, this issue has been discussed in an atmosphere of polemic rather than well-documented evidence, and the topic is thus prone to ideological exaggeration.

The rapid and radical landscape changes prompted by modern agricultural practices has been detailed in Chapter 9. Strong parallels have been drawn between the arbitration role of development controllers in residential and industrial development sectors and the potential role for planning controls in the agricultural sector.

Shoard among others has argued that:

> Agriculture was exempted only because its impact on the countryside was relatively small at the time when the planning system was crystallising and because home food production was considered sacrosanct in the aftermath of the war. Now that agriculture has become a major threat to our environment, however, the most logical way to deal with it within our existing system would be to extend the definition of 'development' to include agricultural activity. The destruction of an ancient wood, a stretch of down or the remains of an Iron Age village matter at least as much to the community as the erection of a new porch on a house.[40]

She progresses from this general supposition to a specific proposal that planning permission should be required for any of the following activities:

(i) taking out hedgerows or drystone walls;

(ii) chopping down trees or woods or coniferising deciduous woodland;

(iii) draining marshes or destroying or damaging the character of ponds, streams, dykes or stretches

of river whether through filling-in, drainage,
piping underground or straightening;

(iv) destroying or damaging the character of tracts
of moor, heath, hay, meadow, down, coastal
marshland, cliff roughland, or any other pieces
of roughland designated by regional countryside
planning authorities or local planning authorities as specially important for recreation or
other uses, whether through ploughing or
through the application of large quantities of
fertiliser or herbicide;

(v) constructing farm roads;

(vi) erecting farm buildings of any size.

This suggested system would not require a farmer to
seek planning permission, or to lose his freedom to
change farming methods or crops, unless the destruction of a landscape feature was involved, and even
then the normal appeals procedure would apply.

These palliative safeguards are hardly sufficient to
temper the wrath of the agricultural and land-owning
fraternities when proposals such as that by Marion
Shoard are aired. They point to the 'mess' which
planners have made in their exploits elsewhere in
allowing urban greed to exploit the land.[41] They
argue that they own the land in trust for the whole
nation and for future generations, and that they are
the best qualified custodians of this heritage.[42]
This line of debate incidentally contrasts markedly
with any use of that land to secure maximum short-
term profit which is a motive which many commentators
would ascribe to farmers. They make every use of
their excellent channels of influence in both central
and local government to express the opinion (or
threat?) that food production will suffer irretriev-
ably if development control is extended in any way to
agricultural land-use.

Strong opposition has already been encountered from
farmers in resisting any extension of the existing
limited planning controls over farm buildings.[43]
Newby pinpoints the central issue here when he
suggested that:

It is not, therefore, simple bloody-mindedness
which will lead some farmers to resist planning controls over the rural landscape; it
will be a defence, however tenuous, of the

interest of private property and that, needless to say, it is an interest which is fundamental to the fabric of contemporary English society.[44]

Blacksell and Gilg[45] have produced interesting case study information from Devon which throws light on the different facets of agricultural land use change (FIGURE 11.2). Outside of the urban fringe, loss of farmland to developed land has been kept well in check by development control powers. However, in each of the four case study areas, significant changes have occurred in those sections where planners have no direct control, even if the bulk of land involved does fall under the (often theoretical) remit of voluntary management techniques (see Section II.4). The authors conclude that in the planning arena where powers are voluntary, advisory or dependent of financial inducement, policies of agricultural expansion have sometimes seriously undermined the efficacy of policies for landscape and wildlife conservation. In those areas outside the influence of even informal planning powers they consider that the growth of unused and unmanaged land is an unaffordable luxury in the British circumstances.

In view of evidence such as this, the extension of development planning principles to agricultural land use and landscape change appears an attractive idea, despite the inevitable opposition. Any enactment of this idea, however, would encounter a series of difficulties. Robins[46] outlines five areas of conflict:

(i) planning authorities do not have the requisite expertise to deal with these new forms of development control;

(ii) the farming lobby is particularly powerful;

(iii) the monitoring and enforcement of conservation measures would be problematic;

(iv) a greater degree of control would antagonise landowning and agricultural interests;

(v) there is no easy method of compensating farmers who are prevented by planning controls from making the most economic use of land.

It seems likely that the procedural problems in this list are not beyond the wit of an admittedly extended planning bureaucracy, but the essentially political

FIGURE 11.2   CLASSES OF DEVELOPMENT UNDER THE USE
               CLASSES ORDER

Class 1   Use as a shop (except hot food shops,
               tripe shops, pet shops, a shop for the
               sale of motor vehicles etc.).

Class 2   Use as an office.

Class 3   Use as a light industrial building
               (light industry is defined as that which
               makes little noise, smoke, smell, dust,
               vibration or other nuisance. It can
               be located in a residential area with-
               out harm).

Class 4   Use as a general industrial building.

Class 10   Use as a warehouse.

Class 11   Use as a hotel or boarding house.

Class 13   Use as a church or for social activities
               connected with a church.

Class 14   Use as an institutional home or hos-
               pital.

Class 15   Non-residential use as a health centre,
               day nursery, clinic or surgery.

Class 16   Use as a library or public hall.

Class 18   Use as a sports or dance hall.

Source: Useful classes were selected by Devon
           Association of Parish Councils, Town and
           Country Planning in Devon (Exeter, DAPC,
           1976).

---

nature of these conflicts are more difficult to
diffuse. The broad concensus of opinion would
appear to follow Newby's view that:

> in the future a diverse ecology will only
> be able to co-exist with an efficient
> agriculture within the context of a planned
> land-use strategy, and such an attempt to
> resolve the various and conflicting demands
> on the countryside cannot be successful
> without farmers surrendering at least some
> of their freedom of action to do as they wish
> with their own land.[47]

Yet a brief recall of the political economy perspective of policy and decision-making in planning
(Section 11.1) should be sufficient to remind the
crystal-ball gazer that the central state maintains
an inbuilt conservatism and has consistently
defended the ideology of landownership. These
status quo tendencies, when added to the unparalleled
influence enjoyed by the National Farmers Union in
its relationship with the Ministry of Agriculture[48],
offer little immediate prospect of a handover by
rural landowners of their freedom of action.

Despite this seemingly entrenched position, there
have been repeated calls for extension of development control powers, particularly in special designated areas. For example, the Highlands and Islands
Development Board[49] have long envied the control
over the acquisition of rural land found elsewhere
in Western Europe, and pleaded for additional powers
to designate areas where they would automatically
be given powers to control land use.

Similarly, the Tourism and Recreation Research Unit's
vast study of the economy of rural communities in
National Parks,[50] after considerable debate as to
the role of agriculture as the natural conservator
of the landscape

> reluctantly recommends that planning control
> be extended to embrace artefacts, landscape
> features and qualitative changes in agri
> cultural land use (for example, reclamation
> of moorland).[51]

This recommendation has been viewed elsewhere as an
equitable redress of the rather over-favourable
position enjoyed by farmers so far as government aid
and policy is concerned.[52]

So, despite the political stone-wall of landowner
freedoms, there remains a growing head of steam for
an extension of planning control over landscape
change, particularly in areas of special status.
Any realistic re-evaluation of policy in this direction, however, will not occur until the currently
favoured technique of informal management (Section
11.4) has been fully reviewed and assessed.

Development Control in Specially Designated Areas

Chapter 8 gives a detailed account of the conflicts

arising between conservation policies and the
management of social resources connected with the
built environment. A short reprise of these issues
is worthwhile in this context both because of the
vast area of rural land (around 50% of England and
Wales) which is designated as worthy of landscape
conservation of one form or another, and because of
the general accusation that development control is
more strictly applied in these areas[53].

Despite a dearth of evidence and well documented
research on these conflicts a recent review has made
some interesting assertions about development control
in designated areas.[54] In <u>national parks</u> there is
some evidence to suggest that recent national park
plans, structure plans and local plans have developed a strong framework for two main trends of development control planning. Not only does it appear
that a more severe interpretation of development
control power is quite likely in the parks, but
paradoxically the national park authorities have as
high an appreciation as any other planning agencies
in Britain of the need to supply disadvantaged sectors of the local population with community facilities and life-style opportunities.

This strange dualism of policy is reflected in the
use of Section 52 Agreements to ensure that new
houses are sold to local people - a strict development control tool linked with an appreciation of
local needs. Unfortunately, the history of rural
planning in Britain suggests that where the incon-
gruous duo of welfare and conservation policies are
due to simultaneous implementation, there is a high
probability of conflict between the two policy
strands, in which case conservation controls will
usually dominate.

<u>AONB's</u> and <u>AGLV's</u> have also been subjected to polemic
debate, particularly concerned with their role as
restrictive influences on both landscape and community. There are considerable methodological difficulties in measuring the exact effect of designations such as AONB or AGLV (or for that matter
national parks) on rural communities. The Standing
Conference of Rural Community Councils[55] highlights
the problems in:

> trying to disentangle what has happened in
> AONB's for what might have happened anyway,
> and separating AONB policies from those

settlement policies which are unlikely to
have as much effect on economic and social
development. It is not easy to see what
would have happened without AONB designation, since many villages within AONB's
include conservation areas and much of
the countryside would be included within
AGLV's.

Analysis of development control data in case study
AONB's [56] suggests that designation does not
necessarily restrict development any further than
levels of control outside the zone, but stresses
that this equality arises from strict standards of
control throughout rural areas rather than form any
laxity of implementation within AONB's. It does
appear, however, that AONB and AGLV designations
can in certain circumstances aggravate pre-existing
problems of population in-migration, pressures on
housing markets and scarcity of employment opportunities. As a minimum, the special status of
these areas represents one additional hurdle to be
overcome by low-income and low-opportunity local
population groups, whose entrance to the housing
market is least aided by development control procedures even in normal circumstances.

Recent research has indicated that a consistent
picture of strictly interpreted development control
exists within green belts. Cherrett[57] suggests 'a
whiff of trench warfare here; the line must be held
at all costs'. Inherent in this holding of the line
is the fact that existing inequalities of area to
housing within green belt areas will be perpetuated.
Similarly, conservation area status tends to act
against the development of small-scale low-price
and mixed tenure residential developments. The use
of strict design conditions on any approval of
applications to build tends to drive up the cost of
the resulting dwelling, and in circumstances where
few new dwellings are permitted anyway, developers
will wish to maximise profit by building for the
affluent and not the disadvantaged.

Methodological and (more importantly) ontological
complexities make it difficult to offer anything
other than inferential evidence of the effects of
strict enactment of development control in designated areas. At the very least it can be asserted
that in some circumstances, these designation policies are capable of exacerbating or even generating

gross inequalities of socio-economic resource
opportunity in their attempts to conserve the rural
heritage. Margaret Anderson[58] points out that the
idea of rigid boundaries for major landscape protection areas grew up alongside the rigid map-
oriented zoning of land use within the early development plans which stemmed from the 1947 Town and
Country Planning Act. While zoning in the statutory
planning system has now been largely discredited
and replaced by more flexible strategic guidelines,
the landscape protection zones have remained and have
even been increased in size and tightened up in their
boundaries with more mortal rural areas.

Anderson poses a very telling question:

> One should perhaps ask why zoning for land-
> scape still holds such a strong place in
> official thinking when other types of zon-
> ing have largely disappeared from the plan-
> ning scene. Could it be that whereas the
> zoning for other activities, such as resi-
> dential and industrial development, broke
> down in the face of increasing public pres-
> sure, the demand for change in landscape
> zones is not sufficiently dominant? Or is
> it that the constraints provided by zoning
> have been so weak that changes have taken
> place regardless of the protective
> envelope?[59]

If the latter explanation is accepted - and it is
difficult to give credence to the former - then it
could just be that the use of reactive development
control planning in sensitive landscapes and settle-
mentscapes has fallen between two stools. Lack of
control over landscape change has nullified some
conservation objectives and surplus control over
the scale and design residential development has
sponsored gentrification processes and therefore
nullified welfare objectives. Clearly, the special
status allotted to these particular rural areas make
them a showcase for the limitations of both
development control exerted, and development control
exempted.

Section 11.4 offers some discussion of the extent to
which informal resource management techniques can act
as a sturdy plank (or even soft landing mat) between
the two stools of conservation and welfare, while
Section 11.3 analyses attempts to build similar

bridges through direct development.

11.3 PLANNING BY DEVELOPMENT

Planning by development control has patently suffered from its inevitably negative tendencies. By
reacting, however worthily, to the development bids
of other (usually private sector) agencies, rural
planners can at best seek goals of constraint,
advocacy and encouragement rather than engaging in
the positive promotion of future planned states
delegated to them either through the democratic
process or through the pursuit of minority welfare
ideals. Dyckman[60] views the very purpose of planning as to release human abilities, to broaden the
field of opportunity, and to enlarge human liberty,
and although it should be recognised that planning
does not have the wherewithall to create human
liberty and dignity, it nevertheless is capable of
promoting the attainment of these attributes, for
both rural and urban communities[61].

Whitby's definition of rural development as 'an
improvement in the welfare of people living in rural
areas'[62] is one which is a useful starting point for
a review of development progress in various nations.
He mentions six policy concerns arising from this
definition:

1.   High unemployment
2.   Low incomes/inequitably distributed
3.   High service costs/unequal access to services
4.   Selective migration into, out of, or between
      rural areas
5.   Externalities imposed by one activity or
      another
6.   Availability of public funds

To these essentially remote area-oriented characteristics may be added the urban-fringe elements arising from urbanisation with resulting land speculation
and other spillover effects which interfere both with
agricultural activity and resident communities.[63]
These development policy concerns, both promotive
and promotive-protective (as required in the latter
case) are interacting and complex. Positive planning
for development has occurred in both sectoral and
comprehensive forms, and has come about through both
direct intervention and corporate co-ordination.
These different approaches are discussed in a little
more detail below.

Direct Intervention

Direct intervention has generally been invoked, even in mixed or capitalist economies, where socio-economic solutions which arise from the rights and obligations which are bargained for in the market-place are found to be socially unacceptable. Lichfield[64], for example, has argued that there is no scope for any significant extension of the market-place in the resolution or implementation of planning problems. Indeed, the opposite applies since many instances of direct intervention are required because market failures necessitate regulation and socio-economic repair.

Nevertheless it is clear from the discussion of planning within political economy (Section 11.1) that the conservatism and internal survival mechanisms within many central states will result in:

(i) a reluctance to sanction any positive action which would be socially progressive or involve a re-allocation of resources, and

(ii) even where direct development is sanctioned, a high degree of variation between and within states in the scale and level of integration of that direct action.

One or two examples from different states within a range of political economies serves to emphasise these characteristics. The U.S.S.R., for example, represents a case of tight central regulation of all rural resources, whereby integrated schemes of direct intervention present few problems to the socialist economy. The rationalisation of rural settlements in the 1960s and early 1970s so that perspekhvnyi (perspective settlements) accommodated population growth while neperspekhvnyi (non-perspective settlements) were phased out over varying time-scales[65] was within the directive capability of Soviet regional planners even though the implementation of these plans was by no means universal.

More recently, a wider perspective of direct intervention in Soviet regional planning has been described by Butusova et al[66] who list seven interacting tasks:

(i) the realisation of projects for industrial complexes conforming with conditions in the region

(ii) the creation of a rational settlement base

(iii) initiation of conservation projects

(iv) forseeing the consequences for nature of agricultural development

(v) estimations of natural reserves

(vi) justification of conservation measures against plundering and pollution of the environment in order to provide for the most rational utilisation of the land and for land reclamation

(vii) differentiation of projects for regional development making short-term projects exact and detailed while leaving open modification of long-term projects with regard to future changes.

This kind of comprehensive agenda for direct intervention in the planning of the entire spectrum of rural resources is only feasible because of the mechanisms and regulations available to planners in a society such as that pertaining in Soviet Russia.

Comprehensive direct intervention should not, however, be viewed as an Eastern European phenomenon. A similar example is found in post-independence Tanzania where an integrated 'villagisation' programme has been implemented which has not only secured a shift of rural populations into growth centres (known as Ujamaa and Development Villages) but has also directly provided running water supplies, dispensaries, primary schools and shops to many of these rural centres. As Kulaba remarks: 'It is political will, backed up actual availability and control over available resources in the country which has made these numerous successes possible'[67].

A third example of 'integrated rural development' is found in the Israel context. Although this term (I.R.D.) has been widely used to describe often conflicting approaches[68], the basic aim of this form of planning has been described by Weitz[69]. He argues that:

> Integrated Rural Development puts a major emphasis on the eradication of poverty, by meeting the basic needs of the entire population of the rural areas through an increase in production, and where necessary, a redistribution of productive assets'.

387

Planning

Meeting the basic needs of rural people is achieved
on the basis of economic growth: agricultural
growth is generated through an increase in the total
employment capacity and an increase in the efficiency
of production; an institutional support system is
provided for marketing, information and community
services, rural industrialisation is prompted so as
to provide markets for agricultural products and to
provide employment; and urban decentralisation into
a system of rural towns is secured.

It would be very simple for those who are culturally
confined to the developed world to scoff at these
development measures as being irrelevant in the hav-
ens of developmental elitism that are Europe, North
America and the 'mature' Pacific regions. Nevertheless the very existence of integrated rural development schemes elsewhere underlines the degree to
which advanced capitalist and mixed economies have
recoiled from comprehensive intervention in rural
planning and have preferred either to restrict their
ambitions for direct action to sectoral scemes or
to adopt the politically pragmatic stance of 'active
inertia'.

The rural resource sector which has perhaps attracted
the most controversial planning intervention is
that of land. From one viewpoint it is argued that
agricultural landowners, for example, have an excellent record both in suiting their activities to the
needs of the national economy, and in demonstrating
a willingness to invest and innovate whilst paying
due regard to conservation ideals.[70] Claims of this
type have been forwarded as an aggressive defence of
private land ownership over the entire spectrum of
land use.

Alternatively, commentators such as Darin-Drabkin
and Darin[71] argue that land should be regarded as a
scarce resource rather than as a commodity, and
that because of the magnitude of the failure of
private sector market mechanisms to ensure an equitable allocation of this scarce resource, state intervention in the land market is required. Indeed,
there are clear indications that capitalist and
mixed economy states have been prepared to act as
land developers,[72] although such schemes appear invariably to operate at the urban scale rather than
as agents of planning by development in rural areas.

In the U.K. rural areas have seen little of the

388

considerable state-initiated lists of development
which were centred first on new and expanded towns,
then on the inner cities. Perhaps the closest equivalent is contained within the work of the Rural
Development Boards in Mid Wales and the Highlands and
Islands of Scotland, where considerable localised
activity has occurred in directly developing advanced
factories, social, economic and cultural facilities,
and, in the case of Mid Wales Development, public
sector housing schemes. Even where planning for
rural development does occur, however, some analysts
remain unconvinced of any advancement in the equity
of planning outcomes in areas of direct intervention.

Planning by direct intervention is generally alien
to the ideologies espoused by western governments.
In situations where this planning mechanism is
counteranced, it is often the metropolitan areas
which are the beneficiaries. Planning by development in rural areas, therefore, is generally undertaken by means of various forms of corporate control
of the development undertaken by other agencies,
either in the private sector, or in the public sect-
or but outside the formal planning institutions.

Co-ordinative Planning of External Decision-makers

A study of social planning in the U.S.A. as viewed
by planning practioners there[74] has produced very
interesting and revealing conclusions as to the
nature of the planning task in that nation. The
authors say of social planners that:

> The jobs they do can be viewed as a set of
> separate job roles defined by the tasks they
> do and the skills they use rather than by
> the substantive policy area in which they
> work. The six job roles identified,
> stated as verbs, are designing, represent-
> ing, directing, advising, policy-making
> and evaluating[75].

This sharply focussed view of social planning as a
process which stops short of any form of implementation is broadly indicative of the favoured approach
to rural planning by development in advanced western
societies. The role of planning is to co-ordinate,
direct and advise other decision-makers through plan-
design, policy-making and outcome-evaluation.
Different configurations of decision-making agencies
occur within different nations with their own

political and socio-economic administrative structures

In the U.S.A., for example, some public sector development has been sponsored by the United States
Department of Agriculture and is managed at the local
level by a co-operative alliance between federal
agencies and local government. Nevertheless it is
realised that much of the development which does
occur is more a consequence of private rather than
public initiative and so organisational systems have
been developed which aim to cope with both sectors[76].

FIGURE 11.3 identifies various elements of society
and government which sponsor development in rural
areas (the behavioural framework), indicates that
participation from individuals and organisations is
crucial to the development process, and highlights
four principal areas of action - human development,
economic development, community facilities, and environmental improvements. The core of this process,
however, is that of co-ordination by planners, both
by control and management methods.

This illustration of co-ordinative planning in
theory should be viewed against the achievements in
practice. Lassey[77] has listed five issues which have
obstructed effective planning for human services in
rural U.S.A.:

(i) county commissioners are often disillusioned
because there are too few resources to init-
iate planned programs which enact the numerous expensive planning studies which exist

(ii) many rural counties suffer from lack of revenue and so each resource allocation decision
assumes crisis proportions

(iii) rural counties are reluctant to employ professional staff to deal with human service planning programs

(iv) federal and state grants are often categorical,
and do not fit local conditions

(v) there are few integrated human resource planning mechanisms available, especially because
of
- an acute rural transportation problem
- limited staffs and budgets for rural social
programs
- a lack of co-ordination between social
agencies

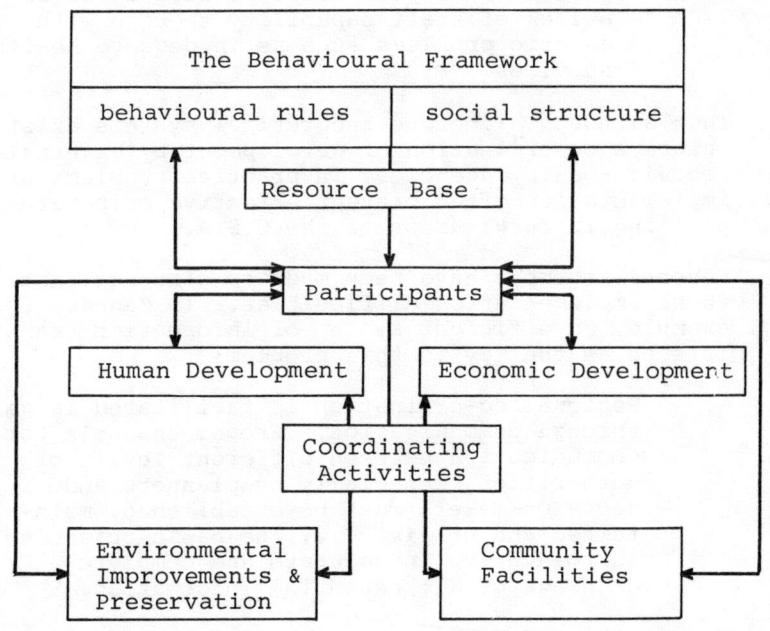

NOTE :

Participants ; include individuals, families, private
associations, firms, government bodies, etc.
Human Development ; includes sociocultural development,
job training, education, health services, care of
elderly, youth activities, income security, etc.
Economic Development ; includes job development,
materials & equipment, credit, markets, taxation, etc.
Coordinating Activities ; includes comprehensive
planning, land use planning & zoning, coordination
among government units, fiscal management, etc.
Environmental Improvements & Preservation; includes
conservation, parks & recreation, forests, wildlife,
farmland, pollution control, population control, etc.
Community Facilities ; includes housing, transportation,
utilities, communication systems, waste disposal and
water supply, schools, churches & public buildings,
shopping & service facilities.

FIGURE II.3 A proposed model of the rural planning system

391

- professional jealousies between agencies
- a lack of staff capability to cope with generic problems such as inadequate health services.

Thus although elaborate theoretical systems exist to ensure a co-ordination of development by external decision-making agencies, in practice problems of implementation often prevent effective corporate planning in rural areas of the U.S.A.

Several attempts have been made to circumnavigate these implementation difficulties. In Canada, for example, an efficient system of information transfer is seen as the key to this problem:

> Regional co-ordination is facilitated largely through <u>communication</u>. Proper channels for communication between different levels of authorities, especially by planners and decision-makers must be established, maintained and utilised.... The basic objective is to achieve an accurate and complete exchange of all essential information.[78]

Yet in the U.K., where the institutional framework for co-ordination is perhaps best developed, analysts such as Cherry[79] speak of ten years' experience in rural planning serving to confirm 'a certain weariness with the imperfections of the system'. He argues that 'the great hope of any form of planning lies in a capacity for <u>programme co-ordination</u>, but the reality of our present machinery is that effective co-ordination is so rarely achieved'.[80] Even in terms of corporate planning between public sector agencies dealing with housing, education, transport, health and so on (supposedly more achievable than the co-ordination of resources governed by the private sector) the gap between social policy and planned implementation remains wide.

This pessimistic account should not hide the achievements which have occurred. In search of a more corporate form of planning, joint committees of public-sector decision-makers now exist so that at least the different parties can talk to each other about potential co-ordination of policy. Indeed, the county structure plans of the 1970s appear to have made significant progress towards mutually responsive policies for rural service provision. The acid test, however, will not be in written statements

of policy but in the implementation of those policies.
Thus far, co-ordinated rural planning appears to have
performed quite well in its negative mode, that is
when control has been the major policy objective.

When positive action has been required, however, co-
ordination has been less successful. Although the
rural service problem has been the recipient of energetic and often active attention, this progress
has often relied for its impact on voluntary effort
and the self-help ethic among rural communities.
Provision of social facilities in areas outside of
zones of market-led growth has therefore often been
coincidental to the co-ordinating promptings of the
statutory planning systems.

Most systems of rural planning, whether sophisticated
or less well developed, can point to success stories
of well integrated joint projects of social or economic provision. In New Zealand, for example, where
regional co-ordination of decision-making agencies
is relatively youthful, there have been many localised advances in co-operative rural planning. A
series of observations from the New Zealand Planning
Council's report on 'rural change'[81] serve to add
flesh to the bones of this contention:
  - in North Canterbury, the hospital board
    provides support for voluntary nursing and
    home-help services co-ordinated by local
    communities
  - the Cheviot Community Committee in partner-
    ship with the local county council is co-
    ordinating social and welfare services
  - a horticultural co-operative in Tikihki
    has evolved to improve access to information
    and advice for its members
  - Southland County Council has established
    special levies to strengthen small and
    medium-sized rural communities in the face
    of depopulation trends
  - the King County Rural Education Activities
    Programme has trained unemployed people in
    wool handling skills and found them permanent
    employment.

Although many of these achievements are small-scale,
they nevertheless represent the types of activity
required as cogs in the wheel of rural development
and co-ordinated management. It is noticeable,
however, that mutual co-operation often appears
simpler to organise between planning agency and

community group rather than between two or more
decision-making and resource-allocating agencies.
If small but locally and cumulatively significant
achievements can be wrought by the planner-people
relationship, how much more so should positive rural
planning be tenable through close planner-agency or
agency-agency relationships? Yet these latter forms
of policy-making integration are inordinately difficult to achieve (for the understandable reasons
analysed in issue Section 11.1).

It is for this reason that the extent to which integrated management of access, services, housing,
employment and farming can become the core of a
coherent planning system has been seen as the most
crucial question for rural planning in the 1980's.[82]
Many planners have pinned their hopes on establishing
systems of greater integration with resultant beneficial outcomes for rural communities.[83] Others
have identified 'planning as co-ordinating external
decision-makers' to be a false hope which ignores
the societal and political contexts which have
spawned fragmented resource allocation agencies in
the first place.[84]

It is certainly clear that as yet, the promise of
co-ordinated rural management has largely been unfulfilled in terms of social resources in the
countryside.

11.4 PLANNING BY AGREEMENT: THE WILDLIFE AND
      COUNTRYSIDE ACT, 1981

One further generic mechanism which offers scope for
resolving conflicts between different rural resource
usages is that of planning by agreement. If the aims
of rural resource management cannot be achieved
through development control or direct or co-ordinated
development, or indeed if these planning tools are
politically untenable for one reason or another, the
last resort is to attempt some form of voluntary or
subsidised agreement between the actors concerned so
as to realise some desired outcome in the countryside.

The issue of planning by agreement raises several
fundamental principles of resource allocation in
situations of conflict between private rights and
public desires. Analysis of the issue here will be
via an important milestone in countryside planning
in the U.K. - the Wildlife and Countryside Act, 1981
- which highlights both conflicts involved and the

vicissitudes of attempting to resolve conflicts in this low-key manner.

The concept of <u>management agreements</u> has been long-standing in British rural planning, having been widely used since the National Parks and Access to the Countryside Act in 1949. Accordingly, a land-owner can enter into some voluntary agreement with the local authority to manage land in a particular way. Commonly some token payment is received by the landowner in compensation for his curtailed freedom of action.[85]

The success of otherwise of management agreements prior to 1981 has been given detailed analysis by Feist[86] and Cawap[87], but in summary three limitations of this planning technique have been emphasised:

(i) management agreements are <u>irrelevant</u> where public sector problems such as conflicting government policy or lack of finance prevail (as they commonly do)

(ii) land ownership and land use conflicts often require <u>legal resolution</u> rather than voluntary agreement.

(iii) management agreements address the <u>symptoms</u> of landscape change but not the causes such as structural changes in marginal agriculture.

These deficiencies were highlighted by the U.K. conservation lobby and successive governments have realised the need for new legislation in this area. The Labour government's Countryside Bill, 1978, which was supersided by events, attempted to designate <u>Moorland Conservation Areas</u> within which agricultural improvements (especially ploughing up) would be prohibited by Moorland Conservation Orders which offered compensation on a once-and-for-all basis. This Bill has been variously viewed as 'a wasted opportunity'[88] and as illustrating 'the growing power of the state over the ways in which private landowners work their estates.'[89] It certainly aroused the passions of the landowner lobby, as represented by the Country Landowners Association and the National Farmers Union, such that when the ensuing Conservative government advanced its proposals for countryside management, their Bill was heavily influenced by landowner views.[90]

The Conservative 'Wildlife and Countryside Act' was

395

placed on the statute books on 30 October 1981,
after nearly a year of parliamentary debate.[91] It
contains a range of provisions, with Part I dealing
with species conservation and Part III covering the
question of public rights of way. It is Part II,
however, which updates the management agreement
concept, permitting relevant authorities to enter
into management agreements with landowners for the
purpose of conserving or enhancing the natural
beauty or amenity land in the countryside or promoting its enjoyment of the public.[92]

The Act has been strongly criticised by several
commentators. McCoubrey, for example, offers the
opinion that 'the act is woefully tentative in its
approach to the most serious manifestations of the
environmental perils, the seriousness of which is
acknowledged by its existence. The overall effect
of the Act appears to be one.....of toothlessness
in the face of the uncaring and the ignorant.'[93]

MacEwen and MacEwen are equally damning:

> The Wildlife and Countryside Act, 1981 is,
> quite liberally, unprincipled. It is a dead
> end, from which another government will have
> to retreat before it can advance by a dif-
> ferent route. It leaves agriculture and con-
> servation on a collision course, but provides
> no way of regulating the conflict except by
> pouring small amounts of money into a bottom-
> less pit.[94]

A string of specific criticisms of the Act have emerged which speak volumes in the context of a more
underspread use of this type of planning procedure.
First, the Act has been seen to introduce what
Cowap[95] calls 'the paradox of compulsory agreement'
which is contradictory in theory and unsuccessful in
practice. Previous experience has shown that any
productive use of management agreements has been
brought about through goodwill and co-operation, but
the notion that conservation authorities should com-
pel landowners to give prior notification of certain
intended land use changes, and then purchase the
goodwill of awkward landowners through monetary compensation removes the Act from the realms of co-
operative husbandry of rural resources into the
realms of profitability of business. Another criticism of the Act is that it is negative in nature,
providing hypothetical machinery to restrict unwanted

changes in the agricultural landscape but offering
little or no scope for securing agreements for
positive management.

These two areas of concern, however, pale into relative insignificance when the factors of scale and
funding are considered. The provisions of the Act
are restricted to small areas of the countryside
including national parks, Sites of Special Scientific Interest (SSSIs) and a few other areas of which
only the Norfolk Broads have so far been designated.
As a consequence, the Act may be viewed as a deliberate attempt to focus upon elitist landscape resources
at the expense of the bulk of the British countryside. Moreover, within these elite areas, the
principle of financial compensation has imposed a
bottomless financial burden on the already hard
pressed management authorities.

MacEwen and MacEwen note that:

'Ministers have sold Parliament in a pig-in-a-poke.
They refused to say precisely what the principles of
compensation would be or to indicate how much money
the Government would provide to enable the conservation authorities to pay the compensation. The
extent of the landscapes or habitats that can be
protected will be determined by the cash available'.[96]
They further argue that ministerial advice on this
matter indicates that landowners should be given
full compensation for any loss of profit arising
from a management agreement, and should be treated
to inflation-proofed annual payments over a 20-year
agreement period.

These financial commitments thrust upon conservation
agencies are not underwritten with any government
guarantee of additional funds to pay for compensation
burdens. Although the matter of securing adequate
government finance for compensation payments remains
under review, it appears most likely that a considerable shortfall will occur. This in turn would
mean that conservation agencies, in cutting their
coat according to their cloth, will be forced to
decide upon their priorities (a case of eliticism
within eliticism) for objection to harmful agricultural schemes. Lack of finance might well prevent
these agencies from objecting at all to land use
changes which they consider to be damaging but
which they cannot afford to compensate for.

The notion of compensation sets a dangerous precedent. Most western societies do not exhibit sufficient political motivation for rural resource
management to provide financial payments to farmers
to conserve the landscape under their control. Paradoxically, most societies do pay farmers to develop
and improve their land, and in the UK the conflict
between generous grant-aid for development by the
Ministry of Agriculture and puny compensation capabilities by conservative authorities is a very one-
sided competition indeed.

Norton-Taylor, in reviewing the first test cases
following the 1981 Act declares that the battle is
already lost:

> The first test involving the Halvergate
> Marshes in Norfolk and the Romney Marsh
> in Kent proved the point: early in 1982
> the conservationists were defeated, the
> landowners won. Some farmers are even
> now putting to the plough land that they
> suspect might be put under conservation
> order, lest they lose their freedom to
> do what they want with 'their' land.[97]

Other commentators are more circumspect, pointing to
the fact that it is now in the interest of landowner groups to make the Act work, since failure so
to do will inevitably lead to stricter measures such
as the extension of development control processes to
cover agricultural land use charge (Section 11.2).

The political nature of rural resource management is
re-emphasised here. The affluent and powerful groups
within rural society are unlikely to sacrifice their
principles of landownership to any great extent
especially when a Conservative central administration
relies heavily upon their support. Even a change
of government would not necessarily bring about any
radical change of emphasis so far as agricultural
power is concerned since the institution structures
of subsidies to farmers are intricate, international
and relatively insensitive to party politics of the
British variety. It is for this reason that the
management of 'damaging' farming activity has for so
long been restricted to rather impotent agreements,
instead of forceful compulsion for the public good.
It requires some rebalancing of landowner strength
and conservation weakness before this situation is
likely to alter noticeably.

The concept of <u>planning by agreement</u> has considerable
relevance in other areas of the rural resource base.
In many ways it is the weakest form of planning,
often adopted from a position of weakness rather
than strength. It panders to the perpetration of
undesirable rural change, and attempts to redress
such change not so much on the grounds of public
benefit but more by appealing to the profit motive
of the already affluent.

We should perhaps draw a fine line here between the
notions of <u>compensation</u> and <u>subsidy</u>. Subsidy is a
widespread method of maintaining or creating needed
resources in rural areas. Local authorities subsidise bus services; nationalised industries subsidise
their rural services by maintaining fixed charges
despite the higher unit costs in rural areas;
government development agencies subsidise new firms
by advance factory building, rent-free periods and
so on; central government subsidises local rural
government through rate support procedures and thereby subsidise positive development in rural areas
through local authority provision of schools, houses,
social services; etc.

Viewed in this way, the upkeep of the socio-economic
fabric in rural areas is heavily dependent upon
external subsidies, without which the life-style
needs of rural people would either be far more
expensive or more distantly located in more economically viable centres. Subsidies, therefore,
maintain or provide services and facilities for
rural people, not as of right, but as a socio-
political act based on generalised grounds of relative equity.

Compensation, although seemingly similar in that
finance changes hands, stands on a different
principle altogether. It suggests that limitation
of an individual's freedom of action requires financial re-balance. It is very important to note that
the 'right' to compensation has been won only by
the powerful landowning groups mentioned above.
Disadvantaged rural families who are forced to move
away from their rural homes because of low incomes,
expensive housing, nationalised in situ services
and lack of public transport are noticeably not
compensated for the limitation on their freedom of
action. There is a grave danger, however, that the
landowner precedent set by the 'Wildlife and Countryside Act' might spread the compensation principle to

other privileged groups, notably those 'suffering'
from restrictions on proposed actions due to development control planning.

The socially polarising distinction between subsidy
and compensation is clear. The use of subsidies to
private sector individuals and firms who are providing services for the public good appears to be
a legimate method of co-ordinating positive planning
in rural areas, although it might be argued that
rather than subsidising the private sector it might
be more efficient to organise direct provision from
the public sector. In the case of agricultural
landowners, such subsidies are already abundant from
the Ministry of Agriculture and the European Economic
Commission.

The use of compensation payments to those who are
sufficiently powerful to flout the public good in
their search for profit-inspired efficiency appears
to be an illegitimate tool for rural resource management. It would surely be far better to organise
subsidies to farmers so that to obtain maximum payments (from whatever central government agency as
long as it is only one agency) both production and
conservation requirements are met.

No individual or group of individuals should be
allowed to play off one planning objective (eg.
agricultural modernisation) against another (eg.
agricultural conservation) as part of a so-called
integrated management strategy. Planning by agreement should therefore make use of subsidies as its
main strength in the improvement of the rural
environment. Moreover, all the forms of countryside
management by planning reviewed in this Chapter are
inobvious need of integration. It is to this theme
that the last Chapter turns.

NOTES AND REFERENCES

1.   D.L.J. Robins, 'Rural Planning', in M. Pacione
      (ed), Progress in Rural Geography (Croom Helm,
      London, 1983): 226.

2.   P. Hall, 'Whatever Happened to Planning?',
      New Society (17 May 1979): 384.

3.   R. Jones, Town and Country Chaos (Adam Smith
      Institute, London, 1982).

4. Ibid, 25.

5. The Royal Institution of Chartered Surveyors,
    Caring for Town and Country (RICS, London, 1979).

6. Royal Town Planning Institute Working Group,
    Planning and the Future (RTPI, London, 1976)

7. D.E. Winfield, 'In Defence of Planning',
    District Councils Review (September 1980): 203.

8. Martin and Vorhees Associates, Review of Rural
    Settlement Policies, 1945-1980 (Martin and
    Vorhees Associates, London, 1981).

9. See S. Barrett and C. Fudge (eds), Policy and
    Action (Methuen, London, 1981) and P. Healey,
    G. McDougall and M.J. Thomas (eds), Planning
    Theory: Prospects for the 1980's (Pergamon,
    Oxford, 1982).

10. P.J. Cloke, 'Policy and Implementation: New
    Focal Points in Rural Planning', Planning
    Quarterly 68 (1982) 15-19.

11. P.J. Cloke and P.J. Hanrahan, 'Policy and
    Implementation in Rural Planning' Geoforum
    16 (1984): 261-269.

12. G.E. Cherry, The Politics of Town Planning
    (Longman, London, 1982).

13. Royal Institute of Public Administration and
    Policy Studies Institute, Party Politics in
    Local Government (RIPA and PSI, 1980).

14. These issues are given more detailed review in
    P.J. Cloke, An Introduction to Rural Settle-
    ment Planning (Methuen, London, 1983).

15. P.J. Hanrahan and P.J. Cloke, 'Towards a
    Critical Appraisal of Rural Settlement Planning
    in England and Wales' Sociologia Ruralis 23
    (1983): 109-129.

16. C. Minay, Implementation - Views from an Ivory
    Tower (Oxford Polytechnic, Oxford, 1979).

17. P. McAuslan, 'The Ideologies of Planning Law',
    Urban Law and Policy 2 (1979): 1-23.

18. As defined by the 1962 Town and Country Planning Act.

19. Cloke, Introduction (Note 14): 204.

20. For a full analysis of structure planning see D.T. Cross and M.R. Bristow (eds) English Structure Planning (Pion, London, 1983).

21. A detailed analysis is presented in P.J. Cloke and D.P. Shaw 'Rural Settlement Policies in Structure Plans' Town Planning Review 54 (1983): 338-354.

22. Salop County Council, Salop County Structure Plan: Written Statement (SCC, Shrewsbury, 1978).

23. Roughly equivalent to the generic title of 'Key Settlements' see P.J. Cloke Key Settlements in Rural Areas (Methuen, London, 1979).

24. Salop County Council (Note 22): 42.

25. Bassetlaw District Council East Bassetlaw District Plan: Draft (BDC, Retford, 1980).

26. A. Alexander, The Politics of Local Government in the United Kingdom (Longman, London, 1982)

27. For a full discussion of this issue see: S.N. Leach, 'Organisational Interests and Inter-organisational Behaviour in Town Planning' Town Planning Review 51 (1980): 286-299.

28. P. Healey, J. David, M. Wood and M.J. Elson The Implementation of Development Plans (Oxford Polytechnic, Oxford, 1982).

29. P. Healey and M. Elson, 'The Role of Development Plans in Implementing Planning Policies' The Planner 68 (1982): 176.

30. J. Lewis and R. Flynn, 'The Implementation of Urban and Regional Planning Policies' Policy and Politics 7 (1979).

31. Working Party on Rural Settlement Policies, A Future for the Village (HMSO, Bristol, 1979).

32. Martin and Vorhees Associates (Note 8): 198.

33.   Blackwell, M. and Gilg, A., The Countryside:
      Planning and Change (Allen and Unwin, London,
      1981).

34.   Lake District Special Planning Board, Draft
      Settlement Policy: Eden (LDSPB, Kendal, 1979).

35.   G. Clark, Housing and Planning in the Country-
      side (Wiley, Chichester, 1982).

36.   D.M. Shucksmith, No Homes for Locals? (Gower,
      Farnborough, 1981).

37.   Department of the Environment, Circular 22/80
      Development Control - Policy and Practice
      (DoE, London, 1980): para 3.

38.   J. Herington, 'Circular 22/80 - The Demise of
      Settlement Planning?' Area 14 (1982): 157-166.

39.   Ibid, 165-6.

40.   M. Shoard, The Theft of the Countryside (Temple
      Smith, London, 1980): 205.

41.   R. Norton-Taylor, Whose Land is it Anyway?
      (Turnstone Press, Wellingborough, 1982).

42.   National Farmers Union and Country Landowners
      Association, Caring for the Countryside (NFU/
      CLA, London, 1978).

43.   R. Westmacott and T. Worthington, New Agricul-
      tural Landscapes (Countryside Commission,
      Cheltenham, 1974.

44.   H. Newby, Green and Pleasant Land? Social
      Change in Rural England (Pelican, Harmondsworth,
      1980): 219.

45.   Blackwell and Gilg, Countryside, (Note 33).

46.   Robins, 'Rural Planning' (Note 1).

47.   Newby, Pleasant Land (Note 44): 219.

48.   G.K. Wilson, Special Interests and Policy-
      Making (Wiley, Chichester, 1977).

49.   Highlands and Islands Development Board,
      Proposals for Changes in the Highlands and

Islands Development (Scotland) Act, 1965
(HIDB, Inverness, 1978).

50. Tourism and Recreation Research Unit, *The Economy of Rural Communities in the National Parks of England and Wales* (TRRU, Edinburgh, 1981).

51. Ibid, 308.

52. P.J. Cloke, 'The Economy of Rural Communities in National Parks: a Review Article', *Journal of Environmental Management* 16 (1983): 281-288.

53. Association of County Councils *National Parks: An Appraisal of some Current Issues* (ACC, London, 1982).

54. Cloke, *Introduction* (Note 14), Chapter 11.

55. Standing Conference of Rural Community Councils *Whose Countryside?* (National Council for Voluntary Organisations, London, 1979): 2.

56. M.A. Anderson, 'Planning Policies and Development Control in the Sussex Dams AONB' *Town Planning Review* 52 (1981): 5-25; M. Blacksell, 'Landscape Protection and Development Control: An Appraisal of Planning in Rural Areas of England and Wales' *Geoforum* 10 (1979): 267-274; M. Blacksell and A. Gilg, 'Planning Control in an Area of Outstanding Natural Beauty' *Social and Economic Administration* 11 (1977): 206-215.

57. T. Cherrett, 'The Implementation of Green Belt Policy', *Gloucestershire Papers in Local and Rural Planning* 15 (1982): 47.

58. M. Anderson, 'Protecting the Landscape' *Town and Country Planning* 51 (1982): 243-4.

59. Ibid, 243-4.

60. J.W. Dyckman, 'Three Crises of American Planning', in R.W. Burchell and G. Stemlieb (eds) *Planning Theory in the 1980's* (Center for Urban Policy Research, Rutgers University, 1978).

61.   J. Muller, 'Promotive Planning: Towards an Approach to Planning for the Disadvantaged', in P. Healey, G. McDougall and M.J. Thomas (eds) Planning Theory: Prospects for the 1980's (Pergamon, Oxford, 1982).

62.   M.C. Whitby, 'The Evaluation and Appraisal of Strategic Choices in Rural Development'. Paper presented to the Regional Studies Association Conference, Newtown, 1983.

63.   D. Berry and T. Plant, 'Retaining Agricultural Activities under Urban Pressures: A Review of Land Use Conflicts and Policies' Policy Sciences 9 (1978): 153-178.

64.   N. Lichfield, 'Land Policy: Seeking the Right Balance in Government Intervention - an Overview' Urban Law and Policy 3 (1980): 193-203.

65.   J. Pallot, Some Preliminary Thoughts on Soviet Rural Settlement Planning (School of Geography, University of Leeds, 1977).

66.   V.P. Butusova, V.V. Vladimirov, P.K. Vladimirov, E.E. Leizerovich, F.M. Listengurt, E.M. Pertsik and Yu. P. Shulenin, 'Division into Economic Districts, Regional Planning and Urban Planning: The Soviet Case' Geoforum 7 (1976): 215-221.

67.   S.M. Kulaba, 'Rural Settlement Policies in Tanzania' Habitat International 6 (1982): 28.

68.   See H.R. Kotter, 'Some Observations on the Basic Principles and General Strategy Underlying Integrated Rural Development' Monthly Bulletin of Agricultural Economics and Statistics 23 (1974): 1-12.

69.   R. Weitz Integrated Rural Development: The Rehovot Approach (Settlement Study Centre, Rehovot, 1979): 8.

70.   W. de Salis, 'Management and Compulsion in the Countryside: Views from the Country Landowners Association'. Paper presented to the Rural Geography Study Group of the Institute of British Geographers Symposium, University of Southampton, 1982.

71.   H. Darin-Drabkin and Darin, 'Let the State

Control!' Urban Law and Policy 3 (1980): 217-227.

72. G. Lefcoe, 'When Governments become Land Developers: Notes on the Public-Sector Experience in the Netherlands and California' Urban Law and Policy 1 (1978): 103-160.

73. G.C. Wenger Mid Wales: Deprivation or Development (Board of Celtic Studies, University of Wales, 1980).

74. G.C. Hemmens, E.M. Bergman and R.M. Moroney, 'The Practitioner's View of Social Planning' Journal, American Institute of Planners 44 (1978): 181-192.

75. Ibid, 186.

76. J.E. Carlson, M.L. Lassey and W.R. Lassey Rural Society and Environment in America (McGraw-Hill, New York, 1981); J.M. Corman and J.P. Madden The Essential Process for a Successful Rural Strategy (The National Rural Center, Washington D.C., 1977).

77. W.R. Lassey Planning in Rural Environments (McGraw-Hill, New York, 1977).

78. Department of Public Works Canada Town Planning Guidelines, (DPW, Ottawa, 1974): 133.

79. G.E. Cherry, 'Rural Planning's New Focus' Town and Country Planning 51 (1982): 240-3.

80. Ibid, 243.

81. New Zealand Planning Council Rural Change: Farming and the Rural Community in the 1970's (NZPC, Wellington, 1982).

82. Robins 'Rural Planning' (Note 1).

83. See, for example, 'Working Party' (Note 31).

84. Hanrahan and Cloke, 'Critical Appraisal' (Note 15).

85. Blacksell and Gilg, Countryside (Note 33).

86. M.J. Feist, A Study of Management Agreements

(Countryside Commission, 1979).

87.   C. Cawap, 'Management Agreements in Rural
       Planning' Gloucestershire Papers in Local and
       Rural Planning 14 (1982).

88.   C. Stoakes and N. Curry, 'The Countryside Bill
       1978: A Wasted Opportunity' Gloucestershire
       Papers in Local and Rural Planning 4 (1980).

89.   H. Clayton, 'Laying down the Law on Moorlands'
       Field 254 (1979): 424.

90.   C. Caufield, 'Wildlife Bill: Bad Law, Good
       Lobbying' New Scientist 30 July, 1981.

91.   A detailed account of these discussions is
       given by G. Cox and P. Lowe, 'A Battle not the
       War: The Politics of the Wildlife and Country-
       side Act' Countryside Planning Yearbook 4
       (1983): 48-76.

92.   An analysis of the legal considerations of the
       Act is found in H. McCoubrey, 'Countryside
       Conservation and the Wildlife and Countryside
       Act, 1981' New Law Journal 132 (1982): 826-8.

93.   Ibid, 828.

94.   A. MacEwen and M. MacEwen, ' An Unprincipled
       Act?' The Planner 68 (1982): 71.

95.   Cowap, 'Management Agreements' (Note 87): 11.

96.   MacEwens, 'Unprincipled Act?' (Note 94): 71.

97.   Norton-Taylor Whose Land (Note 41): 13-14.

Chapter Twelve

INTEGRATED MANAGEMENT STRATEGIES

> One cannot have agriculture, mineral
> exploitation or urban development
> taking place in the countryside as
> single-purpose goals. Often, of course,
> they are the dominant goals, but there
> are always a number of compatible goals
> and the modern technique is to reconcile
> all these different objectives.[1]

12.1 COMPREHENSIVE PLANNING - CO-ORDINATION,
      CONFLICT AND ACTORS

It will be apparent from the preceding chapters that
most countries have evolved planning systems wherein
competing land uses and resource using activities
co-exist in mutual harmony (most of the time), but
wherein co-ordination and comprehensive planning are
conspicuous by their absence. In Britain, for
example, there is no comprehensive planning of
rural land uses embracing the entire spectrum of
resource using activities, and no suitable machinery
for co-ordination of policies and plans between
different countryside users. The lack of a rural
development agency with appropriately wide-ranging
remit has meant that most policies which affect or
are directed towards the British countryside tend to
be sectional, and there is little attempt to inter-
relate and co-ordinate the activities and objectives
of the many different resource-using agencies.

Growing awareness of the dangers and limitations of
piecemeal policies for rural Britain has fueled a
wide-ranging and long-lasting dialogue about the
need for integrated land use strategies in a country
with strictly limited availability of land and
resources. For example, Perring[2] sensed 'a growing

feeling that there is a malaise in the countryside
as a whole which stems from the lack of an integrated
land use policy for the nation', and Paul[3] stresses
the need for a comprehensive enquiry into rural land
use to chart a strategy for the years ahead in order
to combat problems such as the decline of rural
services, changing agricultural landscapes and
pressures from increased country-based recreation.

The Growing Need

Britain has not always lacked a comprehensive rural
planning system. Coppock[4] points to the co-ordinating role played by the major country landowners
during the eighteenth and early nineteenth centuries,
who considered all aspects of their estates and
planned for future generations, but their impact dim-
inished as estates broke up and tenants won greater
freedom of action. The pre-enclosure manorial system
in medieval Europe encompassed similar integrated
land management, with a variety of land uses accommodated within a limited area (creating visual interest and diversity of wildlife habitats) and much
of the land held in common, with rights of access
strictly safeguarded[5]. The switch to private ownership encouraged the fragmentation and dilution of
this integrated resource management.

The mounting need to introduce comprehensive, integrated rural resource management has arisen through
the progressive privatisation of the countryside,
and through growing awareness of the need to adopt
pragmatic but creative approaches to the allocation
of land resources in the face of increased pressure
from population and technology[6]. The need is without
doubt more acute in Britain than the United States
because of differences in population density (225
people per km^2 in Britain in contrast to 22 in the
United States) and thus attitudes to land and
resource availability (the American approach tends
to be less doctrinaire, for example)[7], although from
America too comes the plea for more effective land
use planning to mediate between complete public
control of land use and traditional reliance on
market forces with their attendent imperfections as
a guide to suitable land use[8]. The plea is echoed
in demands for integrated resource management
strategies to ensure the conservation and sustainable use of important areas and landscapes such as
the Table Mountain National Monument in South Africa[9]
(see Figure 4.1).

Conflict and Actors

The need for integrated land use strategies arises from the desire to minimise conflicts between countryside resource-using activities, and from the longer-term goal of enhancing socio-economic opportunities (see Chapter 5.4), optimising productivity and bequeathing an environmental estate for the benefit of future generations (see Chapter 4.1).

Conflict in the countryside has been explored in Chapters 6 to 10, from which it is clear that there is a need to cater for harmonious interaction between the plethora of interest groups who make different demends on the countryside and the various functions which the countryside is obliged to cater for. Functional competition between different uses of the countryside arises from the various levels of compatibility between different resource-using activities (see FIGURE 12.1).

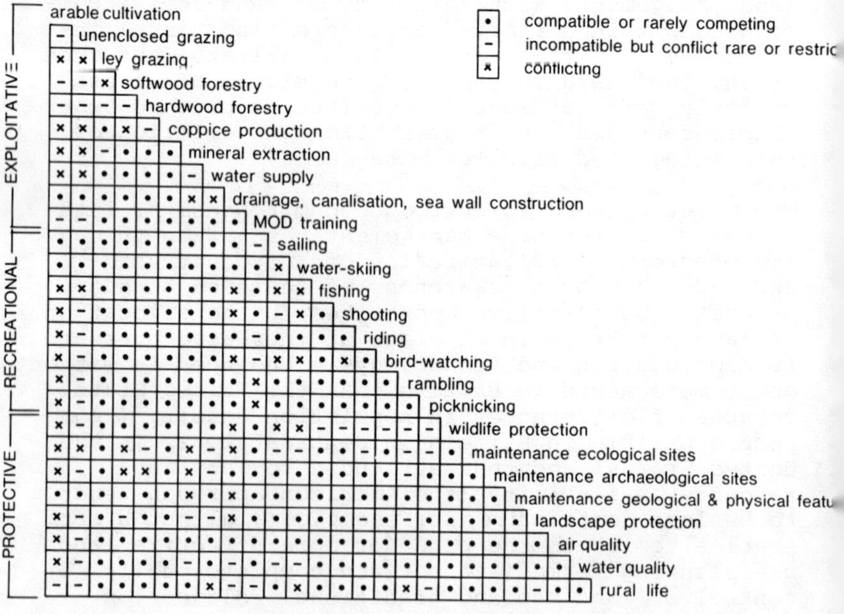
compatible or rarely competing
incompatible but conflict rare or restric
conflicting
EXPLOITATIVE
RECREATIONAL
PROTECTIVE
arable cultivation
unenclosed grazing
ley grazing
softwood forestry
hardwood forestry
coppice production
mineral extraction
water supply
drainage, canalisation, sea wall construction
MOD training
sailing
water-skiing
fishing
shooting
riding
bird-watching
rambling
picknicking
wildlife protection
maintenance ecological sites
maintenance archaeological sites
maintenance geological & physical featu
landscape protection
air quality
water quality
rural life

FIGURE 12.1 Multi-purpose Land Use in the Countryside - Green's compatibility matrix for competing activities

Source: after B.H. Green, 'Countryside planning - compromise or conflict?', The Planner 63 (1977), 67.

Wibberley[10] identifies seven dominant interest groups
in countries like Great Britain (TABLE 12.1) and it
is the interplay between and within these groups,
and be〜〜een them and the functional use of rural
areas (such as for agriculture, forestry, water
supply, minerals, recreation, landscape, employment
and residence, urban limitation and urban reserves[11])
which gives rise to the conflicts. In many ways the
planning system is charged with the resolution of
conflicts between resource-using activities, although
it is accepted that complete resolution is often
impossible. For example, Hall notes that 'planners
have tried in many cases to combine concern for visual aesthetics, economic efficiency and social equity
in their plans; planners and planned now have a
greater understanding of the limited capabilities of
the planning machine to foster all three in
abundance'.[12]

TABLE 12.1   Interest groups in the countryside(after Wibberley)

(a)   those who think that the role of the countryside is
       essentially that of providing outdoor recreation,

(b)   those who are sensitive towards the retention and im-
       provement of the range of natural fauna and flora,

(c)   those who would like the countryside to go back, in
       appearance at least, to what it was when they were young,

(d)   those who want both countryside and rural settlements
       to stay exactly the same, at least in their own partic-
       ular areas, as they were when they first decided to
       live there,

(e)   those who are so harassed by the pace of modern life
       and its tensions that they want the countryside to be a
       refuge for solitude and peace, a sort of wilderness into
       which they can retreat and yet incur no real physical
       danger,

(f)   those who are thankful that the countryside can act as
       a reservoir of land for more urban facilities of all
       kinds, and see it in this form as merely a reserve of
       space and sites,

(g)   those who think that the main function of the country-
       side should be to grow food, and are interested in
       improving technical and economic efficiency in the
       industry of food production.

Yet conflict, within the countryside or any resource
allocation setting, is not a simple concept. Lord[13]
identifies three broadly different types of conflict:

(a)   <u>cognitive conflict</u> (arising through different understandings of a situation of dissonance),

(b)   <u>value conflict</u> (arising through differing assessments of the desirability of ends to be accomplished by actions contemplated), and

(c)   <u>interest conflict</u> (arising because parties to the conflict perceive prospective impacts on their own well being which are desirable for some but undesirable for others).

In the context of this chapter (and the book in general) the <u>interest conflict</u> is the most pressing and merits urgent resolution. Lord proposes that 'resolution of cognitive conflict requires a search for the truth; resolution of value conflict requires a search for the good; resolution of interest conflict requires a search for the acceptable'.[14]

Optimism and Inertia

The need for integrated resource management strategies in the countryside arises in part through a desire to plan effectively for the future, yet Davidson and Wibberley note that within the British countryside 'the mood is still one of cosy optimism, a concern to resolve present conflict rather than to anticipate the future'[15]. But there is a growing body of opinion that such optimism is ill-founded, and an awareness that policies for rural areas are often based on assumptions which are untenable or even destructive. For example, John[16] registers a plea that assumptions that agriculture is the only natural activity in the countryside, that farm amalgamations should be encouraged, that housing and employment should be concentrated in towns and villages, and that sporadic development in the countryside should be resisted, are irrelevant in rural Wales today. The optimism is also ill-founded because of the fragile co-existence of town and country planning in many countries. A meeting of the regional planning ministers of the Council of Europe, held in Vienna in October 1978, concluded that 'at the moment there tends to be a conflict between the interests and aspirations of town and countryside. It is important, therefore, for political bodies and institutions responsible for planning at all levels to have general powers relating to the development of both rural and urban areas in order that the various interests can be dealt with equitably'[17].

Whilst in Britain it is argued that planning has
achieved various successes in the countryside because
there is still a recognisable countryside, the
quality of developments has improved, and planning
acts as an instrument of co-ordination between conflicting interest groups[18], Travis concludes that
'British planners have treated rural planning as
though it has been urban planning writ small'[19] with
policies such as Green Belts, scenic conservation
and the screening of mineral workings representing
a transfer of urban views on amenity and conservation
into the countryside.

12.2 SECTORAL DECISION MAKING AND STRUCTURAL
       LIMITATIONS

One principal reason for the lack of co-ordination
between different resource using activities in the
countryside, and for lack of comprehensive rural
planning is the structure of national government
in general, and its propensity to perpetuate compartmentalised thinking in particular. Wibberley notes
the tendency for the structure of central government
to support the division of activites in the countryside 'because national government either ignores the
countryside or allows it to be administered by separate Government agencies concerned only with one
use.'[20]

Agencies and Responsibilities

More specifically, Coppock sees the treatment of the
countryside as a reflection of 'the way in which
Government responsibilities are organised and in
which users have increasingly come to view the
countryside, for at both local and national levels
the view of the countryside is both narrow and
sectoral. Largely for institutional reasons, there
is a tendency for each component of the countryside
to be viewed in isolation, and this situation is
aggravated by the fact that land use planning, which
is the responsibility of local government, is both
partial and mainly negative, with the major land
uses (farming and forestry) largely outside planning
control. Nobody, nationally or locally, looks at
the countryside in the round'.[21]

The implication of this fragmentation, as pointed
out by Doyle and Tranter, is that 'it is now perhaps
more relevant than ever to reappraise the way we
plan and manage our countryside, and to seek

413

solutions to rural problems arising from the absence
of a national strategy for these areas, and to resolve the current confusion that results from a multiplicity of organisations with rural interests and
powers'[22]. An integrated re-evaluation seems unlikely, given governmental preference for sectoral
approaches and relatively low levels of co-ordination
between agencies.

Minay pinpoints one reason for this <u>sectoral approach</u>
as the problem of resource allocation between agencies: 'the more co-ordination, the more arguments
over resources. Organisations which are reasonably
autonomous can get ahead and implement whatever
seems important to them with the resources they
possess, without arguments that the resources would
be better spent on something else'[23], although
autonomy can lead to duplication of activities,
ineffective and inefficient resource use by the
agencies involved, and compartmentalised thinking,
dissonance and conflict.

The Role of Planning

Part of the responsibility for the fragmentation of
resource allocation decision-making in the countryside must also rest upon the shoulders of planners
at the local level. As Falk stresses, 'the planner
is in a unique position to act as articulator - the
person who establishes what the viewpoints of different interest groups are - and who attempts to
clarify the issues and find what constituent parts
to an issue will settle for where there is conflict'[24]
and Selman[25] adds that the planner is in a unique
position to overview the cumulative results of piecemeal developments. However, formal planning often
lacks the impartiality and rationality, as well as
the breadth of vision and feeling of responsibility
required to perform such a challenging role in conflict resolution.

Batty[26] views planning decision-making as a dynamic
system involving actors (the planners), problems (of
the area of system in question), policies (designed
to alleviate the problems), and factors (describing
the system or area of interest). The typical planning environment involves 'the definition of problems, policies designed to alleviate these problems,
decisions whose outcomes affect the system of interest in spatial or other terms, all set within a
political arena where actors have different degrees

of interest and control over resources (power), and where each actor is trying to optimise some set of goals reflecting preferences and values'[27].

Superimposed on this political/behavioural veneer of decision-making is the fact that for most agencies with responsibility for resource allocation decisions affecting rural areas are often secondary ones if, indeed, they are considered at all. Other objectives are often seen as more important and are thus better defined and more positively addressed.[28]

The problems of planning co-ordination and implement-ation are compounded further by the fact that 'most of the important locational decisions concerning the basic resources which affect rural life-styles are taken outside the formal planning process by agencies other than planning departments and committees'[29], so that the role of private-sector decision-making in rural areas is important in shaping the fabric and lifestyle of rural areas, but is also difficult to co-ordinate in realistic or rational ways.

Policy-making for the countryside thus tends to be compartmentalised and sectoral. Davidson and Wibberley[30] highlight three reasons why such an ap-proach will simply not benefit the countryside in the long term:

(a)   although rural resources may be directly used by only one interest group, resources will be valued (in a less tangible way) by other groups; thus 'the pursuit of single-purpose objectives by different resource interests serves only to curtail the extent to which others may achieve their aims'.

(b)   extra benefits may be derived from co-operation rather than segregation of resource use

(c)   the appearance and functioning of the whole countryside is as important (if not more important) as the working of its component parts (such as forestry or agriculture by themselves).

Nonetheless, single (or dominant) purpose planning of rural resource use has been the rule in Britain during the present century, and Dower notes the growing concern over 'the extent to which the country-side was dominated by great baronies of interest, each pursuing a single major purpose - agriculture, forestry, water supply and so on- and each largely independent of the others'[31].

12.3 BARONIES OF INTEREST AND LEMMING'S RULE

Agriculture and Forestry

The two most dominant 'baronies of interest' in Britain are agriculture and forestry, now the two most important rural industries in the country (see Chapter 9).

They have often been singled out for criticism by proponents of comprehensive planning because they enjoy considerably more freedom from planning restrictions than any other forms of rural land use, for two main reasons pointed out by Whitby and Willis[32]. First, the use of land for agriculture or forestry and the use of existing buildings for that purpose, do not constitute 'development' under the various Town and Country Planning Acts and hence they do not require planning permission. Second, building or engineering operations on agricultural or forestry land are deemed to be covered for planning permission under the General Development Order (1977).

The result is that agriculture and forestry have enjoyed considerable immunity from planning restrictions, and hence they have become powerful forces of change in the countryside. It is interesting to compare a view of 'the rural problem' expressed in 1913 by Harben, who recognised the need for a 'country life movement on the land itself which shall prevent agriculture and all that it represents in the national life being smothered by the neglect of our urban rulers'[33], with the runaway success of agriculture suggested in the conclusion encompassed in the Countryside Commissions New Agricultural Landscapes report that 'the pace of change in agriculture is now so powerful and fast that no environmental policy can be built successfully into agricultural policies'[34].

Indeed, the monolithic power of agriculture has led Wibberley to forecast that without strong planning intervention 'the better agricultural areas will push out all recreational, public access, nature conservancy and landscape considerations from farming practices and policies, and we shall move quickly towards areas of single use, industrialised, food factory development'[35].

Chain Reaction

The 'barony of interest' problem is complemented by what Coleman terms the problem of '<u>Lemming's Rule</u>'[36]. The evidence now available from detailed analysis of the results of the Second Land Utilisation Survey of Great Britain (see Chapter 9.1) shows repeatedly that the existing planning machinery has largely failed to implement its own classical objectives (of containment and conservation), and that the outer displacement of land use changes from urban areas (Lemming's Rule) has occurred widely within the last three decades.

The chain reaction of land use pressures spreading outwards from decaying inner cities like ripples on a pond have led to dislocation of one land use after another; such as the invasion of farmscape land and loss of agricultural land by urban sprawl, intensification of agriculture and loss of wildlife habitats within the countryside[37]. Considerable debate surrounds the availability and interpretation of evidence on land use patterns and changes, and Bowman, Doyle and Tranter[38] point out that effective and appropriate allocation of land resources depends on meaningful and accurate information on land use and capability being available in a suitable form for planners.

The Land Decade Council (1980-90) has been set up in Britain with the task of stimulating discussion on land use, encouraging data surveys, publicising successful land use projects and encouraging initiatives in land use planning[39], although the Council has little power and few resources with which to tackle such a promethean task.

Corporate Planning

Green maintains that shortage of goodwill rather than shortage of opportunity probably accounts for the present lack of initiatives on multi-purpose use of the countryside in Britain; he notes that 'we have grown so used to a patchwork quilt countryside, rich in wildlife and recreational opportunities, largely moulded by the major land uses of agriculture and forestry, that the question is rarely raised whether (such) multi-purpose use is any longer possible, or even desirable'[40].

However, there is evidence from both sides of the Atlantic of growing interest in the introduction of

decision-making systems and planning methodologies
which cater for multiple-path, multiple-choice and
systems-analysis based planning and allocation of
resources rather than with linear and single-purpose
planning[41]. In a wider but nonetheless extremely
relevant context Odum has argued that 'controlled
management of the human population together with the
resources and the life support system on which it
depends as a single integrated unit now becomes the
greatest, and certainly the most difficult challenge
ever faced by human society'[42].

This is matched by the request from Cloke for a
corporate approach to the management of rural areas,
which 'would include a comprehensive form of
decision-making and some form of corporate resource
allocation in rural areas.....Corporate rather than
disparate resource management in rural areas could
become a powerful method for the fulfilment of needs,
and thus an equitable means of isolating and evaluating the priority needs of any rural community is
a vital prerequisite for this new approach'[43]. A
comprehensive planning and corporate resource allocation system for the countryside could also play an
important role in seeking to create more equitable
availability of resources (social and natural) and a
broader range and more balanced distribution of
opportunities in rural areas, as a contribution to
the alleviation of rural deprivation[44].

Such visionary developments seem to be elusive goals
within existing countryside planning systems at least
in Britain, however, because - as Selman stresses -
'the essential nature of the planning process is well
suited to the "timeless" image of a serene and un-
changing countryside, and is abetted in its super-
ficial treatment of resource dynamics by countryside
legislation'[45].

12.4   THE RURAL LAND USE STRATEGY DIALOGUE

Despite the on-going dialogue centred on the need for
integrated approaches to resource management in the
countryside, and in the face of the structural inertia within both central government and local planning systems, there have been few attempts to date
to establish comprehensive and co-ordinated planning
systems at either national or local levels in Britain.

The National Debate

At the national scale the dialogue has recognised the need for a positive land use strategy but largely chosen to ignore such practical issues as how it might be formulated, who would be responsible for formulating and monitoring it, and what factors would need to be encorporated within it.

The debate opened during the Second World War, when the Scott Committee on land utilisation in rural areas recognised three persistent trends in rural areas (urban encroachment, economic depression and population drift from the land) and proposed an extension of facilities into rural areas, the provision of agricultural support subsidies, and the introduction of land use planning into the countryside.[46] All three proposals were incorporated into war-time and post-war legislation, and they have considerably influenced the fabric and functioning of the countryside since. However, the planning developments and constraints were largely piecemeal and sectoral, so that integrated development of the countryside was not directly encouraged.

By the mid 1960's the adverse impacts of these trends were becoming clearly evident, and when the Land Use Study Group set up by the Department of Education and Science reported in 1966, it highlighted the need for rationalisation, integration and co-ordination in countryside planning and predicted the call for a positive land use strategy[47]. A decade later the intergovernmental Countryside Review Committee was to review problems and policies within countryside planning, and to forward the principle of multi-purpose use of rural land as the basis for future developments[48].

Within another decade, the Nature Conservancy Council was to review the links between nature conservation and agriculture, and in doing so to recognise that 'a positive rural land use strategy is becoming increasingly necessary for all users of land'[49]. This was to be the first call for harmonisation of conflicting priorities within the countryside. The Council stressed that 'such a strategy would not infer a system of detailed centralised direction and planning, but would take the form of a statement of intent which would outline the objectives for land use. This would foster a rational approach to resources and would provide a framework within which

the priorities of different land users could be
related and harmonised'.[50]

The Policy Game

This dialogue about the need for a rural land use
strategy has spilled over into the public arena in
recent years. For example, Hall[51] concludes that
a national land use strategy would be disasterous
in practice, regardless of whether it was founded on
strong regulation or weak persuasion.

The form of strategy proposed by the Nature Conservancy Council, based on 'statement of intent', Hall
sees as a weak form of strategy which 'at best.....
can be no more than a set of guidelines possessing
perhaps some propaganda value.' A strong form of
strategy is Coleman's proposal to stick rigidly to
exclusive categories of townscape, farmscape and
wildscape (which would be conserved and improved)
and to reduce land fragmentation and sprawling developments in urban fringes and marginal fringes (which
would be restricted or reduced)[52]. Hall argues that
the strong forms of strategy would be dictated by
central government, and they would engender political
manoeuvring and secretive manipulation of planning
powers and policies, all of which would be unacceptable. He concludes that ' it is surely perverse that
conservationists should advocate the transfer of any
of this power, used or potential, to the centre where
the influence of individuals, voluntary organisations
and communities must be less, rather than press for
the reform of the far-from- moribund institutions
we already have'[53].

Hall calls for a revitalisation of the Structure
Plan machinery, and he argues that its strength lies
in the elaborate public consultation and inquiry procedures which figure so centrally in its implementation. However the development control/structure
plan/public enquiry system is not without its critics
even from within the planning profession (see Chapter
11). For example, Friend, Laffin and Norris have
studied in depth the scope for conflict and collab-
oration between authorities in the handling and publi
examination of structure plans, which they view as
a 'policy game' played out over time among the three
levels of government, with interventions by other
interests which can claim a legitimate stake in
matters of land use policy[55].

The 'game' is played by a range of actors, and the rules allow frequent changes of position through conflict, bargaining and co-operating over land use matters, so that accommodation of public views and opinions is often more apparent than real.

Priority Areas

In Britain the most pressing need for integrated resource planning and management arises in hill-land and moorland areas. Dower outlines the paradox: the problems of land use are most acute in hill lands 'where the best way to secure a beautiful and productive landscape and a stable and prosperous community may be to find a sound balance between farming, forestry, tourism and manufacturing industries. What happens? Each of these complementary activities is the subject of separate and competing government support; subsidies for hill farming, tax incentives for forestry, grants and loans to tourism, advance factories for industry with no machinery to integrate their effects'[56].

Integrated resource planning and land use strategies are also required in urban fringe areas, highlighted by Coleman and others as the scene of recurrent planning conflicts and landscape fragmentation[57], although recent experiments by the Countryside Commission have sought suitable approaches to integrated land management in such areas.

The East Hampshire Study. To many commentators on rural planning in Britain, the most successful attempt at integrated land management to date has been the study in policy formulation for the East Hampshire Area of Outstanding Natural Beauty, which involved a team from the Ministry of Agriculture, Fisheries and Food, the Forestry Commission, the Countryside Commission (then the National Parks Commission), the Nature Conservancy Council (then the Nature Conservancy), Hampshire County Council, and the then Ministry of Housing and Local Government (now the Department of Environment).

The aim of the study was to establish 'a technique whereby rural resources, types of land uses and methods of management could be identified, their relative importance assessed, and their inter-relationships recorded, as a basis for ensuring that demands made on the countryside are capable of maximum fulfilment insofar as they are compatible with other demands and are in accord with national and

421

regional policies'.[58] The study 'brought land use
planning, agriculture, forestry and nature conservation interests round the table to identify land
uses and methods of management'[59], as a reaction to
the normal sectoral and insular planning practices
adopted in land use planning, and it demonstrated
that whereas statutory land use planning is often
ineffective a valid planning and management system
can be achieved through co-operation and co-ordination of public and private interests.

Policy formulation centred on establishing compatible
control policies for zones of greatest potential
conflict and for activities which might be unacceptable to other interests, and general policies for
activities not tied to specific location (such as
agriculture and pleasure motoring).[60]

12.5 COUNTRYSIDE COMMISSION INITIATIVES

Co-ordinated management of countryside resources
has been attempted through the Countryside Management
Projects promoted and supported by the Countryside
Commission in conjunction with local authorities.
These experimental projects aim to resolve conflicts
between recreation, conservation, agriculture and
development in the countryside, and 'to develop a
method of managing areas of the countryside to
benefit, as far as possible, all interested parties'.[6]

Countryside Management Projects

The Countryside Commission is charged with keeping
under review matters relating to the conservation
and enhancement of the landscape and amenity base of
the countryside, and the provision and improvement
of facilities for enjoyment of the countryside, so
that its viewpoint is partisan. But via the provision of grant aid and through agreements, by-laws
and provision of warden services the Countryside
Commission has been able to focus attention on the
prospects of integrated land management in five
sectors of the countryside - the uplands, heritage
coasts, urban fringes, Areas of Outstanding Natural
Beauty and the New Agricultural Landscape at large.

Project officers have been delegated financial and
administrative powers by the Countryside Commission
in conjunction with local authorities, to steer
co-ordinated packages of activities including the
clearance of eyesores (such as derelict buildings),
improvement of landscape (such as via tree planting),

maintenance of key landscape features (such as dry
stone walls), improvement of access (such as via
provision of footpaths and nature trails), traffic
management (such as provision of informal car parks),
provision of new informal recreation facilities
(such as country parks and the repair of damage done
by visitors (to gates, walls etc.)[62].

The Urban Fringe. Integrated land management on the
urban fringe was evaluated through the experimental
project centred on the Bollin Valley on the southern
edge of Manchester between 1972 and 1975[63]. Here a
16 km stretch of farmland and open space along the
Bollin valley has been threatened by conflicts between farming and residential development and the
provision of public utilities (through trespass,
vandalism, illegal shooting, dumping of rubbish,
indiscriminate parking and disturbance to stock by
dogs).

The Project Officer was delegated various tasks, including acting as a link between farmers, landowners,
residents and visitors and reducing conflicts between the various parties (via a programme of small
scale improvements in the valley, a county council
warden service, and a management plan to provide a
framework for future local authority action). The
Bollin experiment proved so successful that a similar approach has since been applied to larger
areas on the fringe of London (135 km^2 in Hertfordshire and Barnet, and 45 km^2 in Havering).

The Uplands. The first land management experiments
carried out by the Countryside Commission focussed
on upland areas (The Upland Management Experiment)
in the Lake District and Snowdonia between 1969 and
1972[64]. The experiments sought to reduce conflict
between farming, conservation and recreation in these
areas, again via project officers (part-time, on
secondment from the Ministry of Agriculture).

The principal task of the project officers was to
maintain close contact with local farmers, and through
this dialogue devise and implement small management
works aimed at conserving key landscape features,
improving the landscape and providing local opportunities for informal recreation[65]. The experiments
fulfilled their two main aims of helping to reduce
visitor pressure on farmland and encouraging farmers
to take more positive attitudes towards conservation
and recreation, and the ideas embodied within them

have since been applied by other National Park
authorities.

Management Agreements. In part the Countryside
Commission approach to multiple land use management
centres around the use of management agreements with
landowners, which are voluntary rather than based on
statutory control. As Fiest[66] points out, management
agreements depend on mutual goodwill and co-operation,
but they do offer a useful means of enlisting the
co-operation of landowners and farmers in the pursuit of particular policy objectives (such as to
safeguard the future of a small wood, to create a
new wildlife habitat, or to enhance the landscape).

Under the 1981 Wildlife and Countryside Act management agreements have been given a central place in
resolving conflicts in countryside resource use,
although Leonard[67] underlines the need to set such
agreements within a better development, policy,
information and management framework. He stresses
the complications surrounding conflict resolution
via financial compensation, and calls for more objective analysis of the economic implications of
management agreements, more refined methods of
calculating compensation and a clearer understanding
of the relationship between conservation and the
assessment of public investment schemes.

The National Parks

National Parks are often regarded as microcosms
of the conflicts in rural land use at the national
scale (see Chapter 10.4) and National Park Plans
represent another area in which integrated management has been attempted.

John Dower's celebrated 1945 report on the objectives
of National Parks in Britain highlighted four areas
of concern - the preservation of characteristic
landscape beauty, provision of public access and
facilities for public open air enjoyment, protection
of wildlife, buildings and places of architectural
/historic interest, and maintenance of established
farming use[68]. Since 1949 there have been mounting
and diversifying pressures on land use and resource
allocation within British National Parks[69], and by
the early 1970's it was becoming clear that more
forward-looking management of the resource base was
required.

From 1974 onwards, each National Park has been
charged with the responsibility of preparing a 5 year
management programme, and of keeping this under constant review in the future. As Potter comments
'these plans are a new concept in local government,
they will provide the basis for the implementation
of management policy geared to management objectives
and budget priorities. The plan will be a considerable elaboration on the many management studies that
have been undertaken for specific areas. It may be
that in time they become the blueprints for management programmes in other rural areas where the need
arises to reconcile conflicting demands on the
resource or to implement specific policies'[70].
Whether the management approaches forwarded in the
National Park Plans could be transferred to other
parts of the countryside remains debatable in part
because of the relative uniqueness of National Park
areas (typified by upland areas on resistant rocks,
dissected by valleys with concentrations of settlements, agriculture and communications[71]). Management
agreements figure largely in the National Park plans,
with compensation payments to be paid to private
landowners if their normal operations are restricted
by National Park policies, if they suffer loss of
profit, if policies reduce the capital value of their
land, if access agreements lead to damage or disturbance, of if policies require a specific agreement for recreational use of their land (eg. for car
parks)[72]. MacEwan, amongst others, criticises the
National Park system in Britain as 'wrongly constituted in the first place', being founded on three
assumptions which have since been proven false.[73]
These are that the planning system would protect the
landscape from undesirable change, that farming
could do no wrong in the countryside, and that the
locally elected planning authority would be equated
with the local interest. He has expressed doubts
over the ability of National Park Authorities to
fairly weigh up local versus national arguments,
short versus long term issues, and economic versus
amenity viewpoints when their objectives differ
from those of either local interest or county
councils.[74]

12.6 MULTI-PURPOSE LAND USE AND RESOURCE MANAGEMENT

Perhaps the ideal way of ensuring equitable but efficient resource allocation in the countryside, in
the face of conflicting demands to use available
resources in different ways, is to strive for

multi-purpose use whereby the same piece of land is used simultaneously for different purposes.

Haggett isolates some of the more important inherent in seeking to introduce multiple use, which 'refers to the integration of major uses like forestry and recreation, often but not exclusively implying publicly owned land..... What kinds of land use can be mixed? Which mixtures provide long-term and stable ways of using the land, and which are the dangerous and short-sighted? And who decides on optimal land use strategy?'[75].

Integrated land management might involve one of two types of approach - the common use of the same tract of land for two or more primary purposes (multi-purpose land use), and the parallel use of land within that tract for two or more primary purposes (land use zoning).

Multi-Purpose Land Use

Multi-purpose land use is rarely possible when the land uses are intensive. Physical limitations on such multi-purpose resource allocation arise because of the inherent incompatibility of certain primary land uses. Clearly some land uses are highly intolerant of others - urban development, for example, is not compatible with recreation, agriculture, forestry, grazing, water management, wildlife or mineral production - so that such land uses could not co-exist on the same tract of land (see FIGURE 12.2). On the other hand many land uses are compatible with others - forestry, agriculture and wildlife conservation can co-exist given goodwill and understanding in the appropriate management regimes, for example.

The prospects for multi-purpose land use thus rest on compatibility of land uses. Green[76] has explored the possible conflicts which arise through interactions of 26 countryside activities (with 625 possible conflicts), and concluded that there would only be 53 major (8.8%) conflicts. Over 80% of the land use mixes seem to be compatible with one another (see FIGURE 12.1), so that there appears to be ample scope for manoeuvre in allocating land to compatible multi-purpose use in the planning process. The main areas of conflict which Green identified centred on the association between recreation and exploitative uses of the countryside (other than intensive

Compatibility with Secondary use for:

Primary Land Use	URBAN	RECREATION	AGRICULTURE	FORESTRY	GRAZING	TRANSPORT	WATER RESOURCES	WILDLIFE	MINERAL PRODUCTION
URBAN	7	0 [a]	0	0	0	1 [c]	0	1	1
RECREATION	0	7	0	2-4	0-1	1	2	5	1
AGRICULTURE	0	1	7	0	0	0	1	2-4	2
FORESTRY	0	6	0	7	0-5	0	0	6	2-4
GRAZING	0	6	0	1	7	0	2-6	6	2-6
TRANSPORT	0	0 [b]	0	0	0	7	0	0	0
WATER RESOURCES	0	2-6	1	1	2-4	0	7	2-6	1
WILDLIFE	0	6	1	4	4	0	2	7	1
MINERAL PRODUCTION	0	2	2	3	3-4	3	2	2-3	7

Level of Physical Compatibility

0 NONE
1 VERY POOR
2 POOR
3 FAIR
4 MODERATE
5 FAIRLY HIGH
6 HIGH

FIGURE 12.2 Compatibility of Primary and Secondary Land Uses within an area

Source: after M. Clawson et al, Land for the Future (Johns Hopkins University Press, Baltimore, 1960).

agriculture), and between most recreational activities and protective functions in the countryside (these are discussed in Chapter 7).

Land Use Zoning

Because of the potential incompatibility of different resource users the most promising prospects centre on zoning of land use for different purposes. Zoning involves the physical separation of land uses within a given tract, with the mixture of uses carefully controlled to minimise conflict and the tract overall managed as a single management unit.

Haggett cites the example of national forest lands in

the United States, where commercial forestry and informal recreation provision are carefully zoned and
managed in an integrated manner to optimise the benefits derived by each group of resource users[77].
Land use zoning has become an important ingredient in
land use planning and countryside resource allocation
in the United States, in response to the problems of
optimising land use mixes and protecting environmental quality of the resource base[78].

Large scale zoning is also practised widely, in
order to allocate available land resources as equitably as possible between competing resource user
groups and for different (and at times incompatible)
functions. In Japan, for example, land protection
on the island of Hokkaido has involved designation
of three major land classes - National Parks, Quasi-
National Parks, and Prefectural Parks - and the
zoning of each into three categories with differing
degrees of development control (special protection
areas; special areas; ordinary areas)[79]. Zoning is
also employed in the Soviet Union as a tool to assist
conservation of valuable landscapes and important
areas of resources. Armand et al point out that the
'main objective of the Soviet economy is the rational
utilisation and expanded reproduction of natural
resources'[80], and to this end a series of 'Terri-
torial Complexes' have been designated and established to protect specific resources such as minerals,
water, wildlife and landscape.

In Britain also the notion of land use zoning is well
established - witness, for example, the recent
nationwide review of existing and potential sites and
habitats by the Nature Conservancy Council[81], which
sought to establish which parts of the countryside
are most in need of protection. Land zoning also
figures prominently in the National Park Plans, as
a basis for designating suitable areas for land
management and a guide to optimum land use mixes
within the National Park areas. In Britain, however,
zoning is generally used as a planning guideline and
its strength lies in encouragement and incentives
rather than formal regulation. The country structure
plans suggest planning guidelines in the form of
zoned land and resource allocations, but the sanctity
of such designations is generally weak in practice.

Land use zoning policies tend to be more effective
when applied to the planning of new developments,
particularly on public (or at least non-private) land.

For example integrated planning of land resources around new inland reservoirs now allows for the water supply function to be complemented by recreation provision, landscape design and wildlife conservation[82]. The integrated development plan for the Chew Valley reservoir, near Bristol, catered for various forms of recreational and conservation interest (such as trout fishing, ornithology, sailing and informal land-based recreation) by zoning of land uses both within and surrounding the reservoir lake to optimise the benefits derived from each resource use and enhance the overall value of the reservoir development.

Evaluation of Alternatives

Whilst recent years have witnessed growing interest in the need to search for more integrated approaches to land and resource allocation, and more wide-ranging dialogues about who might be responsible for such decision-making, there has been relatively little interest in how such decisions might best be made.

Selman[83] notes the lack of attention devoted to techniques of determining multiple use solutions for most rural areas, and the shortage of well-tested and widely accepted approaches to the evaluation of alternative solutions. Such a shortage is to be regretted because, as Jenkins points out, ' a positive advantage of evaluation would be to depoliticise a situation, to provide a cold rational appraisal of policy alternatives or policies per se outside the steam heat of emotion and ideology. Sadly, this is very much a false hope, a product of technocracy and scientism pushed forward by those who hanker after a managerial outlook and who fail to appreciate that there is really no such thing as an apolitical arena'.[84]

Since evaluation of alternative land use mixes and integrated strategies plays so important a role in planning decision-making, it is useful to briefly review the main approaches to evaluation, adopting the frameworks proposed by Selman[85] and Sewell[86]:

Cost-Benefit Analysis. An economic evaluation of alternative schemes or options is often based on cost-benefit analysis of competing uses or mixes of use. For example, Helliwell[87] has used cost-benefit analysis to evaluate the benefits to wildlife and amenity derived from varying combinations of farming

and forestry as primary land uses, and Arad and
Berechman[88] outline the use of similar approaches in
determining the optimum allocation of land use
activities around a new town in the United States.

Despite its widespread use in resource allocation
decision-making[89], cost-benefit analysis has been
heavily criticised in its application on many
grounds such as the frequent failure to include all
relevant actors and sectors of the population in
the evaluation, the failure to include and measure
correctly all costs and benefits for all actors and
sectors, the failure to reflect faithfully the
evaluations for all actors and sectors and the problems of deriving meaningful economic measures of
environmental and social impacts[90]. Hammill argues
that economic methods often create an air of apparent
rationality which is not matched by experience, and
that the lack of substantial agreement over which
econometric models to use weakens confidence in results of cost-benefit analyses[91].

Capability Analysis. An alternative approach is
based on the notion that the most efficient basis
on which to allocate land between competing resource
users is the suitability of that land for different
pruposes. Thus, for example, land most suited because of its physical properties to forestry, ought
logically to be dedicated to growing trees as a
primary function. Capability analysis has been
adopted as a basis for resource allocation in
Canada[92] and Britain[93] and elsewhere, although the
technique is used most frequently to indicate most
productive land use mixes as an element in long term
planning, rather than as a tool of immediate relevance to land allocation.

Much debate surrounds the choice of environmental
ingredients in capability analysis, although there
is general agreement that land quality, existing land
use and existing land management regimes are amongst
the key factors[94]. The Land Use Capability Classification developed by the Soil Survey of Great Britain[95] has been widely used in the assessment of land
capability for agricultural purposes because it is
based on the extent of restrictions placed on the
land by physical limitations inherent in it (such
as wetness, stoniness, gradient, and liability to
erosion); for example Bridges[96] has illustrated the
utility of this scheme in mapping soil distributions
and assessing land potential in Derbyshire. A

similar scheme of land capability assessment has been
developed by the Forestry Commission, to aid their
search for a systematic basis on which to select land
suitable for forestry and tree species most suited to
given areas. The forest capability evaluation is
based on a combination of factors such as soil type,
altitude, rainfall, aspect, slope, exposure, accumulated temperature and frost, potential water deficit and pollution[97].

Existing methods of land classification have been
criticised because some make extremely broad generalisations (and thus they are rarely supported by
ground observations) and others require large-scale,
costly and time-consuming surveys. As a result, recent surveys by the Institute of Terrestrial Ecology
have sought to adopt much broader remits and involve
more sophisticated multivariate analysis. Developed
initially for a survey of part of Cumbria[98], but
later expanded to cover the whole of the county[99],
the ITE Land Classification is based on analysis of
282 environmental attributes (derived from map
nalysis and field augmentation and sampling) on a
1 km^2 grid square basis; 32 land classes have been
established, each with well defined environmental
signatures and well defined patterns of distribution,
and each with established associations with land use,
soil type and assemblage of plant species.

One of the few attempts to adopt a capability analysis approach to overall resource planning in the
countryside is Statham's study of the North York
Moors National Park[100]. This sought to identify
'core areas' of land capability for agriculture,
forestry and outdoor recreation by a sieving/overlay
map analysis, as a basis for the allocation of land
between primary productive uses. This form of study,
based on assessment of the potential of land resources as reflected in land capability, could form a
useful model for other studies of capability evaluation in the countryside at large, although such
useful studies have yet to be undertaken.

Systems Analysis. Birch proposes the widespread use
of systems modelling as 'a more explicitly systemic
approach to resource management ...(it) appears to
provide the most fruitful basis for the development
of computable models through which the likely effects
of decisions can be explored and their consequences
subsequently monitored'[101]. System simulation models
and numerical optimisation techniques have been

widely used in forestry, range and watershed management, fisheries, wildlife and marine biology because
they allow the simultaneous consideration of many
variables and the rapid prediction of outcomes of
given management strategies.

Swartzman and Van Dyne outline the benefits of the
approach thus:

> The simulation models consist of large sets
> of algebraic and differential and difference
> equations. Generally, no analytical solution
> exists for these equations, and in practice
> they must be solved numerically using large,
> high speed digital computers. Operations
> research techniques involve seeking optimal
> action by systematically examining objectives,
> costs, effectiveness and risks of alternative
> management strategies.[102]

Such systems analysis methods have been used in planning resource management strategies for particular
environmental resources such as water[103], and Jeffers
has forecast the likelihood of increased use of
systems modelling in land use planning, which he
stresses 'must be an iterative, dynamic and continuous process' [104].

Perhaps the best illustration of the use of systems
approaches in rural resource allocation in Britain
is Dye's modelling of the economy of a section of
the Yorkshire Dales[105]. The model encompasses data
on land quality and economic factors, in the form
of measures of land class (in-bye land, rough grazing
and moorland), financial reward (economic rent) and
existing land use, and it sought to chart the inter-
linkages within the upland system and to illustrate
how the system would respond to a change in one or
more key variables. It thus proved possible to use
the model in the prediction of possible impacts of
different scenarios for the marginal economy of the
area, by modelling the possible effects of changes
in factors such as land transfers, employment and
income levels.

Goals Achievement Methods. Most of the available
approaches to evaluation and decision-making fail
to accommodate more than a small range of objectives,
and most assume that resource allocation decision-
making can be apolitical, fully rational and capable
of deriving optimum solutions to problems which are

in final analysis somewhat intractable.

There are signs, however, that more realistic approaches might be both possible and preferable, and that these might utilise concepts drawn from management science, operations research and allied fields. For example, Hammill[106] proposed a '<u>rational decision making</u>' process with a series of sequential steps; from initiation of the process, identification of alternative actions, forecasting of the consequences of these actions, statement of objectives, ranking of combinations of actions and their consequences, and formulation of action plans and implementation strategies. Hill[107] outlines a family of common problems in resource management which cannot be catered for using alternative decision-making schemes - such as the need to pursue several objectives simultaneously, the need to juggle with a combination of possible strategies, the need to recognise that goals and strategies vary in relative and absolute importance between different interested parties, and the need to accommodate intangible costs and benefits which cannot readily be expressed in monetary terms.

Approaches based on a '<u>Goals Achievement Matrix</u>', or a form of check-list of success in meeting established goals (a system which is also referred to as 'planning by objective'[108]) thus offer potential for evaluating outcomes of decision-making in the light of initial expectations.

An interesting example is the North Riding Pennines Study[109], which sought to bring together organisations with statutory responsibilities for planning and land use, advisory and voluntary bodies, and representatives of landowners and occupiers and compile a realistic policy dossier which would cater for their views as much as possible and yet also be compatible with the natural potential of the resource base of the area. Some 68 problems and opportunities related to forestry, agriculture, nature conservation, landscape protection, recreation, tourism, and social and economic prosperity were recognised by the study team, who then drew up a series of policy options designed to realise the full potential of the area and meet explicitly stated aims (TABLE 12.2).

TABLE 12.2 Aims of integrated planning stated in the North
            Riding Pennines Study[109]

(a)   to conserve and enhance the quality of landscape
(b)   to conserve and enhance all other physical resources
(c)   to enhance the range of ecological variation and wild-
        life resources
(d)   to conserve soil resources
(e)   to improve employment opportunities
(f)   to improve wage rates, salaries and profits
(g)   to enhance human resources
(h)   to provide adequate public services and facilities
(i)   to provide adequate facilities for recreation and
        leisure.

12.7 INSTITUTIONAL IMPLICATIONS

The lack of a properly co-ordinated and fully comprehensive planning system for rural areas, so
clearly apparent from preceding chapters, needs to
be tackled in a positive way if the social, economic
and environmental problems of the countryside are to
be reduced if not eliminated.

Orchestration of Demand

Coppock has observed that 'there is an increasing
awareness of the dangers of piecemeal policies in
the countryside. What has not yet been achieved is
suitable machinery for co-ordinating policies and
plans, though this topic is likely to receive increasing attention as the difficulties of problem
rural areas become more acute'[110]. This forecast
is indeed proving to be accurate, although the
demand for co-ordination of policies and priorities
is not in itself new.

In 1972, for example, Dower was stressing the need
for 'the general integration of support programmes in
agriculture, forestry, industry, tourism and social
infrastructure, so as to permit a more coherent
attack on the long term problems of land use and
social and economic development'[111], and the Select
Committee on Scottish Affairs was proposing the need
for a Land Use Council supported by a professional
Land Use Unit, charged with co-ordination of land
use planning in the countryside as a whole[112].
Ironically, in 1972 also, the Northern Pennines Rural
Development Board was enjoying its brief spell of
life as a broadly based rural planning agency with

a wide-ranging remit (similar to the Highlands and Islands Development Board) to stimulate, co-ordinate and orientate rural developments within the North Pennines area[113].

Towards the close of the 1970's, however, the demand for co-ordination of rural land planning and resource allocation was being well orchestrated at both regional and national levels. Jones put the case forward at the regional scale, with particular reference to the South Downs Area of Outstanding Natural Beauty; he wrote that 'it is time, therefore, that serious consideration be given to the possibility of establishing a single body with responsibility for managing the South Downs as a unit, with a view to maximising the resource benefits while at the same time separating urban, agricultural and recreation/nature conservation activities. It is imperative that the South Downs, having been protected against the worst kinds of development, should be managed so as to evolve in ways that will maximise benefits, not just to the local populations, but to the south east as a whole'[114]. Doyle and Tranter stress the need for a national review of the ways in which the countryside is planned and managed, and the allied need for 'a rationalisation of the whole rural planning structure, together with a considered land use strategy based on sound information and clearly expressed views on the sort of land use and landscape that people want'[115]. The national need was also articulated by the Countryside Review Committee[116], who outlined the need to view rural problems in an integrated way, and the need to reappraise the present structure of agencies with responsibilities for resource planning and allocation within the countryside, to formulate a national land use strategy and to rank countryside priorities in some meaningful way.

Possible Strategies

Whilst there have been many calls for a nationwide, co-ordinated approach to resource allocation and a parallel nationwide integrated land use strategy, there is a marked lack of concensus over what form these institutional or structural changes would take.

The Countryside Commission, for example, has seen one possible approach to countryside management as taking large areas into public ownership so that full harmonisation of policies and objectives would be

possible[117]. Such a strategy would be costly in
capital, recurrent costs and resources, and extremely
antagonistic to those whose land was taken into
public ownership.

The Commission also saw the possibility of extending
existing development control powers, granted to
local authorities under national planning legislation (see Chapter 11) more widely in the countryside (eg. to include farming and forestry activities
within their remit); but there is a strong feeling
that the overtly negative impacts of such a strategy
would have little effect in stimulating or improving
most parts of the countryside.

A third option viewed by the Countryside Commission
was to persuade countryside owners and users to carry
out improvements for themselves, with appropriate
payments from the public purse - this was the
approach favoured in the Upland Management Experiments (see Section 12.5) for example. Whilst such
approaches doutless lead to improvements in local
landscapes, they are cosmetic in the sense that they
cannot positively encourage beneficial changes in
land use, and ephemeral in the sense that although
they do encourage the more complete integration of
recreation with other countryside uses (in particular
agriculture) their remit is too narrow to encourage
more general integration of land uses and resource
using activities within the countryside.

Institutional Innovation

There is widespread agreement that new institutional
arrangements are required to remove the present sharp
division between agencies which formulate policies
for countryside resource-users (such as forestry,
agriculture and recreation), and to co-ordinate
planning decisions to ensure consistency between rural land transfers and national policies relating to
food, timber, water, energy and so on[118].

Various proposals concerning the most appropriate
forms of institutional arrangement have been made.
For example, a Landscape Planning Council, with four
primary aims, has been called for[119]. This Council
would be empowered to design long term land resource
allocation strategies which promote recognition that
food production should have first priority in rural
land use policies, identification of agriculturally
less-productive land to satisfy other demands on
rural land (linked with a more consistent pattern of

landscape enclosure), differentiation between new
landscapes and retained landscapes (with preference
given to multi-purpose land use rather than exclusive
use by one activity), and creation of interpretative
projects to improve appreciation of landscape and
countryside planning.

Wibberley[120] advocates a marriage of concern and
activities between local planning authorities, farmers and their organisations, and government departments such as the Ministry of Agriculture, the
Countryside Commission and the Nature Conservancy
Council; dialogue, exchange and harmonisation through
collaborative planning of this type would be preferable to the enforced imposition of statutory land
use controls on farmers and landowners which Wibberley sees as the logical alternative.

Other approaches are called for by Green, who concludes that 'we simply cannot afford the present
plethora of independent organisations, both government and private, concerned with landscape, wildlife and informal recreation. Only by a much more
co-ordinated policy of designating country parks,
forests, reservoirs and nature reserves adjacent
to one another, are we likely to protect large enough
zones of wild countryside where these pursuits can be
readily accommodated, without interfering with one
another, and safe from the damaging affects of
sprays, drainage and other forms of intensive husbandry on surrounding agricultural land'[121]. A
policy reorientation away from attempting to maintain
the traditional patchwork quilt landscape towards
creation of new, more polarised landscapes with careful zoning of land use tracts, lies at the heart of
Green's proposals.

Landscape. Without doubt the area over which there
is most agreement in principle is the need to broad-
en the basis of landscape protection in Britain.
This requirement is supported by a wide range of
user-groups in the countryside, such as the conservation lobby who have repeatedly called for a national land use policy which takes full account of
the requirements for wildlife[122], the amenity lobby
who favour increasing the accessibility of all parts
of the countryside, and the statutory organisations
charged with responsibilities for the countryside
(in particular the Nature Conservancy Council and
Countryside Commission).

Perring has proposed a system which recognises a grading of landscape, nature conservation, buildings of architectural and historic interest, ancient monuments, architectural sites and agricultural land and sites under Perring's classification would be sacrosanct; no planning applications, no grants for improvement, and no developments would be considered on these sites and land unless the need for them was agreed by the scheduling body. Whilst the second tier sites would be protected as far as possible by notification procedures, development on these sites and changes in land use might be entertained given suitable justification.[123]

An interesting proposal for a new form of country-side management for the United Kingdom, proposed as part of the UK response to the World Conservation Strategy, has been outlined by O'Riordan[124]. The proposal involves a hybrid approach based on a new countryside classification and the provision of advice and fiscal measures to promote 'management in trust' and the ethos of sustainable utilisation of the countryside and its resources. The scheme would be based on four specially designated countryside categories, which are seen as 'devices for establishing certain priorities regarding resource use, for funnelling funds, tax incentives and specialist advice in particular ways and for prohibiting or penalising certain activities regarded as being incompatible with agreed objectives'[125]. The categories are Heritage Sites (with strongest protection), Conservation Zones, Agricultural and Forestry Landscapes, and Areas of Local Conservation Importance, and the O'Riordan scheme demands the zoning of large tracts of countryside according to these categories.

12.8 CONCLUSIONS

It was pointed out at the beginning of this chapter that co-ordination and comprehensive planning and allocation of resources within the countryside are conspicuous by their absence. Whilst there have been repeated calls for the creation of a rural development agency with wide-ranging powers and responsibilities, and for a national land use plan and strategy, there have to date been few innovations in this direction.

Land zoning appears to be more common and simpler to organise and manage than more comprehensively multi-purpose land use, although the evidence suggests that

within the countryside as a whole there are relatively few intractably incompatible land uses which
could not co-exist in mutual harmony if there were
sufficient need and goodwill for this to be encouraged. There are clearly organisational and institutional constraints on the extent to which fully
integrated land use strategies will be possible in
practice, related in part to the present sectoral
and partisan policies favoured by the individual
agencies responsible for resource allocation and
management in the countryside.

A completely monolithic allocation strategy is
possibly not conceivable without the extremes of
complete or wholesale public ownership of countryside resources, which would be both undesirable and
unviable. Nonetheless it does seem feasible that
integrated strategies will be needed more and more
in the future as pressures on existing land and
natural resources in the countryside continue to
diversify and intensify.

In final analysis what is required is the sort of
'image of an integrated countryside' which was explored in Chapter 1, in which all elements in the
rural system are seen in a realistic light and the
strength of certain resource users (in particular
agriculture and to a lesser extent forestry) is not
allowed to dominate in resource allocation decision-
making. What form this decision-making system assumes will be a matter for debate and compromise.
A planning system which balanced social and economic
issues alongside physical and environmental issues,
and which defined policy options for each on the
basis of detaned survey and evaluation procedures,
is required. A further requirement is the rational
evaluation and selection of alternative strategies.
Examination of the proposed plan in public, followed
by monitoring and adjustment whilst the plan is
being implemented, are also key elements in an integrated rural planning system.

NOTES AND REFERENCES

1.   R.E. Boote, 'Only one earth; it's no longer
       why conserve - only how', Wildlife 18 (1976):
       443-5.

2.   F.H. Perring, 'Conflicts in rural land use',
       1-12 in M. Mellanby (ed) Conflict in Rural

Land Use - the need for a national policy (Institute of Biology, London, 1980).

3.   R. Paul, 'A major enquiry into land use', Field 254 (1979): 223.

4.   J.T. Coppock, 'The challenge of change; problems of rural land use in Great Britain', Geography 62 (1977): 75-86.

5.   Perring, Conflicts (Note 2).

6.   W. Burns, 'Managing the nation's land resources' Chartered Surveyor 109 (1976): 47-53.

7.   J. Zetter, 'Attitudes to land and planning in the U.S.A.', Planner 62 (1976): 170-5.

8.   J.W. Maxwell, 'Land use and the planning process', 36-9 in Transactions of the 35th Federal Provincial Wildlife Conference, Canada.

9.   E.J. Moll, B. McKenzie, D. McLachlan and B.M. Campbell, 'A mountain in a city; the need to plan the human usage of the Table Mountain National Monument, South Africa', Biological Conservation 13 (1978): 117-31.

10.   G. Wibberley, 'Conflicts in the countryside', Town and Country Planning 40 (1972): 259-64.

11.   M. Dower, 'The function of open country', Journal of the Town Planning Institute 50 (1964): 132-40.

12.   J.M. Hall, The Geography of Planning Decisions (Oxford University Press, London, 1982).

13.   W.B. Lord, 'Conflict in federal water resource planning', Water Resources Bulletin 15 (1979): 1226-35.

14.   Idem, 1227.

15.   J. Davidson and G. Wibberley, Planning and the Rural Environment (Pergamon Press, Oxford,1977).

16.   B. John, 'A plea from the Welsh wilderness', Town and Country Planning 50 (1981): 256-60.

17.   Anon, Planning 289 (1978), 13 October.

18. J. Foster, 'Planning in the countryside', _The Planner_ 59 (1973): 417-21.

19. A.S. Travis, 'Policy formulation and the planner', in J. Ashton and W. Harwood Long (eds) _The Remoter Rural Areas of Britain_ (Oliver and Boyd, Edinburgh, 1972).

20. G.P. Wibberley, 'Rural resources development in Britain, and environmental concern', _Journal of Agricultural Economics_ 27 (1976): 14.

21. Coppock, Challenge of change (Note 4): 78.

22. C. Doyle and R. Tranter, 'In search of vision - rural land use problems and policies', _Built Environment_ 4 (1978): 289-98.

23. C. Minay, 'Four types of planning implementation', in C. Minay (ed) _Implementation - Views from an Ivory Tower_ (Department of Town Planning, Oxford Polytechnic, 1979).

24. N. Falk, 'A research base for planning', _The Planner_ 60 (1974): 850.

25. P. Selman, 'Environmental conservation or countryside cosmetics?', _Ecologist_ 6 (1976): 333-5.

26. M. Batty, A political theory of planning and design, _University of Reading Geographical Papers_ 45 (1976): 68pp.

27. Batty, Political theory (Note 26): 8.

28. M.J. Moseley, _Accessibility: the Rural Challenge_ (Methuen, London, 1979).

29. P.J. Cloke, 'Resource evaluation and management', in M. Pacione (ed) _Progress in Rural Geography_ (Croom Helm, London, 1983): 199.

30. Davidson and Wibberley, _Planning_ (Note 15).

31. J. Dower, 'Who plans the countryside?', _Town and Country Planning_ 40 (1972): 253.

32. M.C. Whitby and G.G. Willis, _Rural Resources Development - an economic approach_ (Methuen, London, 1978).

33. H.D. Harben, The Rural Problem (Constable, London, 1913): 5.

34. Countryside Commission, New Agricultural Landscapes - a discussion paper. (HMSO, London, 1974).

35. Wibberley, Rural resources (Note 20): 13.

36. A. Coleman, 'Land use planning in a world of shrinking resources', Long Range Planning 11 (1978): 47-52.

37. A. Coleman, 'Land use planning -success or failure?', Architects Journal 19 January (1977): 93-134; and A. Coleman, 'Last bid for land use sanity', Geographical Magazine 50 (1978): 820-824.

38. J.C. Bowman, C.J. Doyle and R.B. Tranter, 'Why we need a co-ordinated land use policy', Town and Country Planning 46 (1978): 405-8.

39. Coleman, Last bid (Note 37).

40. B.H. Green, 'Countryside planning: compromise or conflict?', The Planner 63 (1977): 67.

41. See, for example, P. Weiss, Renewable Resources, National Research Council Publication 1000A (Washington, D.C.).

42. E.P. Odum, 'Ecosystem strategy in relation to man', in L. Russwurm and E. Sommerville (eds) Man's Natural Environment: a systems approach (Duxbury Press, Massachusetts, 1974): 31.

43. Cloke, Resource evaluation (Note 29): 221.

44. P.J. Cloke and C.C. Park, 'Deprivation, resources and planning; some implications for applied rural geography', Geoforum 11 (1980): 57-61.

45. Selman, Conservation (Note 25): 334.

46. Scott Committee, Report of the Committee on Land Utilisation in Rural Areas (HMSO, London, Cmnd.637B, 1942).

47. W. Ellison, Forestry, Agriculture and the

Multiple Use of Land, Department of Education and Science Land Use Study Group Report (HMSO, London, 1966).

48. Department of Environment, The Countryside - Problems and Policies (HMSO, London, 1976).

49. Nature Conservancy Council, Nature Conservation and Agriculture (Nature Conservancy Council, London, 1977).

50. Idem.

51. C. Hall, 'Who needs a national land use strategy?', New Scientist 90 (1981): 10-2.

52. A. Coleman, 'Is planning really necessary?', Geographical Journal 142 (1976): 411-36.

53. Hall, Who needs (Note 51): 12.

54. See, for example, J. Underwood, 'Development control - a review of research and current issues', Progress in Planning 16 (1981): 178-242; and J. Rowan-Robinson, 'The big public enquiry', Urban Law and Policy 4 (1981): 373-390.

55. J.M. Friend, M.J. Laffin and M.E. Norris, 'Competition in public policy - the structure plan as arena', Public Administration 59 (1981) 441-63.

56. Dower, Who plans? (Note 31): 253.

57. For example, Coleman, Planning? (Note 52).

58. Countryside Commission, Rural Planning Methods (Countryside Commission, London, 1968).

59. Foster, Planning (Note 18): 420.

60. Hampshire County Council, East Hampshire AONB: A Study in Countryside Conservation (Hampshire County Council, 1968).

61. Countryside Commission, Local Authority Countryside Management Projects (Countryside Commission, London, 1978).

62. Idem.

63. Countryside Commission, <u>The Bollin Valley: a Study of Land Management in the Urban Fringe</u> (Countryside Commission, London, 1976).

64. Countryside Commission, <u>Upland Management Experiment</u> (Countryside Commission, London, 1974).

65. Countryside Commission, <u>The Lake District Upland Management Experiment</u> (Countryside Commission, London, 1975).

66. M. Fiest, 'Management agreements: a valuable tool of rural planning', <u>The Planner</u> 65 (1979): 3-5.

67. P. Leonard, 'Management agreements: a tool for conservation', <u>Journal of Agricultural Economics</u> 33 (1982): 351-60.

68. J. Sheail, 'The concept of National Parks in Great Britain: 1900-1950', <u>Transactions of the Institute of British Geographers</u>, 65 (1975) 41-56.

69. M. MacEwan and A. MacEwan, <u>National Parks</u> (George Allen and Unwin, London, 1981).

70. D.N. Potter, 'The National Parks of England and Wales - management of a limited resource', <u>Planning and Administration</u> 5 (1978): 53-62.

71. I.G. Simmons, 'Protection and development in the National Parks of England and Wales - the role of the physical environment', <u>Geographia Polonica</u> 34 (1976): 279-90.

72. Potter, National Parks (Note 70).

73. M. MacEwan, 'Britain's National Parks - why haven't they worked?', <u>Architects Journal</u> 166 (1977): 434-5.

74. M. MacEwan, 'Future of the National Parks II: a need for strength and vigilance', <u>Country Life</u> 60 (1976): 182-4.

75. P. Haggett, <u>Geography - a Modern Synthesis</u> (Harper and Row, New York, 1972): 142.

76. Green, Countryside planning (Note 40).

77.   Haggett, Geography (Note 75).

78.   See, for example, T. O'Riordan, 'Land use man-
       agement in the United States - the problem of
       mixing use and protecting environmental quality'
       209-12 in J.W. Watson and T.O'Riordan (eds) The
       American Environment - Perceptions and Policies
       (Wiley, London, 1976); and W.A. Malone, 'Plan-
       ning practice and techniques', Journal of Soil
       and Water Conservation 28 (1973): 21-4.

79.   I.G. Simmons, 'The protection of ecosystems and
       landscapes in Hokkaido, Japan', Biological
       Conservation 5 (1973): 281-9.

80.   D.L. Armond, I.P. Gerasimov, K.A. Salishchev
       and Y.G. Sanshkin, 'The role of geographers in
       the study, mapping, economic appraisal, util-
       isation, conservation and renewal of the
       natural resources of the USSR', Soviet Geog-
       raphy 1 (1973): 3-10.

81.   D.A. Ratcliffe, A Nature Conservation Review
       (Cambridge University Press, London, 1977).

82.   Countryside Commission, Recreation at reser-
       voirs (Countryside Commission, London, 1973).

83.   P. Selman, 'Alternative approaches to the
       multiple use of the uplands - a review', Town
       Planning Review 49 (1978): 163-74.

84.   W.I. Jenkins, Policy Analysis - Political and
       Organisational Perspective (Robertson, London, 1978).

85.   Selman, Alternative approaches (Note 83).

86.   W.R.D. Sewell, 'Broadening the approach to
       evaluation in resources management decision-
       making', Journal of Environmental Management 1
       (1973): 33-60.

87.   D. Helliwell, 'Priorities and values in nature
       conservation', Journal of Environmental Manage-
       ment 1 (1973): 83-127.

88.   R.W. Arad and J. Berechman, 'A design model for
       allocating interrelated land use activites in
       discrete space', Environment and Planning A 10
       (1978): 1319-32.

89. J.T. Coppock and W.R.D. Sewell, 'Resource management and public policy - the changing role of geographical research', Scottish Geographical Magazine 91 (1975): 4-11.

90. See, for example, N. Lichfield, 'Cost-benefit analysis in planning - a critique of the Roskill Commission', Regional Studies 5 (1971): 157-83.

91. L. Hammill, 'The process of making good decisions about the environment of man', Natural Resources Journal 8 (1968): 279-301.

92. J. Burbridge, 'Methods of evaluating rural resources: the Canadian experience', Journal of the Royal Town Planning Institute 57 (1971): 257-9.

93. D.C. Statham, 'Natural resources in the uplands' Journal of the Royal Town Planning Institute 58 (1972): 468-77.

94. J.A. Taylor, 'The ecological basis of resource management', Area 6 (1974): 101-6.

95. J.S. Bibby and D. Mackney, Land Use Capability Classification, Soil Survey of Great Britain Technical Monograph 1 (1969).

96. E.M. Bridges, 'Land use limitations in the area north of Derby', East Midland Geographer 4 (1966): 31-8.

97. R.D.L. Tolman, 'Soil survey and site appreciation in forests in the South Wales Coalfield', Welsh Soils Discussion Group Report 13 (1972): 129-60.

98. R.G. H. Bunce, S.K. Morrell and H.E. Stel, 'The application of multi-variate analysis to regional survey', Journal of Environmental Management 3 (1975): 151-65.

99. R.G.H. Bunce and R.S. Smith, An Ecological Survey of Cumbria (Cumbria County Council/Lake District Special Planning Board, Kendal, 1978).

100. Statham, Natural resources (Note 93).

101. J.W. Birch, 'Geography and resource management'

Journal of Environmental Management 1 (1973): 3-11.

102. G.L. Swartzman and G.M. Van Dyne, 'An ecologically based simulation-optimisation approach to natural resource planning', Annual Review of Ecology and Systematics 3 (1972): 347-98.

103. A.G. Wilson, 'Toward systems models for water resource management', Journal of Environmental Management 1 (1973): 65-81.

104. J.N.R. Jeffers, 'Systems modelling and analysis in resource management', Journal of Environmental Management 1 (1973): 13-28.

105. A.O. Dye, 'Upland sub-regional planning using a simulation model', Journal of Environmental Management 1 (1973): 169-99.

106. Hammill, Good decisions (Note 91).

107. M. Hill, 'A goals achievement matrix for evaluating alternative plans', Journal of the American Institute of Planners 34 (1968): 19-25.

108. Selman, Alternative approaches (Note 83).

109. North Riding County Council, North Riding Pennines Study: Study Report (North Riding County Council, Northallerton, 1975).

110. Coppock, Challenge of change (Note 4): 85.

111. Dower, Who plans? (Note 31): 254.

112. Select Committee on Scottish Affairs, Report of the Select Committee on Scottish Affairs, House of Commons Paper 511, Volume 1 (HMSO, London, 1972).

113. J.W. House, 'The Northern Pennines Rural Development Boards: an interim report', Appendix A34, Select Committee on Scottish Affairs (HMSO, London, 1972).

114. D.M.C. Jones, 'The Downland that is England', Geographical Magazine 52 (1980): 623.

115. Doyle and Tranter, Search of vision (Note 22): 293.

116. Department of Environment, The Countryside (Note 48).

117. Countryside Commission, Upland Management Experiment (Note 64).

118. Doyle and Tranter, Search of Vision (Note 22).

119. Anon, 'Recommendation for a rural settlement agency', The Architects' Journal 3 (1976): 143-6.

120. Wibberley, Rural resources (Note 20).

121. Green, Countryside planning (Note 40): 69.

122. D. Goode, 'The threat to wildlife habitats', New Scientist 89 (1981): 219-23.

123. F.H. Perring, 'Conflicts in rural land use', 1-12 in K. Mellanby (ed) Conflicts in Rural Land use; the Need for a National Policy (Institute of Biology, London, 1980).

124. T. O'Riordan, Putting Trust in the Countryside, Report 7 of Earth's Survival: a Conservation and Development Programme for the UK (Nature Onservancy Council, London, 1982).

125. Idem.

EPILOGUE

The adoption of a resource management approach in this book has encountered a series of problems in the integration of social and physical issues.

One group of problems centres around the type of resource use characteristic of rural areas. Many of the resources being extensively used at the present time are <u>non-renewable ones</u> (such as mineral resources). Krutilla[1] argues that many of the problems of resource use stem from the irreproducibility of unique phenomena such as natural landscapes and habitats. Whilst for many such rural resources supply cannot readily be enlarged, the utility of them to man (and hence the economic values placed on them and the pressures to develop them) is doubtless increasing.

A second suite of problems derives from differing <u>compatibilities</u> of rural resource use. The countryside is a mosaic of interacting resource-using activities, and inevitably the use of some resources automatically devalues or destroys others. Extraction of mineral resources generally reduces scenic quality, for example. Hall[2] comments that 'planners have tried in many ways to combine concern for visual aesthetics, economic efficiency and social equity in their plans; planners and planned now have a greater understanding of the limited capabilities of the planning machine to foster all three in abundance'.

Problem three concerns <u>evaluation</u>, both in theory and practice[3]. Natural resources can be evaluated in monetary terms because market forces are generally of central importance in determining resource use and allocation. Non-utilitarian resources, however, cannot be evaluated unambiguously in monetary terms

449

(such as the European Communities Common Agriculture
Policy, or the forthcoming Community Directive on
the Environmental Assessment of Projects). Balance
also arises through the need to include factors other
than simply economic criteria in resource allocation.
Social impacts, environmental repercussions, strategic implications and political acceptability are
amongst the more important factors which must be
considered.

The final problem area combines ideology and expediency, and it concerns <u>allocation procedures</u> and
<u>intervention</u>. For most rural resources allocation is
generally based in part on market forces of supply
and demand, but intervention in the planning system,
and the public responsibility and accountability
which this implies, are fundamental factors. Intervention is an inevitable outcome of the need to
balance forces such as national policies and strategic issues; regional priorities and objectives;
local development control interests; political opinion (local, regional and national); social impacts;
environmental impacts; and economic incentives and
constraints. Intervention is also required to introduce welfare and equity considerations into
rural planning. We have argued elsewhere that 'the
aims and objectives of rural planning and management
could be redirected towards redressing the inequalities causing (rural) deprivation... Ultimately the
problem becomes one of resolving conflicts within
the rural resource system, particularly those arising from basic deprivation of opportunity occasioned
by social and environmental forces within the country
side'[5].

In the final analysis, the implications of this book
- that physical and social resources can be viewed
from a central standpoint; that conflicts between
them can be resolved within a resource management
framework; and that integrated planning techniques
can be developed wherein the physical and the social
have equal stature and opportunity for goal achievement - are found to be 'imbued with dream-like
qualities' rather than being couched in the practical
realities of present-day society. Most of us have
in-built predilections for the 'physical' or the
'social' within the countryside, based on value-laden
education, culture and ideology. If pressed to
enunciate 'the most important problem in the countryside', there is considerable doubt as to whether the
reader who approaches this book from the social

despite attempts to include intangibles such as
environmental quality, loss of habitat and extinction
of species into conventional cost-benefit analyses[4].
Conflicts involving both natural and non-utilitarian
resources (such as the conflict between open-cast
mining and landscape protection) thus involve many
value judgements and -ultimately - ethical decisions.

A fourth set of problems relates to the <u>balance of
factors</u> in resource-use decision-making. This
balance is important in terms of scale, because local
scale plans might need to accommodate national or
even international scale objectives and strategies
science stance will - having read it - be led to
integrate the social priorities with physical resource
issues, or vice versa.

It is perhaps noteworthy that having adopted a common
approach to the description of resource bases
(Section I) and resource conflicts (Section II) within this book, we as authors have in effect returned
to our initial biases by the time we come to discuss
'<u>integrated</u>' resource planning. The social scientist
seeks answers to human deprivation in Chapter 11, and
in doing so integrates the physical rural environment only when it serves as an explanatory factor in
the causation or continuation of that deprivation.
Similarly the environmental scientist, when discuss-
ing integrated management strategies (Chapter 12),
seeks to avoid environmental deprivation by regulating conflicting land uses, and the condition and
life-style of rural people becomes a secondary consideration to that of resolving the interests of
land users. It is likely that these differences will
always be so. After all, the social scientist <u>is</u> a
social scientist because of an inate concern for the
social condition - similarly the environmentalist
with the environmental condition. Indeed, the two
may drift further apart as the environmental planner
seeks rationality in resource management while the
social planner often scorns this approach in favour
of ideology and neo-systems.

This book does not, therefore, offer solutions to
problems. It merely encourages a co-ordination of
approach by adopting a resource management perspective within the bounds of the individual's constrained
interests and political priorities. Resource management <u>per se</u> is not the panacea of rural planning, but
it might just offer a useful framework in which to
evaluate and organise conflicts and priorities such

that human and physical resources may be viewed <u>not</u> as mutually exslusive, but as symbiotic and worthy of mutual consideration within any management process.

NOTES AND REFERENCES

1.   J.V. Krutilla,'Conservation reconsidered' <u>American Economic Review</u> 67 (1967): 777-86.

2.   J.M. Hall, <u>The Geography of Planning Decisions</u> (Oxford University Press, London, 1980).

3.   N. Lichfield, P. Kettle and M. Whitbread, <u>Evaluation in the Planning Process</u> (Pergamon, London, 1975).

4.   D.R. Helliwell, Priorities and values in nature conservation, <u>Journal of Environmental Manage-ment</u> 1, (1973): 85-127.

5.   P.J. Cloke and C.C. Park, Deprivation, resources and planning - some implications for applied rural geography, <u>Geoforum</u> 11 (1980): 57-61.

LOCATION INDEX

INDEX

458

467

Upland Farm Landscape Survey 277
Upland farming 276-78
Upland Management Experiment 208, 422-25, 436
Urban, development process 47; environment 5, 20;
    system 125; planning 413; space-time order 132
Urban fringe 25, 27, 28, 368, 379, 385, 421-23
Urbanization, process 20, 25; extension of urban
    land 27, 135, 166, 268, 270, 332; demand for
    aggregates 68, 174, 177; demand for water 70;
    effect on water quality 77
Use Class Order 366, 380

Value, conflict 4, 5; judgement 79, 102; rural
    values 133; social values 126; wildlife 80;
    landscape 91, 96-101
Vegetation, zonation 206; removal 76; tolerance to
    trampling 202
Vehicle densities 197
Vehicles, see access, mobility and car ownership
Village, definition 7; general 3, 55; population
    size 11; isolation 13; settlement form 20, 124;
    expanding 28, 142; new villages 233;
    agricultural 229; commuter 28; tourist 28;
    desertion 140; preservation 240-42, 244, 250-51
Village of Special Overall Character 241
Village planning, objectives 252; development
    control 370-77, 412
Village shop 330-31
Villagization Programme 387
Visitor behaviour and trampling 204
Visitor centres 191, 213
Visitor density 192, 290; see carrying capacity,
    crowding
Visitor management 114, 196, 208, 336-38, 345-50

Water Authorities 74
Water grid (National Water Plan) 75
Water pollution, see pollution
Water quality 76
Water resources, general 42, 48, 51, 60; overview
    69-77; value 69-71; allocation and management
    71-4, 75-8, 81; dynamics 74-5; user conflicts
    187-8
Water Resources Act (1973) 73
Welfare Economics 38, 43
Wetland habitats, conservation 76; recreational use
    202; access 335; agriculture 266, 279, 281, 287,
    377, 398
Wilderness, overview 108-114; definition 108, 110;
    general 8, 42-3; preservation of 109-110;
    distribution 111; recreation 112-14, 194-7, 291;